UTOPIA FOREVER
Visions of Architecture and Urbanism

gestalten

ESSAYS
—
On Utopia and Beyond

004. This Time Tomorrow
by LUKAS FEIREISS

014. 49 Cities
by DAN WOOD and AMALE ANDRAOS (WORKac)

062. Productive Dystopia
by DARRYL CHEN (Tomorrow's Thoughts Today)

112. Utopia Generator
by GEOFF MANAUGH (BLDGBLOG)

158. They Promised Us Jetpacks!
by MATTHIAS BÖTTGER and LUDWIG ENGEL (raumtaktik)

200. A Project on Visionary Cities
by ULF HACKAUF (The Why Factory)

CHAPTERS

On Worlds to Come

I
GREAT SCAPES
Extensive Thinking
Across Large-Scale Planes

PP. 012–59

The opening chapter looks at contemporary large-scale architectural proposals, which span diverse environments from the countryside to the urban realm. Here, seemingly limitless building systems, of vast dimensions, explore a whole new scale of architecture and urbanism against the backdrop of a wide range of landscapes, including mountainous regions, vast arid deserts, coastal areas, as well as urban landscapes.

II
RISING TIDES
Exploring the
Consequences of Global
Sea Level Rises

PP. 060–109

Focusing on the issue of the global rise of sea levels—one of the most critical impacts of global warming—this chapter, seeks to present speculative design solutions to this significant climatic challenge from the perspective of architects and urban planners.

III
ECOTOPIA EMERGING
Alternative Speculation On
Ecologically Sound Worlds

PP. 110–155

This chapter sets out to portray radical, ecologically-sound counter-cultures somewhere in an alternate future. The projects conjured are characterized and inspired by the vivid imaginings of the alternative lifestyles they propose.

IV
TECHNOLOGY MATTERS
Reflecting Upon
the Impact of
New Technology

PP. 156–197

The projects shown here investigate new technologies suffused with utopian energy, and consider their significance in the way we might live and work in the future. Many of the architectural projects gathered in this chapter rely on technology that does not yet exist, or spin-off technology that is derived from existing models or ideas.

V
SKY HIGH
Elevating the
Possibilities of
Vertical Habitation

PP. 198–249

Taking the utopian idea to new heights, this chapter engages in the discussion of vertical architecture and the city, and proposes advanced aviation systems for the future. The chapter explores the possibilities and the implications of high-rise living in all its kaleidoscopic, creative facets, and looks at new kinds of spatial and functional relationships between tall, habitable buildings and the voids between them.

THIS TIME TOMORROW

On the Value of Speculation On Present Futures to Come

by LUKAS FEIREISS

Lukas Feireiss is a curator, writer, artist, and teacher, whose interdisciplinary creative practice, *Studio Lukas Feireiss*, focuses on the discussion, mediation, and re-evaluation of architecture, art, and visual culture in the urban realm.

Once Upon an Island

On the night of December 13, 1847 a group of spiritualists rejoiced and celebrated in the town hall of Utopia, a small settlement founded by followers of French utopian socialist and philosopher, Charles Fourier, in Clermont County on the northern bank of the Ohio River. Disregarding the warnings of locals and the fact that the river had flooded its banks dramatically, and despite the fact that they had already been forced to evacuate their homes, and that the water was drawing dangerously close to the town hall, the spiritualists, nevertheless came together to dance and cheer in joyous anticipation of a 35,000 year-long period of peace in which, according to their belief, the oceans would turn to lemonade. But the merry party was interrupted violently, when the brick structure of the newly erected building gave way to the deluge of water which rushed over them. All but a few of the party of spiritualists were swept away by one of the biggest floods of the nineteenth century, to drown or freeze in the icy Ohio River. Until today, the place at the river bank where the spiritualists drowned that night is rumored to be haunted by their ghosts.

What began as a cooperative community inspired by utopian ideals, was relentlessly put to an end by the powers of nature. Neither utopian ideals nor higher visions were able to withstand the inevitable reality of existence. Reality bites, and here it bit back hard. Sure, this example might seem somewhat exaggerated and lemonade oceans might seem rather farfetched, but is this not the fate all utopian endeavors have to face eventually: the unwillingness of the real world to embrace higher ideals—no matter how grounded or far off they might appear to be? But then again, can a utopia unequivocally prove its value, only by its ultimate success or failure? What is it that makes a utopia worthwhile regardless of its potential applicability in reality? Is it not, perhaps, precisely this *inapplicability* that is at the heart of utopia's inspiration? Is it not the expression of the human spirit sowing ideas, whose speculative fruits future generations might harvest; the ghosts of utopia that continue to haunt us? Admittedly there are more questions than answers to be found when engaging in the discourse on the phenomena of utopia and its manifold influences, however, the endeavor is worthwhile nonetheless.

Renaissance English writer and philosopher, Thomas More's book, *Utopia*, published almost 500 years ago, in 1516, not only named the aforementioned spiritual community on the banks of the Ohio River, but probably serves as the most influential paradigm and measure for all other utopian enterprises to follow, whether they were situated in real life or imagined in fictional worlds. Our general understanding of the notion of *utopia* today, as a token for a concept of a complete political and social ideal, is still based on More's narrative—through the words of his fictional wanderer and pilgrim, the eternal student, Raphael Hythloday—who describes an amazing island in the Atlantic Ocean, named Utopia, whose inhabitants learned how to cure the ills of human society. Interestingly enough, one still discovers in many interpretations of utopia today, some version of this initial search, or quest, for a place isolated from the rest of the world, a refuge from the mundane aspects of the everyday; a sheltered island far away. Utopia as society's dream-image is often envisioned as an island: a Galapagos of the mind, an incommunicado of ideas, or a metaphor for paradise itself—the land where rivers of milk and honey flow. Examples of this archipelago of paradisiacal territories are as numerous as they are diverse, and range from More's *Utopia*, to Daniel Defoe's *Robinson Crusoe,* Aldous Huxley's *Island*, all the way to Buckminster Fuller's intuitive visions of a *One World Island* and the mostly, short-lived alternative communities founded in the late 1960s and early 1970s as small islands in the deserts of New Mexico and Arizona—too mention only a few of the numerous other places across the globe.

Whether intentionally sought after, or accidentally stumbled upon, across unmapped oceans, in endless deserts and deep valleys or even high on the summit of mountains, the notions of *escapism* and *exceptionalism* is what unifies all ruminations on utopia. While the road to these utopias all too often leads to failure, it is the utopian impulse and quest itself which is of the greatest value. Despite utopia's intentional isolation from the commonplace and from reality, it remains the imaginative springboard for achievable change in the here and now. As the famous British writer, Oscar Wilde, famously put it: "A map of the world that does not include Utopia is not worth even glancing at, for it leaves out the one country at which Humanity is always landing."

The World to Come

In the field of architecture and urbanism, utopias have always been confronted with the same complexities and paradoxes inherent in the search for the perfect world. Of the arts, it may well be architecture that provides the most substantial vehicle to imagine possible futures due to the inherent notion of progress in the discipline, which is naturally linked to the discourse on utopia. In fact, the entire discipline is consequently focused on the future world—from basic building process all the way to the inevitable configurations of social and political space.

However, until recently, there has been relatively little discourse in the discipline with regard to utopian ideas. While it seemed almost compulsory for architects to design a utopian city in the 1960s and early 1970s, it vanished completely from the architectural discourse after the collapse of twentieth century's grand ideologies, and the subsequent disillusionment of the ideas in the decades thereafter. To some it seemed as if the entire Modern Project had failed completely: architects' zealous, but misled systemization and mechanization of social and urban problems in utopian grand schemes had contributed to the creation of many cheerless places around the world. Think for instance of Japanese architect, Minoru Yamasaki, who unwillingly became the enigmatic composer of utopia's architectural requiem with his infamous *Pruit-Igoe* public housing project in St. Louis, Missouri. Whilst it was hailed as a great advancement at the time of its construction in 1958, it fell victim to disrepair, vandalism, and crime only a few short years later. With its publicly televised implosion in 1972, it became an immortal icon of failure; as American architecture theorist, Charles Jencks, wrote in *The Language of Post-Modern Architecture*, a symbol of the death of Modern architecture: "Modern architecture died in St. Louis, Missouri on July 15, 1972 at 3.32 pm (or thereabouts) when the infamous *Pruitt-Igoe* scheme, or rather several of its slab blocks, were given the final coup de grace by dynamite." In the profound volte-face of its initial utopian spirit, it has hindered the meta-narrative of progress. It is only now, a decade into the twentyfirst century, that we can witness a resurgence of utterly new, otherworldly concepts in architecture and urbanism, and complex and far-reaching visions of possible future scenarios that challenge present building conventions. Today, utopia seems to be on everyone's lips. London's Barbican Art Gallery recently revisited the most radical and experimental architecture to have emerged in the past 50 years in the exhibition held there, *Future City. Experiment and Utopia in Architecture*, the History Channel, initiated a competition on the *City of the Future* a century from now, the MoMA envisioned speculative projects for New York's waterfront in its exhibition, *Rising Currents*, and another entitled, *Megastructures Reloaded*, examined the visions of megastructuralists in the 1960s, they were tested for their currency and relevance to solve the problems of contemporary urban design. And this is just the tip of the iceberg! But what is it that has made *utopia* such a hot topic once again? Following the social utopias imagined in the 1920s such as Le Corbusier's *Radiant City*, Frank Lloyd Wright's *Broadacre City*, or Ebenezer Howard's *Garden City* as well as the second wave of utopian architecture in the 1960s that focused on emerging cultural and political conditions with Archigram's *Walking City*, Constant Nieuwenhuys' *New Babylon*, Yona Friedman's *La Ville Spatiale* or the Metabolist's capsule buildings—in what way do contemporary utopias differ from their predecessors? Or are they inherently reconfiguring already existing schemes in a paradoxical inversion of utopia, as a nostalgic groping for what was before, rather than what might be in the future? An utopian "mannerism" so to speak? Against the backdrop of the global realities the world is facing today at beginning of the new, urban millennium with ever increasing mega-cities across the globe, and the "impossible" already made possible everyday in the deserts of Dubai and Masdar, or across China's mushrooming urban landscapes; what novel ideas can really be formulated that challenge the boundaries of human imagination? What is left for utopia to strive for if nothing seems too farfetched or out of reach any longer? If architecture competitions now call for housing projects on the Moon, private entrepreneurs engage in personal air-travel in outer space, and the incontestable consequences of global climate change urgently demand long-term thinking in time-spans of a century, then what effect might that have on utopian ideals?

Without even attempting to come to a conclusive answer to all these questions, let alone assess the projects featured in this volume; this book rather strives to bring together today's architectural and urban visions of possible futures that rise above the disillusionment of the present, and expand the imaginative horizons of human potential, whilst at the same time, reveal the conflicts this architecture provokes and outlines the potential implications for this world. From magnificent master plans, floating islands and flying fortresses, to visionary cityscapes and extraordinary habitats, *Utopia Forever*, showcases the best examples of experimental architectural propositions to have originated in recent years. Some are ironic yet critical, others affirmative yet progressive; but all are rather ambiguous and exploratory. Around 70 projects from around the globe are presented in this book. The projects have been subdivided under five thematic headings in order to create a novel image of utopian thinking in architecture today. These thematic headings are intended to invite reciprocal exchange as the ideas remain essentially open to foster a dialogue of ideas. Whilst the opening chapter, *Great Scapes,* looks at a number of large-scale projects across primarily uninhabited landscapes, the following chapter, *Rising Tides,* looks at ideas responding to the rise in sea levels—one of the most critical impacts of global warming. The third chapter, *Ecotopia Emerging,* conjures ecological utopias that are characterized by their lively imagination of alternative and ecologically sound ideals. The chapter, *Technology Matters,* investigates new technologies that are suffused with utopian energy, and their significance in the way we might live and work in the future. Finally, the chapter *Sky's the Limit,* engages in a discussion of vertical architecture and the city, including advanced aviation propositions for the future. *Ecotopia Emerging,* conjures ecological utopias that are characterized by their lively imagination of alternative and ecologically sound ideals.

In addition to the numerous projects presented in this book, *Utopia Forever,* moreover provides a selection of essays by various architects and theorists that critically discuss numerous questions associated with the subject of architectural utopias. In their thorough analysis of several centuries of unrealized urbanism, from the ideal Roman city to the great utopian projects of the twentieth century, New York-based architectural firm, Work AC, re-engages cities as the sites of radical thinking and experimentation in an essay on their 2009 exhibition and accompanying book, *49 Cities,* at the Storefront for Art and Architecture in New York. Berlin-based architect and theorist, Matthias Böttger from raumtaktik—office from a better future, together with the futurologist, Ludwig Engel, address the task of critically analyzing urban utopias focusing on the origins of utopia in *They Promised Us Jetpacks. Of Futures and Utopias*, while Darryl Chen of London-based studio, Tomorrow's Thoughts Today, offer a provocative perspective on the surplus of dystopia in their essay, *Productive Dystopia or An Architecture of Unintended Consequences.* Furthermore, BLDBLOG's Los Angeles-based writer, Geoff Manaugh, contributes with a thought-provoking game to further architectural conjectures, urban speculations and landscape fictions in his ingenious *Utopia Generator*. Ulf Hackauf of the newly formed think-tank *The Why Factory* at Delft University of Technology, elaborates on the research and production of models and visualizations of our urban futures. The wide array of works and ideas which are featured in *Utopia Forever* proves the lasting relevance of utopian thought for the discipline of architecture today, as both a tool for envisioning the future, as well as a motivation for the present. Utopia remains architecture's "dirty secret," as Dutch architect, Rem Koolhaas and author of the seminal book, *Delirious New York* alleged: "Deep down all architecture, no matter how naive and implausible, claims to make the world a better place."

News from Nowhere

What is this better place though? Ever since Sir Thomas More invented the word "utopia" all those years ago, it has adopted manifold interpretations and incarnations. To some it is the happy, ideal place, while others consider it as an impracticable place; its existence impossible. It is often given both meanings simultaneously, creating more confusion. It is worth noting here that More's term "utopia" inherently suggests this dual nature: the Greek term "utopia" contains both "eutopia" or "good place" and "outopia" or "no place." As if that were not enough, art historian, Edward Rothstein, has taken it even further by postulating in his spirited essay, *Utopia and Its Discontents,* that: "If you look too close at any utopia, you begin to shiver at the possibility. One man's utopia is another man's dystopia." Utopia always presumes its apparent opposite, dystopia, with regards to the impracticality of realization, and the impossibility of fulfilling most of the ideas conceived. This is the crux of the matter: those who envisage creating "heaven on earth," Austrian-born political and social philosopher of science, Karl Popper, denotes in his essay, *The Open Society and Its Enemies,* "will only succeed in making hell."

As the pendulum of time swings back and forth relentlessly, whatever is hailed as progress today, might be condemned to failure tomorrow. There are no prefect blueprints for everlasting utopia on earth, as they cannot ever fully respond to the complexity, and contradiction of reality. This unpredictability is probably the only predictable aspect of human experience. Yet, Rothstein rightly remarks yet again: "The unpredictable is just what a utopia is unprepared for." Though a modicum of predictability is what all complex working systems depend and rely on! In particular in utopias, where proportions are carefully designed, contradictions eliminated, and outside intrusions minimized. In actual fact, to achieve a utopian ideal of let us say, harmonic cohabitation in peace, freedom and justice, a set of mandatory rules and definite organizing principles is imperative. Yet, with respect to these rules and principles, the borderline to force and control, rather than to allow collective happiness to emerge is alarmingly thin here; a perfectly beautiful utopia can also gradually degrade into a repressive and controlled dystopia.

Moreover, as utopias tend to see the world differently in their vision of a better place in the future, their inherent demand for change and transformation in the here-and-now, carries a radical revolutionary impetus; utopia, perhaps, as a fundamental change in power or organized structures, or utopia, as a withdrawal from short term solutions in favor of a comprehensive solution that dramatically shakes the foundations of society? Many such revolutionary calls have been made throughout history. In the realm of architecture, one only needs to think of Le Corbusier's rallying cry at the end of his book *Vers une Architecture*: "Architecture or Revolution" of 1923, which threatened political upheaval if modernist design was not upheld; all the way to the Congrès Internationale d'Architecture Moderne's (CIAM) self-righteous claim of the *Athens Charter*: "By which the destiny of the cities will be set right," or Buckminster Fuller's less portentous, but every bit as utopian assumption, in his famous *Operating Manual for Spaceship Earth*, that the time was ripe in our social systems for politicians and financiers to hand over control to designers, engineers, and artists. Recently, the German philosopher, Peter Sloterdijk, picked up on Fuller's appeal to the spirit of creativity and revolutionary jargon, when he controversially spoke of the necessary turn-over of the present model for civilization, of global industrial culture, at the 2009 Climate Conference in Copenhagen.

So whether "utopia," "eutopia" or "dystopia"; at the heart of all utopian thoughts lies thorough understanding of the need for the rigorous alteration of present conditions. Even though utopias might never be realized, we should be careful not to overlook them or condemn them, since they are indicative of the great capacity of the human imagination that might otherwise be restrained. The thoughts produced might give birth to ideas that may mature in more realistic and practical circumstances. Their claim being an elemental expression of humankind's will to shape history, and thereby our ability to change it?

Cornflakes or Cadillacs

As the concept of utopia—in its inevitable promise of revolution and transformation—incorporates the notion of progress, it draws nearer to one of society's and culture's essential driving forces, namely technology. As much as utopia, in its reflection of the impact of imagined innovation in science or technology, is suffused by technological thinking; technology, in fact, seems saturated with utopian energies as well— from the electric light bulb, to the telephone, right up to the World Wide Web. New technologies have been the breeding ground for the formulation of new utopias. Technology, after all, is the science of transforming society through invention. As with any exploratory or revolutionary process, its outcome remains uncertain or unknown. There are inevitably failures as well as successes, no matter how well formulated the initial idea might be, but technology remains a means of change. It is an implacable force that gathers power as it advances and swiftly transforms society.

In the 1968 cult film *2001: A Space Odyssey*, Stanley Kubrick ingeniously displays the effect technology has for the good and the bad of human evolution. At the beginning of the movie, the dawn of man is depicted. After discovering that a bone can be used as both tool and weapon, and subsequently dispatching the leader of a rival group with the bone-club, an ape-man roars in victory and hurls the bone-club skyward. In what is often hailed as one of the most famous match-cuts in film history, the picture cuts from the tumbling bone to an orbiting spaceship, and aligns in one scene four million years of human evolution through technology.

Against the backdrop of investigating the profound impact technology and media have on the way we live and work, and especially how we will live and work in the future, the work of Canadian "high priest" of media culture, Marshall McLuhan, provides the most original example. His worldwide bestseller, *Understanding Media*, first published in 1964, focuses on the media/technology effects that permeate society and culture. He defines media generally as technological extensions of man, ranging from skin, clothing and architecture, to mass media such as radio and television. Central to his study, and most commonly known as the famous dictum: "The Medium is the Message," is the concept that a medium affects the society in which it plays a role, not by the content delivered through the medium, but also by the characteristics of the medium itself: "In terms of the ways in which the machine altered our relations to one another and to ourselves, it mattered not in the least whether it turned out cornflakes or Cadillacs." As we shape our technologies, they shape us, in a constant feedback loop that produces our everyday physical, social, and cultural environment.

Today, with technology and human knowledge exponentially growing, we are confronted with the need for answers to questions that we can hardly formulate. Technology also provokes new fears. Whether or not Buckminster Fuller is correct in his critical observation, that: "Humanity is acquiring all the right technology for all the wrong reasons," the speed of technological developments has already outstripped our collective capacity to develop appropriate moral approaches and social and environmental policies for their application. In correlation with these technological and cultural revolutions, the utopian thought gains, once again, significance in its attempt to invoke, direct, and shape the development of the future. French philosopher, Raymond Ruyer, even observed a structural similarity between scientific and utopian descriptions of the world in his book, *L'Utopie et les Utopies*—the so called *mode utopique*. In his understanding, utopian thinking is not so much about its contents, such as the far-away islands or possible futures, but far more about its mode of thinking about society: utopia, as a cultural model of understanding, a unique method of comprehension, which employs imaginary elements, in order to try to grasp the present.

Over the Rainbow

In the introduction to the German philosopher, Ernst Bloch's, peerless opus magnum *The Principle of Hope*—a comprehensive account of human strivings for utopia throughout history, coupled with the philosopher's own vision of the possibilities for a real utopia questions the reader existentially: "Who are we? Where do we come from? Where are we going to? What can we expect? What is expected of us?" "It depends on," he continues in answer, "whether we learn to hope." To him, hope is never ending as it is obsessed with success not failure. The book was originally planned to be published under the title, *Dreams of a Better Life, The Principle of Hope,* and is, in a sense, a practical guide to living with hope. For Bloch, hope permeates everyday consciousness and is articulated in cultural forms, ranging from simple daydreams, to the fairy tale and to the great religious, philosophical and political utopias. For Bloch, individuals are ever-changing, we are animated by "dreams of a better life," and by utopian longings for fulfillment. This anticipatory element and unconscious dimension of the future, is what he calls the *not-yet-conscious*. It contains emancipatory moments which project visions of a better life that question the organization and structure of life as we know it. Bloch thereby makes a key distinction between an "abstract" and a "concrete" utopia. The first denoting a wishful thinking of better places, as it occurs in most utopian traditions throughout history, the later describes utopias, that anticipate, and affect the future, and have the potential of being realized.

However, the future is always a long time in coming, is it not? All things considered utopia—both as model as well as method—can therefore be described as an optimistic process of possible realization, in which the particular determination of the future carefully formulates itself, experimenting with the promise of the horizon. However, the out-of-reach utopias featured in this book are, in creating images and visions of tomorrow, become part of the actual creation of our future to come. In order to push things forward we need to use our imagination. The rest will then follow. French writer and aviator, Antoine Saint-Exupéry, adequately puts it as follows: "If you want to build a ship, don't drum up people together to collect wood and don't assign them tasks and work, but rather teach them to long for the endless immensity of the sea."

GREAT SCAPES

※

Extensive
Thinking
Across
Large-scale
Planes

Recalling the avant-garde of the 1920s and 1930s, and the great structuralist proposals of the 1960s, the opening chapter, *Great Scapes,* looks at contemporary large-scale architectural proposals, which span diverse environments from the countryside to the urban realm. Here, seemingly limitless building systems, of vast dimensions, explore a whole new scale of architecture and urbanism against the backdrop of a wide range of landscapes, including mountainous regions, vast arid deserts, coastal areas, as well as urban landscapes. The projects featured range from the architect, Behring Behnin's adaption of solar-chimney power generators—a prominent theme in many projects featured in this book—Behnin's horizontally stratified *Stack City* located in the Gulf region, to Matsys Design's futuristic *Sietch Nevada,* which envisions a city of complex underground networks of tunnels and canals in the arid planes of the American Southwest. Also featured is Magnus Larson's *DUNE* project, in which he proposes a 6,000-kilometer-long stretch of compacted sand dunes as habitable spaces in the Sahara Desert, Mad Architects' *Superstar,* a mobile three-dimensional star which could house 15,000 people and includes lakes, spas, sport facilities, and even a cemetery. Combining both their physical origins and the cultural overlay of human presence, these built landscapes ingeniously reflect the living synthesis of people and place vital to local identity. Inherent to all of these super-complexes, is a mighty grandeur, an understanding of spacial immensity and the ability for human-made transformation of enormous scope that make these designs extreme examples of speculative and exploratory architecture today.

"HOW BIG CAN WE THINK?"

BUCKMINSTER FULLER

22. *Multiplicity* by John Wardle Architects and Stefano Boscutti
25. *The Hanging Cemetery of Baghdad* by NaJa & deOstos
26. *Consistenze & Persistenze* by Giacomo Costa
28. *Urban Skylink* by David A. Garcia
30. *Silk Road Map Evolution* by OFL Architecture
34. *The Berg* by Mila Studio (Jakob Tigges)
36. *Lace Hill over Yerevan* by Forrest Fulton Architecture
40. *Recovering Berlin* by Protocol Architecture (Yuval Borochov, Lisa Ekle, Danil Nagy)
42. *Sietch Nevada* by MATSYS
44. *Dune—Arenaceous Anti-Desertification Architecture* by Magnus Larsson
46. *Stack City* by Behrang Behin
50. *Green Desert Mine* by CDMB Architects (Christophe DM BARLIEB)
51. *IP2100 (Island proposition 2100)* by Scott Lloyd, Aaron Roberts (Room11), Katrina Stoll
52. *Self Defense* by Stéphane Malka Architecture, Michael Kaplan digital images
53. *Roller Coaster Warsaw* by Kobas Laksa
54. *Slave City* by Atelier Van Lieshout
56. *Dead Websites Archive* by David A. Garcia
57. *Happy Consensus Land* by Speedism
58. *Doomdough* by Speedism

49 CITIES

by DAN WOOD and AMALE ANDRAOS

Dan Wood and Amale Andraos are co-founders of New York-based WORK Architecture Company (WORKac), that develops architectural and urban projects that engage culture and consciousness, nature and artificiality, surrealism and pragmatism.

Throughout history, architects and planners have dreamed of "better" and different cities—more flexible, more controllable, more defensible, more efficient, more monumental, more organic; taller, denser, sparser, and greener. With every new plan, radical visions were proposed; visions that embodied, not only the desires but also, the fears and anxieties of their time.

With the failure of the suburban experiment and the looming end-of-the-world predictions—from global warming to post peak-oil energy crises and uncontrolled worldwide urbanization—architects and urban planners find themselves once more at a crossroads; a place fertile for visionary thinking. Today's meeting of intensified environmental fears with the global break down of laissez-faire capitalism has produced a new kind of audience; one that is ready to suspend disbelief and engage in fantastic projections to radically rethink the way we live.

Recognizing the recurrent nature of our environmental preoccupations and their impact in shaping utopias, WORKac embarked upon a research project to re-investigate, rediscover, and redefine these utopian visions. *49 Cities* inscribes our time within a larger historical context, re-reading seminal projects and visionary cities of the past through an ecological lens of the present that goes beyond their declared ideology, to compare and contrast their hypothetical ecological footprint. And while both terms constituting the research—that of *city* and that of *ecology*—are purposefully reduced to an almost naïve level, however they are still powerful enough in their striking simplicity to reveal that many of the radical propositions from bygone eras are closer than we are today in boldly articulating the challenges we face and offering inspiring possibilities to meet them.

Born from our "eco-urbanism" research seminar at Princeton University's School of Architecture, *49 Cities* emerged as a means to re-engage our thinking about the city and reclaim the imagination of architects towards re-inventing the way we live. While initially focused on the present condition, analyzing current trends in green architecture and urbanism, our interest gradually gravitated back in time, towards the long tradition of prolific visionary thinking about the city that was lost sometime in the mid-1970s. Encouraged by the "amateur-planner" status of those who dreamed of the most influential plans—from Frank Lloyd Wright and Le Corbusier, who were architects, to Ebenezer Howard, who was a stenographer—and unconvinced by more recent professional manifestos such as those of the New Urbanists, we set out to find ways to move beyond mapping our "urban-on-speed" condition, to rediscover alternate modes to re-project and re-work the city.

The 49 cities were selected from more than 200 cases studied. The choice was based on the city's ability to capture an era and an ambition; either by best representing their contemporaries or by being radically advanced and ahead of their time. While some cities were built either partly or in one form or another, most of them remained on paper. And yet today, many have nevertheless, indelibly influenced our global urban landscape. While the repercussions of *Radiant City*, ● see opposite page *Broadacre City*, and the *Garden City* have been widely acknowledged, it is interesting to compare recent developments in China and the United Arab Emirates to some of these visionary urban plans, ranging from the more utilitarian to the more exuberant. These parallels, however, stop at *form:* while today's urban developments are almost always shaped by capital flows, the 49 cities were all shaped by ideology and an ambition to recast society's modes of being and operation, an ambition that produced widely varying results, depending on their time and their context.

Beyond their particularities and specific preoccupations, there are two characteristics that most of the 49 cities share. The first lies in the embrace of scale and the radical abstraction they have, in order to question their impact on the planet as a whole. A "better city for the future" always seems to imply a redefined relationship to nature and to the environment, a relationship whose form—whether it requires sprawl to embrace wilderness or compression to minimize impact—depends on the broader ideology it embodies. The second characteristic is that each of the 49 cities is conceived as a reaction to the urban conditions and fears of its time: overpopulation, sprawl, chaos, slums, pollution, war.

With today's heightened fear of imminent environmental disasters, "ecological urbanism" seems the natural "first" utopia of the twenty-first century. Projecting today's questions

Le Corbusier's *Radiant City*

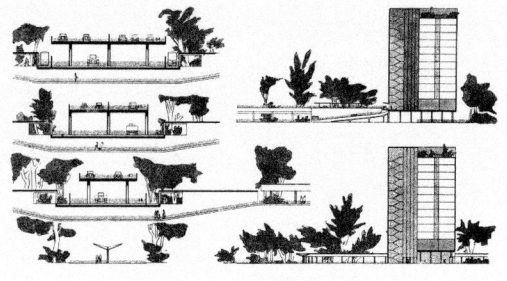
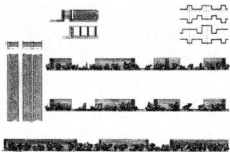
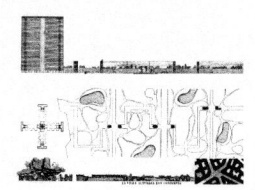

Le Corbusier's *Radiant City* attempted to open the city to light, air and nature, while simultaneously achieving extremely high residential densities. The park-like ground plane of the city was completely open to the pedestrian, crisscrossed by elevated highways and dotted with towers on pilotis. Horizontally, the city was zoned into specific areas of residential, administrative/business and industrial functions. Residents inhabited superblocks, self-contained residential neighborhood-buildings of 2,700 residents that had communal amenities and recreational facilities. Cruciform office buildings in the business zone of the city were to be forty-stories tall, housing 3,200 workers per building. The plan was highly influential in residential and commercial planning for decades after it was introduced.

TOTAL SITE AREA (2-D; IN M²)	**114,290,621**
TOTAL GREENSPACE (M²)	**114,290,621**
Area: Greenspace: agriculture	0
Area: Greenspace: lawn	0
Area: Greenspace: park	54,689,799
Area: Greenspace: wilderness	59,600,822
AREA OF WATER (M²)	**737,602**
AREA OF INFRASTRUCTURE (M²)	**12,854,154**
TOTAL BUILT AREA (FOOTPRINT; M²)	**8,479,819**
Area: Housing (footprint)	2,066,675
Area: Industrial (footprint)	5,618,460
Area: Public (footprint)	794,684
TOTAL POPULATION	**2,073,600**
Total number housing units	829,440
Number of people per housing unit	2.50
TOTAL AREA (3-D; IN M²)	**255,324,701**
Number of Floors: Housing	13
Number of Floors: Industrial	8
Number of Floors: Public	70

AREA: TOTAL BUILT	**127,442,324**
Area: Housing (3-D)	26,866,770
Area: Industrial (3-D)	44,947,684
Area: Public (3-D)	55,627,870
Area: Open Space (Greenspace + Water + Infrastructure) (3-D)	127,882,377
FAR: 3-D AREA/2-D AREA (X)	**2.23**
DENSITY: total population/site area (2-D) (people per km²)	**18,143**
DENSITY: total population/total area (3-D) (people per km²)	**8,121**

2-D PERCENTAGES

Greenspace	100%
Agriculture	0%
Lawn	0%
Park	48%
Wilderness	52%
Water	1%
Infrastructure	11%
Built Area	7%
Housing	2%
Industrial	4%
Public	1%
Total % of land use (can exceed 100%)	119%

3-D PERCENTAGES

Greenspace	45%
Agriculture	0%
Lawn	0%
Park	22%
Wilderness	23%
Water	0%
Infrastructure	5%
Built Area	50%
Housing	11%
Industrial	17%
Public	22%
Total % of land use	100%

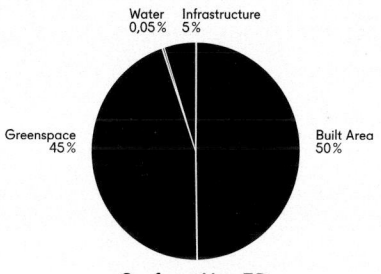

Surface Use 3D

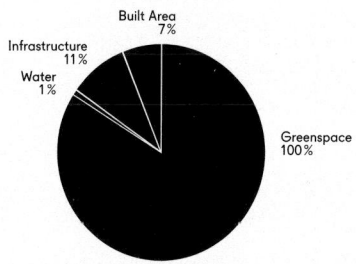

Land Use 2D

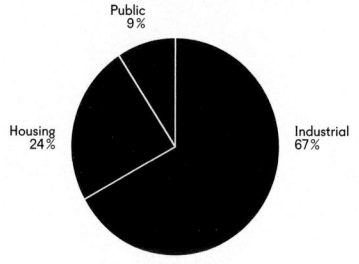

Built Space

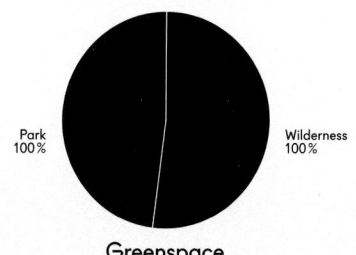

Greenspace

Buckminster Fuller's *Tetrahedral City*

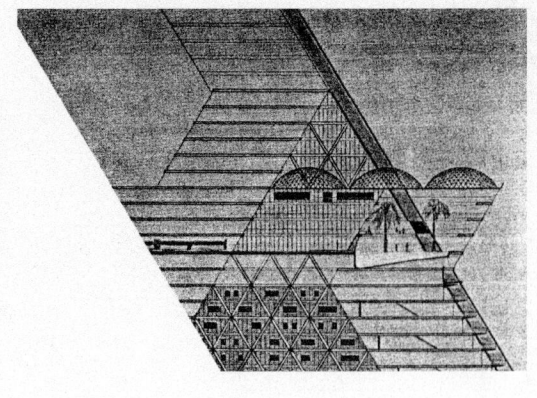

Proposed by Buckminster Fuller for multiple locations, including San Francisco and Tokyo, *Tetrahedral City* was to be a floating or land-based residential pyramid that could grow to accommodate one million inhabitants. The building was to have three triangular walls and a total of 300,000 living units, 200-stories tall with two-mile long walls at its base. Large openings in the structure would occur every fifty stories, allowing sunlight to enter the public garden at the bottom of the interior. Three city centers would ring the structure at different levels. Each of these featured "a community park, complete with lagoon, palms, and shopping center in geodesic domes." Fuller employed the tetrahedron shape due to its having the most surface per volume area of all polyhedra, and therefore its ability to provide the most living space with full access to the outdoors.

TOTAL SITE AREA (2-D; IN M²)	4,486,024
TOTAL GREENSPACE (M²)	2,768,724
Area: Greenspace: agriculture	0
Area: Greenspace: lawn	0
Area: Greenspace: park	2768724.04
Area: Greenspace: wilderness	0
AREA OF WATER (M²)	0
AREA OF INFRASTRUCTURE (M²)	366366
TOTAL BUILT AREA (FOOTPRINT; M²)	4,600,556
Area: Housing (footprint)	1,831,832
Area: Industrial (footprint)	0
Area: Public (footprint)	2,768,724
TOTAL POPULATION	1,000,000
TOTAL NUMBER HOUSING UNITS	300,000
NUMBER OF PEOPLE PER HOUSING UNIT	3.3
TOTAL AREA (3-D; IN M²)	252,246,346
Number of Floors: Housing	200
Number of Floors: Industrial	0
Number of Floors: Public	4

AREA: TOTAL BUILT	249,111,255
Area: Housing (3-D)	241,801,824
Area: Industrial (3-D)	0
Area: Public (3-D)	7,309,431
Area: Open Space (Greenspace + Water + Infrastructure) (3-D)	3,135,090
FAR: 3-D AREA/2-D AREA (X)	56.23
DENSITY: total population/site area (2-D) (people per km²)	222,915
DENSITY: total population/total area (3-D) (people per km²)	3,964

2-D PERCENTAGES

Greenspace	61%
Agriculture	0%
Lawn	0%
Park	61%
Wilderness	0%
Water	0%
Infrastructure	8%
Built Area	103%
Housing	41%
Industrial	0%
Public	62%
Total % of land use (can exceed 100%)	172%

3-D PERCENTAGES

Greenspace	1%
Agriculture	0%
Lawn	0%
Park	1%
Wilderness	0%
Water	0%
Infrastructure	0%
Built Area	99%
Housing	96%
Industrial	0%
Public	3%
Total % of land use	100%

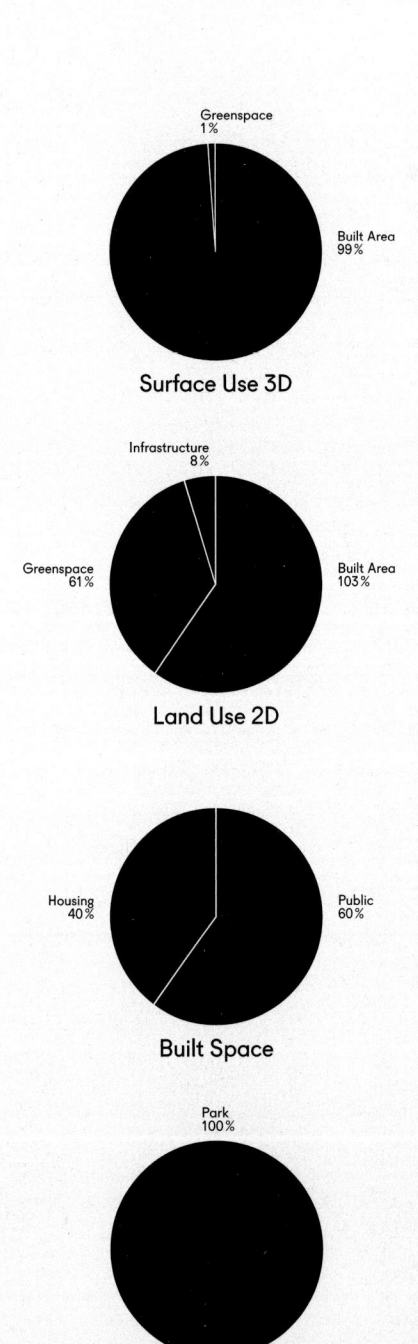

Surface Use 3D — Greenspace 1%, Built Area 99%

Land Use 2D — Greenspace 61%, Infrastructure 8%, Built Area 103%

Built Space — Housing 40%, Public 60%

Greenspace — Park 100%

about what constitutes an ideal "ecological city" on to the idealized cities of the past, *49 Cities* examines a variety of relationships—from the relationship of form and ideology, to that of form and performance—generating a fresh outlook and a new framework from which to re-engage the discourse on the city today.

Each of the 49 cities was categorized in terms of the cities' overall form or layout (linear, grid, radial or irregular), as well as "fear-factor"—the predominant conditions that each city is imagined to have to overcome or to alleviate (invasions, sprawl, urban chaos, slums, inflexibility, pollution or waste). Each city was carefully re-drawn, utilizing a standard color code for types of greenery, building typology, infrastructure, etc. in order to be able to easily compare the cities with one another.

Using these drawings and available information, each city was subjected to a quantitative analysis, calculating the overall area, population, amount of green-space, water and infrastructure as well as floor-area-ratio and both two-dimensional (i.e. footprint) and three-dimensional (i.e. surface area) densities. The cities were then ranked according to a number of categories—from 1 to 49—in order to compare and contrast the different approaches.

Form

The ultimate expression of urbanity, the grid, appears time and again, recognizable as the dominant urban form in as many as 21 of the 49 cities. The grid has been used as the basis of urban layouts in an attempt to combat everything from pollution to inflexibility. The grid configuration transcends time and geography, serving the basis for projects as diverse as Wright's *Broadacre City* and Le Corbusier's *Radiant City*. In an unintended symmetry, the most recent of the 49 cities, Norman Foster's *Masdar*, takes many of its urban design cues from the most ancient conurbation, namely, the Roman city.

The grid is the preferred form utilized when the fear-factor is *foreign invasion* or *warfare;* this connection dates back to the Roman Empire which sought high levels of control and organization. The diversity of uses and expressions of cities based on a grid system however, from the Conquistadors in Latin America to *Archizoom*, is testament to the grid's ultimate flexibility, suiting the needs of both colonialists and radicals alike.

Ten of the 49 cities chosen have irregular urban plans, for example Kitutake's *Ocean City*, (which was inspired by organic structures, and which follow the city's informal historic development), to Haussmann's radical rearrangement of Paris. Given the identification of irregular forms with informality and open-endedness, it is ironic that almost all of the authors of these cities conceived of them as antidotes to perceived urban chaos or sprawl. Many of the more geometric or tightly organized cities have a greater density or potential to expand, however nevertheless showing the danger of becoming seduced by organic growth when searching for a more balanced state of urban coexistence with nature.

Ten of the other cities analyzed are organized in a linear manner. *Roadtown*, built in the first decade of the last century, is the earliest example, and in many ways still the most revolutionary, designed as a continuous collection of row-houses, railway tracks and a highway stretching from Baltimore to Washington. Later examples, such as the projects by the Metabolists, use the linear form within an organic structure, organizing the city into *trunk*, *branch*, *stem*, and *leaves*. Linear cities are, however, inherently inflexible; they are only able to expand in one dimension and are singular in expression, yet all of them share a fascination with infrastructure, making them potential models for future ecological cities where infrastructure systems will inevitably require reinvention.

The radial urban form is most rarely used, appearing in only seven of the cities studied. However, from Claude-Nicolas Ledoux's *Saltworks* to the *Communitas* projects of Paul and Percival Goodman, it provides perhaps the most compelling "visionary" form; one that combines the structure and flexibility of a grid with the curved, organic forms of nature. The limit to endless radial expansion can, in some sense, be a benefit, allowing for new settlements to be separated by open space, agriculture or wilderness such was originally proposed by Howard for his *Garden Cities*.

Density

No urban quality reflects the ecological promise of visionary cities better than *density*. As more and more people populate the planet, and migrate to cities, it is imperative to find innovative ways to occupy less space with more people. Urban visionaries from Constantinos Doxiades to the Dutch architectural practice, MVRDV, and many of the authors of the 49 cities trumpeted denser cities as the solution to any number of societal and ecological ills.

Topping the list of the densest urban plans was Buckminster Fuller's *Tetrahedral City* ● see previous page designed in 1965. Fuller postulated that a pyramidal structure 200-levels high, containing a giant public park within it, would not only be able to house one million people in 300,000 apartments, but that the structure would also be light enough to float! (He proposed this city could continuously travel between Tokyo and San Francisco.) Cedric Price's *Fun Palace* was the second densest urban plan, followed by Archigram's 1964 *Plug-in City*. Both of these projects herald the High-Tech Movement by incorporating small, efficient modules that are able to accommodate great numbers of people on a reduced footprint. Completing the top five densest city plans are Superstudio's *Continuous Monument* and Archizoom's *No-Stop City*, both highly theoretical projects which aim to transform the lives of vast numbers of people on one level—Superstudio stated that the *Continuous Monument* should house the global population—and on another level were meant more as social critique than as a serious urban plan concept.

No-one, in the 1960s and 1970s, championed the environmental city and the merits of density more than the visionary architect, Paolo Soleri. He introduced his book *Arcology: City in the Image of Man* (1969) with the statement: "Miniaturize or die." Analyzing the two Soleri projects included in *49 Cities*, *Noahbabel*, ● see next page and *Mesa City*, it is therefore somewhat surprising that neither project has been designed to be particularly dense. *Mesa City*, is, ironically, one of the least dense schemes in terms of surface area to accommodation ratio.

FAR

Floor-area-ratio, or *FAR*, represents the number of times the entire urban footprint is duplicated in total built area. Cities with a high FAR also inevitably have a high three-dimensional density. For the projects that are designed with mega-structures—such as Peter Cook's *Mound* or Cedric Price's *Fun Palace*—FAR simply corresponds to the number of floors; these projects have the highest FAR values. (Fuller's *Tetrahedral City*, once again, tops the list—it is tricky to beat a 200-storey pyramid!) Existing cities like *Fort Worth* or *Dome over New York* also score highly in their FAR calculations, as both of these projects cover commercial centers with little or no open or green-spaces.

What Soleri's projects lack in density they make up in FAR, as this is because Soleri's *Arcologies* are often limited to the structures themselves, with little attention to their surrounding areas, which are assumed to be wilderness. High density/high FAR design ideals can conceivably be combined with larger and more generous allocation of open space, while still accommodating large populations: a possible viable approach to the design of cities in the future.

Population

Total population is the stated, or calculated, number of people for which the city has been designed. It shows the breadth of ambition of the project, and can also be read as analogous to the ego of the visionary architect. Some projects are absolutely vast in terms of pure numbers. Kenzo Tange's *Tokyo Bay* project, for instance, is designed for five million people, and can be expanded to accommodate ten million. Furthermore, the Goodmans' *Communitas* projects are envisioned as cities accommodating six million people, all engaged in what they call "efficient consumption." Ludwig Hilberseimer's pre-suburban dispersal plan for Chicago calls for displacing four million people from the city center, in order to minimize the potential damage of a nuclear bomb dropped in the downtown core. Soleri and Le Corbusier both tackle cities of approximately two million inhabitants. A few projects—such as Isozaki's *Clusters in the Air* designed in 1962 or Edgar Chambless' *Roadtown*—actually have far smaller capacities than one would imagine.

Open Space

In all of the 49 cities studied, open space is clearly as important a focus as built space—whether the two aspects are intertwined or whether one is compressed to allow for the other's expansion. There are also cities which focus consciously on rural areas, such as Kurokawa's *Agricultural City*, Richard Snibbe's *Handloser*, or Howard's *Garden City* as well as the projects by Communitas, which imagine a harmonious balance between surrounding open land and developed cities. Le Corbusier's *Radiant City* calls for every building to have both public space on the rooftops and *pilotis* on ground level, allowing the ground to continue fluidly beneath the buildings. *Radiant City*, thus creates a city with 100% of the footprint dedicated to open and green-space; this is equaled only by Peter Cook's *Mound* proposal—a city completely submerged into a hillside.

Averages

While ecological cities cannot be measured solely by data; density, population, FAR and proportion of green-space may not be the only, or the most important measure of sustainability, it is obvious that a green city of the future has to address all of these issues head-on.

It is useful, therefore, to examine the cities that achieved consistently in all the categories. This was achieved by taking an average score of their rankings. Surprisingly, Le Corbusier's *Radiant City* scored the highest average, followed closely by Fuller's *Tetrahedral City*. The two visionaries are in many ways at the opposite ends of the rationalist spectra: Fuller, the scientist/inventor, was convinced that geometry and efficiency provided the keys for a future society based on equality and temperance, whilst Le Corbusier, the artist/architect, whose intuitive drive to discover the essence of the new modern world drove him to imagine a city of sunlight and open spaces, while at the same time, ironically, providing the foundation for the inert and oppressive regime of faceless, urban redevelopments of the 1970s. While Fuller is often hailed as a genius ahead of his time, Le Corbusier remains vilified in many quarters for his urban visions: a quote from *Radiant City* provides the introduction to the New Urbanist tract, *Suburban Nation*, which goes on to lay America's urban problems at the door of the Swiss master-planner.

While it is perhaps, no surprise that Fuller's musings led to one of the densest, most efficient (and strangest) visions of urbanity in *49 Cities*, *Radiant City*'s vision seems to create an opportunity to rediscover and perhaps re-interpret the project through a new, ecological lens. Consistently referring to his project as *La Ville Verte* (The Green City), Le Corbusier discusses his plan as a means to combat pollution, provide light, and open green-space, as well as to house vast numbers of people in humane conditions. Setting aside his insistence on the clear separation of zones of use, one can envisage the *Radiant City* being promoted as a means to combat climate change and deal with our current pace of urbanization.

There are also unexpected deviations in some of the most familiar elements of Le Corbusier's *Ville Radieuse*, beginning with the notion of *Towers in the Park*. Le Corbusier's green-spaces are far different from the pale grass plazas of 1970s housing blocks. Instead, the architect describes a city surrounded by vines and dense thickets with a multitude of plant life: a city in a wilderness, not a city of tended, green lawns. He envisaged the weaving together of the urban and natural worlds that has intriguing possibilities for us today once again.

Le Corbusier's fascination with fitness and sports was well known. Lesser known, however was his vehement and coherent argument in favor of urban farming. In many ways, the urban farm is the holy grail of sustainable cities, providing both green-space, as well as places for community interaction combined with locally grown food. While farming is a major component of many of the urban schemes featured in *49 Cities* (from Fourier's *Phalènsteres* to Wright's *Broadacre City*), few of them bring agriculture within the heart of the urban realm. Le Corbusier, however, proposed 150 m² "kitchen gardens" for each resident, linked together to create communal gardens, equipped with automatic irrigation and overseen by a resident farmer for every 100 allotments. Each day after sports would be the time for farming—an important aspect of the *Radiant City* that is often overlooked or ignored.

This closer re-reading, of just one of the chosen 49 cities, reveals the wealth of information and inspiration that can be gleaned from the rich history of visionary planning. Every city has its own forgotten story—with clarity of vision that seems breathtakingly innovative even today—ready to be rediscovered. *49 Cities* is a call to re-engage cities as the site of radical thinking and experimentation, moving beyond "green building" towards an embrace of ideas, scale, vision, and common sense; this all combined with unbridled imagination in the pursuit of empowered questioning and the re-invention of new cities for tomorrow.

Paolo Soleri's *Noahbabel*

 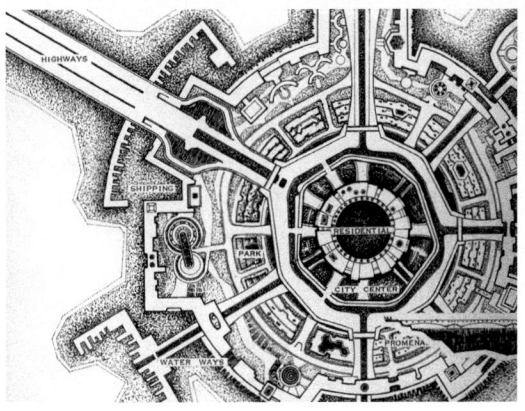 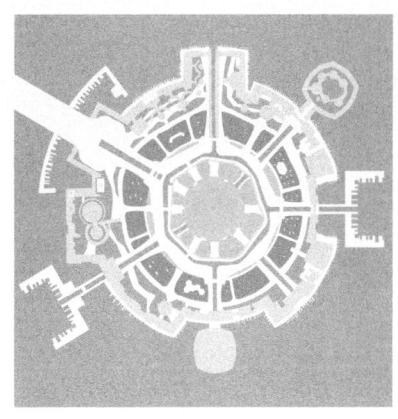

Noahbabel, one of Paolo Soleri's Arcology projects, followed the design principles laid out in his book, *The City in the Image of Man*. These principles called for a hyperdense city designed to maximize human interaction and access to shared cost-effective infrastructural services like water and sewage. The *Arcologies* proposed in the book attempt to minimize the use of energy, raw materials and land; reduce waste and pollution; and allow interaction with the surrounding natural environment. *Noahbabel*, an aquatic *Arcology*, features apartments and residences near vertical cores of structure, and is rigidly zoned into work, housing, leisure, and transportation functions.

TOTAL SITE AREA (2-D; IN M²)	3,459,858

TOTAL GREENSPACE (M²)	204,933
Area: Greenspace: agriculture	0
Area: Greenspace: lawn	0
Area: Greenspace: park	204,933
Area: Greenspace: wilderness	0

AREA OF WATER (M²)	1,452,510
AREA OF INFRASTRUCTURE (M²)	1,166,342

TOTAL BUILT AREA (FOOTPRINT; M²)	841,006
Area: Housing (footprint)	344,813
Area: Industrial (footprint)	159,791
Area: Public (footprint)	336,402

TOTAL POPULATION	90,000
TOTAL NUMBER HOUSING UNITS	30,000
NUMBER OF PEOPLE PER HOUSING UNIT	3.00

TOTAL AREA (3-D; IN M²)	17,505,755
Number of Floors: Housing	30
Number of Floors: Industrial	8
Number of Floors: Public	9

AREA: TOTAL BUILT	14,683,969
Area: Housing (3-D)	10,344,377
Area: Industrial (3-D)	1,278,329
Area: Public (3-D)	3,061,263
Area: Open Space (Greenspace + Water + Infrastructure) (3-D)	2,823,786

FAR: 3-D AREA/2-D AREA (X)	5.06

DENSITY: total population/site area (2-D) (people per km²)	26,013
DENSITY: total population/total area (3-D) (people per km²)	5,141

2-D PERCENTAGES

Greenspace	6%
Agriculture	0%
Lawn	0%
Park	6%
Wilderness	0%
Water	42%
Infrastructure	34%
Built Area	24%
Housing	10%
Industrial	5%
Public	10%
Total % of land use (can exceed 100%)	106%

3-D PERCENTAGES

Greenspace	1%
Agriculture	0%
Lawn	0%
Park	1%
Wilderness	0%
Water	8%
Infrastructure	7%
Built Area	84%
Housing	59%
Industrial	7%
Public	18%
Total % of land use	100%

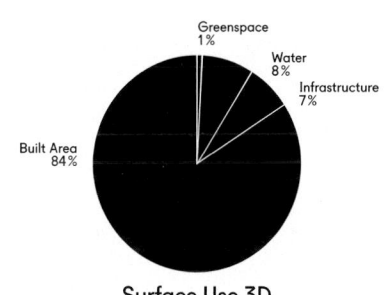

Surface Use 3D

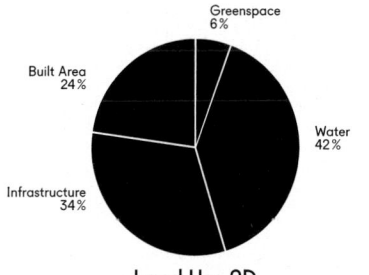

Land Use 2D

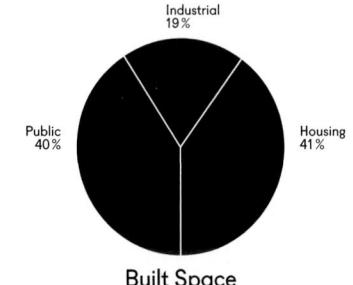

Built Space

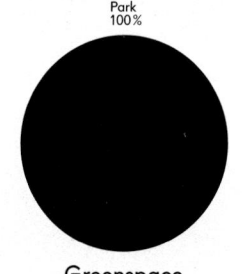

Greenspace

Ж. CHPT. I — 49 CITIES

Project Title:
MULTIPLICITY
Architect:
John Wardle Architects and Stefano Boscutti
Envisioned Project Location:
Melbourne, Australia
Envisioned Completion Date:
2110

WHERE AND WHEN

The modern Australian city is simply unsustainable. The project, *Multiplicity,* proposes that we can no longer afford any more growth at the periphery. In order to maximize our resources we need to grow together, not apart. *Multiplicity* assumes that by the year 2110, new planning initiatives in Melbourne will have incubated a self-sustaining city of hyper-density. Growth will be germinated from the heart of the city. Melbourne has not yet grown further out into a suburban sprawl, but rather upwards and downwards. Air-rights within the city grid have opened up a completely new scenario. The densification this project proposes through its layering continues below ground as potential new space, which could accommodate large entertainment venues, supermarkets, and concert halls. The new three-dimensional city grid could be organic and non-hierarchical. Technology would be fragmented, converged and merged with the private, corporate, political, and public spheres into a seamless field. Technology would diffuse civic institutions into the public realm. Communities and cultures would blur the conventional dividing lines of wealth, privilege, and ethnicity.

BASIC CONDITIONS

Cities tell stories. In the future Melbourne will also have multiple stories to tell—a bundle of narratives and possibilities, a place where "form follows fiction." A recurring theme in fiction is the idea of the existence of parallel worlds. *Multiplicity* proposes a new parallel city above the old, and poses the question of how the two might co-exist. Will they be populated similarly? How will the two meet? Will the upper city be residential and separated from the corporate city below? Will the new city supersede the old?

KEY PRINCIPLES

In *Multiplicity*, the vaulted dome of Renaissance cathedrals like St Peter's in Rome would be replaced by an equivalent dome that would cover the whole city, rendered in lightweight materials. This urge to recreate the vault of the sky is extended to form a field across the entire city. *Multiplicity* is a city of architectural membranes with millions of constantly changing screens: pixel as address, home as multiplex, life as *mise-en-scène*. This architecture of information, of media, art, and advertising, is embedded within the fabric of the new city. The

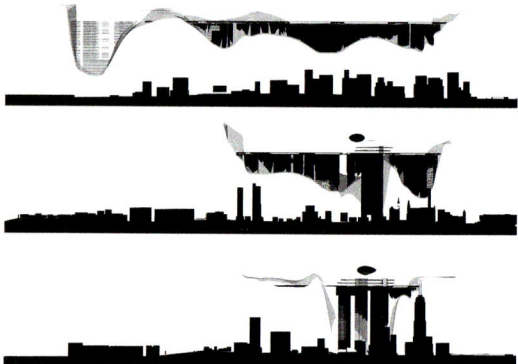

curtain screen is replaced by the pixel to control transparency and privacy. Structural pylons would support the new city above. They would be the umbilical links between the "mother" and the "offspring" city. The upper plane would thermally cool the multiple cities below like an enormous canopy to shade the city from climate change. Solar cell micro-fiber edges would convert prevailing winds and sunlight into power. Energy production would be embedded into the sheer fabric of the city. Food production through mosaic farming and rainwater harvesting on the topmost level, would create a city of agriculture. Airships would transport millions of travelers every day, to and from, the upper city.

Project Title:
THE HANGING CEMETERY OF BAGHDAD
Architect:
NaJa & deOstos
Envisioned Project Location:
Baghdad
Envisioned Completion Date:
Non-applicable

WHERE AND WHEN
The Hanging Cemetery of Baghdad is a speculative architectural project. Since its sketchy inception dating back to the summer of 2004, NaJa & deOstos have tried to explore what architecture could possibly generate when faced with extreme cultural and political scenarios like the current crisis in the Middle East. As with the rest of their work, the focus of the project is less about a final, complete object, and more about a kind of script that is inserted into the city.

BASIC CONDITIONS
Although architects typically design for clients, the *Hanging Cemetery of Baghdad* is not for, or about the people of Baghdad, who are located over 4,100 km away from the London-based NaJa & deOstos. As the architects say: "About them (the users) we know almost nothing. But it is about a city represented and portrayed daily through international TV and newspapers." A place that seems almost fictional due to the huge amount of attention that it generates, but equally one so far removed from our immediate physical reality in central Europe or America. Through the medium of television, the imaginary clashes between a predatory West and a stereotyped East are reduced to spaces, architectural inventions and structural uncertainty. Consequently the project, or story, reveals itself through the duality of both television cameras and spectators, searching for an understanding of the colossal, suspended apparatus.

KEY PRINCIPLES
The main driving force behind the *Hanging Cemetery of Baghdad* is to consistently explore the ambiguities that surround our current lives through an inventive design proposal, not only as producers of space, but also as global spectators.

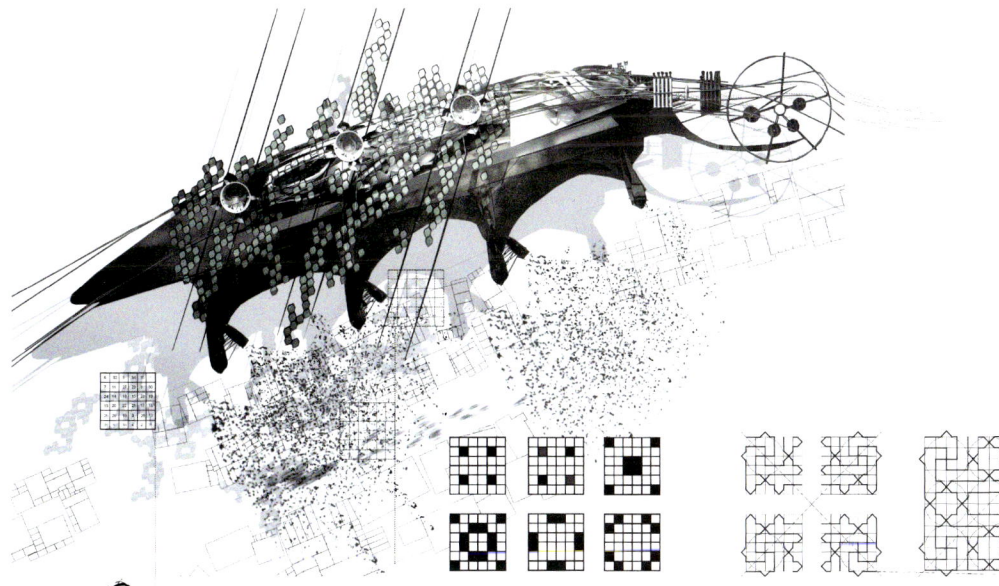

PERSISTENZE   GREAT SCAPES

Project Title:
CONSISTENZE & PERSISTENZE
Artist:
Giacomo Costa
Envisioned Project Location:
Urban realm worldwide
Envisioned Completion Date:
An alternative future

WHERE AND WHEN
The fantastic worlds created by Giacomo Costa, at turns historical as well as contemporary, real and imagined, seem to be situated in a post-catastrophic scenario.

BASIC CONDITIONS
In *Consistenze & Persistenze*, a cityscape is punctured by amorphous, alien mega-structures. The project portrays both the city and the structures at various stages of deterioration, with half submerged infrastructure emerging from the debris. The surrounding desolate urban fabric appears to be free of any habitation or maintenance.

KEY PRINCIPLES
Employing sophisticated digital techniques borrowed from the world of cinema, the artist, Giacomo Costa, reinterprets the collective imagination of the metropolis, creating imaginary cityscapes, spaces with vast vistas that include spectacular ruins and amazing architecture. Suspended between tradition and modernity, both real and dreamlike, the images echo the genre of science fiction. At the same time the images are layered with meticulous detail, they appear as the fruits of a contemporary reinterpretation of the most classic topos: that of the ideal, utopian city.

URBAN SKY LINK   GREAT SCAPES

Project Title:
URBAN SKY LINK
Architect:
David A. Garcia
Envisioned Project Location:
New York, USA
Envisioned Completion Date:
2020

WHERE AND WHEN
The sites chosen for this proposal, *Urban Sky Link*, are alongside the East River edge, close to the UN building in Manhattan, and also along the opposite shore of the river, at Hunters Point in the Queens area. This is a relevant test scenario, partly because of the existing density and high proportion of skyscrapers in Manhattan, and also, primarily due to the strong geographic barrier that the East River creates. Currently an industrial site with in-full development, Hunters Point is far from a lively city district. Nevertheless, it is the site of a vital railroad link and train station, with breathtaking views of the Manhattan skyline, and a water's edge full of potential, waiting to be developed. The building would become an extension of Hunters Point and would reach downtown Manhattan and become a continuation of East 39th Street into Queens.

BASIC CONDITIONS
Urban Sky Link tries to challenge the traditional concept of the skyscraper, and aims to transform the typology of the high-rise into an asset for the user and the city. The history of the skyscraper is inherently linked to that of the elevator. It is interesting to note that although, structurally speaking, the skyscraper has evolved enormously it is still a vertical structure, dictated by the elevator, which in its vertical trajectory only arrives at a dead-end. The lack of alternative methods of traversing levels (the elevator's inability to curve) has determined the typology of the skyscraper for the last century. This proposal attempts to expand the constraints of high-rises beyond a high floor-to-area ratio, or simply extruding the floor plan x-times. The proposal's primary concept is fairly straightforward: the idea of moving upwards in a building design can equally mean that one could move in a different direction in the urban fabric, taking the pedestrians' relationship to the city as a decisive design factor. The concept converts the traditional high-rise structure into a double-sided skyscraper, making it rise and fall again, linking the two sites and transforming the structure into a kind of wormhole in the cityscape. The structure would also become a public transport system, as well as an accessible cityscape. The skyscraper would link unconnected sites, or overcome topographic barriers such as rivers, or even link different levels within a city.

KEY PRINCIPLES
The skyscraper functions as an extension of the street, offering leisure, office space, hotels, and apartments, as well as outdoor areas and energy parks. Rising gradually to an apex of 260 m high, set between other high-rises on the Manhattan riverside, the Skylink would rise parallel to the neighboring structure for the initial 50 floors, then curve towards the East River and "arrive" on Hunters Point on the far side. At ground level, the footprint of the Skylink is relatively small, only the structure would be visible. The site is a public park, where access to the skyscrapers would be possible via elevators that would run at an incline, or gondola lifts. Immediately above, the levels will be used for office space, hotels, and apartments distributed around a central core or a central atrium where each function would be separated by an atrium garden. The apex of the structure, given its geometry, would function primarily as a public space enlivened by restaurants, cafés, and shopping areas. On the descent

offices and living space, will be separated by a park and an aviary. A series of empty levels without glazing, would allow the wind to ventilate the structure, rotate air turbines, and generate energy. To solve the challenge of circulation in a curved high-rise, the architects looked at existing technologies related to large spans, such as Gondola lifts, that could be used to circulate to designated destinations/stations along the skyscraper. Inclined elevators and escalators would transport people to different levels.

Project Title:
SILK ROAD MAP EVOLUTION
Architect:
OFL Architecture
Envisioned Project Location:
Silk Road Route
Envisioned Completion Date:
The near future

BASIC CONDITIONS

Silk Road Map Evolution is a project conceived from the desire to re-establish and rebuild the current Silk Road link through a social, economic, political, and architectural rehabilitation of the old Silk Road route. The new Silk Road becomes a driving force for the creation of small urban projects. It is a new way of conceiving urban sprawl (linear), where larger cities help smaller cities. Silk Road is a project that strongly links architecture and infrastructure

KEY PRINCIPLES

Silk Road Map Evolution is a kind of global metropolis for the future based on the idea of designing a set of highly differentiated, sustainable, and habitable towers. These small living worlds are organized into rounded skyscrapers according to program, habitants and the proximity to the railway line and the countryside. The proposal consists of two urban, ecologically integrated systems which will be developed vertically and horizontally respectively. The

WHERE AND WHEN

Silk Road Map Evolution is the winning proposal for the Silk Road Map International Competition organized by New Italian Blood and open to Italian and Chinese professionals and students. The Silk Road is an extensive interconnected network of trade routes across the Asian continent connecting Asia with the Mediterranean, North and Northeast Africa, and Europe. The Silk Road has been given its name from the lucrative Chinese silk trade, a major reason for the connection of trade routes to an extensive transcontinental network. As such, the Silk Road was also historically important as a route for cultural, commercial, and technological exchange between myriads of different people: traders, merchants, pilgrims, missionaries, soldiers, nomads, and urban dwellers.

through a new main railway line, which will follow the current Silk Road route that will run from Venice to Xi'an in China through several countries en route, extending its "arms" across an infrastructure network, commercial services, and new housing. The route will bring new impetus to ailing and luckless economic regions in its vicinity. The 15,000-kilometer-long Silk Road will be interspersed with several bionic towers constituting the new conurbation's core, while new cities, configured like routes, will run from the main branch (the main Silk Road line) linking smaller disadvantaged and unconnected towns and cities. The system is conceived as a kind of a pump, which will feed the small disadvantaged cities along the new Silk Road with economic lifeblood, which will revive them economically and socially.

first element, the complex of towers, will be composed of three different types of skyscrapers that will have an average height of 400 m. The second element, the Silk Road railway system, will form the main line of the Silk Road and will serve as a line of commercial transport with trains travelling on new railways lines based on gravitational, polarized fields, thereby merging the East with the West. The outer membrane of the complex, towers and tunnel, will consist of a unique and innovative system constructed with a high standard ecological concrete based on titanium dioxide that will help to significantly reduce air pollution and, via synthetic chlorophyll, generate a photo-catalytic reaction producing 500 million liters of oxygen (clean air) per day.

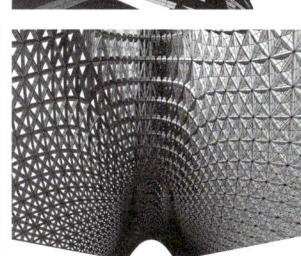
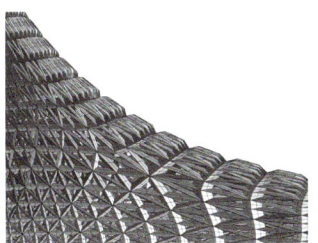

Project Title:
THE BERG
Architect:
Mila Studio (Jakob Tigges)
Envisioned Project Location:
Berlin-Tempelhof, Germany
Envisioned Completion Date:
An alternative future

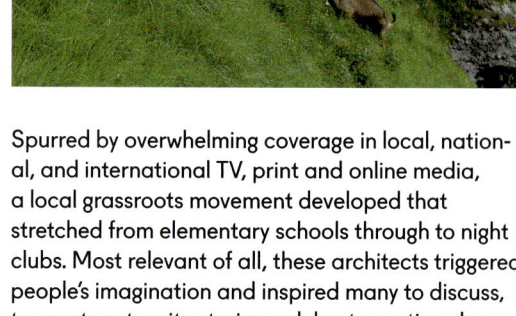

Spurred by overwhelming coverage in local, national, and international TV, print and online media, a local grassroots movement developed that stretched from elementary schools through to night clubs. Most relevant of all, these architects triggered people's imagination and inspired many to discuss, to create art, write stories, celebrate parties, draw portraits—to ultimately see in their mind's eye, *The Berg*, an imaginary attraction that created a new symbol of the many virtues of contemporary Berlin.

WHERE AND WHEN
While big and wealthy cities in many parts of the world challenge the limits of possibility by building gigantic hotels with fanciful shapes, erecting sky-high office towers or constructing philharmonic temples that hover, Mila's project, *The Berg*, envisions a 1,000-meter-high mountain at the heart of the city of Berlin, covered with snow from September to March.

BASIC CONDITIONS
In 2008 Berlin's famous Tempelhof Airport was closed as it had become defunct. Already a decade ago the city's department for urban development put together an uninspired plan for the use of the airfield after the airport's closure. The original master-plan proposed the creation of five new neighborhoods around a central park. Unlike in the developing world, Berlin has a stagnant population, so there is no need for new apartments, and there are plenty of vacant building sites located even more centrally than the Tempelhof Airfield. The airport is also indebted by more than 60 billion Euro! Jakob Tigges' proposal was to imagine the most beautiful mountain on the site and to speculate on the project's potential to provoke discussion. The core body of the project was formed by the reactions it provoked.

KEY PRINCIPLES
This projects aims to provide a struggling city with a breath of new energy by creating a colossal icon—one that suits Berlin both financially and culturally. According to Tigges: "This icon would need to play with the alleged defects of the people of Berlin, namely their presumption and their plainness." Furthermore, it had to be something that people yearned for and that inspired them—a common reference point. With this project Tigges managed to achieve two things simultaneously: give joy to disillusioned Berliners and replace mediocre urban reality with a fantastic container for individual projections in the classic utopian tradition.

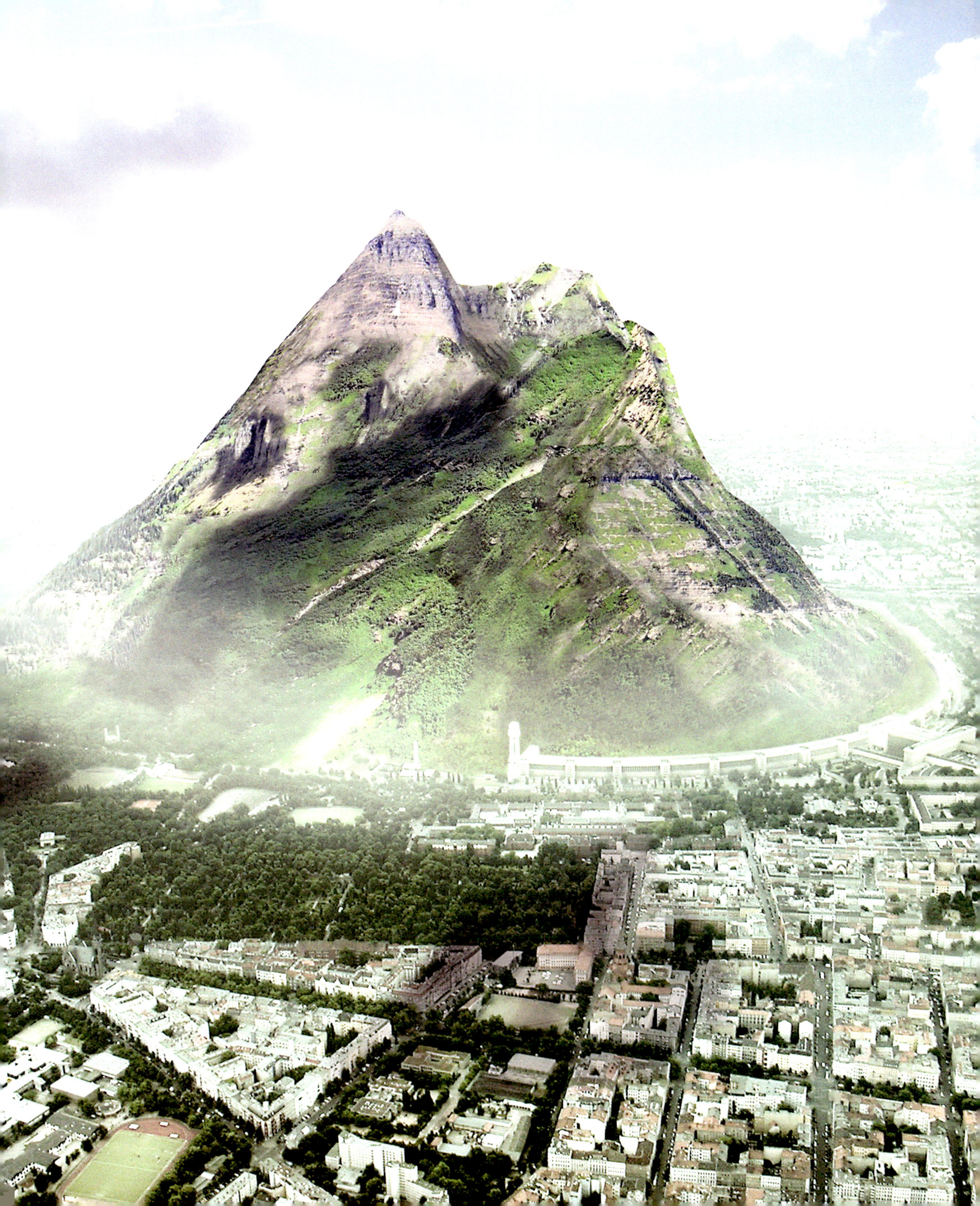

Project Title:
LACE HILL OVER YEREVAN
Architect:
Forrest Fulton Architecture
Envisioned Project Location:
Yerevan, Armenia
Envisioned Completion Date:
The near future

WHERE AND WHEN
Lace Hill over Yerevan is an 85,000 m² proposal for a new model of development for Armenia's capital city, Yerevan. The site has unique genus loci; it is dense with overlapping natural and urban phenomenon and looks across at the iconic Mount Ararat.

BASIC CONDITIONS
The project attempts to tie the adjacent city and the landscape together to create a place that will support a holistic, ultra-green lifestyle, somewhere between rural hillside living and dense cultured urbanity. To create a new, firmly rooted architectural urbanism, *Lace Hill* morphs the ubiquitous urban element of Yerevan, the superblock, to the site on a truncated hill along the natural amphitheater of Yerevan.

KEY PRINCIPLES
Native plants irrigated with recycled grey-water cover the hill. Intricate perforations recalling traditional, delicate Armenian lace provide terraced exterior areas with natural ventilation, and views along the promenade, in the hotel rooms, apartments, and offices. Unlike a monolithic tower block that dominates the landscape from the city below, the delicate, "lacy," inhabited hill seduces visitors to enjoy the promenade walkway with a succession of tower-voids. The tower-voids act as dramatic cooling towers in Yerevan's semi-arid climate. As one moves toward the cooler center, the hill opens to the sky. With the atmosphere of a soaring cathedral in its scale and its light quality; watery pools and tree-topped hills fill these flowing public spaces. The primary structure is the perforated concrete exterior load-bearing façade, which creates column-free and beamless spaces that can be configured flexibly. The undulation of the surfaces form structurally efficient vaults and arches, while creating an array of views, as well as maximizing the area. Orientation and views informed the location of living and working activities. All living spaces are strung along the elongated, meandering southern slope of the hill, maximizing direct sun, creating terraces, and providing incredible views. Offices, which favor indirect light, are less reliant on having spectacular views and are therefore situated along the northern slope of the hill. A narrow, stepped floor plan for the office spaces provides adequate, diffuse daylight. Stores, restaurants, exhibition halls, cinema, and fitness center line the promenade on the ground level. Pedestrians and cyclists access the hill via a park at the south, east, and west edges of the site. A potential greenway along the amphitheater to the west links the hill to tourist sites and additional pedestrian and bicycle routes.

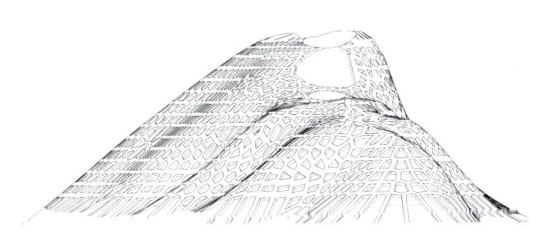

East elevation

West elevation

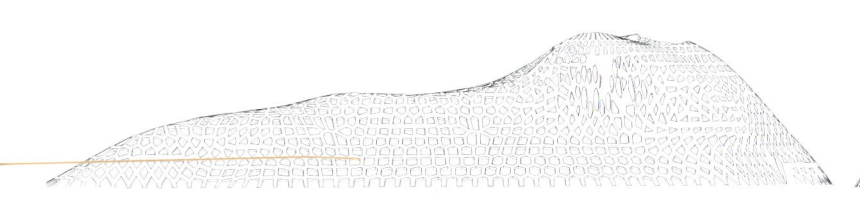

North elevation

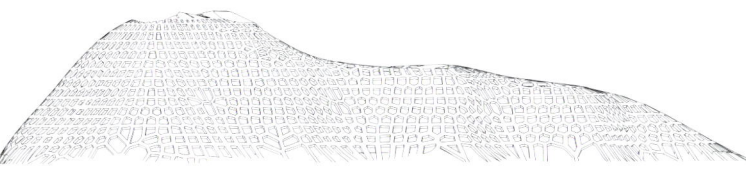

South elevation

Ж. CHPT. I

37

LACE HILL OVER YEREVAN

Ж. CHPT. I

39

Project Title:
RECOVERING BERLIN
Architect:
Protocol Architecture (Yuval Borochov, Lisa Ekle, Danil Nagy)
Envisioned Project Location:
Berlin, Germany
Envisioned Completion Date:
2050

40   RECOVERING BERLIN   GREAT SCAPES

WHERE AND WHEN

This project, by Protocol Architecture, is set in Berlin in 2050, where, in four decades from now, Germany and Western Europe's rapidly declining population will have lead to large-scale abandonment of Berlin's urban infrastructure.

BASIC CONDITIONS

The City of Berlin decided to commission Protocol Architecture to apply their research towards a new approach to city planning; an approach that is not contingent upon development or growth. In order to address this issue within the context of recent advances in bio-technology, Protocol Architecture devised a radical plan for Berlin that would harness the geological power of earthquakes to strategically de-stabilize the physical landscape, demolishing sections of the abandoned city, while simultaneously creating the potential for a new form of urbanism beneath the ground. In the course of their research, the architects discovered several historical documents that collectively produce a geopolitical history and technological basis for recovering Berlin. A recurring thread in each history is the bacillus pasteurii, a microbe able to transform sand into sandstone by depositing calcite (calcium carbonate) throughout the granules, fusing them together. This microbe became the driving force behind much of their research.

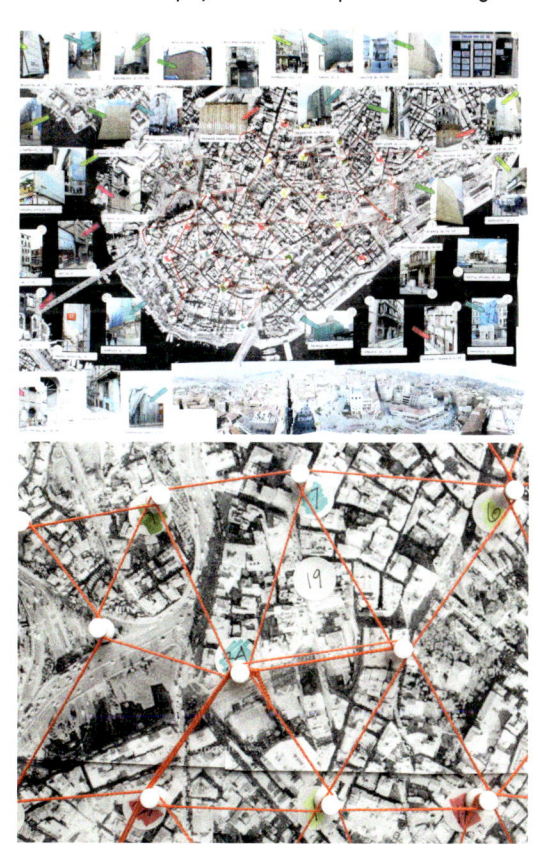

Document 641.17: *The Nesin Map* (2017)
Author: Harem Nesin, Turkish Journalist. Description: Map created by Nesin, recording disguised locations of state-led injections of soil-stabilizing bacteria in order to mitigate predicted destruction from the imminent 2019 Istanbul Earthquake. Conclusion: First implementation of the genetically modified bacteria on an urban scale, pursued without the cooperation of the populace.

Document 641.02: *The Rühmann Notebook* (2000)
Author: Martina Rühmann, urban planner for Berlin. Description: Documented hidden network of bio-technological research labs, later discovering their use was a collaboration between Soviet and Western Scientists prior to the fall of the Berlin Wall. The potential of bacillus pasteurii was being tested at the time. Conclusion: The notebook reveals human initiative for communication in spite of socio-political context, particularly for advancements in the sciences.

KEY PRINCIPLES:

Recovering Berlin will utilize innovations in bio-technology to implement the first highly networked earth-based bio-supercomputer. Using modified bacteria-based technology, the project will weave together a complex and highly refined computation network, similar to the neural network of the brain. The bacteria will be delivered into the Earth by injecting large amounts of specialized fluid into several sites throughout Berlin. The "injections" will induce tremors, which will cause liquefaction of the soil, thereby destroying vacant buildings and allowing the distribution of the *Shewanella* bacteria and its micro-filaments. Following the tremors, the re-settled soil will leave behind cavernous spaces underground, which will be structurally reinforced and prepared for habitation by the activity of the bacteria *bacillus pasteurii*. A new kind of real-estate speculation will arise from the combination of geological conditions and technological capacities deposited within the soil. The underground caverns, now latent with vast computational power, will begin to be excavated by humans and adapted for inhabitation. The value of the space will depend not only on its size and layout, but also the amount of computing power generated from the activity of bacteria with metal deposits in the earth beneath Berlin. This new subterranean urbanism, occurring within an ultra-conductive and highly networked ground, would allow humans to interact more directly with this new technology and with each other, creating a vibrant new urban fabric within old Berlin.

Bio-processor network
Stabilized earth, pre-occupation

- bacteria
- paths of information transfer
- concentrations pf micro-conductive material in the soil

Bio-processor network
Post-occupation activation

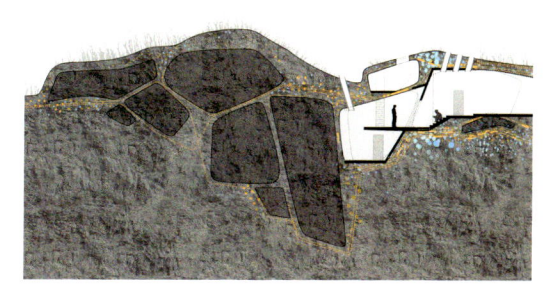

- bacteria
- paths of information transfer
- concentrations pf micro-conductive material in the soil

Project Title:
SIETCH NEVADA
Architect:
MATSYS
Envisioned Project Location:
Nevada, USA

WHERE AND WHEN
Envisioned for the American Southwest, *Sietch Nevada,* is a futuristic urban prototype consisting of a complex underground network of tunnels and canals.

BASIC CONDITIONS
In Frank Herbert's famous 1965 novel *Dune*, he describes a planet that has become almost completely desertified. *Dune* is regarded as the first ecological novel and forecasts a dystopian world that has hardly any water reserves. In the novel, the few remaining inhabitants have secluded themselves from their harsh environment in subterranean oases. Far from idyllic, these havens, known as *sietch*, are essentially underground water storage banks. Water is the currency of wealth in this alternate reality. It is preciously conserved, secretly hidden, protected, and rationed with strict authority. Although this science-fiction novel sounded completely alien in 1965, the concept of a water-poor world is fast becoming a reality; for example in the American Southwest. Lured by cheap land prices and the promise of endless water supplies via the powerful Colorado River, millions of Americans have made this region their home. However, the Colorado River has been desiccated by both heavy agricultural cultivation and global warming, to the point that the river now ends in an intermittent trickle in Baja, California. Towns that once relied on the river for water have increasingly begun to dig underground boreholes for use in emergency drought conditions. However, as droughts are becoming more frequent and more severe, these water banks will become more than simply precautionary for emergency situations, but will be necessary for everyday use.

KEY PRINCIPLES
Sietch Nevada projects "water-banking" as the fundamental factor in future urban infrastructure in the American Southwest. *Sietch Nevada* is an urban prototype that makes the storage, use, and collection of water essential to the function of urban life. Inverting the stereotypical southwest urban patterns of dispersed structures open to the sky, the *Sietch* proposes a dense, troglodytic community. A network of storage canals would be covered with undulating residential and commercial structures. These canals would connect the city with vast aquifers situated deep underground; the aquifers would provide transportation, as well as agricultural irrigation. The underground caverns would brim with dense, urban life: a kind of subterranean Venice! Cellular in form, these structures constitute a new neighborhood typology that would mediate between the subterranean, urban network, and the surface-level activities of water-harvesting, energy-generation, and urban agriculture and aquaculture. However, the *Sietch* is also a bunker-like fortress, which prepares for the inevitable wars which will be fought over water in the future.

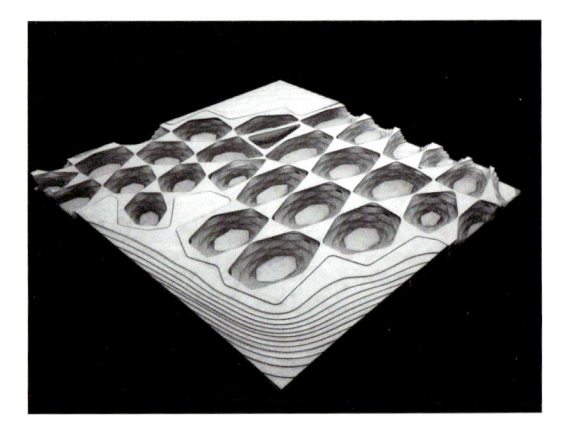

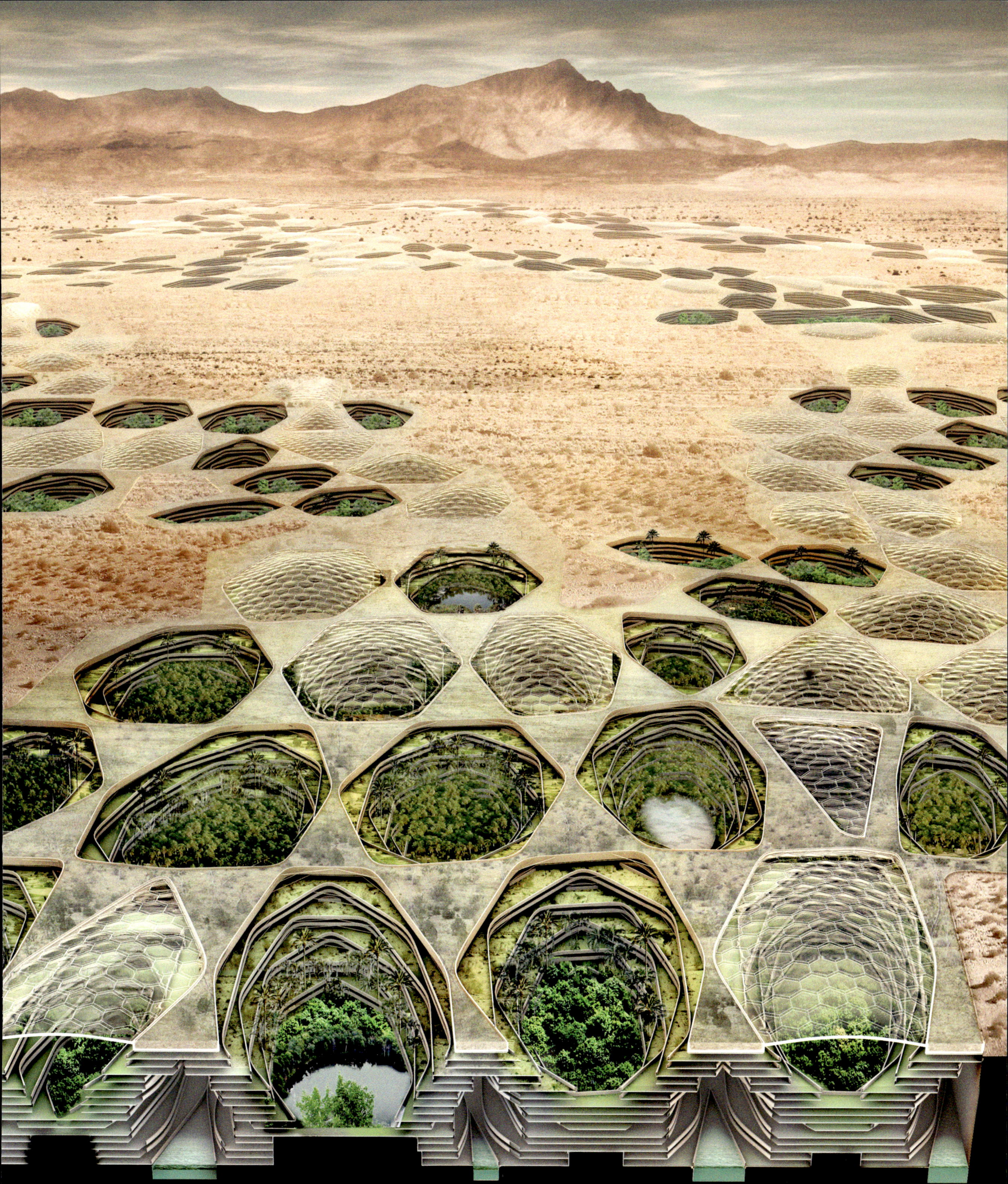

Project Title:
DUNE—ARENACEOUS ANTI-DESERTIFICATION ARCHITECTURE

Architect:
Magnus Larsson

Envisioned Project Location:
Sahara Desert

Envisioned Completion Date:
The near future

44 DUNE GREAT SCAPES

KEY PRINCIPLES

Dune is an architectural proposition that suggests precisely such an elemental manipulation of the landscape. The design also advocates a radical shift in structural thinking, away from pre-fabricated or in-situ construction, and towards localized production of granular materials into cement. Localized cementation of desert sand is achieved through microbial induced carbonate precipitation (MICP) using the micro-organism *Bacillus pasteurii*, an aerobic bacteria pervasive in natural soil deposits. The bacteria's enzymatic catalyst, hydrolyses urea, that—when the process occurs in a calcium-rich environment—generates calcite, which binds the individual grains of sand together. The solidification of the sand would be arranged in a narrow, roughly 6,000-kilometer-long pan-African city with the capacity to withstand the shifting sands of the Sahara Desert. *Dune* would evolve into a micro-environmental support structure for the *Great Green Wall* for the Sahara and Sahel Initiative. Investigating a more climate-conscious architecture that points toward adaptive responses to the potential threats of extreme environments, *Dune* creates a framework for an innovative architecture that applies controlled bio-cementation processes as a strategy to mitigate the continual migration of sand dunes in the arid lands of Saharan Africa. The final outcome would be a habitable anti-desertification process made from the desert itself; a sand-preventative device created from sand itself.

WHERE AND WHEN

The project, *Dune*, presented here is an architectural speculation aimed at creating a network of 6,000-kilometer-long solidified sand dunes in the Sahara Desert.

BASIC CONDITIONS

A single grain of sand might seem insignificant: a tiny splinter of rock, a miniscule fragment of a shell, the residue of a microcosmic event. Myriads of grains joined together, however, can transform into almost anything: mesmerizing landscapes or vast deserts. Sand is a fluid material capable of being transformed into solid structures, and ultimately even into flourishing cities. In grains of sand, one can find fascinating forms and emerging patterns, interlocking angular quartz grains; possibilities of the formation of other morphologies. In short, we find a constant unfolding of interactive opportunities. Architects work in the mineral world, in which all design is fundamentally about aggregation and erosion. Even the most austerely minimalist structures present aggregations of elements and densifications of matter that did not exist before. Through additive processes, materials assembled together become buildings that, in turn, can develop into cities. At its most fundamental level, architecture is about the manipulation of landscape.

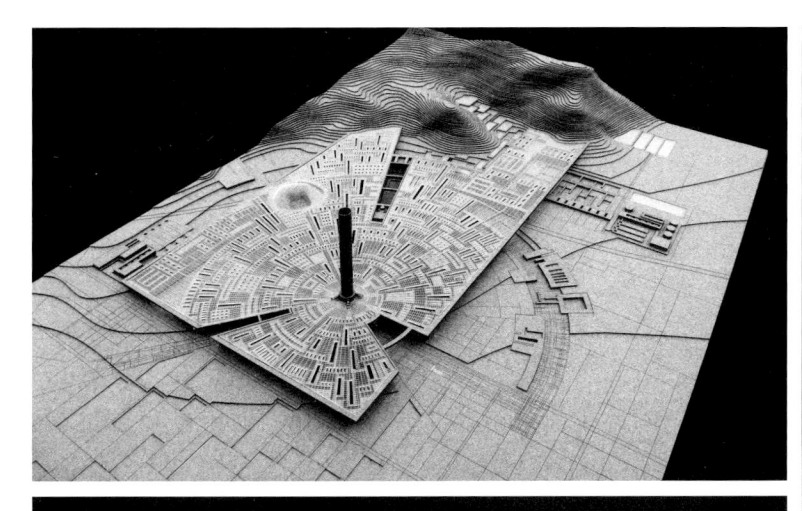

STACK CITY GREAT SCAPES

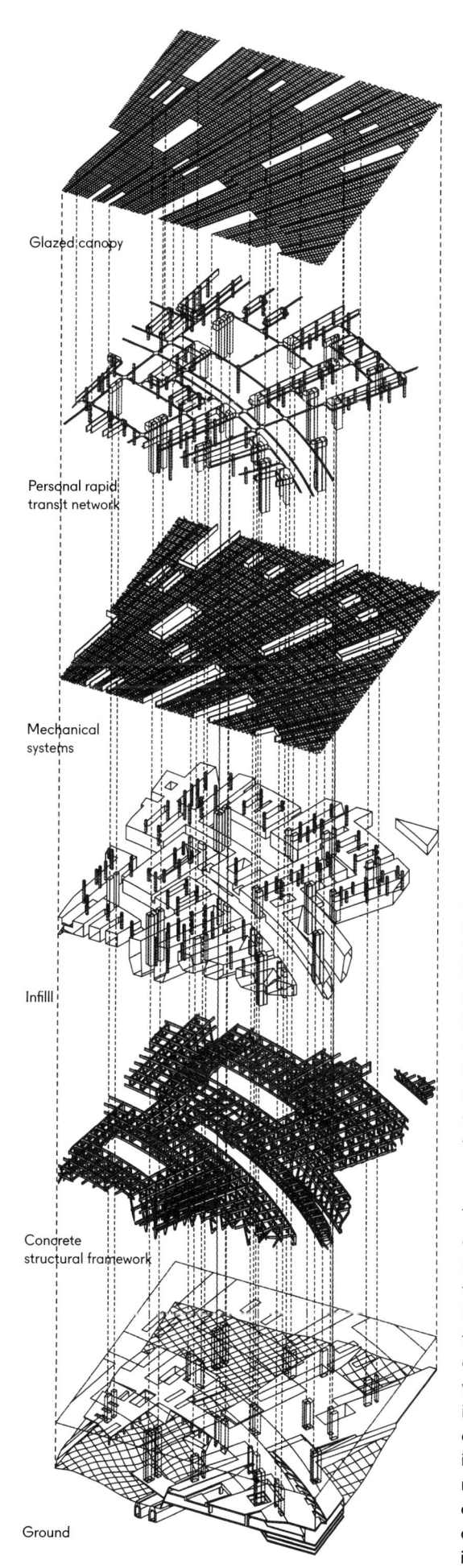

Glazed canopy

Personal rapid transit network

Mechanical systems

Infill

Concrete structural framework

Ground

Urban Stack

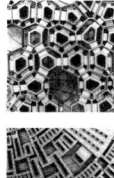

Project Title:
STACK CITY
Architect:
Behrang Behin
Envisioned Project Location:
United Arab Emirates
Envisioned Completion Date:
2050

WHERE AND WHEN
Stack City takes place in a future where irrepressible market forces and massive rural migration into urban centers tempt us to build even more cities, while the possibility of a human-caused environmental catastrophe compels us to reconsider how we construct our urban centers. *Stack City*'s departure point is the Gulf Emirate city, Ras al Khaimah, in the year 2006—a time of rapid urban development, in a place where ambitious plans for new cities provided a platform for experimentation with new urban forms and infrastructure.

BASIC CONDITIONS
The United Arab Emirates (U.A.E.) was chosen as a site not because it reflects the current state of urbanism, but rather as it provides a warning of things to come. The extreme environmental conditions of the U.A.E. portend the extreme temperatures and weather catastrophies we are likely to experience over the next century. Furthermore, while the "Dubai-style" development model, with its predilection towards self-contained, branded, and master-planned new cities rather than slow, incremental, organic growth, is problematic for many reasons: its appeal to investors and state department agencies seeking to spur growth and capture part of the global economy will not diminish. Despite the recent economic downturn, new cities and large-scale developments will continue to be planned and to be built in the manner we have seen in the U.A.E. It is worth asking, then, what forms of urban infrastructure might emerge from within the development logic of the Gulf to address the environmental concerns that go hand-in-hand with an expansion of its urban fabric.

KEY PRINCIPLES

Stack City combines solar-driven thermal updraft mechanisms with a flexible, pleasant, and "scalable" urban fabric to produce a highly efficient infrastructure framework and a novel urban environment. The solar-thermal updraft system, a modification on Jörg Schlaich's solar-chimney power-generators, employs the very conditions that make the desert so inhospitable (excessive heat and solar radiation) in order to make the city self-sufficient and inhabitable. Waste heat from photovoltaic panels and solar collectors at the city's uppermost layer drive a centralized airflow towards and through a single super-tall stack tower, pulling cooled air into the inhabited spaces of the city through a series of underground earth ducts. This system helps to shade and cool both private and public spaces in the otherwise intolerably hot and humid climate of Ras Al Khaimah, while also providing for the city's energy needs. Driven by physics (i.e. the buoyancy of heated air), this system encourages the sectional stratification of the city into three habitable layers: (1) The uppermost layer is a continuous solar-collector which captures energy and supports the flow of heated air towards the stack tower. Openings in the continuous solar-collector layer lead to courtyards and open spaces in the city below and are oriented to minimize wind-drag. As a kind of "connective tissue" of the city, the uppermost layer also provides a flexible zone, which can be reconfigured, for the city's other infrastructure needs. This includes a Personal Rapid Transit (PRT) system which provides automated, reliable transportation from any location to any destination within the city. (2) The secondary layer contains a structural framework which is in-filled with cellular spaces containing most of the programmed spaces of the city, including residential and commercial development. The density of this layer supports a heterogeneous and interconnected set of programmatic functions, reducing the ecological footprint of its inhabitants, while suggesting a departure from the suburban, isolated lifestyles promoted by neighboring new cities in the Gulf. (3) With the upper two strata of the city overhead, the ground is liberated, providing a cooled, shaded, continuous, and automobile-free surface for pedestrian movement and communal gathering. The ground is lifted in some areas to provide for limited vehicular routes, parking, large-scale retail, and communal programs. Beneath the ground, a series of earth ducts act as the city's air intakes, cooling the incoming air by exposing it to the earth's thermal mass. Timed control of airflow through these ducts takes advantage of diurnal and seasonal swings in temperature to keep the thermal mass beneath the city at a relatively cool temperature.

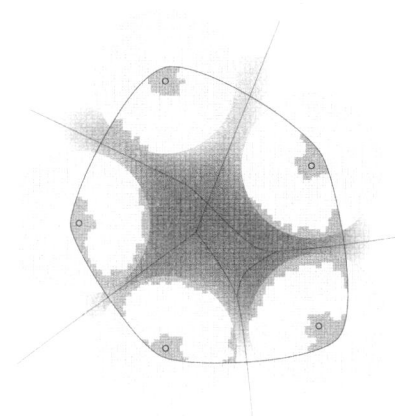

Urban-Scale possibilities within the framework of the updraft tower

Satellite city arrangement

Polycentric conglomeration

Linear arrangement based on transport infrastructure

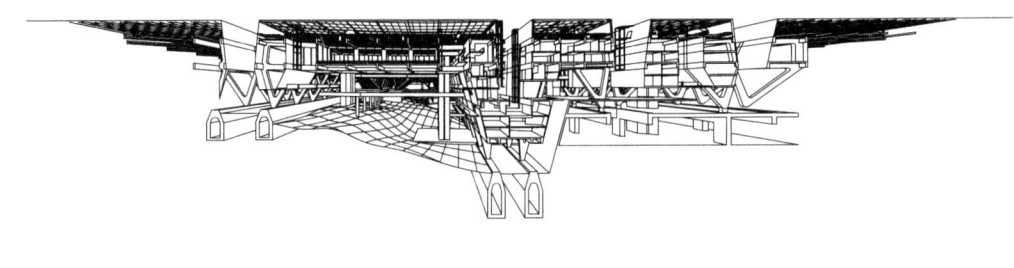

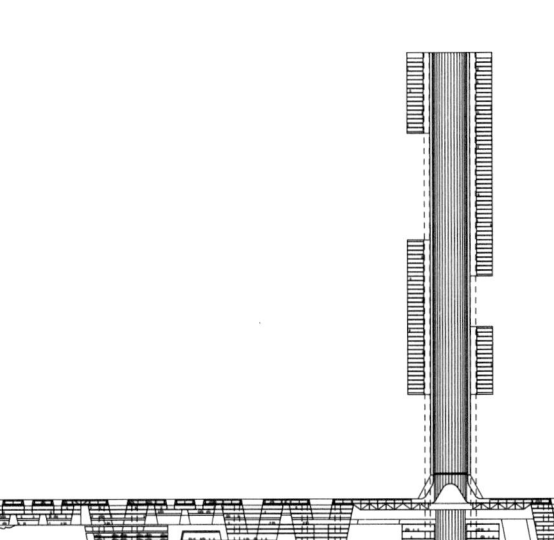

Ж. CHPT. I

Project Title:
GREEN DESERT MINE
Architect:
CDMB Architects/ Christophe DM BARLIEB
Envisioned Project Location:
Desert regions
Envisioned Completion Date:
The near future

WHERE AND WHEN
The *Green Desert Mine* envisions the transformation of arid desert areas across the globe into fertile lands, rich with biodiversity, and adapted to modern lifestyles.

BASIC CONDITIONS
It appears as if geology, water supply, population growth and climate change will play a major role in the future. Globalization will most likely produce massive migratory flux between poorer and more affluent nations, which will most likely lead to new social and political tensions. Faced with the "over-exploitation" of inner and outer regions of megacities, one will witness two forms of desertification: the destruction of fertile land and the subsequent migration of populations suffering from it. This would adversely affect the two billion people who currently live in arid regions of the globe.

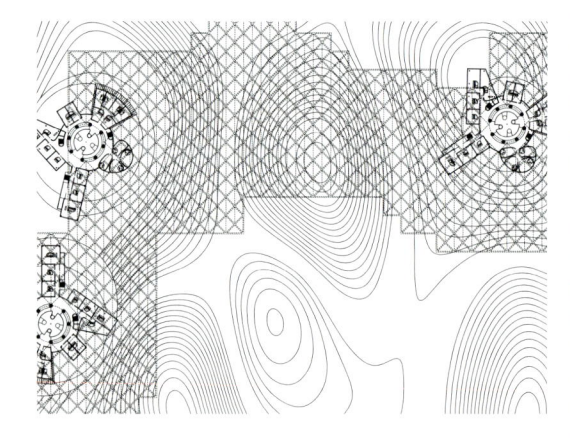

KEY PRINCIPLES
The project, *Green Desert Mine*, proposes a series of thermal chimneys, which would capture solar radiation and recycle heat generated by machines, bodies, and the environment. The bases of the chimneys would provide a new economic and urban landscape by concentrating citizens around the towers' super-structures and by elevating the functions of the compact city and elevating the properties above the ground. The total impact on the proposed 4 hectares area is thus limited to a 1,000 m² footprint housing 1,400 inhabitants. The remaining 3.9 hectares of land would be used to combat desertification: a garden would be created. The "garden" would be covered by a double membrane capable of collecting solar energy on the one hand, and transmitting thermal energy to the chimneys' turbines, on the other. The grey-water produced by the city would be filtered over an extensive portion of the "garden" using biological and mineral filtration systems. The evaporated water from the vegetation and the lakes would be collected at the top of the greenhouse, condensed, and channeled into cisterns located at the base of each tower. An extensive biodiversity would be introduced to enhance the oases. To achieve this effect, colonies of birds and aquatic animals would be given a fertile salt-water habitat, which would also promote other species adapted to this environment. By planting dates, palm trees, lavender and roses, etc.… the stage would be set for insect populations, such as bees and butterflies, to flourish. A drip irrigation system would bring water from the surrounding hills, which would provide excellent water management and higher crop yields. As for the city's infrastructure, the facilities necessary for education, work, leisure, and consumption would be placed in the commercial zones of the structure. This would imply working in close proximity to one's home. Such a system would suggest an urban university, a biotech research facility, etc. The system's autonomy could export energy, water, agriculture, as well as financial/technical services. A Maglev system near to the surface would ensure rapid connections between regional and urban centers.

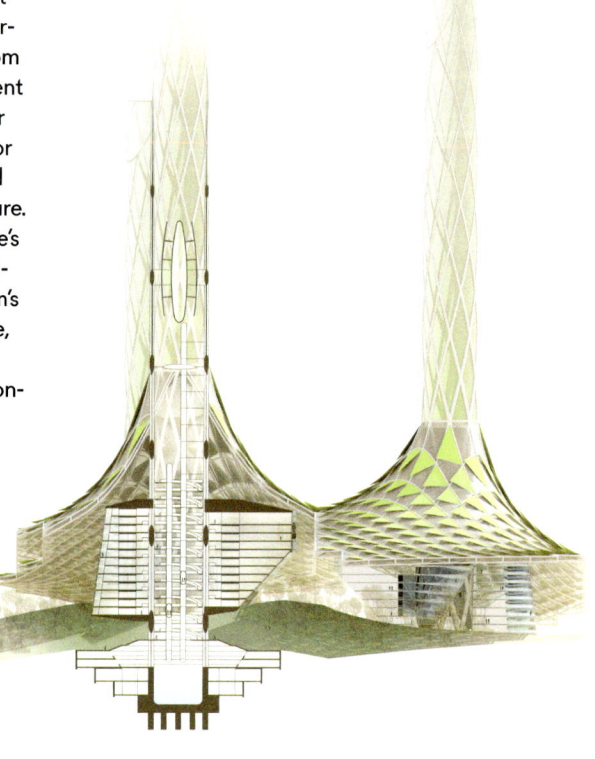

Project Title:
IP2100 (ISLAND PROPOSITION 2100)

Architect:
Scott Lloyd, Aaron Roberts (Room11), Katrina Stoll

Envisioned Project Location:
Australia

Envisioned Completion Date:
2100

WHERE AND WHEN

The *Island Proposition 2100* proposes an infrastructure spine as an instrument to connect Australia's regions to a sustainable metabolic system, initiating a symbiotic relationship between urban centers and their supporting territories. Connecting Melbourne and Hobart by the year 2100, the spine will carry the physical and virtual flows of exchange, allocate stocks, transform processes, and demarcate future urban development along its linear axis. New urban typologies for living, industry, and commerce will develop, countering sprawl, and increasing natural spatial reserves.

BASIC CONDITIONS

IP2100 responds to a future context shaped by non-linear building. This method sources long-term data projections by research institutions, and applies them in order to set off foreseeable trends in society. In short, the conditions of the year 2100 are shaped by a society still optimistic about technology, hybrid forms of private/public governance, and a precarious shortage of natural resources. An increasing demand for mobility and connectivity, coupled with the continued reliance on physical density to create and sustain culture, completes the context. A balanced system of migration, information, material, energy, water, and capital will flow in a steady stream along the spine, efficiently distributing stocks to solve predicted shortages of resources in specific regions. High-speed magnetic levitation and other emerging technology will be implemented to transport people and cargo along the spine and to adjoining subsystems. In addition to functioning as a means of transporting material and circulation flows, the spine will operate as a model of efficient hybrid infrastructure by harvesting energy on site via solar, wind, and tidal mechanisms, cleaning grey water with embedded wetlands and performing as a rainwater catchment. These services will plug into the loop, sending inputs to urban centers and receiving outputs in the form of nutrients, from compostable waste and grey-water, that will return to the midlands agricultural region to complete the cycle. *IP2100* incites the next great planning project by connecting Australian cities to achieve territorial equilibrium within the vast continent.

KEY PRINCIPLES

The *IP2100* spine contains a looped system of composite infrastructure, which will produce an extensive network on the multi-regional scale. It is a scalable modular system designed to reactivate regional territories by providing for social demand flows, managing circulation of resources, improving energy and water efficiency, transforming waste, managing spatial reserves, and increasing the resilience of the urban "metabolism." By connecting formerly disparate regions, the spine will be able to efficiently distribute surplus and cover predicted regional shortages, thus transforming specific regions into vital components of the metabolic system. The route of the spine will be drawn to access the major population densities, sources of abundant fresh water, natural energy potentials, and arable lands for agriculture. The spine will form a structure in constant flux, modified by the movement of materials and the constructions and the "deconstructions" of its inhabitants. In its current form, it will produce a segment with two fixed points which will terminate in Hobart and Melbourne. However, the potential of a composite intelligent infrastructure capable of reacting to the evolving complexity and extended context of urban systems, is infinite.

were attending school. Malka has completed this design in an effort to unite the forsaken and the marginalized: refugees, the Roma, demonstrators, dissenters, hippies, utopians, and the stateless of any kind. He describes this conceptual design as a "colonization" of neglected public spaces by the participation of a non-specialized labor collective that appropriate prefabricated and hijacked construction systems. He argues: "My methodology seeks to promote public participation as an act of resistance against urban restrictions."

KEY PRINCIPLES

Malka seeks to create an "architecture for the people" and an urban strategy of parasitic explorations. Motivated by the desire to create a new, social scenario, the *Pocket of Active Resistance (PAR)* system is a modular complex providing an alternative to the defiant lifestyle, by positioning itself in a permanent state of insurrection. Its growth is articulated by the vitality of its spontaneous community to create a pocket of active resistance created by welcoming the discontented. This act of guerrilla architecture sets out to hijack the "great arch of fraternity" and unite the forsaken.

Project Title:
SELF DEFENSE
Architect:
STÉPHANE MALKA ARCHITECTURE
Envisioned Project Location:
La Défense, Paris, France
Envisioned Completion Date:
The near future

WHERE AND WHEN

This study by Stéphane Malka, imagines the hijacking of a building that is symbolic for its monumentality and its location: the *Grande Arche De La Défense* in Paris. The *Grande Arche De La Défense* is an arch on axis with the *Arc de Triomphe* on the famous shopping promenade, *Les Champs Elysées*.

BASIC CONDITIONS

The time-frame of the project, *Self Defense,* takes place after the 2009 strikes and the social upheavals in France due to the difficult politic issues of the "sans papiers," illegal immigrants, who were relocated on a massive scale and sent back to their countries of origin. Immigrants were even relocated when they had children born in France, who

Project Title:
ROLLER COASTER WARSAW
Artist:
Kobas Laksa
Envisioned Project Location:
Warsaw, Poland
Envisioned Completion Date:
An alternative future

WHERE AND WHEN
This project by the artist, Kobus Laksa, is envisioned in Poland's capital city, Warsaw. A city known for struggling with finding its urban identity in a process of constant rebuilding and—often problematic—architectural experimentation. This is the setting of a roller-coaster ride that would span the city.

BASIC CONDITIONS
Laksa's *Roller Coaster Warsaw* creates a simulated environment that utilizes Google Earth's virtual tours, where any location, regardless of its proximity, close or far-flung, can be experienced virtually. A 360 degree spherical panorama represents a futuristic version of central Warsaw in a state of flux; a chaotic state of never-ending construction.

KEY PRINCIPLES
The primary motif of a roller-coaster weaved into the city landscape blurs boundaries between functionality and entertainment as the residents can ride to work, drink coffee on a merry-go-round, and warm up in a communal solarium. Entertainment, a privilege demanded and expected by industrialized society, is simply caricaturized as an amusement park.

Project Title:
SLAVE CITY
Artist:
Atelier Van Lieshout
Envisioned Project Location:
Various locations
Envisioned Completion Date:
An alternative future

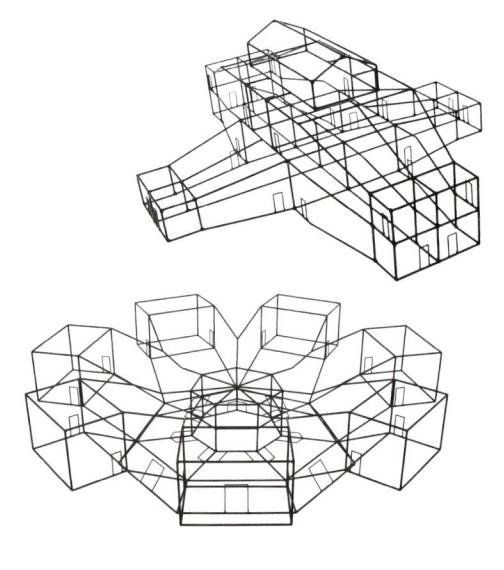

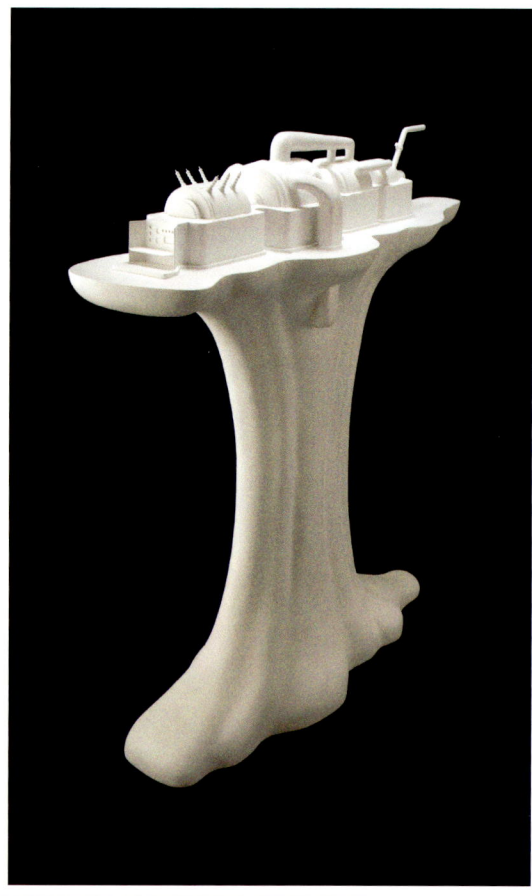

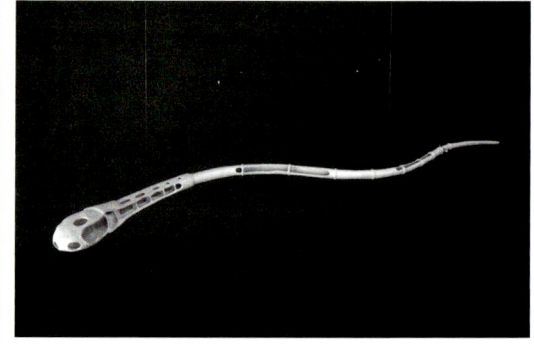

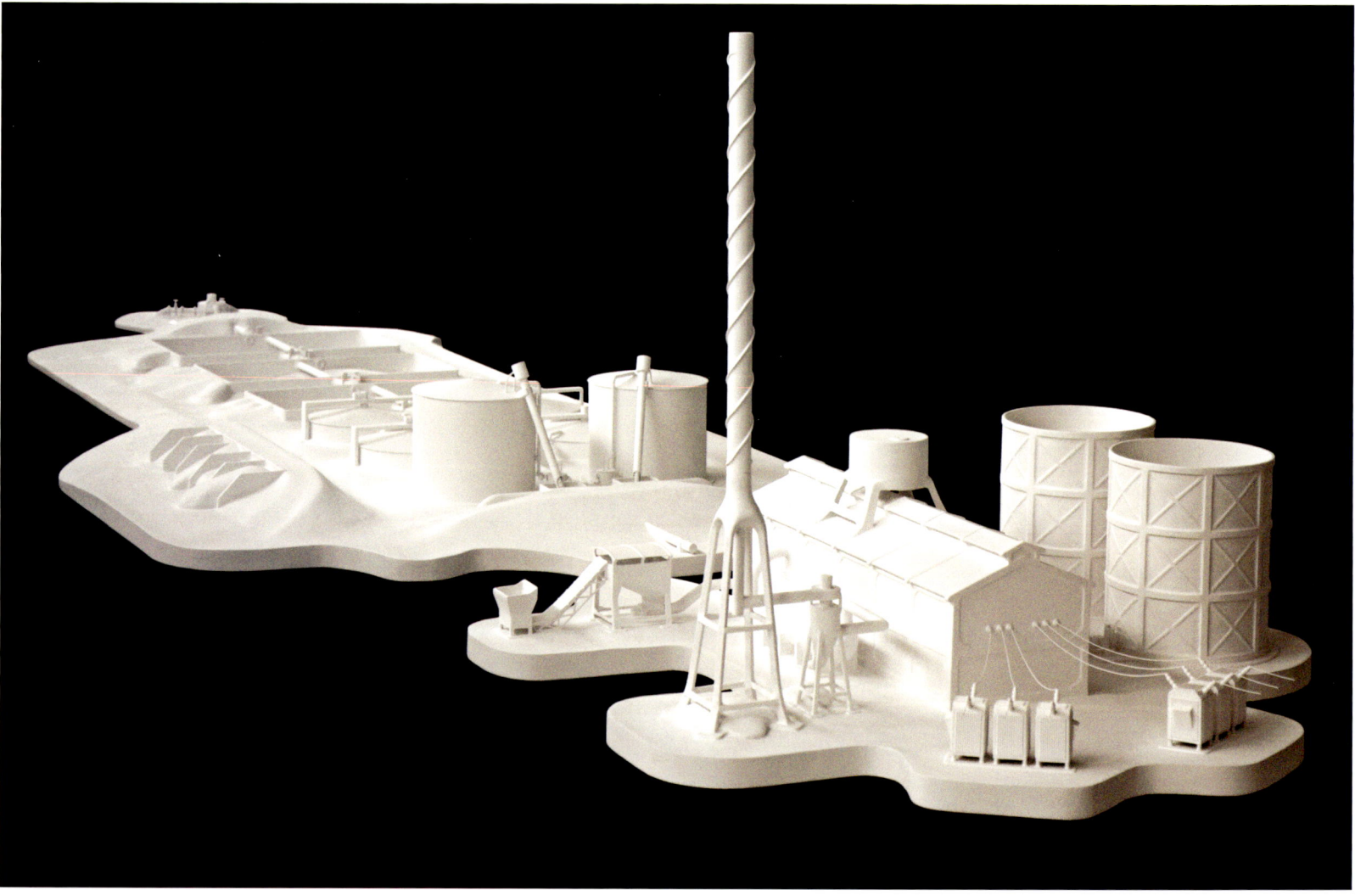

54   SLAVE CITY   GREAT SCAPES

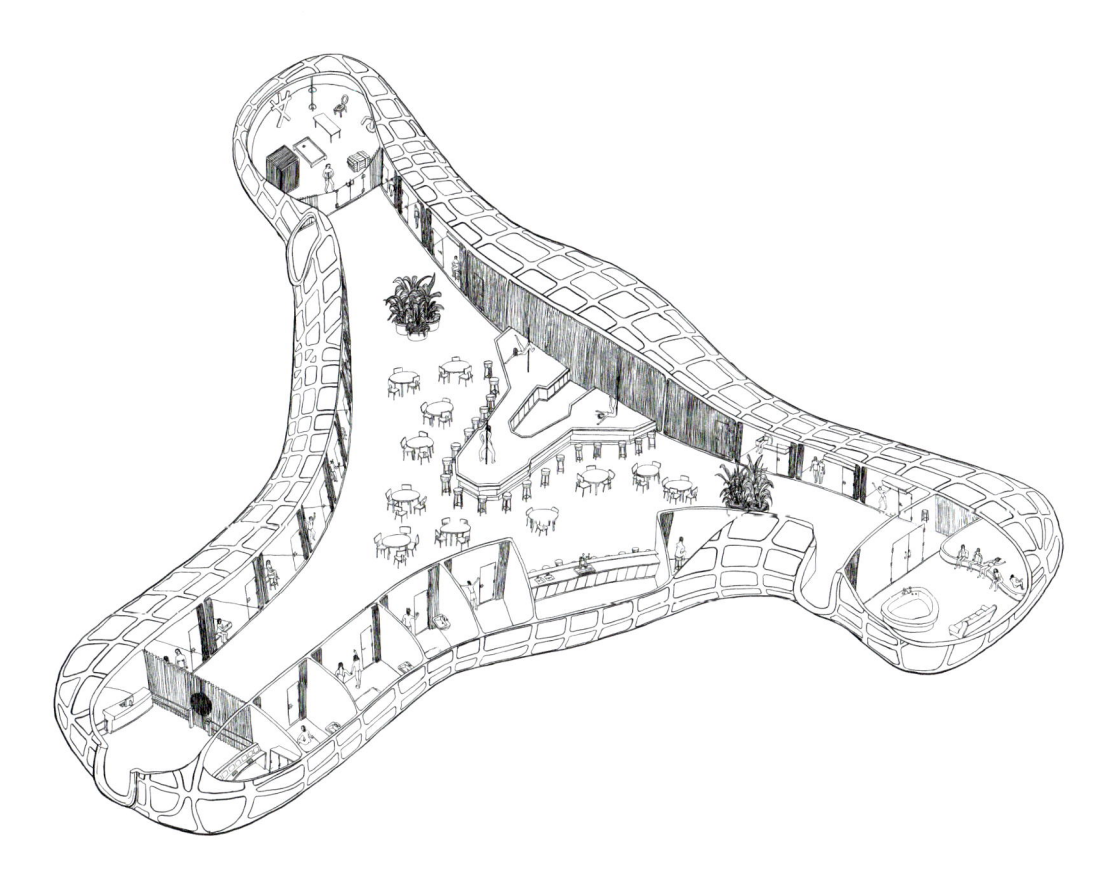

work in the Call Center. This Call Center would be the *Slave City*, an up-to-date concentration camp made out of the latest technology and with the most up-to-date management methods. The highly profitable *Slave City* (7 billion Euro net profit per annum) is provided with all necessary facilities to make sure that the inhabitants (called "participants" here) are as efficient as possible. Values, ethics, aesthetics, morals, food, energy, economics, organization, management, and markets are turned topsy-turvy, upside-down, and reformulated into a city. The participants would work seven hours per day on tele-services such as customer service, ICT, telemarketing, computer programming etc. Thereafter, they would work another seven hours on the fields or workshop, whilst the the rest of their time would be used for education, sleep and other necessities. This *Slave City* would be a self sufficient "green town" which would not use or waste the world's resources and would not produce any waste material thanks to efficient recycling.

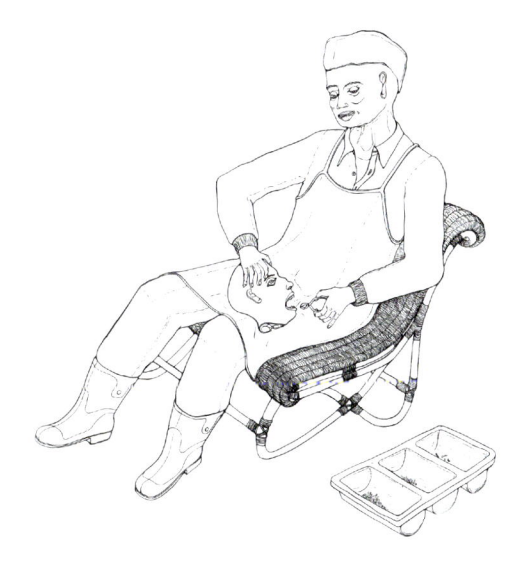

WHERE AND WHEN
Atelier van Lieshout's *Slave City* is an urban project, which has been designed to maximize rationality, efficiency, and finacial profit of a city.

BASIC CONDITIONS
Slave City works with contemporary ethical and aesthetic values, ideas on nutrition, environmental protection, organization, management and markets, in order to recombine and reinterpret them. The project proposes collectively organized forms of working and living that circumvent conventional categories. It presents a perfectly conceived city, with comprehensive infrastructure that includes services buildings, health centers, villages, brothels and museums, consuming an area of 60 km² with a population of 200,000 people. The city's only source of energy will be self produced: biogas, solar and wind energy, working to build a "cradle-to-grave" situation in which everything works as a closed circuit recycling system; where there is no waste.

KEY PRINCIPLES
Before entering *Slave City* and becoming an inhabitant of the city, one would have to pass the *Welcoming Center*. In this large building, participants would be selected for their suitability to work in *Slave City*. Old, cripple, sick and people with bad taste would be recycled in the biogas digester. Healthy, but unintelligent people, would be recycled in the meat processing factory. Young and healthy people, however, would be able to take part in the organ transplant program. Healthy, clever people would be able to

Ж. CHPT. I

55

Project Title:
DEAD WEBSITES ARCHIVE
Architect:
David A. Garcia
Envisioned Completion Date:
2015

WHERE AND WHEN
The bridge-like structure, *Dead Websites Archive* center hovers over Europe's largest cave in Croatia. The Munizaba Cava in Gracac is more than 600 meters deep and several kilometers long.

BASIC CONDITIONS
Hundreds of websites are shut down daily, constantly eliminating traces of our present culture. Although services exist which make random "back-ups" of internet websites, they are only as robust as the media they are saved on to, and digital media has a frighteningly short lifespan. This archive of "dead websites," converts what was once virtual and plural while in use, to a physical and single reality when it has been removed from the Web.

KEY PRINCIPLES
The Archive's center will select the relevant shut-down-websites, and proceed to laser cut the contents of the full site into polycarbonate A4 sheets. Researchers can stay and work in the central building, and descend to the cave when access to the archive is required. In the depths of this natural hollow, the "website sheets" are arranged chronologically, placed directly upon the topography, lit by LEDs, and visited as one would a library. Down here, websites become unique realities, housed in a single location, guaranteeing a lifespan of hundreds of years; an alternative to the fleeting existence of a hard disk. The cave allows the user to select and photocopy an archived "web site" from the cave floor, or project it on large screens for group study. Arduous work is required to move about in such an impressive, natural space, and becomes a contrast to the easy access and plural digital reality that defined the website when it was "alive." Within the cave, projector screens allow the visitors to enlarge the "website" plates for an onsite study or collective discussion. The engraved polycarbonate plates, visualizing the discontinued websites, are place chronologically on the cave floor. The visitor can navigate through time, and search with in the catalogue. Traditional photocopy machines are found throughout the cave. Keeping in line with the analogue world that this archive represents, users can copy the polycarbonate sheets on to paper for their own use.

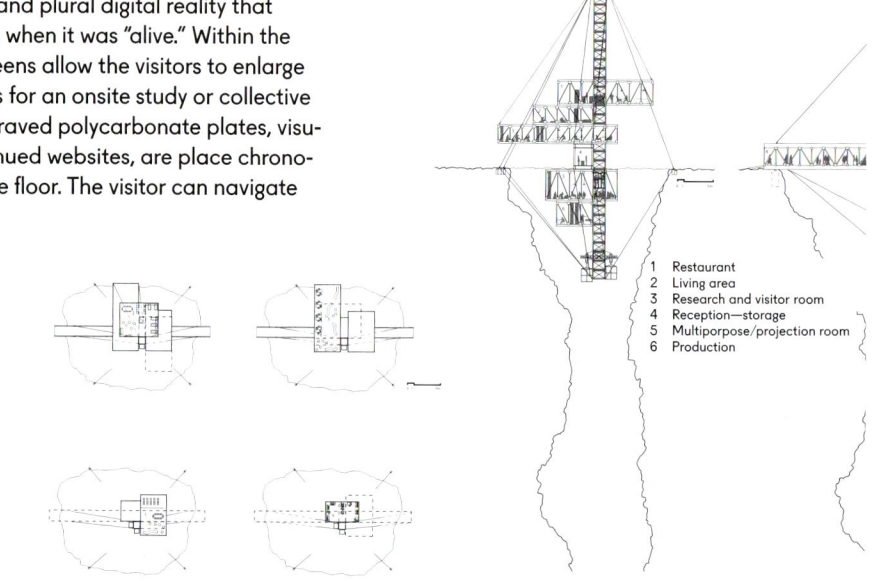

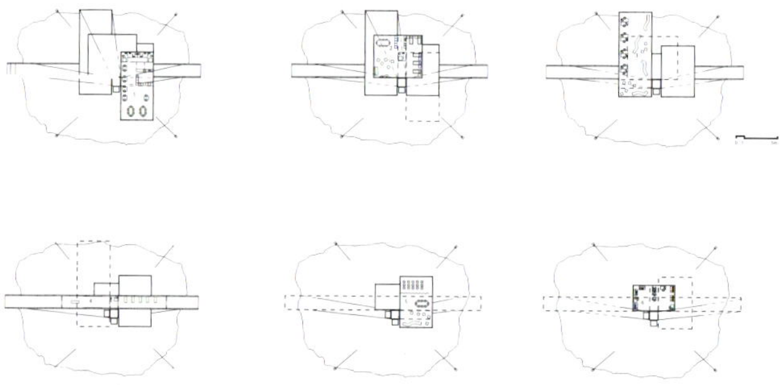

1 Restaurant
2 Living area
3 Research and visitor room
4 Reception—storage
5 Multiporpose/projection room
6 Production

DEAD WEBSITES ARCHIVE   GREAT SCAPES

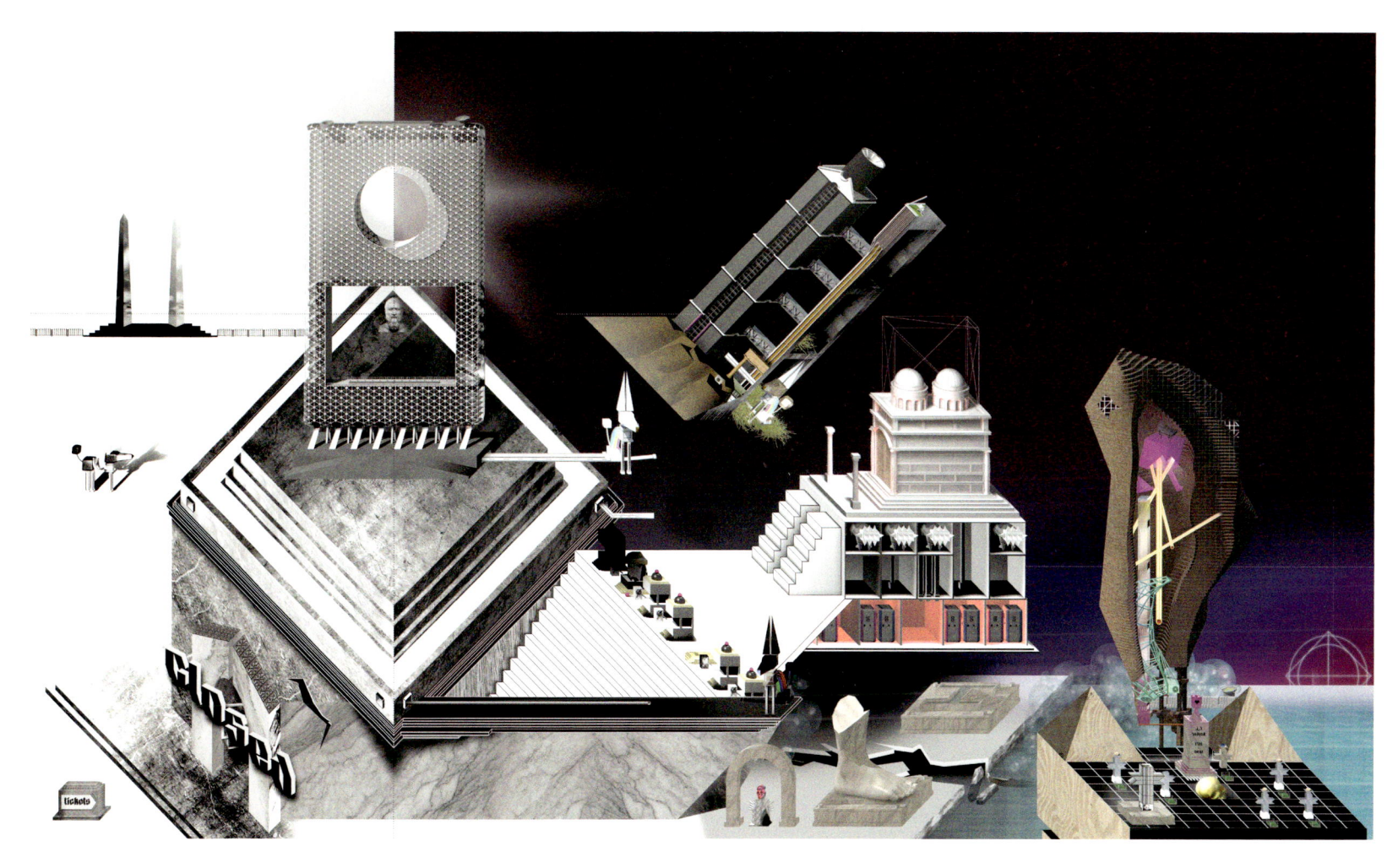

Project Title:
HAPPY CONSENSUS LAND
Architect:
SPEEDISM
Envisioned Project Location:
Happy Consensus Land
Envisioned Completion Date:
Today + 1

WHERE AND WHEN
Happy Consensus Land is the spectacular future of Doomdough *see next page*, an abandoned theme-park that transforms into a theme-park for architects, which is fine-tuned as the private playground of Plato, the cosmic speculator, and Edna, the doom drag-queen, the stage for their disputes and for their cooperation.

BASIC CONDITIONS
The basic cultural, architectural, theoretical, and aesthetic conditions of all Speedism projects are the general conditions we face today in developed cities. These projects can be applied as theoretical landscapes; story-boarded wastelands paved with endless journeys towards the limits of architecture.

KEY PRINCIPLES
Welcome to *Happy Consensus Land*! In the aftermath of Happy Doom's clash with the Dream Panorama, both fight but love one another too. Here ordered cosmos meets wild and colorful chaos. "Consensus" embraces "Nonsenus." Welcome to conflict, beauty, emotion, stress, and change. A future awaits you, where Dream and Doom have become one… Slowly we approach the entrance.

Do we arrive at Consensus Land? No, it is Nonsensus Land now! What seemed to be white and shiny in the glistening distance is now grey and dull, abandoned and decayed. Only wild poodles roam the empty streets and plazas. They ignore the sign at the gate "C.L.O.S.E.D" … The Solomon Temple, a huge souvenir shop, dominates the entrance-area.

Project Title:
DOOMDOUGH
Architect:
Speedism
Envisioned Project Location:
Feng City
(Beijing, Shanghai, Doom fiction)
Envisioned Completion Date:
Today + 1

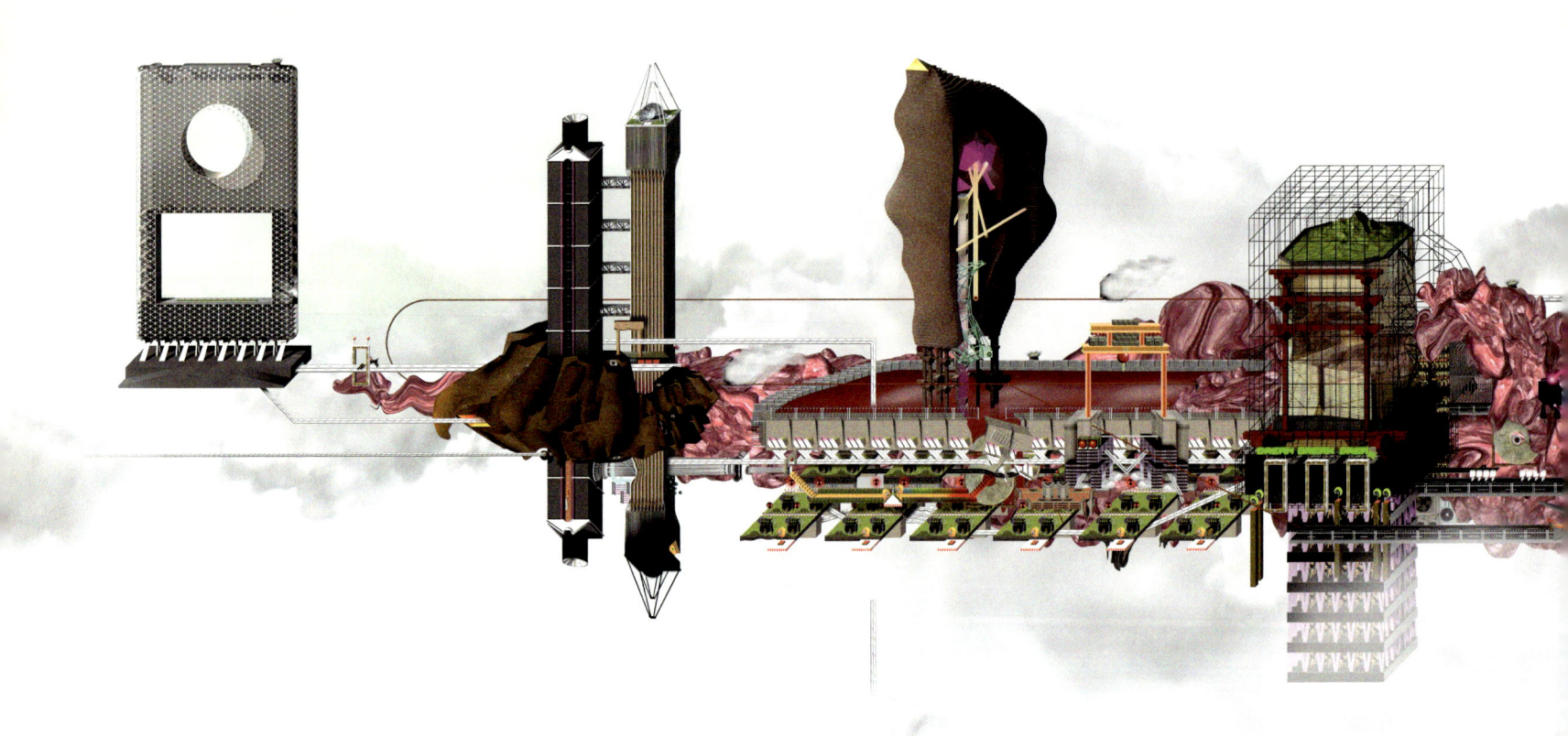

WHERE AND WHEN
Doomdough is a post-heroic scenario for the Chinese Dream. *Doomdough* is a post-heroic scenario against the Chinese Dream. *Doomdough* is a post-heroic magic ingredient to maintain the Chinese Dream.

BASIC CONDITIONS
Speedism's graphic architecture is conceived in pixel form and translated to paper. Their projects emerge out of a mysterious and monstrous software designing process. Techno-enthusiast theory and catastrophist prophecy at the same time, Speedism somewhat embodies seventies avant-garde. Speedism's convergence architecture occupies an intersectional space where architecture and its popular representations (cinema, literature, gaming, comic books) meet.

KEY PRINCIPLES
The Chinese future looks bright. Architects, theorists, researchers, and lobbyists put a lot of hard work into the "Chinese Dream" to try and give it a perfect panorama. Speedism moves into the dreamscape, heads towards the finish, and peeks behind the D*R*E*A*M panorama, where the dream will be 100% real and where nothing will happen. The counterpoint to this sad "dream-bubble-void" of dream ambition is Speedism's *Happy Doom*. *Doomdough* takes us 8+1 steps deeper into a happy future where doom and dream are united as one. The 8+1 highrise architect-protagonists follow the steps that propel us into eternal being. No doom, no dream…

Ж. CHPT. I

RISING TIDES

≈

Exploring the
Consequences
of
Global Sea
Level Rises

Focusing on the issue of the global rise of sea levels—one of the most critical impacts of global warming—*Rising Tides,* seeks to present speculative design solutions to this significant climatic challenge from the perspective of architects and urban planners. During the next century, increasing global temperatures will result in sea-level rises due to both the thermal expansion of water, as well as through the increase of the volume of water to the oceans due to the melting of land-ice, such as mountain glaciers, ice caps and ice sheets from regions like Greenland and Antarctica. These sea-level rises would lead to potentially catastrophic changes for coastal communities in the next century, resulting in the need for massive storm-surge defenses for countless cities across the globe, in order to avoid displacement of these numerous coastal populations. The possible impact on coastal systems, due to the rise in sea levels, are various and frightening: ranging from coastal erosion, higher storm-surge flooding, inhibition of primary production processes, increase in coastal inundation, changes in surface water quality and groundwater characteristics, increased loss of property and coastal habitats, increased flood risk and potential loss of life, loss of cultural resources and lowered land values, impact on agriculture and aquaculture through decline in soil and water quality, and loss of tourism, recreation, and transportation functions. Against this bleak backdrop, the projects featured in *Utopia* range from Anne Holtrop's artificial floating islands with their gardens and spa, to Vincent Callebaut's self-sufficient, floating city, *Lilypad,* an "ecopolis" for climate refugees; all the way to Off Architecture's *Bering Strait* proposal for a habitable bridge descending to the bottom of the ocean connecting Russia to America, or IwamtoScott's *Hydro Net,* an underground network of tunnels for hydrogen-powered, hovering vehicles and a forest of towers sprouting from lowland areas inundated by rising sea levels. At the intersection of *pressing needs* and *abstract prophecies,* all of the featured works engage in the creation of futuristic visions for the ocean and the endangered coastlines, where the ocean meets the shore.

"TIME IS AN OCEAN, BUT IT ENDS AT THE SHORE"

BOB DYLAN

- 66. *Aqualta* by Studio Lindfors
- 68. *Floating Gardens (spa)* by Anne Holtrop
- 70. *Varde Arks* by CDMB Architects (Christophe DM BARLIEB)
- 72. *Cruise City, City Cruise* by NL Architects
- 74. *Micro-utopie* by IaN+
- 75. *Quarantined Library* by David A. Garcia
- 76. *Flooded London* by Anthony Lau
- 80. *Physalia: A Positive Amphibious Energy Garden to Clean European Waterways* by Vincent Callebaut Architecture
- 82. *Syph. The Oceanic City* by Arup (Alanna Howe and Alexander Hespe)
- 84. *Giant Water Lilies* by The Why Factory
- 85. *Lilypad: A Floating Ecopolis for Climate Refugees* by Vincent Callebaut Architecture
- 88. *Green Float* by Shimizu Corporation
- 89. *Turbine City* by Leon Rost, ONOFFICE
- 90. *Lake Effect – Chicago 2106* by Strawn.Sierralta
- 91. *Skygrove* by Hollwich Kushner LLC (HWKN) (Matthias Hollwich, Marc Kushner)
- 92. *City of the Future: Hydro-Net SF 2108* by IwamotoScott Architecture (Lisa Iwamoto, Craig Scott)
- 94. *Saturation City* by McGauran Giannini Soon (MGS) with Bild Architecture, Dyskors and Material Thinking
- 96. *Aquatown* by NH Architecture & Andrew Mackenzie
- 97. *Future North: Ecotariums In The North Pole* by Terreform ONE + Terrefuge
- 98. *Gandara/Guild Wars Nightfall* by Daniel Docio
- 100. *The Religious City* by Silu Yang
- 102. *Towards a New Antarchitecture* by Taylor Medlin
- 104. *Sustainable Iceberg Living Station* by David A. Garcia
- 106. *Rethinking The Bering Strait* by Off Architecture

PRODUCTIVE DYSTOPIA

by DARRYL CHEN from Tomorrow's Thoughts Today

Designer, urbanist, critic, and curator, Darryl Chen, founded, together with Liam Young, the London-based think tank *Tomorrow's Thoughts Today*, exploring the consequences of fantastic, perverse and underrated urbanisms.

The Problem with Utopia

"A great epoch has begun."
• Le Corbusier

A four-kilometer-long complex of six storey concrete blocks extends relentlessly along the coast of the Baltic Sea on the island of Rügen. This beach front "paradise" in Prora built between 1936 and 1939 was the brain-child of the Nazis as part of their "Kraft durch Freude" or "Strength through Joy" initiative. The enormous complex was to house 20,000 holiday-makers as a resort for soldiers and workers of the Third Reich. Stretching as far as the eye can see, this huge complex proclaims its makers' insistence that the health properties of the sun and sea would be an integral part of servicing the new society. The complex now lies half-crumbled in a progressive state of ruin. Its dominant physical presence on the island coastline creates a continuous monument to a particular brand of utopians whose vision of a new society remains unrealized. Forever confined to the imagination is the picture of thousands upon thousands of white bodies practising open air aerobics, their calisthenic poses synchronized against the pristine beachside backdrop. The complex is an imposing edifice to health and happiness as much as to "good" genes—it is however a delusional trinket on the mantelpiece of an utopian project doomed to failure.

Le Corbusier's *Ville Radieuse* represented a gleaming blueprint for a paradigm shift in ways of living in the twentieth century—nothing short of a radical New Architecture. Requiring the wholesale demolition of cosmopolitan cities, his plans effected the rebuilding of a new generation of slums, twenty, thirty, forty storeys-high and starkly devoid of adornment—as though ornamentation were a kind of moral transgression. A solution to the claustrophobic squalor of the slums of the ancient regime, Le Corbusier's propositions tell us more of the problems of his present day reality than a plausible way to design cities.

The utopian project is premised upon the correction of some injustice or suffering, like a tumor of the human condition that requires a bold dose of radiation therapy to restore its health. The pure white light of a radical solution throws the current circumstances into relief—it is the most pure, abstract, and singular solution that best exposes cancerous tumors.

Utopia is more dysfunctional than functional. Failure is written into its DNA. How could anything so pure and so all-encompassing ever be taken seriously as a realistic blueprint for the future? We might already have realized this with our present hindsight. In fact, so accustomed and preconditioned are we to registering its inevitable limitations, that we simply overlook the elaborate hoax that it really is. And yet the power of the speculation continues to lure us, enrapturing us with amazing tales and thrilling, wonderous stories. There is still power in the speculation, but utopia ain't what it used to be.

Utopia ain't What it Used to Be

"Today we have computers that enable us to answer some very big questions if all the relevant data is fed into the computer and all the questions are properly asked."
• Buckminster Fuller

"This is the voice of World Control. I bring you peace. It may be the peace of plenty and content or the peace of unburied death... In time you will come to regard me not only with respect and awe but with love."
• Colossus: The Forbin Project

The American futurist designer, Buckminster Fuller, believed the problem of solving the world's greatest and most enduring problems was a simple matter of mathematics. Fuller's *World Game* used scenario-building and hypothesizing to formulate solutions to poverty and global food distribution as though balancing arithmetic equations. The belief in the project was second only to the totality of the vision. According to Buckminster, technological progress, supposedly unhindered by ideology, would offer a rational entry-point to liberating humankind.

The demise of the social welfare state in 1960s America coincided with a crisis of confidence in world markets, a shocking postscript to the *summer-of-love*. The *ensuing era* was marked by a retreat of the social ideal into the individualism of the 1970s. The social liberation of the collective transcendental trip gave way to the paradise of the privatized kick. The genre of the *paranoia* film emerged as cinema-goers sought a vicarious suffering on-screen. Combining this with science fiction, the big-screen expressed the naiveté of many visions of a technology-led nirvana. In the film Colossus: *The Corbin Project,* a number-crunching computer (Buckminster's veritable dream machine) was supposed to guarantee peace to humankind by defending him from his worst enemy. Ironically, when his worst enemy is found to be humankind itself, drastic measures have to be taken to guarantee that peace. Missile strikes against cities are warnings that any interference in Colossus' plan for world peace will be met with the nuclear-armed fist of discipline. In a bitter ending, the computer enslaves its creator and presumes that in time Colossus will be an object of love to all mankind.

Somewhere along the way we had lost our innocence and realized our optimism, left unchecked, had defeated our better judgement. However, neither the naïve simplicities of our problem-solving endeavours, nor the equally totalitarian hopelessness of the paranoid state offered in its wake, are adequate to provide the sum of our fears and hopes for the future.

Utopia is powerful because of its ability to abstract and crystallize a problem into a concise and internally consistent solution. Dystopia is similarly single-minded in projecting a series of consequences, albeit that run headlong into an abysmal, nightmarish conclusion. Ironically the two poles are interlinked in that the simple totalitarian aspect of utopia is precisely the form of the other, with the simple addition of one fatal flaw—a seemingly insignificant oversight with enough destructive potential to collapse an entire civilization. Head far enough west and you end up east. The utopian and dystopian impulses stem from the same place; they are two sides of the same coin. Though the question emerges as to whether we have managed to move beyond this bipolar condition into the light of a clearer day?

Post-pessimism

"Oh, Frank, you're the best, you're the champ, you're the master...!"
• Patricia Cornell, The Stepford Wives, 1975

Eighty-six percent of the British public lives in the suburbs. In a country that invented the idea of the *Garden City* the ubiquity of the suburb is a strange twist to a kind of utopia everywhere. The suburb developed over the last century and has survived successive generations of technological development producing no more than a flaccid urbanity which sorely disappoints Ebenezer Howard's original assertion. A place that aspires to embody both town and country becomes neither.

Terrace after terrace of speculatively built cottages, replete with faux-pastoral ornamentation and pre-fab DIY sheds, establish the ultimate template for individual expression—each man an island, each home a castle—each contributing to a wasteland of monotony, where a lack of density destroys any seeming sense of collective spirit.

Is there something latent within this cultural vacuum that creates the perfect conditions for experimentation on an unimaginable scale? Do the by-products of our urban civilization form the perfect petri dish for our psychological fantasies? Mega-malls, car mania, the cult of home improvements and the feminist critique that was latent as early as the claustrophobic depiction of suburbia in the film *The Stepford Wives,* first released in 1975, have elucidated on an emergent suburbia that surpasses a mere town and country fusion. However, even more startling developments are taking place. London's temple to energy self-sufficiency lies not in the heart of the capital, but ten miles south of the center, on the commuter line, where wide-eyed day-trippers can visit the nation's first zero-carbon housing project. Plans are now under way for a fully-fledged eco-town, a self-sustaining enclave that turns its back on the rest of the city and threatens to create a new class hierarchy based not on wealth or education, but on carbon usage. Are we witnessing a breakaway, a kind of rebellion in slow motion? And what would happen if these new eco-separatists had their way?

Moving away from the totalizing poles of u/dys/topias opens up a whole new field of critical enquiry where design decisions are motivated not only by morality, but by the rich and latent territory between. We emerge on the other side of pessimism and paranoia with a mature, informed gaze into the future. Where past attempts have failed, the detritus left behind only fuels the new, in a continual redefinition of the future.

Is it possible to dismantle the utopian project without abandoning our ability to usefully excavate a knowledge of the future through design and speculation? Or more radically, can we recover some raw material for a productive design practice from the dystopian, from our waste landscapes, and from our technological errors? Dystopia is not merely the cautionary tale, but becomes the context in which the extraordinary can happen.

Dystopia and its Discontents

"Your rules are really starting to annoy me."
• Snake Plissken, Escape From L.A., 1996

"Game? This wasn't meant to be a game. Never!"
• Rusty, Rollerball, 1975

Los Angeles has become a prison-state, disconnected from the rest of the United States and a repository for an ever growing population of prisoners, outcast by a fanatically moralistic state. A weapon designed to wreak havoc on the world's electronic devices has fallen into the wrong hands and is wanted back by a dictatorial president who does not want to get his hands dirty. There is only one man who can do the job…

A man emerges from the fiery wreckage of a military helicopter. Out of the smoke and twisted metal he strides forward, injured and battle-scarred, but undefeated. The man is instantly met by uniformed personnel, who create a firing-squad formation around him, but he does not flinch as he draws the weapon's activation device from his pocket. In John Carpenter's 1996 film, *Escape from L.A.*, Los Angeles is an underworld; Snake Plissken, a cold and violent ex-convict, the most notorious of a ragtag group of tricksters, conmen, and outcasts who inhabit this new crime-ridden city. After fulfilling his mission to recover the weapon, Plissken confronts the blackmailing president, though instead of handing the weapon back, he wreaks his own revenge by activating it himself—and not without some caustic banter for comic effect. Justice will have its day but the world is not spared from electronic meltdown.

The fictitious dystopian world initially offers a compelling setting for conflict and adventure, as well as room for the "hero," or the character who is even more ingenious than the dystopia itself. The hero understands that even the most perfect dystopia is not flawless, and that the flaws are there to be exploited. The hero is the character who beats the system at its own game—the unexpected survivor. Like cockroaches in the post-nuclear scenario, these heroes are agile adapters in a twisted ecosystem whose strengths are intensified by new environmental conditions.

The condition of dystopia gives birth to its protagonist, and consequently, it is the protagonist who relies on the dystopia as their raison d'être. The means of triumphing in the face of an oppressive and hopeless set of circumstances comes from within the system itself. The scenario is instrumentalized in order to demonstrate its own weakness—the dysfunction within the dysfunctional, the game that requires cheating.

In this way the dystopia is far more than merely the context or the narrative foil, but an active participant in the drama being played out. The rules become a set of terms to be negotiated, characters become interchangeable assets, and the physical space becomes something molded and redeployed in new and novel ways.

The fiction is the place where the impossible becomes possible. The rules for the game are a framework that implies a labyrinth of potential latent within. The main character in *Escape from L.A.*, Snake Plissken, lies, cheats, kills, intimidates, and satirizes on his journey to a conclusion that undermines his original, flawed mission. The rules of his deployment may be annoying, but they anticipate some nail-biting plot twists.

There's no Place Like Non-place

*"Welcome to Westworld…
where nothing can possibly go wrong!"*
• Advertising poster, Westworld, USA

"Modern technology… offers an endless field-day to any deviant strains in our personalities."
• JG Ballard

Macau now hosts more casinos in a geographically defined territory than any other place in the world, surpassing Las

Vegas as the biggest global gaming-room of the twenty-first century. In the context of the Chinese state, this economic zone is very "special" indeed. Like the Hong Kong of free commerce that offered an incubator of trade before being subsumed into the opportunistic regime of the motherland, Macau was the incubator of hedonism and vice dressed in Portuguese colonialist guise. Politics aside, it is perverse that sealed-off perpetual daytime interior environments should dominate a subtropical island. After a slow-burner of a coming-out decade, Macau now boasts a gambling revenue that fuels as much as three quarters of the state economy. A handful of multi-millionaire entrepreneurs are courted to bring in the heady mix of poker, strippers, and poolside cocktails. Ever increasing amounts of capital have established a grotesque topography of ostentatious architecture, concrete causeways, and luxury leisure enclaves.

In the West, infrastructure often leaves gaping holes in urban environments after technologies are rendered obsolete, resources expended, or societal fashions have run their course. Shopping malls, like the electronic products they stock, have a built-in obsolescence. Currently the pioneering shopping malls of the postwar era are being heritage listed—a palliative gesture preserving relics in perpetuity—while the vast majority of structures are demolished by bulldozers to make way for urban redevelopment, or are even left to decay slowly in wastelands of devalued real estate. Returning to the elements, these mega-structures of previous boom-times become unusual habitats for creatures who unwittingly build their nests in bargain bins, checkout counters, and automatic photo booths. Like a perfect study in decomposition, they create a microcosm of our emerging world, where the artificial and natural become indistinguishable from one another.

Our narrative is modernity, and our dystopias are the super-planned, re-planned, and unplanned environments of the modern world. The aberrations and abandoned spaces of our modern environments, the margins that are squeezed by the excesses of development, the new natures that are produced in lieu of what was natural, the waste that is left behind after the flight of capital—these are the instable interstices of modern life. They are latent territories that are both the unforeseen consequences of our modern impulse, as well as the raw material for a renewed project on the city.

Like a private detective covertly sorting through the trash of a client's ex-lover, so we find in the wastelands of our modern existence a potent indicator of our cultural habits. These rogue byproducts of our modern existence even threaten to play an active role in the progress of our urbanism. There is in this deduction, the possibility to recover something from the ruins of the present in the formulation of the future.

An Architecture of the Unintended

"There's another world outside! We've seen it!"
● Jessica, Logan's Run, 1976

The dystopic vision is invoked in practice by subverting existing norms in order to form an instrumental knowledge of them. Design speculation on these grounds is able to make critical diagnostics on what this means for users and for society. The opening up of a broader field from which to unearth the visions of tomorrow does not entail working towards a predetermined result, but rather extrapolates the consequences of the present. In so doing, we can free ourselves from the impossibility of reverse engineering an ideal state, and instead build speculations out of the resources we have at our disposal. The "consequential" is the uncovering of what is latent in emerging technology—technology regarded in the broadest sense as capturing social, biological, geographical, jurisdictional, and technical phenomena.

An exploration of consequences cannot escape from judgment or criticism. By its very nature it ought to be critical—that is, of our present society's norms and forms. It is a game of persuasion where the power of speculation rests not on how it will solve problems, but instead on how it will capture our imagination, and by its ability to seed further exploration. Powerful architecture transcends the merely moral and embraces the sublime, the grotesque, the monstrous, and the radical.

The present can be mined for those critical projects that turn the perverse, fantastic, and underrated phenomena of our modern world into design platforms. This vast material at our disposal can be projected into the future in order to let wild imaginings roam free and test speculations against our own fragile notions of what should be real. This activity is tangential to the spectrum of morality. It both provides a lens on the future and provides a critique of the present, and in so doing collapses future and present into the same time-frame unearthing tomorrow's thoughts today.

AQUALTA　　　　　　　　RISING TIDES

Project Title:
AQUALTA
Company Name:
Studio Lindfors
Artist/Architect:
Ostap Rudakevych
Envisioned Project Location:
New York/Tokyo
Envisioned Completion Date:
The near future

WHEN AND WHERE
The *Aqualta* series of images imagines how New York and Tokyo might look in a few centuries from now as a result of global warming and rising sea levels.

BASIC CONDITIONS
The title of the project, *Aqualta,* is a play on the Italian expression "acqua alta," or the increasing high tides which periodically flood Venice. *Aqualta* is a series of speculative images, which visually explore what a coastal metropolis might feel like a hundred years from now, due to rising sea levels. The images illustrate two cultural and financial epicenters—Tokyo and New York—which adapt to, rather than resist, the rising waters.

KEY PRINCIPLES
Aqualta reveals an adaptable city infrastructure capable of acclimatizing to nature. It imagines city dwellers migrating to higher and dryer altitudes as water levels gradually rise. Piers, boardwalks, and systems of navigable canals re-establish the transportation network lost below. Residents appropriate rooftops for farms and greenhouses. Wetland ecologies and oyster-beds thrive and take root to create a better layer of protection to coastlines from future storms. The cities are shown without combustion—engines, power plants, all emissions are rendered obsolete—resulting in cleaner, quieter cities.

FLOATING GARDENS (SPA) RISING TIDES

Project Title:
FLOATING GARDENS (SPA)
Architect:
Anne Holtrop (in collaboration with Roderik van der Weijden)
Envisioned Project Location:
Lake IJsselmeer, Amsterdam, Netherlands
Envisioned Completion Date:
2012

WHERE AND WHEN
The *Floating Gardens,* which are envisioned to be completed around 2012, are situated in the IJsselmeer Lake—one of the biggest fresh-water lakes in the Netherlands, northeast of Amsterdam.

BASIC CONDITIONS
Dutch architect, Anne Holtrop, has collaborated with green-technology firm, Studio Noach, and botanist, Patrick Blanc, for this proposal of an artificial floating island containing gardens and a spa. By constructing a habitable landscape on a lake, the project examines the element of water as a possible design surface for the construction of floating environments. It questions what kind of architectural forms can be found for a structure on the water surface. The project also investigates how an amorphous architecture with faceted surfaces can create an exterior landscape of artificial hills and valleys. The interior would, thereby assume the counter form of the constructed landscape. As a visitor strolls from space to space, he or she experiences a sequence of baths, panoramic saunas, treatment rooms and relaxation areas. From the within, the windows frame the landscape and provide access to outdoor terraces and pools. From the terrace, paths continue over the hills and through the valleys connecting different spaces through the landscape. Those who walk here would see a combination of water, plants, and architecture, which would gratify their human desire for a world that is concrete and tangible.

KEY PRINCIPLES
Essential to this project—where interior and exterior, landscape and architecture all meld into one—is the creation of a floating sustainable biotope, constructed using recycled materials with a vegetative, green covering that literally breaths oxygen and wellness from its pores. *Floating Gardens* (spa) will be made completely from GreenRexwall, which is a recycled polystyrene composite. The vegetation will grow on the façades and ceilings using Patrick Blanc's soilless system, and will grow on the mineral-rich water of the lake. The vegetation will be a breeding ground for birds, butterflies, and insects. The innovative technical installations will provide substantial energy savings. The surrounding water will act as a heat-exchanger; the converse of how a refrigerator works. It can serve as a heat, and a cooling source, and is up to 70% more efficient than conventional energy systems.

Project Title:
VARDØ ARKS

Architect:
CDMB Architects/
Christophe DM BARLIEB

Envisioned Project Location:
Vardø, Norway, The Arctic Circle

Envisioned Completion Date:
Only time will tell

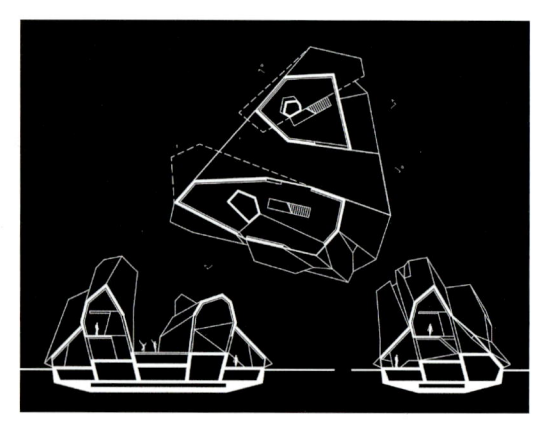

Typical Vardø Ark: Section AA and section BB

WHERE AND WHEN
Vardø is a small island on the northern fringes of Europe; the island is situated well within the Arctic Circle where climate change is more visible than elsewhere.

BASIC CONDITIONS
CDMB asks pertinent questions: "What will happen to Vardø, and its inhabitants if sea levels rise? Will they retreat inland, or will they go out to sea and explore new opportunities?" Climate change tends to be regarded as having a negative impact on our lives. While the effects of climate change are difficult to imagine, our entire planet will have to pay the price for change, and we might have to pay the price to adapt to new environments. *Vardø* is the contemporary version of the epic biblical tale of *Noah's Ark;* however unlike Noah the architects propose to "save" his human friends too!

KEY PRINCIPLES
Vardø's Arks proposes a contemporary collage of urban elements. The design forms public and private spaces, islands within the town, streets, dwellings, and bridges. Each urban component would float and would anchor itself to a neighboring component. Neighborhoods would be able to be reconfigured in no time; the entire town could change overnight. *Vardø's Arks* would be built from dismantled houses, while storage facilities could be constructed from the harbor's old infrastructure. In time, more structures would be converted into floating units. Vardø is an ideal stopover en route to Greenland or Canada. The new urban settlement would testify to the change of time, and to our adaptability by embracing new opportunities. In many ways the project reflects the ancient tale of social and environmental events affecting our daily lives. In the worst case scenario, where the island is flooded and submerged, Vardø would simply form a "mothership" consisting of all its arks. They would eventually drift through the northern seas like an iceberg populated by a small community on a quest for a homeland.

Ark Typologies

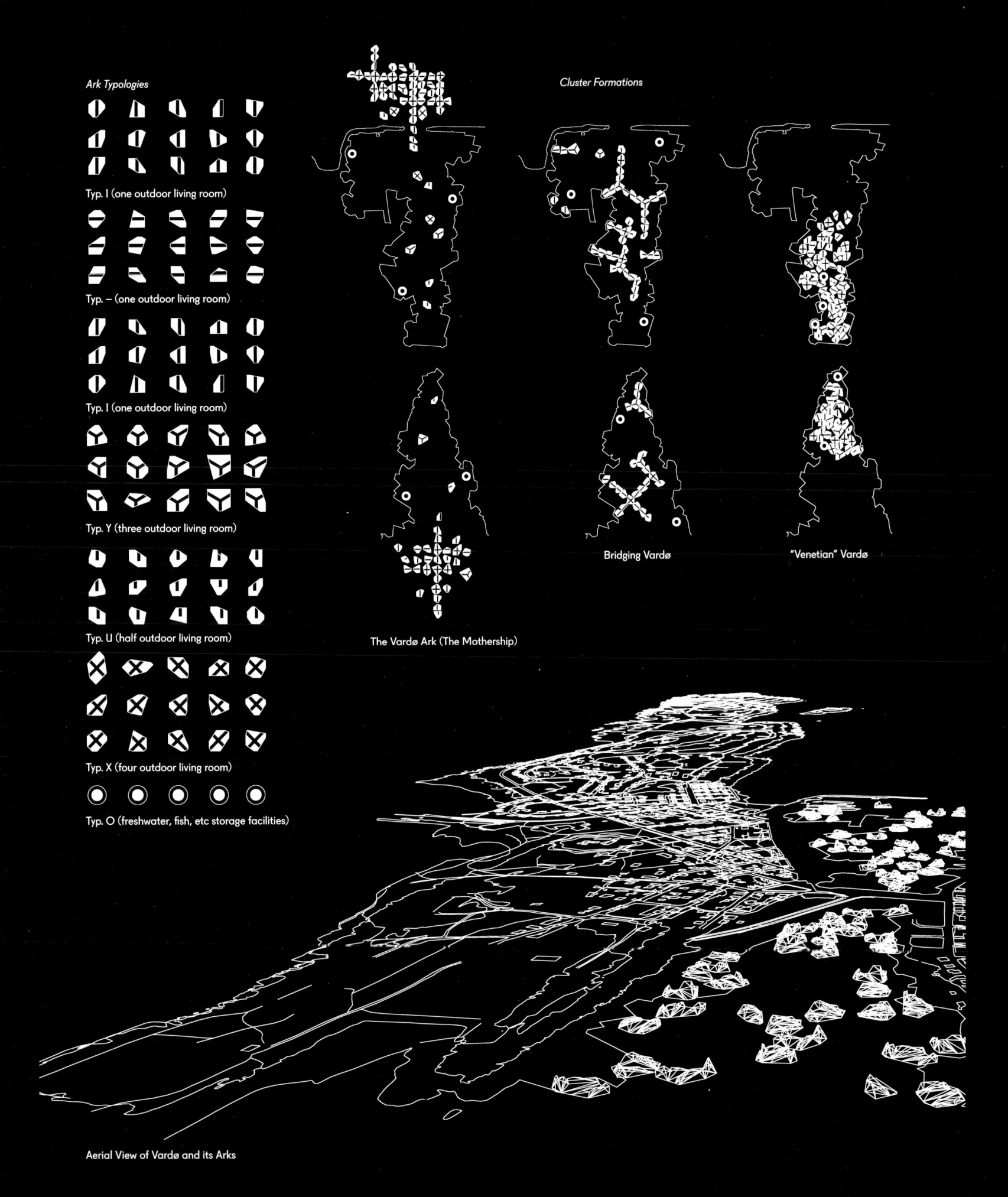

Typ. I (one outdoor living room)

Typ. – (one outdoor living room)

Typ. I (one outdoor living room)

Typ. Y (three outdoor living room)

Typ. U (half outdoor living room)

Typ. X (four outdoor living room)

Typ. O (freshwater, fish, etc storage facilities)

Cluster Formations

The Vardø Ark (The Mothership)

Bridging Vardø

"Venetian" Vardø

Aerial View of Vardø and its Arks

Project Title:
CRUISE CITY, CITY CRUISE
Architect:
NL Architects
Envisioned Project Location:
The world's oceans
Envisioned Completion Date:
An alternative future

WHERE AND WHEN
Sometime in the near future, roaming aircraft carriers will be transformed to amusement parks that will cruise the world's oceans.

BASIC CONDITIONS
Tourism constitutes one of the largest industries in the world today; the project, *Cruise City, City Cruise*, tries to take advantage of this fact by exploring the idea of transforming a cruise-liner into a moving tourist destination by transplanting an entire city and amusement park onto the decks of aircraft carriers.

KEY PRINCIPLES
Weighing over 70,000 tons, these warships belong to the largest naval vessels ever built. In *Cruise City, City Cruise*, the enormous scale and naval character is employed for pleasure voyages, where the voyage itself and the discovery of different destinations en route, as well as the ship's amenities become part of the experience. The project questions the parasitic nature of cruise ships on the cities ports they rely on. The project poses the question, whether some form of reciprocity might be introduced, where a two-way relationship or connection might be established between the ships and the harbor-cities they visit.

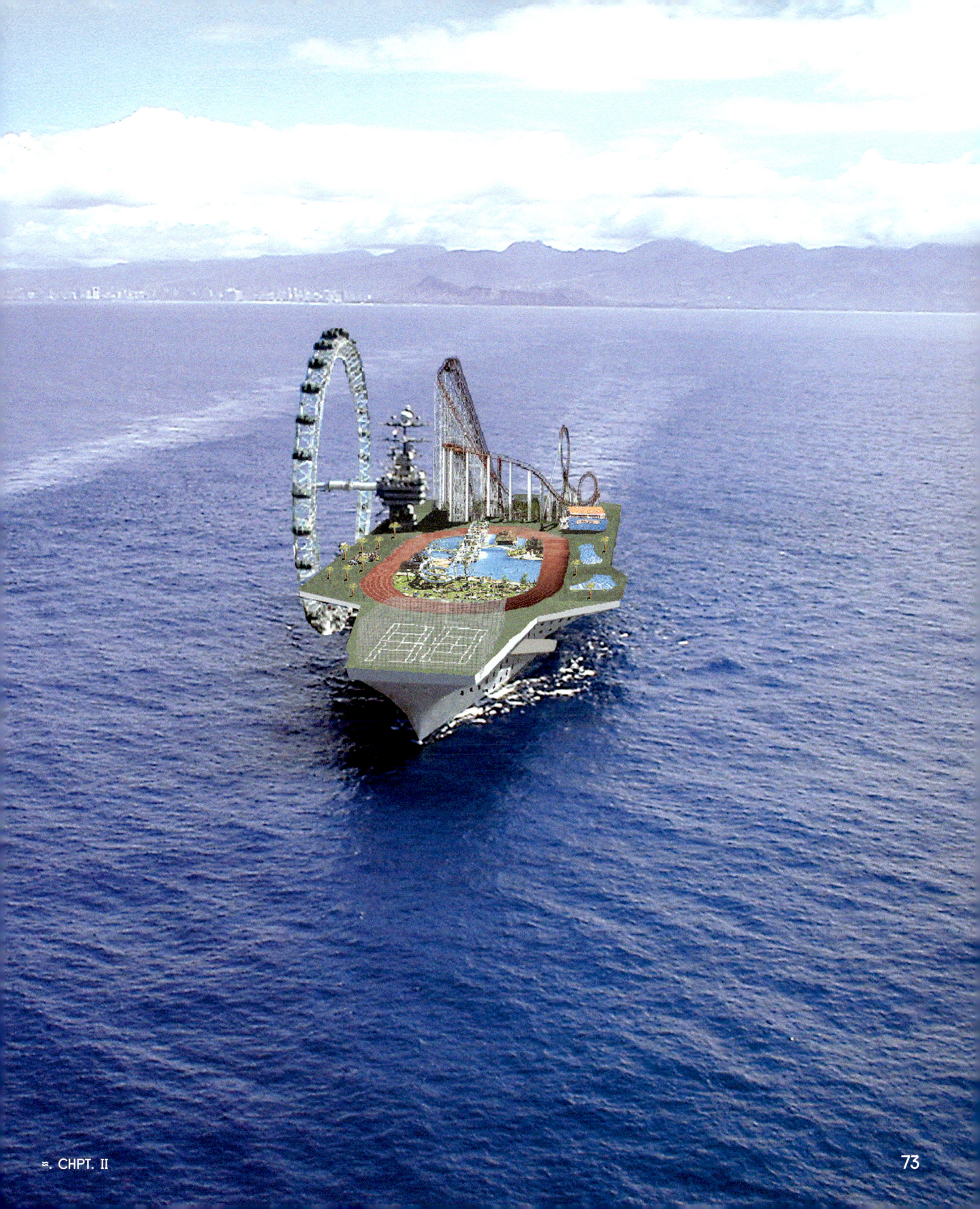

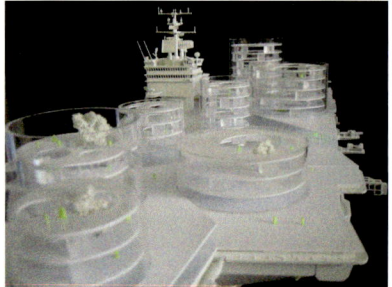

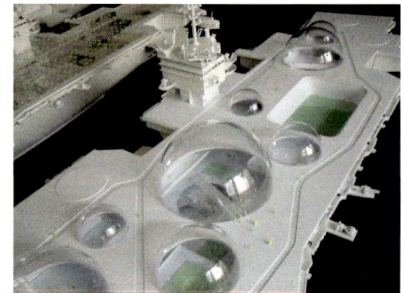

Project Title:
MICRO-UTOPIE
Architect:
IaN+, Marco Galofaro
Envisioned Project Location:
The world's oceans
Envisioned Completion Date:
The near future

WHERE AND WHEN
Micro-utopie is the name given to IaN+'s idea to use aircraft carriers for civil use in critical areas. As military aircraft carriers are sent to certain areas to threaten the opponent, civil aircraft carriers would be sent to areas where needed, to temporarily take care, wherever required, of services, housing, cultural, and/or recreational areas.

BASIC CONDITIONS
An aircraft carrier is a large warship whose main role is to transport airplanes to operation areas: it is a movable air-base that can adapt to various geographic conditions. Aircraft carriers are used strategically and act as an off-shore airbase and as a deterrent. The architecture of aircraft carriers is conducive to change: *Micro-utopie* takes advantage of this adaptability: to create a moveable architecture which could provide logistical support to any city in need.

KEY PRINCIPLES
Aircraft carriers are considered to be special devices (huge and strongly symbolic), which react to conflict situations in a particular territory; the forces occupying it are obliged to engage with the culture and heritage of the region it is involved with. The converted aircraft carriers represent the boundary between two specificities: they are no longer warships but would gain a completely new association. IaN+ have coined names for the various conversions: *Artscape* would convert the carrier into a museum, *Housescape* would convert the carrier into a housing scheme to shelter the homeless and displaced in emergency circumstances after a natural catastrophe, *Sportscape* would be a theme park, and *Landscape* would convert the aircraft carrier into a nature park. *Micro-utopie* aircraft carriers are simultaneously able to be global as well as to be able to adapt to the specific context of the local.

Project Title:
QUARANTINED LIBRARY

Architect:
David A. Garcia

Envisioned Project Location:
World's oceans

Envisioned Completion Date:
2015

BASIC CONDITIONS

Some texts can be dangerous, not because of their content, but because they are, simply, contaminated. Others are deemed dangerous—their words liable to "infect" or "pollute" any person who reads them. They are deemed high risk by authorities, and have therefore been censored. Some information is eternally "quarantined" and kept secret within us, never confessed, exposed or shared; but rather becoming a burden.

KEY PRINCIPLES

This *Quarantined Library* collects these three typologies of isolation in an abandoned cargo ship: an archive of infected and radioactive books from around the world, where users are obliged to wear a bio-hazard suit to view the content of any contaminated books. These books are held in silo-formed shafts, where in case of extreme pollution in the archive, they can be ventilated. Secondly, there will be a library of confessions and secrets, where people at each port can leave their confessions anonymously under the quiet of a tree. Adjacent to this space, secrets will be engraved some days later on large wooden signage boards by a robotic arm. These boards, infected with termites, will be exhibited; visitors will have access and be able to read the engraved secrets, for as long as the wooden panels last. This method of delayed and inevitable erasure gives the archive a limited lifetime; its longevity controlled by a parasite. Lastly, there will be a collection of historically censored books, piled up on top of each corresponding country on a large world map attached to the floor. The user will be able to navigate chronologically through each nation's history of book censorship, whilst the landscape becomes an expression of a forlorn past and present.

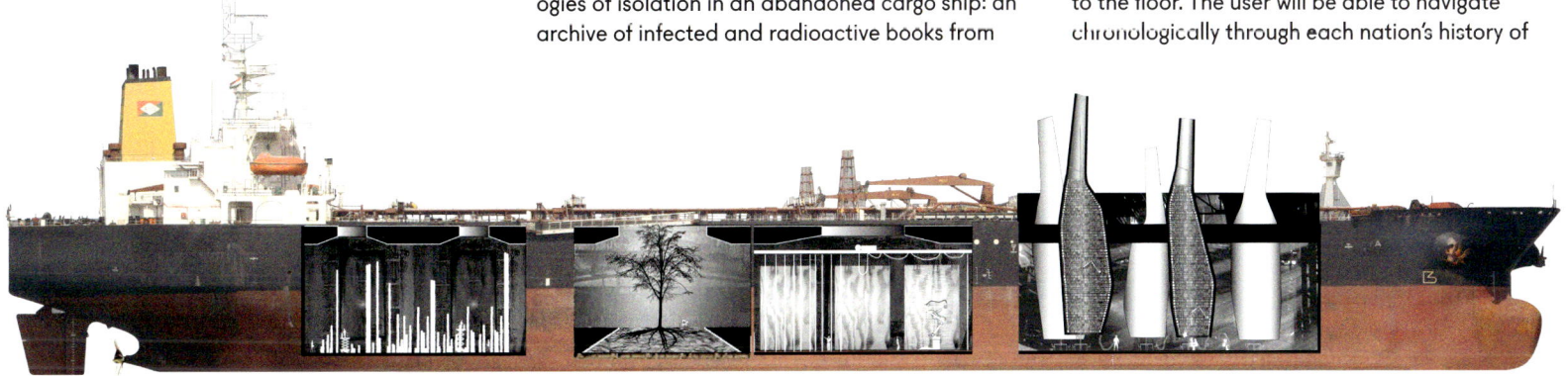

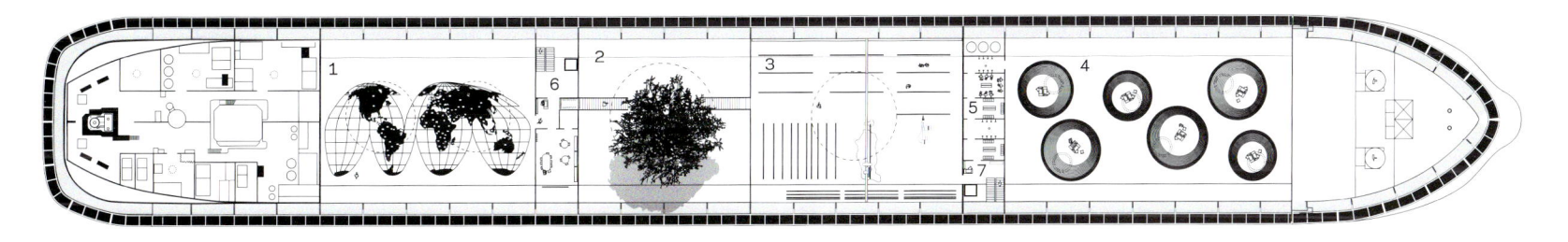

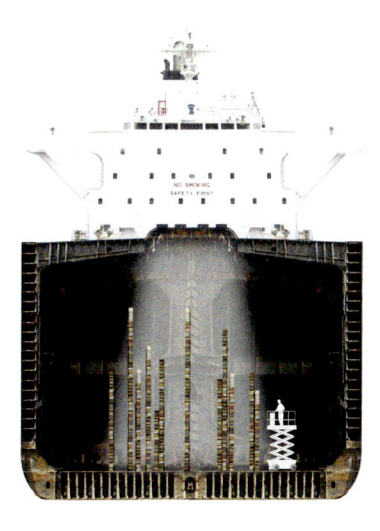

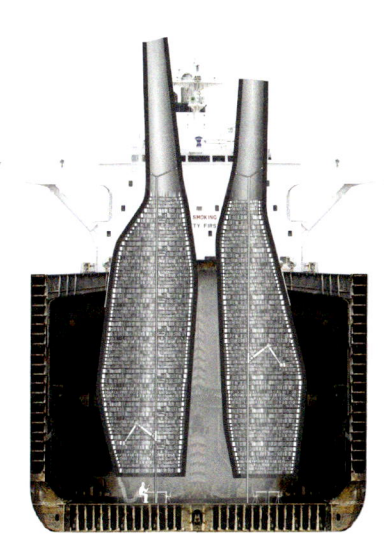

WHERE AND WHEN

Playing on the custom of ships as carriers of diseases between seaports, the *Quarantined Library* as a vessel, travelling in eternal quarantine on the world's great oceans, would collect and display rejected, dangerous, and secretive documents.

Project Title:
FLOODED LONDON
Architect:
Anthony Lau
Envisioned Project Location:
London, UK
Envisioned Completion Date:
2030

WHERE AND WHEN
Flooded London proposes a floating city, made from decommissioned ships and oil-rig platforms on the Thames Estuary, London in 2030.

BASIC CONDITIONS
With the pressure of increasing population and urbanization, cities do not have any choice but to build on flood plains or on low-lying areas. The consequence of humanity's rapid expansion and a climate that is changing due to global warming, is resulting in rising sea levels and extremer weather conditions. The conflict between expansion and climatic change threatens coastal cities around the world. One tenth of the world's population live in coastal cities, most of which are situated in low-lying coastal areas in poorer, developing nations, as well as affluent cities, like New York and London. Even a sea-level rise of 1 m would result in widespread economic and social disaster. The future of human habitation and expansion is obliged to adapt to living on water.

KEY PRINCIPLES
Every year, hundreds of ships and other floating structures are defunct and left for scrap. *Flooded London* proposes breathing new life to decommissioned ships and oil-rig platforms by converting them into hybrid homes adapted for aquatic living. The Thames Estuary has been chosen as the site for aquatic urban expansion, and is an alternative solution to the current plans to build 120,000 new homes on flood plains in the Thames Gateway. The regeneration of the riverside through the reuse of dockyards, plus increased river transport and the reversion to a natural hydrology of flood plains will bring nature and life back to the River Thames. Sustainability through the reuse of marine structures and the reduction of energy use and waste will be a high priority when living on the water. By utilizing the submerged landscape, a floating city of offshore communities, mobile infrastructure, and water transport will allow the city to reconfigure through "fluid" urban planning. Wave, tidal, and wind energy will be ideal for this offshore city; the inhabitants will live alongside the natural cycles of nature and the rhythms of the river and tides. Most modern floating architecture involves new-build modular systems for mass production. Although this may be the most efficient for spacial planning, it often lacks architectural character. The multitude of hull shapes and sizes will inspire unique and inventive designs. The proposal aims to express the beautiful forms and internal steel structures of the hulls. The hulls will serve as nautical reminders of the ship's past and our previous proximity to water, which we will now have to embrace once again. This strategy for creating a self sufficient floating city by reusing ships and marine structures can also be applied to island nations such as the Maldives. Over 80% of its 1,200 islands are a mere 1 m above sea level. With sea levels rising around 0.9 cm per year, the Maldives could become uninhabitable within 100 years. Its 360,000 citizens will be forced to adapt to their new conditions; they could become one of the first floating nations.

Global application
This strategy for creating a self sufficient floating city by reusing ships and marine structures can be applied to island nations such as the Maldives. Over 80% of its 1,200 islands are around 1 m above sea level. With sea levels rising around 0.9 cm a year, the Maldives could become uninhabitable within 100 years. Its 360,000 citizens would be forced to adapt and they could become the first floating nation.

FLOODED LONDON   RISING TIDES

CHPT. II

Project Title:
PHYSALIA: A POSITIVE AMPHIBIOUS ENERGY GARDEN TO CLEAN EUROPEAN WATERWAYS

Architect:
Vincent Callebaut Architecture

Envisioned Project Location:
Europe's waterways

Envisioned Completion Date:
The near future

and water conservation on a geopolitical level, on a European scale, in order to verify strategic solutions to water networks. *Physalia* is a truly nomadic hydro-dynamic laboratory which will be dedicated to implement an international network of scientific partnerships; it will also develop new prototypes of environmental resources and which will demonstrate its most advanced studies regarding water consumption and waterway transport.

made from aluminum which would cover the steel hull structure. This silver-plated cladding would be covered by a TiO_2 layer of shaped anatase that would react to ultraviolet rays enabling the reduction of water pollution. In addition to being a self-cleaning vessel, *Physalia* would be able to absorb and recycle using the photo-catalytic effect; the chemical and carbonated waste from the water would be rejected by traditional boats. Furthermore, *Physalia* is crossed by a hydraulic network that would enable the vessel to filter water and to biologically purify it thanks to its planted green-roof. When the system of automatic irrigation functions, the structure would seem to disappear into the atmosphere. In actual fact, the project would metamorphoze into a kind of a foggy cloud with an indistinct contour. The *Physalia* would, therefore, become a sweet-smelling "evaporation" space that would seem to engulf the visitors suspended inside. The architecture of the futurist ship would reveal a perfect balance between its cantilevered masses, making it seem to hover lightly on the water surface. The curved forms are refined and subtle. The lines of the vessel elegantly show the innovation and the stylish aesthetic of the design. The interior scenography of *Physalia* ignites the debate on the future of water habitation. *Physalia* divides the scheme into four thematic gardens dedicated respectively to the four elements, symbiotically bringing their inherent aspects to the fore in the amphibious landscape.

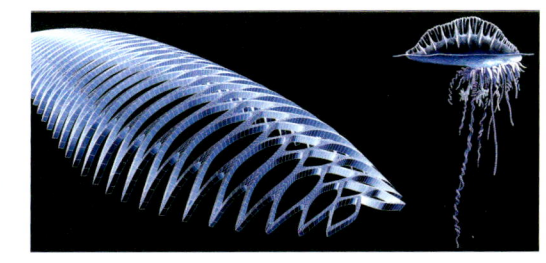

WHERE AND WHEN
The *Physalia* vessel navigates the main European rivers between the Danube and Volga, the Rhine and Guadalquivir, and between the Euphrates and Tiger rivers.

BASIC CONDITIONS
The World Forum of Water held in Istanbul in 2009, was attended by ministers, scientists, and ecologist fighters from 120 countries. The participants studied ways to avoid water crises, which according to UN and the World Water Council, will affect as much as half of the world's population in the next 20 years. In this context, the project, *Physalia* is an architectural prototype that aims to react to the pooled knowledge regarding the sustainable management of water resources. It is a semi-aquatic and a semi-earthly amphibious vessel; a floating *agora,* which aims to deal with ecology

KEY PRINCIPLES
Physalia is a vessel that will be completely energy self-sufficient. The vessel's bionic structure is inspired by the pneumatophorous, known also as *Physalia physalis,* from the Greek *physalis,* meaning "water bubble." This aquatic pneumatophorous, is noteworthy due to its perfect symmetry, its elegant, oblong shape, and its translucent shell. The architecture of Physalia is designed ecologically from renewable energy and would have carbon-zero emissions. It is designed as a prototype that would produce positive energy, meaning that it would produce more energy than it consumes. Thus, it is covered with a double pneumatic membrane which would be adorned with smooth photovoltaic solar cells like the scales of a fish. Beneath its hull, hydro-turbines would transform the energy of the fluvial stream into hydro-electricity and would be able to adjust the fine navigation. The surface of the vessel would be

SYPH. THE OCEANIC CITY   RISING TIDES

Project Title:
SYPH. THE OCEANIC CITY
Architect:
Arup
(Alanna Howe, Alexander Hespe)
Envisioned Project Location:
The world's oceans
Envisioned Completion Date:
2050

WHERE AND WHEN
The ocean city concept—as a way of life underwater—is envisioned in a landless future where land, as a resource, will be scarce due to the rise of sea levels.

BASIC CONDITIONS
As part of the Australian Pavilion's exhibition "Now + When Australian Urbanism" at the 12th International Architecture Biennale 2010 held in Venice, this project looks at a dramatically changed world forty years from now. The Oceanic City project, *Syph*, by Arup proposes an underwater city against the backdrop of an era when land will begin to disappear, the value of remaining land will increase drastically, and people will be unable to afford to live on land any longer. As a result, people will migrate from land to sea, providing an opportunity to develop completely new cityscapes.

KEY PRINCIPLES
Syph is spawned from a rise in the interest in biomimetic practices and materials in the advent of climate change. The design evolves into a collection of organisms, or pods, with specialized functions, like energy generation and sustainable food production that would work in unison to form an underwater city.

Project Title:
GIANT WATER LILIES
Architect:
The Why Factory
Envisioned Project Location:
Phuket, Thailand
Envisioned Completion Date:
The near future

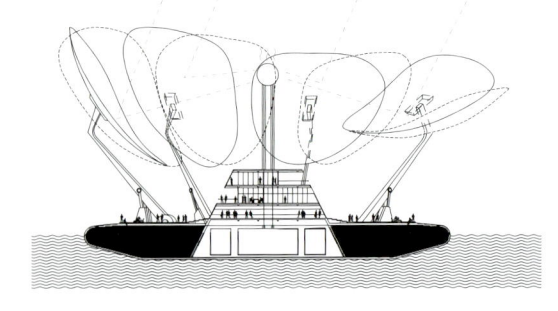

WHERE AND WHEN
This project conceived by Ulf Hackauf, Pirjo Haikola, and Gonzalo Rivas for The Why Factory at Delft University of Technology, is based on a design that the inventor, Bill Gross, presented in his lecture in 2003. This newly created biotope, *Giant Water Lilies,* would be a tourist attraction off the coast of Thailand. The project celebrates "new green" design that ignores any notion of "artificial versus natural." The project proposal is large in scale and clearly visible, economic and effective; it is intended to amaze and dazzle with its beauty.

BASIC CONDITIONS
The Why Factory imagined giant water lilies, floating on the sea; over the course of the day, the flowers would slowly open and close their reflective petals, which would catch the sunlight and transform the sun's rays into valuable, clean energy that would feed the needs of the coastal towns nearby. The *Giant Water Lilies* would be a landmark beacon of a new green infrastructure that goes beyond bio-mimicry and that creates its own aesthetics from nature's instrinsic logic.

KEY PRINCIPLES
Giant Water Lilies uses the tested principles of solar-thermal energy generation: the flower's petals are designed as large mirrors that would reflect sunlight and focus its rays on an absorber in the center of the structure. At the central focus point, temperatures of 500 degrees Celsius, and more, could be achieved. Within the structure molten salt would be used as heat transfer fluid, transporting the captured heat down into the base of the flower. Here, gas turbines would transform the heat into electricity, which would be brought to the coast by cables under the seabed. The solar-thermal generation of energy is not the same as photovoltaic techniques. Photovotaic cells generate electricity directly, which can be tricky and expensive to store. Solar-thermal structures, however, generate heat which can be stored easily with little loss of energy. With the aid of good insulation, molten salt can retain its heat for several days, allowing the flowers to provide electricity reliably even during the night and on overcast days. Underneath the large blossom-leaves, there could be artificial beaches, restaurants, and even hotels.

Project Title:
LILYPAD: A FLOATING ECOPOLIS FOR CLIMATE REFUGEES

Architect:
Vincent Callebaut Architecture

Envisioned Project Location:
The world's oceans

Envisioned Completion Date:
2100

WHERE AND WHEN
As a result of the increase of the world's ocean levels due to the melting of the ice caps of the Antarctic and Greenland, and the melting of continental glaciers, there has been a significant loss of land all over the world and millions of people have lost their homes, if not their entire country, by the year 2100.

BASIC CONDITIONS
Facing the worldwide ecological crisis, this floating *Ecopolis* or *Lilypad* has the duel objective, not only to increase levels of sustainability in the offshore territories of the most developed countries but also, more importantly, to provide housing to future climatic refugees of imminent submerged ultramarine territories such as the Polynesian atolls. New biotechnological prototypes of ecological resilience dedicated to nomads and urban ecology in the oceans, *Lilypad* will float on the water surface of the oceans, from the equator to the poles following the warm marine currents which ascend off the Gulf Stream or else the cold currents descending off the Labrador. *Lilypad* is like a true amphibian, half aquatic and half terrestrial. It will be able to accommodate as many as 50,000 inhabitants and will also invite biodiversity by developing its fauna and flora around a central lake of sweetwater, which will collect and purify rainwater. The lake will be entirely immersed and thus ballast the city. It will enable inhabitation in the heart of the aquatic depths. The multi-functional program is centered on three marinas and three mountain peaks which are dedicated respectively to the provision of offices, shops, and leisure. The entire structure will be covered with a stratum of planted housing with suspended gardens, crisscrossed by a network of streets and lanes which will create an organic edge. The aim is to create an environment where both human-beings and nature can coexistence harmoniously. Furthermore, the architects have explored new modes of sea habitation by building communal spaces in close proximity, which encourage social inclusion and are conducive to the meeting of all the inhabitants—local or foreign-born, young or old.

KEY PRINCIPLES
The floating structure of the *Ecopolis* is divided into petal-like forms which were inspired by the ribbed leaves of the great lily-pads of *Amazonia victoria regia* enlarged 250 times in scale. Belonging to the family of *Nympheas*, this aquatic plant with its exceptional elasticity was first discovered by the German botanist, Thaddäus Haenke, and dedicated to Queen Victoria of England in the nineteenth century. The double-layered membrane is made from polyester fibers covered by a layer of titanium dioxide (TiO_2) like an anatase, which, by reacting to ultraviolet rays, is able to absorb atmospheric pollution by a photo-catalytic effect. Entirely auto-efficient, *Lilypad* responds to the four central challenges launched by the Organization for Economic Co-operation and Development, (OECD) in March 2008: climate, biodiversity, water, and health. *Lilypad* will reach a positive energy balance with zero carbon-emissions thanks to the integration of all the renewable energies (solar, thermal and photovoltaic energy, wind energy, hydraulic, tidal power, osmotic energy, biomass) thereby sustainably producing more energy that it will consume. This "true" biotope will be entirely recyclable; this floating *Ecopolis* tends therefore, towards positive eco-calculations by producing oxygen and electricity, by recycling CO_2 and waste, by purifying and biologically treating grey water and by integrating ecological niches, aquaculture fields, and biotic corridors, on and beneath its structure, in order to meet its food requirements.

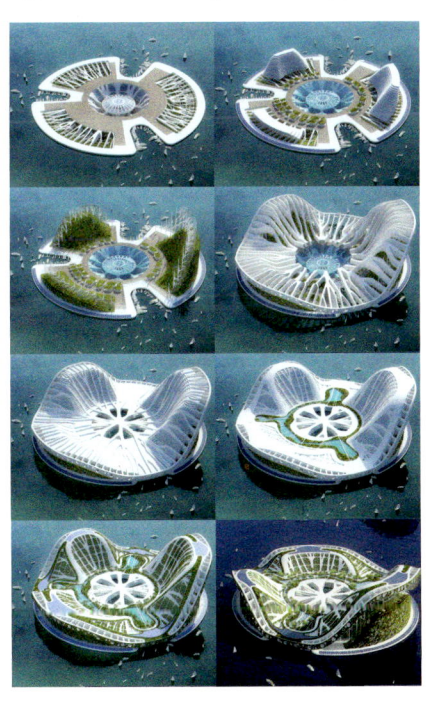

LILYPAD RISING TIDES

=. CHPT. II

Project Title:
GREEN FLOAT
Architect:
Shimizu Corporation
Envisioned Project Location:
Equatorial pacific
Envisioned Completion Date:
The near future

WHERE AND WHEN
The *Green Float* is a botanical future-city concept for an environmental island floating on the equatorial Pacific.

BASIC CONDITIONS
The point of departure for the project, *Green Float*, is the observation that the majority of the Western world lives remarkably convenient lives in cities that have developed economically and physically. Yet, apart from focusing on material wealth, the project aims at the ideal of living harmoniously with nature and passing time at a leisurely pace in cultural pursuits. Born from these aspirations, the project envisions the development of the city, like a single plant, that would embody these principles. The entire complex of the *Green Float* is imagined as an environmentally-friendly, self-sufficient, and carbon-negative island that would continuously absorb CO_2 like a plant, using sunlight for photosynthesis. Here, advanced technology of the future is created amid nature.

KEY PRINCIPLES
The environmental island *Green Float* would have a 3 km diameter and would float on the ocean like a flower petal. The plan is shaped like an inverted cone to maximize surface exposure to sunlight. The

Green Float is conceived as a vertical city in the sky, a village-scale community with a 1 km diameter and green, aquatic open spaces bathed in sunlight. The numerous different facilities accommodated would range from a beach resort, a marine city of low-rise townhouses on the outer circumference with links to the beach resorts, as well as an extensive plant greenhouse equipped with cutting-edge biotechnology situated at the center of a tower. The residential zone of the marine city, along the exterior circumference waterfront, would house as many as 10,000 inhabitants. The greenhouse/nursery would provide jobs for 10,000 people and would act as a new industry incubation-station for future business that would merge nature and technology. At the same time *Green Float* would provide food production at close quarters. Furthermore, there would be a biologically-rich forest as an estuarine zone, where sea water and fresh water would mix, as well as a marine forest formed from seaweed and other marine vegetation in a bio-diverse lagoon. In addition, the so called "city in the sky," would encompasse a residential zone at an elevation of 700 m at the top of the tower. Offices, research facilities, such as a typhoon monitoring station, stores, convention centers, hotels, and other facilities would be clustered in the center. The vertical living area would encompass approximately 30,000 inhabitants on 30 levels. For the overall energy supply, facilities in geosynchronous orbit will be used to collect energy from sunlight and to transmit it to Earth in the form of microwaves. This would provide a stable solar energy supply available for use throughout the day and the night. The quantity of energy that will be produced is calculated to be 5 to 10 times greater than that on land.

Project Title:
TURBINE CITY
Architect:
ONOFFICE
Envisioned Project Location:
North Sea, near Stavanger, Norway
Envisioned Completion Date:
The near future

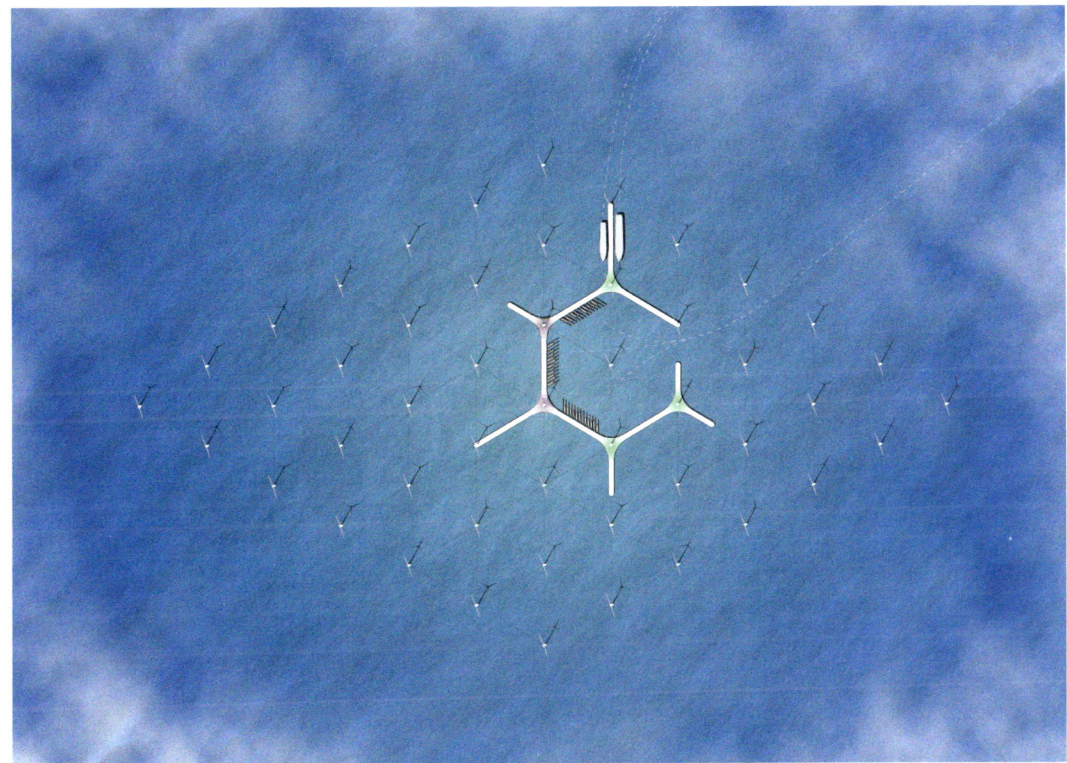

WHERE AND WHEN
Turbine City will be located off the coast of Stavanger, which lies exactly at the point where the Norwegian coastline is constantly barraged by high-speed winds. The fourth largest city in Norway, Stavanger, is a well-connected tourist destination.

BASIC CONDITIONS
The European Union is committed to deriving 20% of its total energy consumption from renewable sources by 2020. The Guarantees of Origin (GoO) system has created a new tradable commodity within the EU: renewable energy. Norway carries the geographic and economic potential to even surpass its renewable energy goals and become a major exporter of "GoO energy." The country already possesses everything required to achieve this end: the longest, most windy, undeveloped coastline in Europe. Furthermore, Norway also possesses expertise in establishing offshore installations, has immense investment capital from the state oil industry, and a battery of hydropower plants to supplement wind power. This potential is already been utilized; Norway has already begun to realize an ambitious 8000 Mega Watt, $44 billion speculative venture. Unfortunately, offshore wind farms are being met with strong resistance, mainly due to misinformation, skepticism, and fear of the dominance of wind turbines on coastal landscapes due to their sheer size.

KEY PRINCIPLES
Turbine City is a flagship project promoting wind farms and celebrating investment in wind power. Wind-energy is the fastest developing renewable energy source. The enormous scale the structures have reached means that they can accommodate habitable space within them. A great mast with a 10 m diameter is no longer merely a pole; it becomes a tower. Against this backdrop, the *Turbine City* offshore wind-farm would be able to accommodate a hotel, spa, and museum within its tower. In order to power the facility, only 1 Mega Watt of the 8 Mega Watt energy the turbine's produce, would be needed. By attracting tourists, sailors, and offshore oilrig-workers to *Turbine City*, people will be able to experience the advantages and the dramatic spectacle of the turbines firsthand, thereby increasing awareness and support. By combining tourism with wind-energy production, the energy debate is taken out of town halls and is, instead, contextualized within the majestic ocean landscape of the wind-farms. Furthermore, *Turbine City* aims to "rebrand" Stavanger—known as the oil capital of Norway—in time for the "sustainable revolution," to create a significant landmark that will rank among the architectural symbols of renewable energy throughout the world.

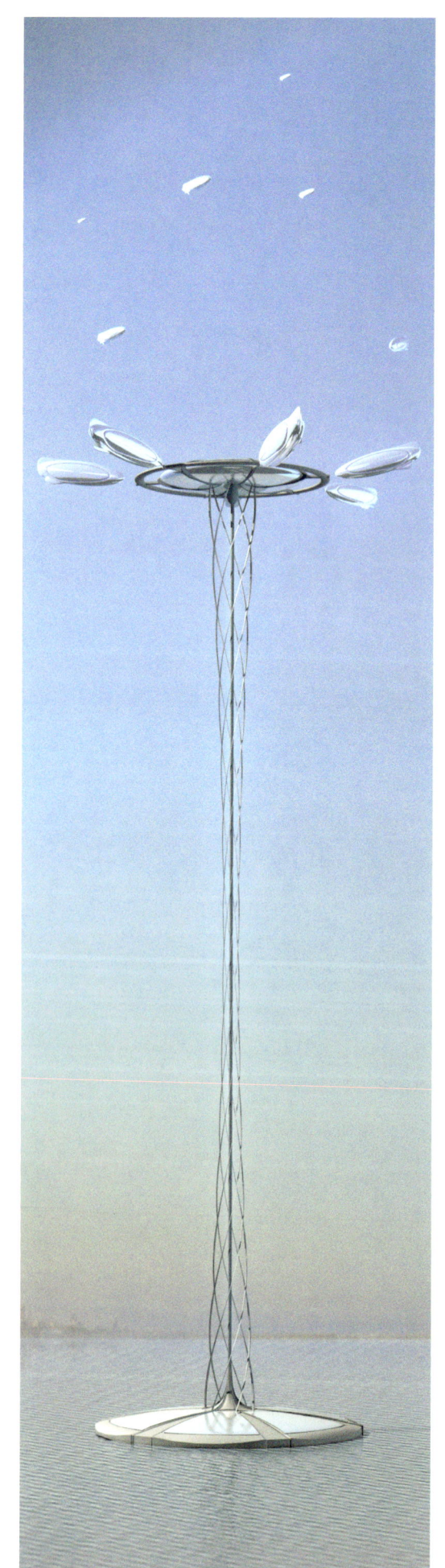

Project Title:
LAKE EFFECT – CHICAGO 2106

Architect:
Strawn.Sierralta

Envisioned Project Location:
Chicago, USA.

Envisioned Completion Date:
2106

WHERE AND WHEN
The project, *Lake Effect*, envisions the city of Chicago in a century from now. In the future, cities will survive thanks to, and in balance with, the natural environments that surround them. Chicago's proximity to Lake Michigan, one of the largest bodies of fresh water in the world, provides large populations with clean water, renewable energy, and expansive waterfront living.

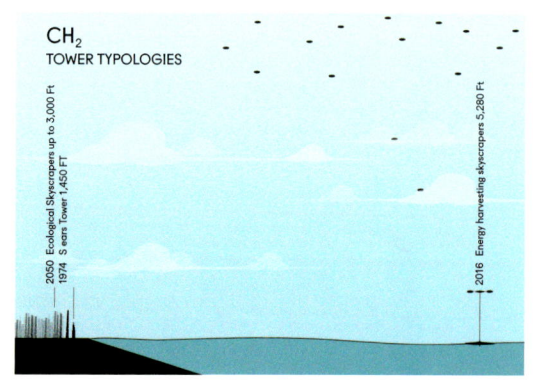

BASIC CONDITIONS
One hundred years from now, in 2106, Chicago's population is predicted to have tripled in size and diversified even more. Chicago will have developed into a poly-centric region where inhabitants live in multiple, interconnected, super-dense centers. These new city centers will operate with maximum efficiency by utilizing horizontal and vertical space over the 24 hour continuum. "Super-density" would free up space for natural ecosystems to be restored. Former urban areas and brown-field sites could be reclaimed by co-op farms, wetlands, and wilderness preserves. Open space and new green corridors would create a network across the region. Green piers would stretch out along the shoreline and new human-made waterways, and water boulevards would expand waterfront living opportunities. In 2106, the inhabitants of Chicago will carefully monitor everything they consume, while producing their own energy and maintaining a level of zero waste-consumption.

KEY PRINCIPLES
A new typology of *energy-harvesting skyscraper* will dominate the skyline by 2106. A renewable energy grid of floating, mile-high towers on Lake Michigan will collect, convert, and store hydrogen to generate 75% of the region's energy needs. The lake will provide a secure location for Chicago's hydrogen infrastructure (CH_2), as well as provide a location close to the city for the practical distribution of stored energy. Combined transportation systems of *mass automated transit*, *on-demand vehicles* for personal use, and air and water taxis will run on the expanded Chicago grid. New typologies such as *automated valet towers* and *inter-modal transfer intersections* will appear in the urban environment. Multi-use, ecological skyscrapers will become the predominant building typology on land. Real-estate will be based in cubic meters and zoning based on 4 dimensions. Spaces will be used, adapted, and transformed from day to night. Individual living units will include *protein cultivators*, *hydroponic gardens*, *temperature alteration pods* and three-dimensional printers. Buildings will produce 25% of their own energy, offer 10% of their floor plan to planted open space, treat their own sewage, and act as city-scaled air filters.

Project Title:
SKYGROVE

Architect:
HOLLWICH KUSHNER LLC (HWKN)
(Matthias Hollwich, Marc Kushner)

Envisioned Project Location:
Costal areas of America/
New York, San Francisco, USA

Envisioned Completion Date:
The near future

WHERE AND WHEN
Envisioned for the coastal areas of America, such as New York and San Francisco, the *Skygrove* project proposes an answer to the future rising of sea levels and stormier weather conditions—as a solution to the interface between the city and the sea.

BASIC CONDITIONS
Today's coastal relationship of dry land in "opposition" to the sea will become blurred in the future by rising sea levels, persistent coastal flooding, storm surges, and tsunamis. *Skygrove* occupies this new nebulous coastal zone and is designed to protect against the dangers rising water poses, as well as to capitalize on its potential.

KEY PRINCIPLES
Skygrove proposes a new high-rise typology conceived to operate in a world of higher water levels. Partly environmental infrastructure and partly vertical office park, *Skygrove* is designed to house corporate employees and business operations in a future where the environment is "predictably unpredictable." Each level would be a self-sufficient entity designed for independent survival in maximum disaster conditions. Different levels will be connected via a compartmentalized matrix façade that will contain all services, from vertical circulation to water, energy, and air supply.

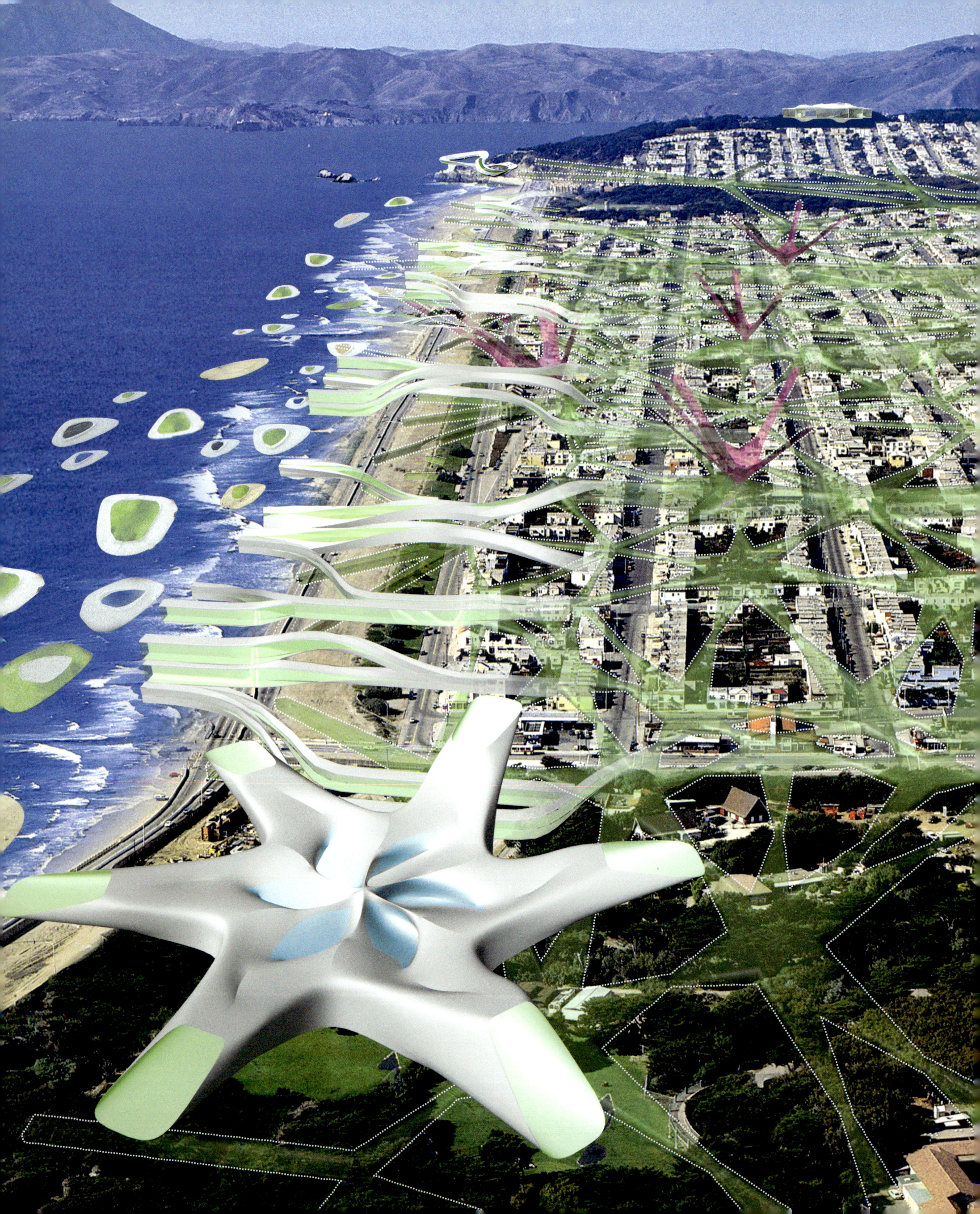

Project Title:
CITY OF THE FUTURE: HYDRO-NET SF 2108

Architect:
IwamotoScott Architecture (Lisa Iwamoto, Craig Scott)

Envisioned Project Location:
San Francisco, USA

Envisioned Completion Date:
2108

WHERE AND WHEN
Envisioned for San Francisco a 100 years from now, IwamottoScott's, *Hydro-Net,* imagines new programmatic potential with its subterranean nodes and above-ground tendrils, which would co-exist and evolve alongside the existing urban city of San Francisco.

BASIC CONDITIONS
The *Hydro-Net* project speculates that cities of the future will need to be evermore interconnected, yet also more self-reliant at the same time. In order to accommodate the projected doubling of population by the year, 2108, while avoiding further outward sprawl, the Bay Area and San Francisco will together require a new, more efficient infrastructure network that will be able to collect and distribute water, power, fuel, goods, as well as to accommodate the transport of residents and tourists alike.

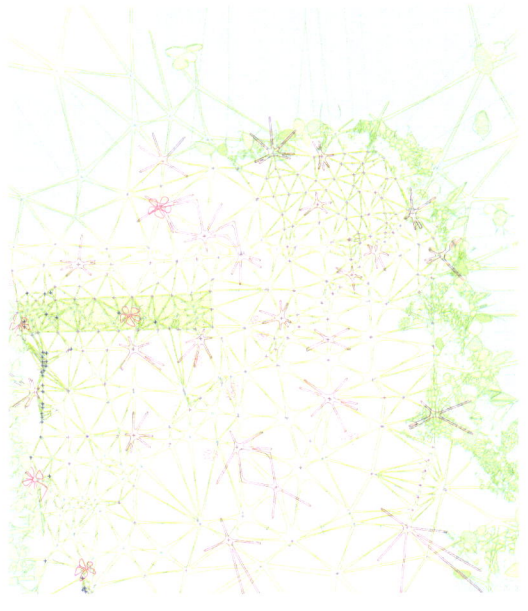

KEY PRINCIPLES
Symbiotic and multi-scale, the *Hydro-Net* project is proposed as a habitable infrastructure that organizes critical flows of the city. It would provide an underground arterial circulation-network for hydrogen-fueled hover-crafts, removing the necessity for higher speed traffic from city streets. *Hydro-Net* emerges at the waterfront and also at multiple nodal points. Here, new kinds of architecture will bloom at key locales in the form of enterprising "urban caves, reeds and outcroppings" that would link the upper and the lower worlds, fostering new social spaces and urban forms fed by the resources and connectivity provided by *Hydro-Net*. The scheme also serves to simultaneously collect, distribute, and store freshwater (H_2O), geothermal energy and hydrogen (H_2) fuel. Built with automated drilling robots, *Hydro-Net*'s tunnel walls would be structured using carbon nano-tube technology. Algae ponds would re-occupy areas along the bay impacted by the projected 5 m water level rise of global climate change. This new aquaculture zone would provide the raw material for the production of hydrogen fuel that would be stored and distributed within the nano-tube tunnel walls. New, high-density housing, would coexists with this aquaculture zone as a forest of sinuous towers. *Hydro-Net* will become a device to tap the vast reserves of water and power housed within the earth beneath San Francisco, storing and distributing energy and fresh water from existing underground geothermal fields and aquifers stretching from Golden Gate Park to the city's airport. Replacing today's street surfaces so that rainwater run-off will be channeled into the sewers, new porous sidewalks will allow rain to refill the aquifers. *Hydro-Net* will also link to an array of fog harvesters, diversifying sources of water.

Project Title:
SATURATION CITY
Architect:
McGauran Giannini Soon (MGS), Bild Architecture, Dyskors, Material Thinking
Envisioned Project Location:
Australia
Envisioned Completion Date:
2050

WHERE AND WHEN
The *Saturation City* project was developed in response the curatorial proposition of the Now&When exhibition for the Australian pavilion of the 2010 Venice Architecture Biennale: a request to imagine the future of urban space in Australia 40 years from now. In order to explore the future of Australian urbanism, the architects imagined a crisis situation—a rise in sea levels of 20 m. The team concentrated their hypothesis on the area around Melbourne and Port Phillip Bay.

BASIC CONDITIONS
Today, Australia is one of the most urbanized continents on Earth, with 93 % of the population living in cities. Against this backdrop, the project acknowledges that significant social and urban change tends to occur during, or in response, to periods of crisis. While Australian urbanism is at a crossroads, due to rapid population growth, diminishing water resources, as well as other issues, the continent has not yet reached a crisis-point that would require dramatic urban upheaval. The conundrum for Australian urbanism is not that there is a dearth of land, but rather that there is too much space for development—its cities expand on huge tracts of productive farmland and tenuous ribbons of infrastructure, stretched to breaking point. By hypothesizing a possible future scenario, an exaggeration of the saturated coastal zone; a critical evaluation of urban value is performed. Some zones would be preserved, modified, or transformed, while others would be dismantled to return to landscape.

KEY PRINCIPLES
Four key Australian urban typologies: the park or garden, the CBD, the suburb, and the coastline, are subjected to dramatic densifications in response to the rise in water, acknowledging that future urbanism will be both fundamentally informed by existing models and will be modified by emerging requirements. Melbourne, and indeed Australia's, urban heritage is intrinsically tied to the coastline culturally, psychologically, and geographically. The shoreline is the epitome of the symbolic "in-between," peripheral place; ephemeral and nebulous. The coast is a saturated space, both solid and viscous, a status symbol, a place of recreation, a protected, yet desired asset. The shoreline is the location where the contemporary environmental debate plays out: the ongoing climate change dialogue implies a rise in sea levels necessitating global change. The shoreline is not static, whether through natural incursion, human imposition, or the inevitable evolution of coastal form, its location, proximity, and character are in a state of constant flux. These future urban spaces are born of this in-between state; a coastal city, but one born of an architectural and tectonic palette of forms, clearly linked to the context of the coastal zone.

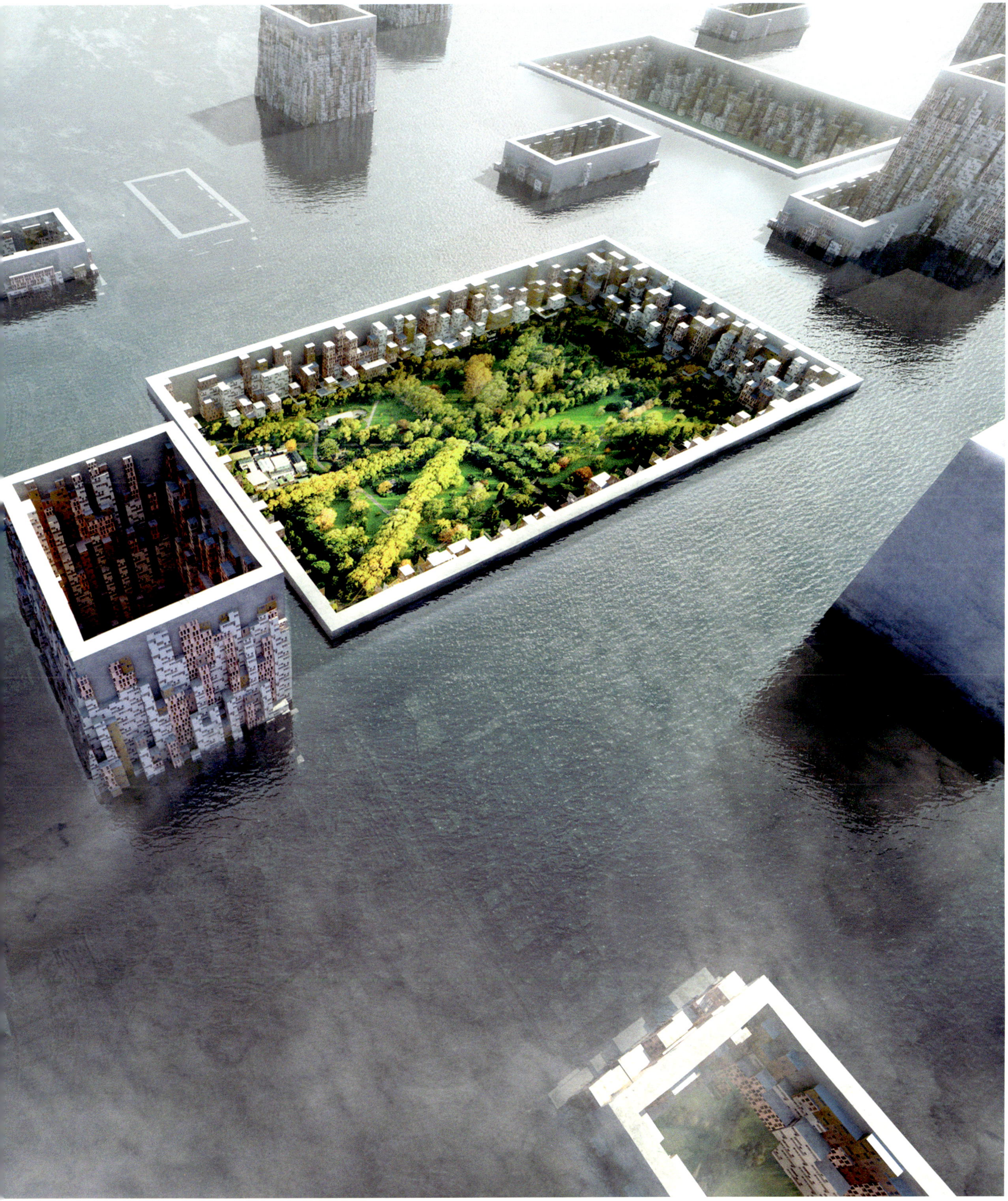

Project Title:
AQUATOWN
Architect:
NH Architecture & Andrew Mackenzie
Envisioned Project Location:
Australia's eastern coastal zone
Envisioned Completion Date:
2050

WHERE AND WHEN
By 2050 aquatic extremes will have forced the fundamental rethinking of established colonial settlement plans. Development along Australia's eastern coastal zone will create new water-based infrastructure that will decouple agriculture, food production, manufacturing, and residential patterns from the land. Australians will remember what ancient cultures never forgot: that water is the key to life.

BASIC CONDITIONS
Water will define the future of Australia. There will be relentless droughts and regular floods which will disturb old colonial settlement patterns. By 2050 Australia will not only abandon the Outback, but also swathes of established inland settlements, turning rather to the coastal zone.

KEY PRINCIPLES
A series of new, artificial urban-forms will be developed—as much infrastructure as architecture. Seasonal monsoon-like northern floods will push development completely off the land, in the form of new *seaburbs*. Rural drought in the south will result in massive population growth in Melbourne, which will lead to the development of a *Dockworld* in Melbourne Bay. In the center, the Gold Coast's leisure economy will extend the already established tradition of coastal formations, to create a Central Beach District. Each will be an artificial urban response to aquatic extremes. Connecting these will be a twenty-first century aqueduct which will bring life to the linear east-coast conurbation, allowing medium density development over 1,000 km along the coast. This "water spine" will create a completely artificial water supply, decoupling agriculture and settlement from climate conditions.

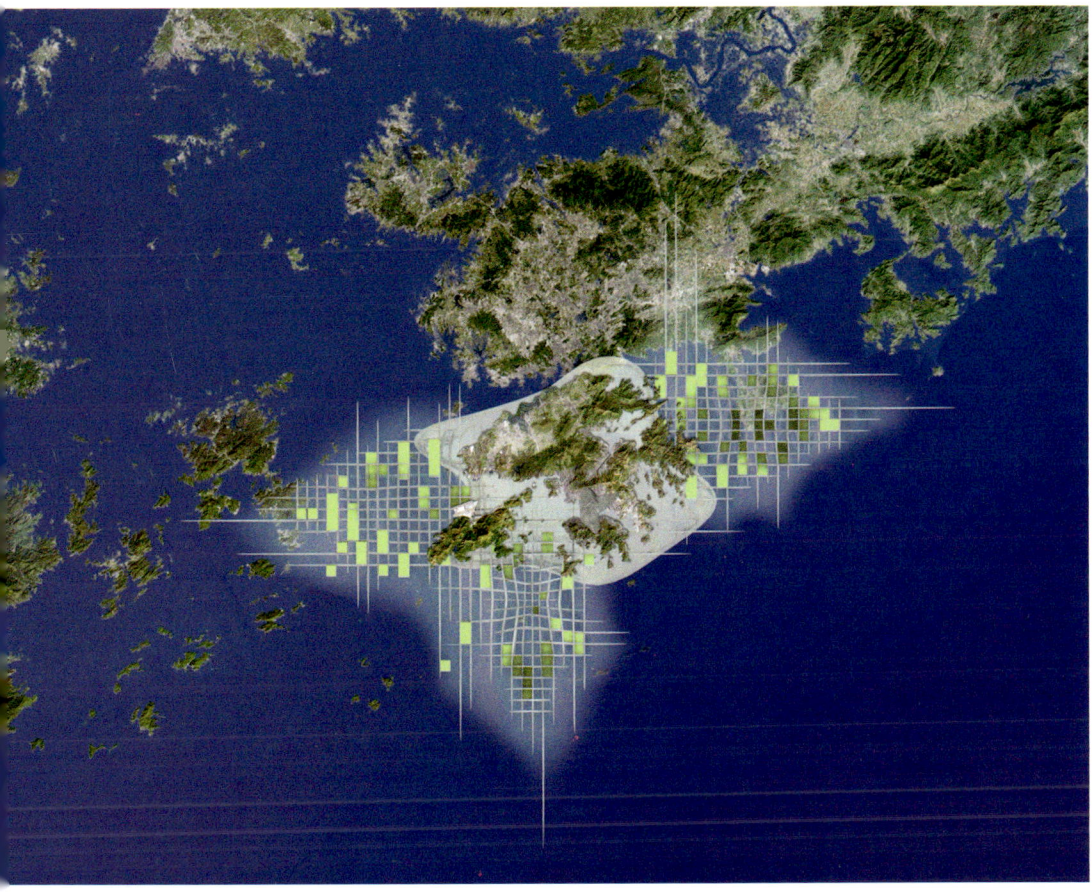

Project Title:
FUTURE NORTH: ECOTARIUMS IN THE NORTH POLE

Architect:
Terreform ONE + Terrefuge
(Mitchell Joachim, Maria Aiolova, Jane Marsching, Makoto Okazaki, Melanie Fessel, Dan O'Connor)

Envisioned Project Location:
The North Pole

Envisioned Completion Date:
2110

WHERE AND WHEN
Future North anticipates the end results of global warming. Millions of people will need to migrate into areas where there is a more hospitable climate as the polar caps melt.

BASIC CONDITIONS
The *Future North Ecotarium* project is based on the premise that within the next century our climate will be irreversibly altered. Massive migrations of urban populations will move north to escape severe flooding and increased temperatures. Areas inside the Arctic regions will warm up significantly, making the occupation of them possible and even desirable. Real-estate wealth will shift to privileged northern climates that were formerly almost devoid of human inhabitants.

KEY PRINCIPLES
To underscore the disruption and upheaval of such a global shift, entire cities will have to be moved. The prospect of hundreds of millions of people relocating their respective centers of culture, business, and livelihoods is almost incomprehensible. In its polemic representation, this project will impact our perception of the future.

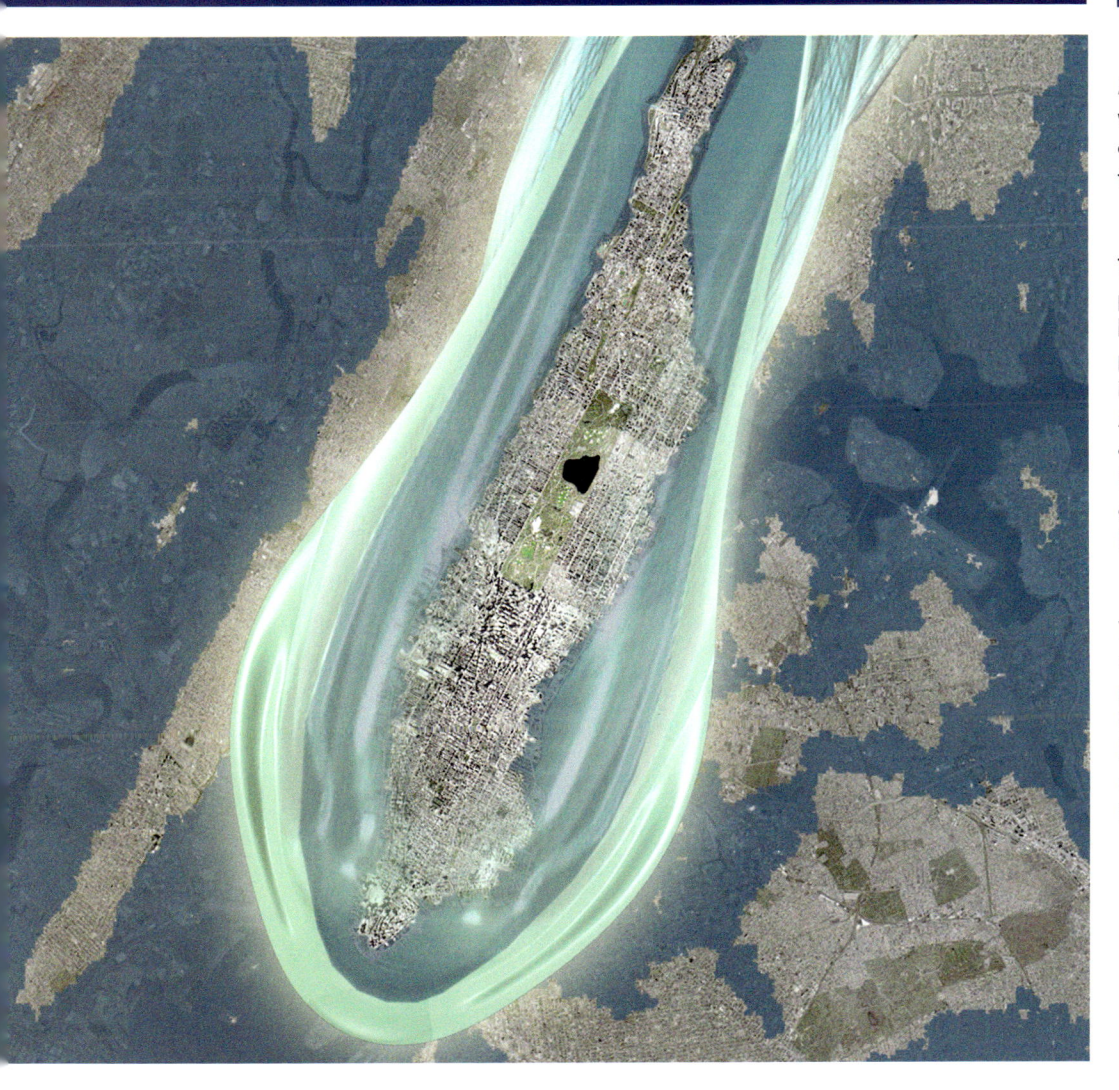

Project Title:
**GANDARA/
GUILD WARS NIGHTFALL**
Artist:
Daniel Docio
Envisioned Project Location:
Kourna Province/Elona
Envisioned Completion Date:
An alternative future

WHERE AND WHEN
As war marshal, Varesh Ossa's seat of power at the mouth of the Elon River, this crescent-shaped fortification allows Ossa to monitor all river traffic, as well as provides protection from any potential naval threat. Previously, the river culminated in a wide delta, but the ruling war marshals sealed off the lesser tributaries and dredged the main channel. The result provided irrigation to the lower Elon valley and gave *Gandara's* owner total domination of the river-mouth. *Gandara* is divided between barracks, warehouses, and bureaucratic offices. It is also home to Ossa's palace, which houses the legendary Kournan Plaza of the Five Gods.

BASIC CONDITIONS
Gandara's high walls and reinforced doors protect its garrison soldiers from threats of invasion. Plenty of natural sunlight and fresh air is able to flow through the fortress' winding corridors. Spacious and sprawling, the fortress possesses enough arms and supplies to continue operating even during heavy sieges. Some of the larger courtyards are planted with local flora, giving this battle-ready structure a friendlier, more tranquil atmosphere.

KEY PRINCIPLES
The fortress is built primarily out of brick and stone from the region to save costs; also chosen due to their proven durability against the region's blistering temperatures and merciless sandstorms. The bulk of materials for its construction were purchased from neighboring towns and cities to ensure rapid construction, as well as to support local economies. The money saved by using local materials offset the cost of shipping in the few goods transported from distant provinces.

Project Title:
THE RELIGIOUS CITY
Architect:
Silu Yang
Envisioned Project Location:
Los Angeles, USA
Envisioned Completion Date:
The near future

WHERE AND WHEN
Los Angeles is a city based on material artifice and fantasy; the glitzy, glamorous city takes the juxtaposition of culture and nature to its utmost extreme. *The Religious City* imagines a meteorite shattering this opposition in a single dramatic stroke, allowing the reality of the natural world to literally flood the city in the form of a devastating tsunami, like some kind of divine vengeance.

BASIC CONDITIONS
Their material lives lost and destroyed, the citizens of Los Angeles have to find a new life on the last surviving island in Los Angeles' former port. In the narrative of this project, the idea of Armageddon, or the "end of the world," takes hold of the imagination of these few remaining citizens.

KEY PRINCIPLES
The new inhabitants of the island gradually evolve a new *Salvationist* religion, which fortifies them psychologically from the unpredictable forces of nature. Created from the wreckage of the old city, the new settlement is formed from a palimpsest of reorganized debris, religious ritual, and the ordinary requirements of daily urban life.

CHPT. II

101

Project Title:
TOWARDS A NEW ANTARCHITECTURE

Architect:
Taylor Medlin

Envisioned Project Location:
Marie Byrd Land, Antarctica

Envisioned Completion Date:
The near future

WHERE AND WHEN
Antarctica is known as a remote location that experiences some of the harshest conditions on the face of the earth. Currently, Antarctica's isolated location—the freezing and desolate southernmost tip of the globe—results in a gross misuse of materials from a construction and logistical point of view. It is the aim of the *Towards A New Antarchitecture Coalition* (TANAAC) and its *Terra Nova II Expedition* to prove that it is not only possible to build in Antarctica with minimal external resources, but that it is also the beginning of a new era of construction for the continent. The research station is envisioned in the Marie Byrd Land area of Antarctica, one of the last completely undeveloped regions of the world.

BASIC CONDITIONS
Two of the biggest challenges faced by current research stations in Antarctica are building construction and longevity; together with the ability to continuously heat the interior spaces given the sub-zero temperatures. An average building in Antarctica lasts only around ten years, and most large stations take roughly three to five years to construct. Comparing the lifespan of the buildings to the relative time required for their construction highlights the incredibly high life-cycle cost; with the construction time alone sometimes taking as much as half the amount of time as the overall life span of the buildings. Heating is another major concern; it is primarily achieved by super-insulating the building to roughly four times the U-value (overall heat transfer coefficient) of buildings in the United States. The temperature outside can plummet down to -20°C, while the interior temperature is usually kept around 18°C. That means there is almost a forty degree difference between inside to outside temperatures that is mitigated by a thin wall construction. The power necessary to make up this drastic temperature fluctuation is substantial. Furthermore, almost all electricity on the continent is still generated by diesel, which is powered by fuel transported laboriously from the over on the mainland.

KEY PRINCIPLES
The proposed building system consists of three distinct parts: prefabricated utility cores geared for survival (Life Support Units), an exterior wall element made from local materials (Ice 9 System), and a series of inflatable living quarters (Habitation Pods). The prefabricated *Life Support Units* house key facilities such as rest rooms and cooking stations

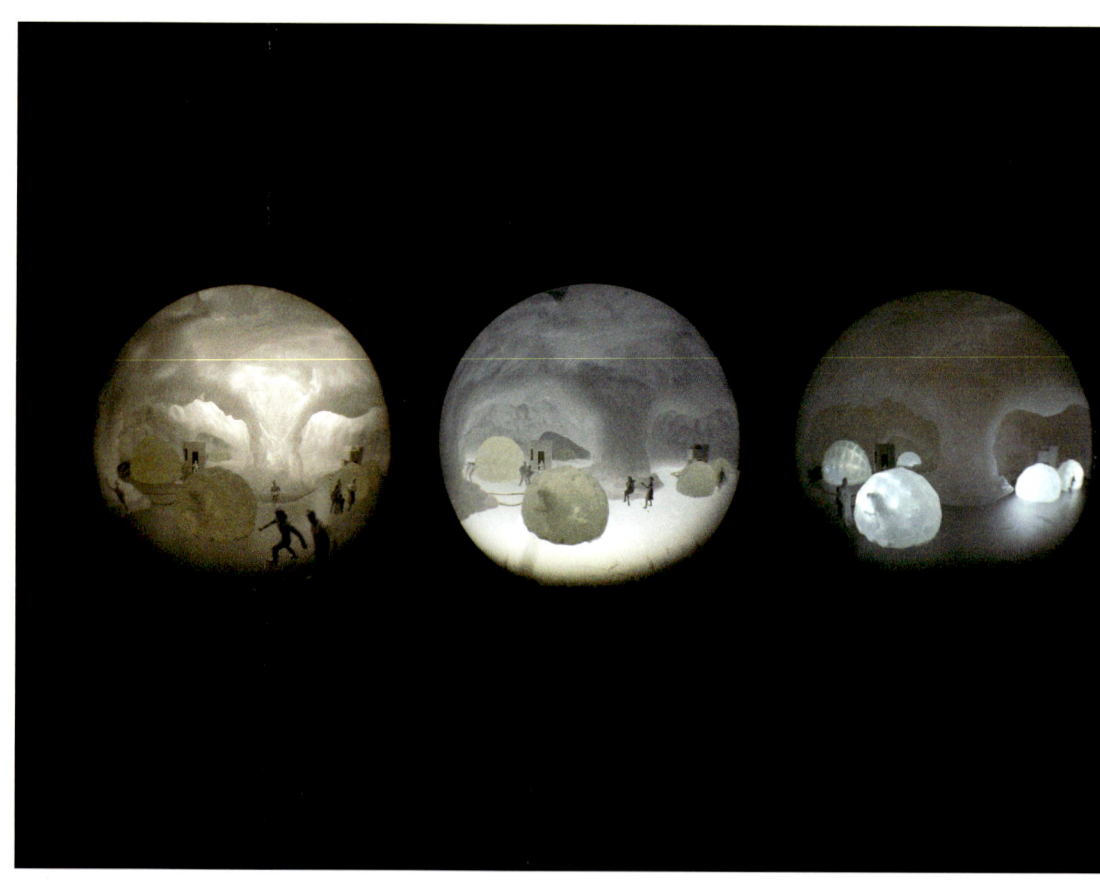

To achieve funding for the upcoming expedition, a presentation viewing chamber named, *The Ark,* was created to facilitate resource procurement.

that would be instantly connected to the internet, to provide utilities and power for the construction process as well as the eventual habitation of the units. Prefabricated procedures are used to hasten on-site construction as well as to limit material waste. The proposed modules are made up of materials able to withstand the wear-and-tear of the extreme weather conditions prevalent in Antarctica. The modules are dimensioned to fit snugly within the cargo hold of an HERC LC 130, one of the only cargo planes capable of making the trip to Antarctica. *TANAAC* proposes, furthermore, the use of a new construction technique, code-named the *Ice 9 System*, which consists of an inflatable formwork, powered and made possible by the *Life Support Modules* delivered to site in Marie Byrd Land prior to the construction time. Once the modules are hooked up to the generators

Outer puncture-proof layer
Coupling cable
Straplink
Membrane
Reflective coating

Wet rooms

Food preperation

Combo breaker

Power/Heating

Dry heating

Temperature Variations

-70°F
-30°F
Current: Antarctic stations
Up to 140 degree temp. difference from exterior to interior

Snow build-up = extra insulation
Heat radiated back inside
32-50°F   60°F   70°F
Wind
Proposed: TANAAC
+/- 100 degree temp. change | Inflatables only have to make up roughly 10 degrees! | Hibernation areas smaller and easier to insulate

CHPT. II

and are receiving electricity, air will be pumped into inflatable parabolic forms, (requiring only 0.5psi), to maintain rigidity during the next step in construction; the spraying onto the inflatable forms. The *Ice 9 System* employs a similar technique to shot-crete, where concrete is sprayed onto forms via a large hose at a high pressure, which compacts the concrete further and increases the strength of the material due to the force of the projection. The difference, in the case of the *Ice 9 System,* is that *pykrete*—a combination of sawdust and water that is then frozen, producing an extremely strong form of ice—will be used in place of regular concrete. On the *Terra Nova II Expedition*, large free-spanning vaults will be made possible by spraying layer after layer of thin pykrete onto the inflated formwork. In response to the challenge of lack of direct sun light, *TANAAC* plans on embedding ultra low-heat emitting LED's (Light Emitting Diodes) into the pykrete shield, thereby creating the impression of exterior surfaces, even in the interior.

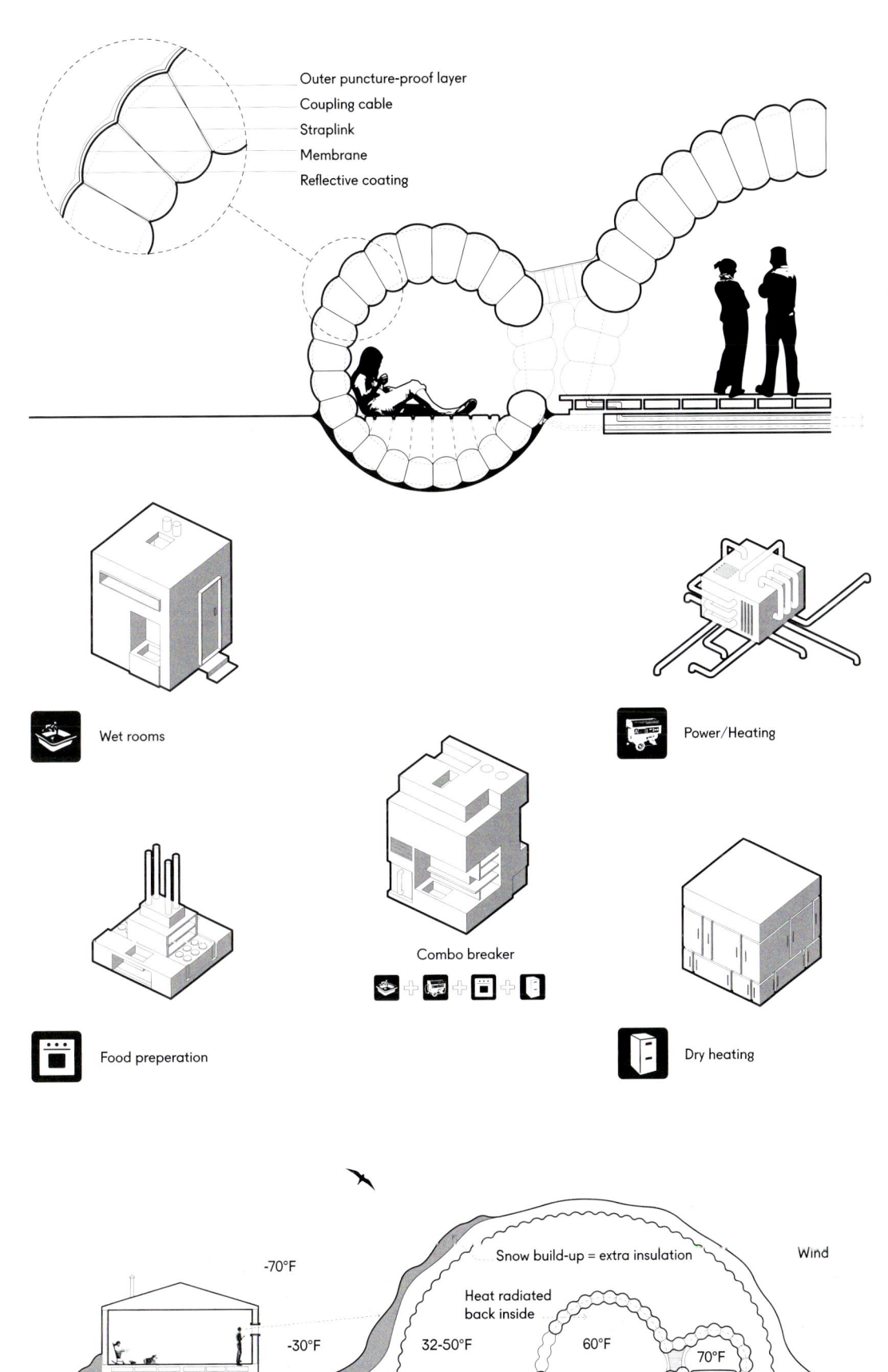

Project Title:
SUSTAINABLE ICEBERG LIVING STATION

Architect:
David A. Garcia

Envisioned Project Location:
Antarctica

Envisioned Completion Date:
2015

WHERE AND WHEN
Icebergs are created by highly compacted snow, which only become ice at a depth of 25 m. As Inuit igloos have demonstrated, snow provides very efficient insulation. Against this background, the project *Sustainable Iceberg Living Station*, proposes a sustainable living station for 100 visitors within an iceberg in Antarctica, which would have minimal environmental impact.

BASIC CONDITIONS
Buildings and base stations have mushroomed in the last couple of decades in the Antarctic. In 2010 alone, around 80,000 tourists are expected to visit the South Pole; whilst an average of 5,000 researchers are based on the mainland during the summer season.

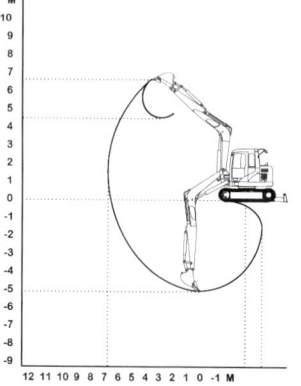

Mini Hydraulic Escavator

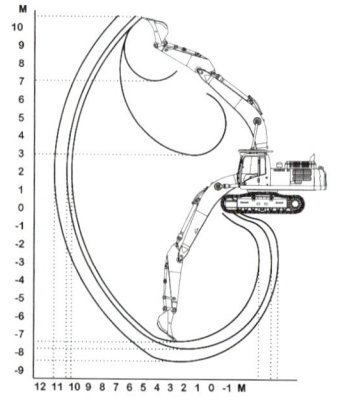

Large Hydraulic Escavator

KEY PRINCIPLES
To avoid transporting building materials foreign to the continent—which might never leave Antarctica again—the architecture of the living station is, instead, carved out of an enormous iceberg (about 1.5 m² in area), which would eventually melt within an estimated decade. Caterpillar excavators, traditionally used in the Antarctic to move and clear snow, would carve out spaces deep within the iceberg. The geometric trajectory of the movement of these machines, used to "design and cut" the spaces, would create the curved "walls" of the interiors. Two access ramps (one for pedestrians, the other for vehicles) would give access to the main hall and canteen, with access to kitchen, medical services, and bathrooms. From this public area the living station would grow into an array of passages, which would give access to the sleeping quarters, clustered in groups of eight or nine rooms, around a common lounge. A lecture/conference hall would accommodate cultural activities. Containers would transport food, reusable solar cells as well as energy equipment, and would be used to store waste and grey-water residue, which could be shipped away regularly. The energy infrastructure would be completely reusable and could be transported away once the iceberg is abandoned at the end of the iceberg cycle—whilst the "architecture" would simply melt away into the ocean.

CHPT. II 105

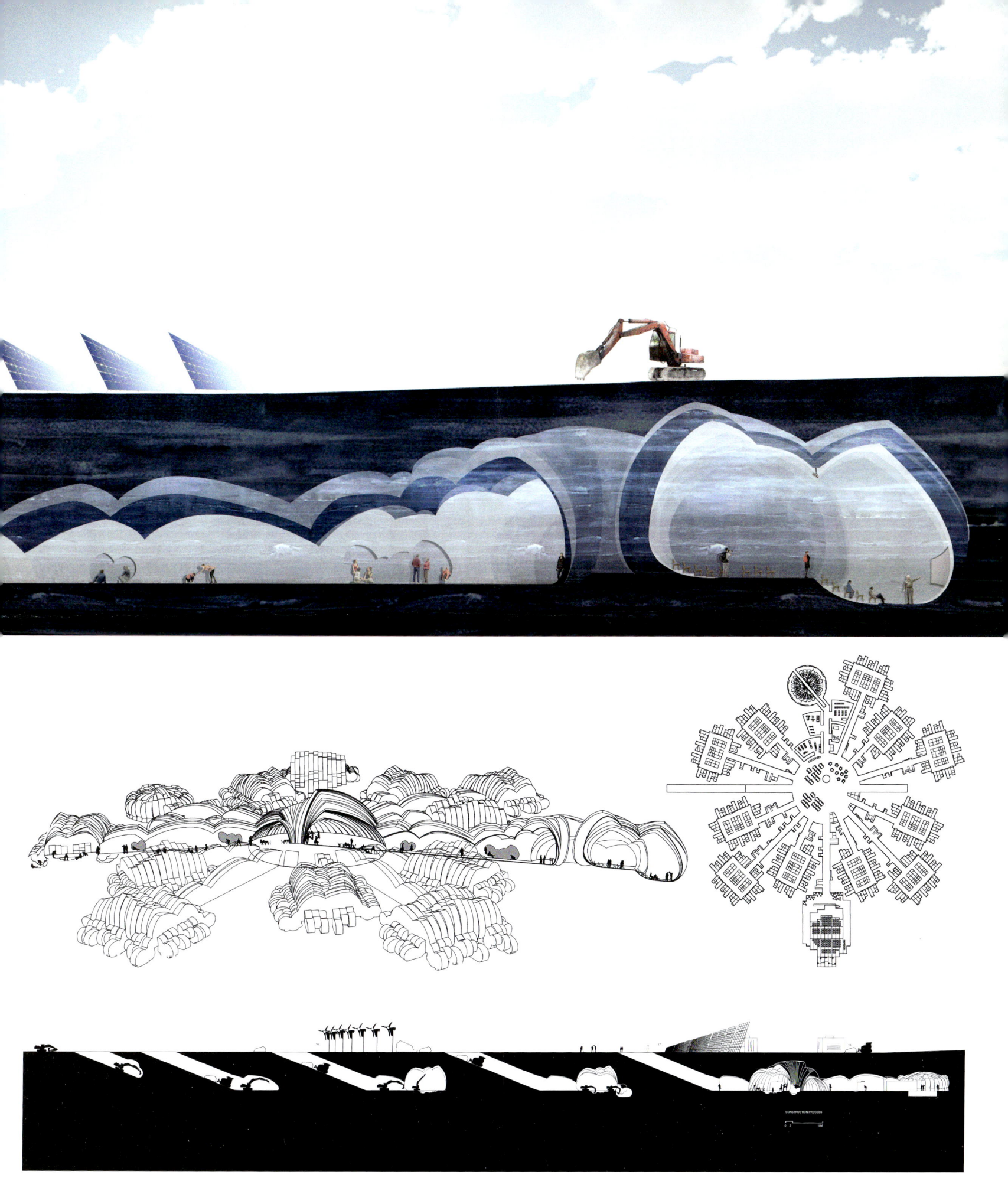

Project Title:
RETHINKING THE BERING STRAIT

Architect:
OFF Architecture

Envisioned Project Location:
Siberia/Alaska

Envisioned Completion Date:
2070

CHPT. II 107

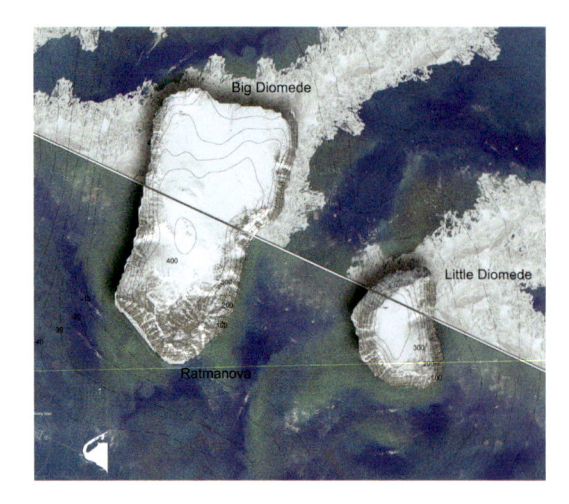

WHERE AND WHEN

The threshold between the Arctic and the Pacific Oceans, the Bering Strait, has a highly fragile and sensitive micro-climate, which is linked to the creation of ice, and acts as a significant zone for the global climate. A unique ecosystem connected to the climatic conditions is found there; composed of extremely rare and delicate species: including belugas, walrus, polar bears, blue whales, dolphins, and orcas, to name a few. The project, *Rethinking the Bering Strait*, envisioned for 2070, does not simply concern itself with the construction of a commercial or railway link, or a bridge connecting one continent to another. The amplitude, site, geopolitical context, as well as global ecological awareness, call for a far more audacious proposal: a "pro-active" project, which would be sensitive to the unique conditions of the site.

BASIC CONDITIONS

The project, by OFF Architecture, is a winning entry of a competition launched by the UIA, and the Foundation for Peace and Unification. The structure of the project takes advantage of the existing currents in the channel. Perforations in the structure would act as ocean current turbines, which would accelerate water movement and currents. Because the water level in the Bering Strait is relatively shallow, current flows tend to be faster, generating more energy. Due to their large scale, the turbines would rotate at a slow pace, which would allow marine fauna to be able to pass through; diminishing any chance of negative repercussions on marine life. The energy produced from this rotation would be channeled into various programmatic zones of the scheme.

KEY PRINCIPLES

Due to the Strait's relatively shallow water levels; the proposed structure would be able to descend to the bottom of the ocean, with only a few meters that would project above water level. The structure would work in compression. Two parallel walls would cut through adjacent bodies of water, and would be held apart with bracing, which would be habitable in places. Each wall would be 10 m wide, and would provide train and vehicular infrastructure on their upper surfaces. The massive structure would need to be straightforward; an attribute only achievable by having a direct line that connects the two sides of the strait. The interstitial space created by this huge separation gap, which would span 50 m, would become an interface for human passage and exchange, providing visitors and inhabitants the opportunity to traverse the strait even by foot—as was originally intended by early civilizations. Extensive views of the marine landscape, which would travel across the perforated tubes and "pierce" the linear horizon of the space, thereby constructing a new ground plane, submerged 50 m below water level. The project envisages a place dependant on green-energy, which would take advantage of the site and its natural currents, in order to install a completely ecological and renewable system. The delicate ecosystem embodied in the site would be enriched through the result of the perforations in the main structure, across which local fauna could permeate. This would provide laboratories situated there direct access for research, as well as would invite the public to explore and witness this unique habitation. A protected space would thus be created for these ecologies to flourish.

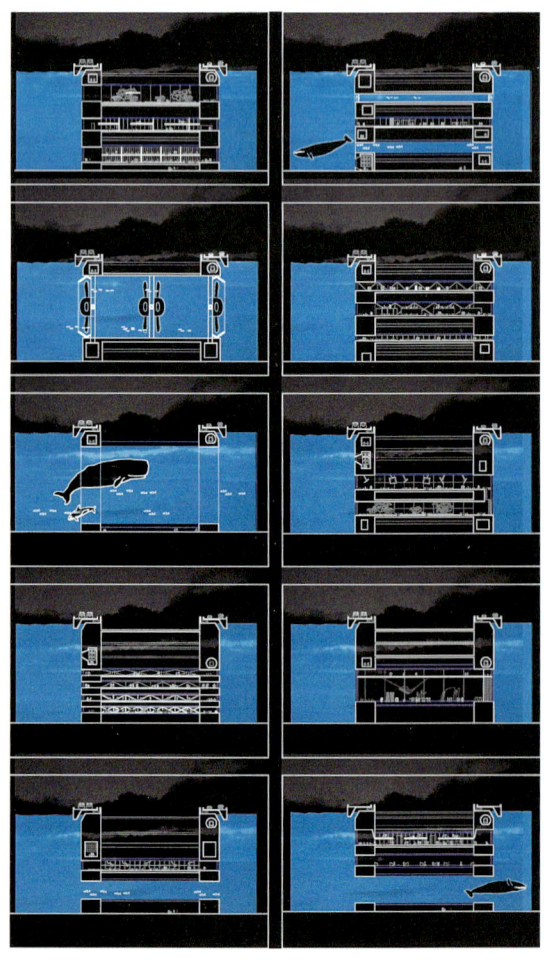

Life inside the structure

CHPT. II

109

ECOTOPIA EMERGING

Alternative Speculation On Ecologically Sound Worlds

This chapter pays tribute to Ernst Callenbach's seminal 1970s utopian novels, *Ecotopia* and *Ecotopia Emerging*, and sets out to portray radical, ecologically sound countercultures somewhere in an alternate future. The projects conjured in this chapter are characterized and inspired by the vivid imaginings of the alternative lifestyles they propose. Yet, in these projects' devotion to the prevailing subject of ecological change and adaptation caused by humankind's interventions into existing ecosystems, the interbreeding of biology and technology give birth to strange new environments. The projects offer a view of the future inhabitation of our augmented designs. From CTRLZ's *For All The Cows*, which proposes the growth of generous interconnected social spaces and a completely transparent model of energy and production above a level dedicated solely to the grazing of cows and cultivation, to HWKN's enigmatic *METreePolis* project, that is based on projecting real-life developments in the field of genetic manipulation into the future of city planning, all the way to the team, Tomorrow's Thoughts Today's fictional exploration of a community in *Where The Grass is Greener* that constructs itself around high ideals of sustainability and conservation that closes itself off from the ugliness of the hugely consumptive world we inhabit, allowing its citizens to live in blissful, idyllic ignorance. Here we deal with ecology in the broadest sense, as the science of how living creatures relate to one another and to their environment. The projects featured in *Utopia* depict absolutely new kinds of architecture and radically innovative concepts of urbanity that might well become reality in years to come.

"ONE TOUCH OF NATURE MAKES THE WHOLE WORLD KIN."

WILLIAM SHAKESPEARE

116. *Where the Grass is Greener* by Tomorrow's Thoughts Today
120. *MEtreePOLIS* by Hollwich Kushner LLC (HWKN) (Matthias Hollwich, Marc Kushner)
121. *Urbaneering Brooklyn 2110 City of the Future* by Terreform ONE, Terrefuge (Mitchell Joachim, Maria Aiolova, Melanie Fessel, Dan O'Connor, Celina Yee, Alpna Gupta, Sishir Varghese, Aaron Lim, Greg Mulholland, Derek Ziemer, Thilani Rajarathna, John Nelson, Natalie DeLuca)
122. *The Transcendent City* by Richard Hardy
124. *Soak City* by Crab Studio (Peter Cook, Gavin Robotham, Lorene Faure)
126. *Vegetal City* by Luc Schuiten
130. *The Eco-Commune* by Richard Hardy
132. *For All The Cows* by CTRLZ Architectures (Francesco Cingolani, Massimo Lombardi)
133. *City Pig* by The Why Factory
134. *The Mobile Mountain City Zoo* by Tomorrow's Thoughts Today
135. *Zoo of Infectious Species* by David A. Garcia
136. *Dochodo Zoological Island* by JDS Architects
138. *Natwalk 2.0* by Remote-controlled (Anton Markus Pasing)
140. *Specimens of Unnatural History: A Near Future Bestiary* by Tomorrow's Thoughts Today
141. *Acoustic Botany* by David Benqué
142. *AmesMM* by 'AMID* architecture [cero9] (Cristina Díaz Moreno, Efrén García Grinda)
144. *Evolving Skyscraper* by Vahan Misakyan
146. *Freshwater Factory* by DCA/Design Crew for Architecture (Nicolas Chausson, Gael Desveaux, Jiaoyang Huang)
148. *400k Pods* by Elia De Tomasi, Filippo Mazzaron, Federico Pedrini, Alessandra Pepe, Silvia Sandor
149. *SeaWater Vertical Farm* by studiomobile (Antonio Girardi, Cristiana Favretto)
152. *Galije* by MVRDV
153. *Hualien Beach Resort* by BIG/Bjarke Ingels Group

The following *Utopia Generator* requires one a die and a pad of paper to play.

The rules are simple: when it is your turn, roll the die at the top of each column to see if you are required to choose an item from that column.

If you do not need to choose anything, simply move on to the next column—and so on, until the end.

Along the way, write down each aspect of utopia you have chosen—and, within no time, you will have created your own speculative myth of a perfect human community!

POSSIBLE LANDSCAPES OF UTOPIA:

Choose three pairs from this column, then one item from each pair

- ◊ Surrounded by water vs. a city of canals
- ◊ In a swamp vs. in a desert
- ◊ Located entirely within a mega-structure vs. entirely outdoors
- ◊ On an island vs. spanning an archipelago
- ◊ Heavily forested vs. on the plain
- ◊ In a dark valley or gorge vs. on a mountain peak or summit
- ◊ On Mars vs. on an as-yet-unknown earthly planet
- ◊ Amidst rolling hills, (Hobbit-like landscape) vs. within a day's walk of an large inland lake

UTOPIA'S RELATIONSHIP TO THE PLANETARY SURFACE:

Choose one item from this column if you roll 1–5

- ◊ Underground
- ◊ Underwater
- ◊ Surface-dwelling
- ◊ Airborne
- ◊ Outer-space
- ◊ A combination of all the above

POSSIBLE WEATHER CONDITIONS IN UTOPIA:

Choose one item from this column if you roll 1–4

- ◊ Mediterranean
- ◊ Baltic
- ◊ Arid
- ◊ Humid continental
- ◊ Hurricane prone
- ◊ Tornado prone
- ◊ Artificially generated by huge machines on the periphery of the city

UTOPIA GENERATOR

by GEOFF MANAUGH

Geoff Manaugh is the author of *BLDGBLOG* (bldgblog.blogspot.com) and *The BLDGBLOG Book*, former senior editor of *Dwell magazine,* and a contributing editor at *Wired UK*. He lives in Los Angeles

UTOPIA'S PHYSICAL SIZE:	POSSIBLE RESIDENTS OF UTOPIA:	AVERAGE AGE, IN YEARS, OF THE RESIDENTS:	POSSIBLE CAUSES OF DEATH:
Choose one item from this column if you roll 1–3	*Choose two items from this column if you roll 1 or 2; choose one item from this column if you roll 4 or 5*	*Choose one item from this column if you roll 3–5*	*Choose one item from this column if you roll a 2*
◊ 1 acre	◊ Clones	◊ Embryonic: not yet born	◊ Nothing: people don't die in utopia
◊ 5 acres	◊ Vegetarian	◊ 10	◊ Suicide
◊ 50 acres	◊ Orphans	◊ 17	◊ Dementia
◊ Three-times the size of Manhattan	◊ Celibate	◊ 21	◊ War
◊ Continental	◊ Addicted to sex	◊ 35	◊ A medically unidentified disease of the central nervous system
◊ Planetary	◊ Blind	◊ 50	◊ Hemorrhagic fever
◊ Galaxial	◊ Bodybuilders	◊ 72	◊ Natural disaster
◊ Universal	◊ Deaf	◊ 99	◊ N/A: no one has died yet
	◊ Nostalgic	◊ 250	
	◊ Violent	◊ Immortal	
	◊ Illiterate		
	◊ Gossips		
	◊ Monastic		
	◊ Actors		
	◊ Robots who don't know that they are robots		
	◊ Irrationally obsessed with the possibility of time travel		

THE POLITICAL SYSTEM:	THE HARSHEST CRIMINAL OFFENDERS:	YOUR UTOPIA'S CITIES ARE DOTTED WITH:	YOUR UTOPIA'S ARCHITECTURE:
Choose one item from this column if you roll 2–5	*Choose one item from this column if you roll a 6*	*Choose one item from this column if you roll 5–6*	*Choose one item from this column if you roll a 1, 3, or 6*
◊ Representative democracy	◊ Thieves	◊ Gymnastia, parks, and sports stadiums	◊ Romanesque
◊ Military dictatorship	◊ Rapists	◊ Aquariums	◊ *Videogame moderne*
◊ Market socialism	◊ Murderers	◊ Sprawling, genetically-modified forests teeming with remote-controlled robotic birds	◊ Futurist
◊ Neoliberal free-market	◊ Runaways		◊ Parametric in the "Patrick Schumacher" sense
◊ Communist anarchism	◊ Adulterers	◊ Large, open squares and cobblestone piazzas lined with benches	◊ Parametric in the "Thom Mayne" sense
◊ Depends on who is asking	◊ Arsonists	◊ 24-hour media screens run by the state	◊ Biomorphic
◊ Agrarian self-rule	◊ Hackers	◊ 24-hour media screens run by private companies	◊ 1930s International Style
◊ Colonial	◊ Counterfeiters		◊ Celtic/megalithic
◊ Post-colonial	◊ No criminals: there is no crime in utopia	◊ Re-assembled dinosaur skeletons sealed behind bullet-proof glass and installed at the center of every intersection	◊ Vaguely neo-Gothic in a *Dungeons & Dragons* way
◊ Federal republic	◊ Insomniacs		◊ Hsian Japanese
◊ Constitutional monarchy	◊ Hecklers	◊ Small community garden plots and family farms	◊ "Angkor Wat-like"
◊ Dynastic empire	◊ Smugglers	◊ Planetariums	
◊ Theocracy		◊ Interactive holograms	
		◊ Subway entrances to an underground system that flooded long ago	
		◊ Elaborate cinemas	
		◊ Reflecting pools	
		◊ Ruined transmitting equipment of an unknown purpose	
		◊ Ongoing archaeological digs	
		◊ Elaborate cemeteries	
		◊ Animals freed from the zoo	

THE HOUSES IN YOUR UTOPIA ARE PRIMARILY BUILT WITH:	YOUR UTOPIA'S BUILDING STOCK IS MOST LIKELY TO BE INFESTED BY:	TRANSPORTATION INFRASTRUCTURE IN YOUR UTOPIA RELIES ON:	IN ONE MILLION YEARS YOUR UTOPIA WILL BE:
Choose one item from this column if you roll a 3 or 6	*Choose one item from this column if you roll a 2*	*Choose one item from this column if you roll 2–3 or a 6*	*Choose one item from this column if you roll a 6*
◊ Coral	◊ Nothing, it is utopia: there are no infestations here	◊ High-speed trains	◊ Entirely forgotten
◊ Brick	◊ Spiders	◊ Footpaths	◊ Written about in myths and legends
◊ Granite	◊ Octopi	◊ Hydrogen-powered cars	◊ Archaeologically rediscovered beneath the foundations of a future utopia
◊ Red oak	◊ Jellyfish	◊ Light air travel, including personal hang-gliders	◊ Dismissed as kitsch by graduate students in architectural theory
◊ Limestone	◊ Bats	◊ Public hovercraft	◊ Swallowed up by plate tectonics
◊ Geo-technically stabilized soil	◊ Rats	◊ Moving sidewalks	◊ Still thriving: it is utopia
◊ Storms of controlled air pressure	◊ Ants	◊ Underground tunnels with spectacular ventilation structures	
◊ Ferrofluids	◊ Cockroaches	◊ Motorboats and canoes	
◊ Stacked skeletons of extinct megafauna	◊ Bees	◊ Teleportation	
◊ Catenary arches made from any material available	◊ Electro-magnetic interference of unknown origin		
◊ Unvarnished plywood	◊ Bio-luminescent algae		

UTOPIA GENERATOR

Permacultural Hinterland

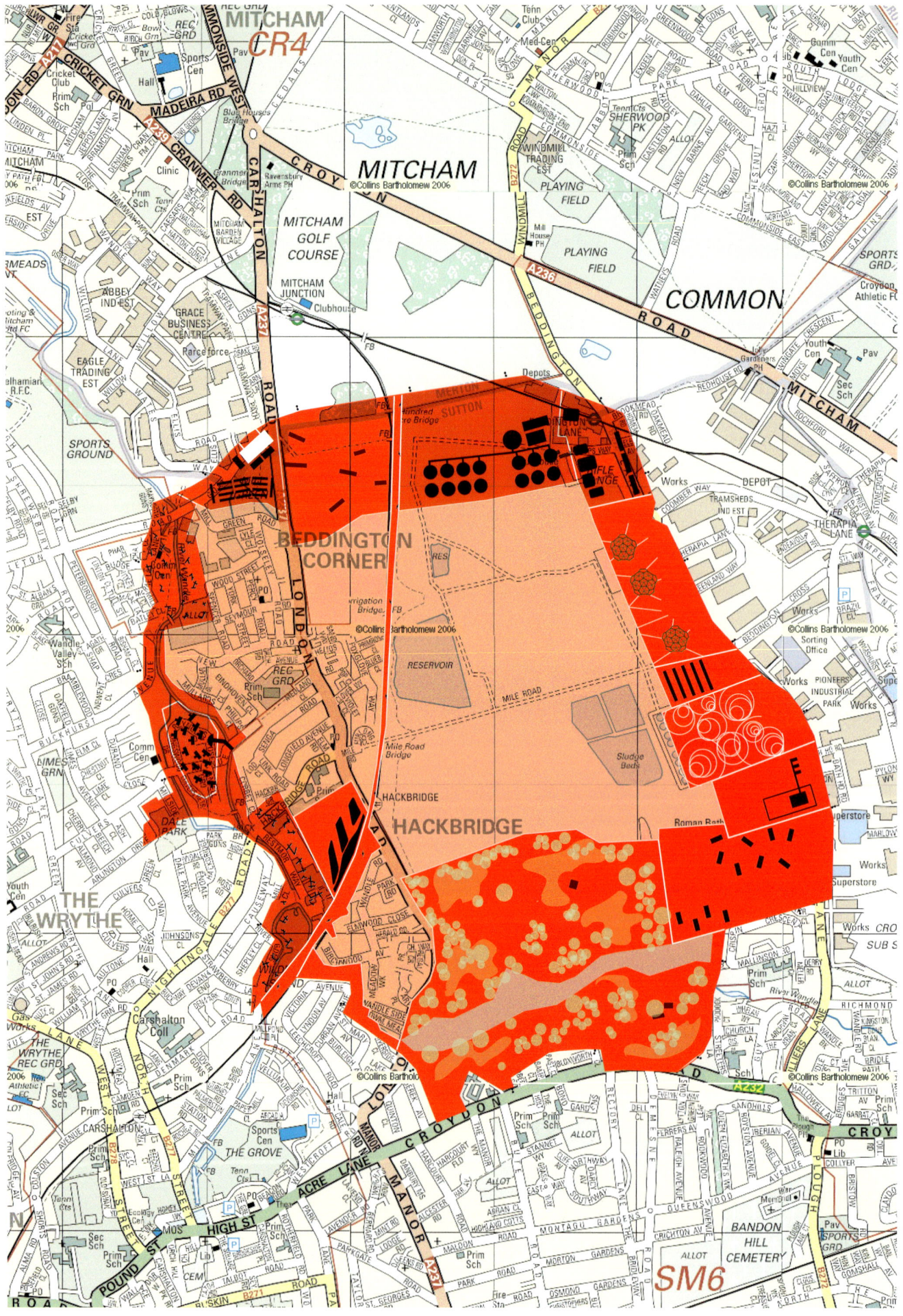

116 WHERE THE GRASS IS GREENER ECOTOPIA EMERGING

Project Title:
WHERE THE GRASS IS GREENER

Architect:
Tomorrow's Thoughts Today

Envisioned Project Location:
London, UK

Envisioned Completion Date:
An alternative future
WHERE AND WHEN

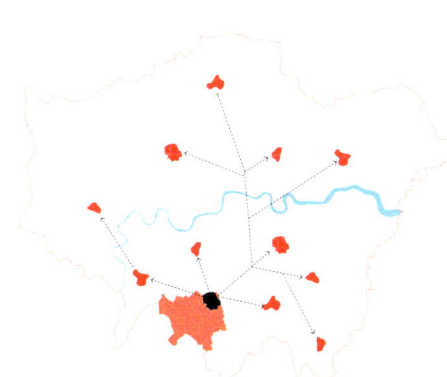

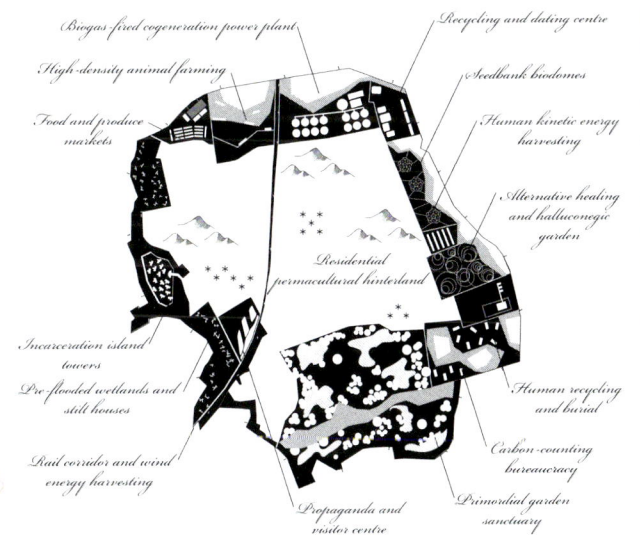

Where the Grass is Greener is set in the outer suburbs of London where a community has voluntarily separated themselves from the rest of society, and has taken up the mantle of sustainability in an extraordinary way.

BASIC CONDITIONS
Driven by a set of ethical beliefs that places the community in radical opposition to the bulk of the rest of London, they decide to adopt a lifestyle that effectively makes them a carbon-sink for the remainder of the city. They consolidate existing geographical patterns to create a giant ring of infrastructure which contains a series of productive and social programs comprised of terra-forming, hybridized architecture, natural obstructions, and electronically surveiled barriers. This sophisticated urban edge would become a new kind of urbanism—a fortress that would shelter a community of "carbon-positive" altruists, and would reserve a place within the chaotic fabric of suburban London for idealism—where the grass is greener…

KEY PRINCIPLES
Carbon-counting bureaucrats would expose this utopian community's ability to offset as much as 19,000 ton of CO_2, whilst simultaneously producing 68,800 MWh/year surplus heat and electricity. This amazingly productive powerhouse could effectively represent 22% of the borough's residential energy requirement, whilst also recycling and methane-harvesting the borough's waste. Clearly the potential of this urban intervention to replicate itself across London's suburbs is self evident. Not surprisingly some of the greatest supporters of the project are the residents of the adjoining districts who are responsible for a large amount of waste and who would be more than happy to give them a "raison d'être." There will be little chance for civil unrest between these two extreme poles of the demographic spectrum. The project's border will be ingeniously constructed so that little contact is needed to be made with the outside world at all. With years until any adequate assessment of the concept can be made, debate will rage as to whether the community belongs in the category of *Visionary Pioneer* or to the long lineage of failed utopian experiments. For the time being, we can only say we have been offered a glimpse of "salvation by urbanism"—where the grass is greener…

Heating: 62,000 MWH/year

Electricity: 15,600 MWh/year

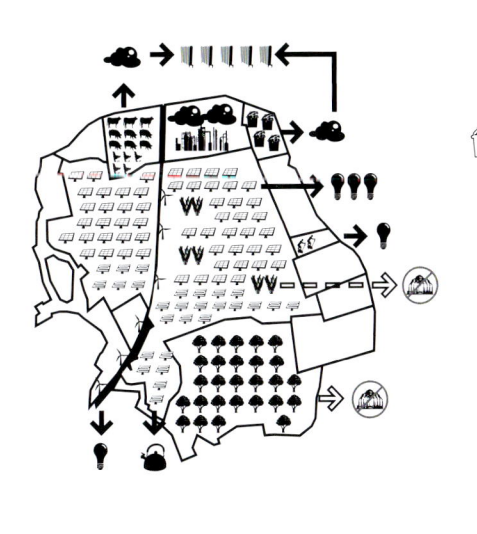

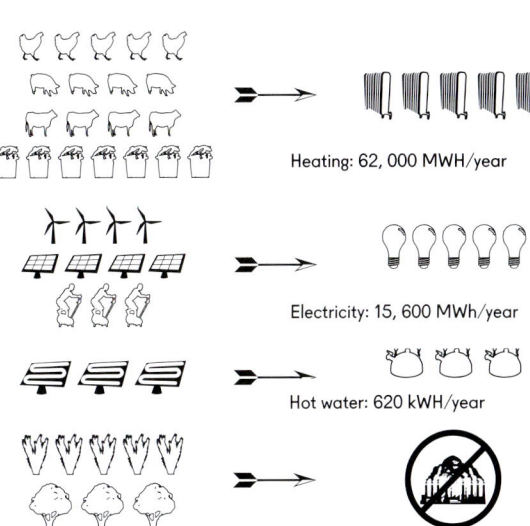

Hot water: 620 kWH/year

CO_2 absorption: 2,906 t

118 WHERE THE GRASS IS GREENER ECOTOPIA EMERGING

Đ. CHPT. III

119

Project Title:
METREEPOLIS

Architect:
HOLLWICH KUSHNER LLC (HWKN)

Envisioned Project Location:
Atlanta, USA

Envisioned Completion Date:
2108

WHERE AND WHEN
MEtreePOLIS is a project based on projecting scientific developments in the field of genetic manipulation into the future. By the year 2108, Atlanta's downtown buildings could be retrofitted with so called *power-plants*, taking the city center off the energy grid. These *power-plants* would harness natural energy resources, which would significantly impact on the urban fabric as we know it.

BASIC CONDITIONS
The *MEtreePOLIS* city of the future, will be a prosperous and pleasant place to live. The fusion of landscape and cityscape would introduce opportunities for recreational and nature activities into the daily routines of its citizens. *Power-plants* would eliminate wasteful urban energy consumption—which accounts for as much as 40% of today's total energy needs—while simultaneously cleaning the atmosphere. The city of the future will owe its economic and intellectual wealth to the richness and diversity of enhanced nature—and to the genius of today's creative thinkers. Only through meaningful progress will we be able to undo the damage of the past. Recent discoveries suggest that a shift from technical to biological innovation might well give us hope that this might indeed be feasible. It is the responsibility of architects, engineers, and visual artists to communicate and promote these new ecological ideas that surpass sustainability, to create an entirely new conception of the way people will interact with the natural world in the future.

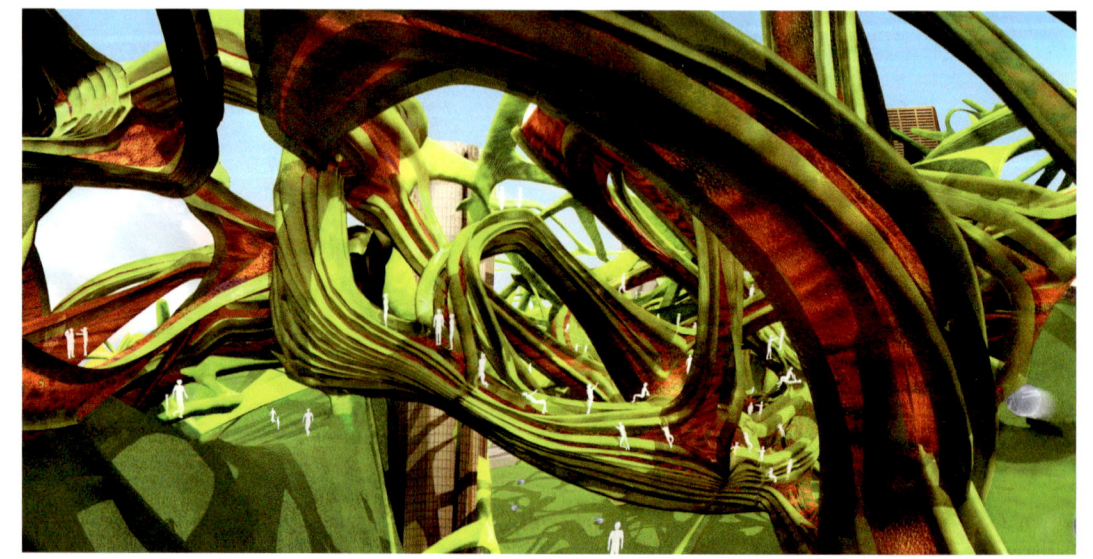

KEY PRINCIPLES
Like a forest, the cityscape, *MEtreePOLIS*, is best understood in terms of strata. At the top level would be a canopy of biologically enhanced *power-plants* that would capture energy from the sun and water from clouds. The canopy would be low in open, suburban areas, and lift higher off the ground in dense areas of urban central business districts. No longer simply a twenty-first century city of high and low-rise, skyscraper and street; *MEtreePOLIS* would create a mid-level datum that would extend urban life along a new dimension, creating a new city-wide "fun-scape." The undifferentiated surface of the landscape would enable new types of hyper-efficient traffic organization. Hydrogen-powered pods would roll along the landscape using swarm intelligence, thereby creating semi-natural conditions, like river-banks, that could be enjoyed by the inhabitants of the city. Unlike vehicles of today, pods would be scaled to the specific needs of the users in order to maximize efficiency. A series of autopilot mail carriers, private vehicles, and larger pods would slowly move through the shaded underworld of the *MEtreePOLIS*, turning transportation into an opportunity for social interaction. *MEtreePOLIS* proposes a new chapter in the evolution of cities that would grow from the historical fabric of the built environment. Old forms, and traces of the past, would be absorbed into the new "organism." Thanks to this combination, the past would be updated and preserved. The surviving, existing buildings would be adapted to this bio-grid and would survive from the energy the grid would provide. The forms simultaneously contain both built and natural constructs. They would have transformed from resource consumers to power producers. The bio-web would spread out evenly over the city and along with it, the population will follow. The city of the future will not be composed of segregated urban and suburban enclaves, but it will rather be a tapestry of demographic richness, where different socio-economic groups will live in harmony and mingle in the horizontal public canopy. Construction in the next century will be highly innovative thanks to advances in the cultivation of *power-plants*. The structures will be symbiotic towers that engage the mighty root-system of the bio-grid to lift off of the Earth's surface to the sunny green-scape of the canopy above. Traditional single-family dwellings would have evolved into a new non-segregated typology of communities that will coexist harmoniously with nature.

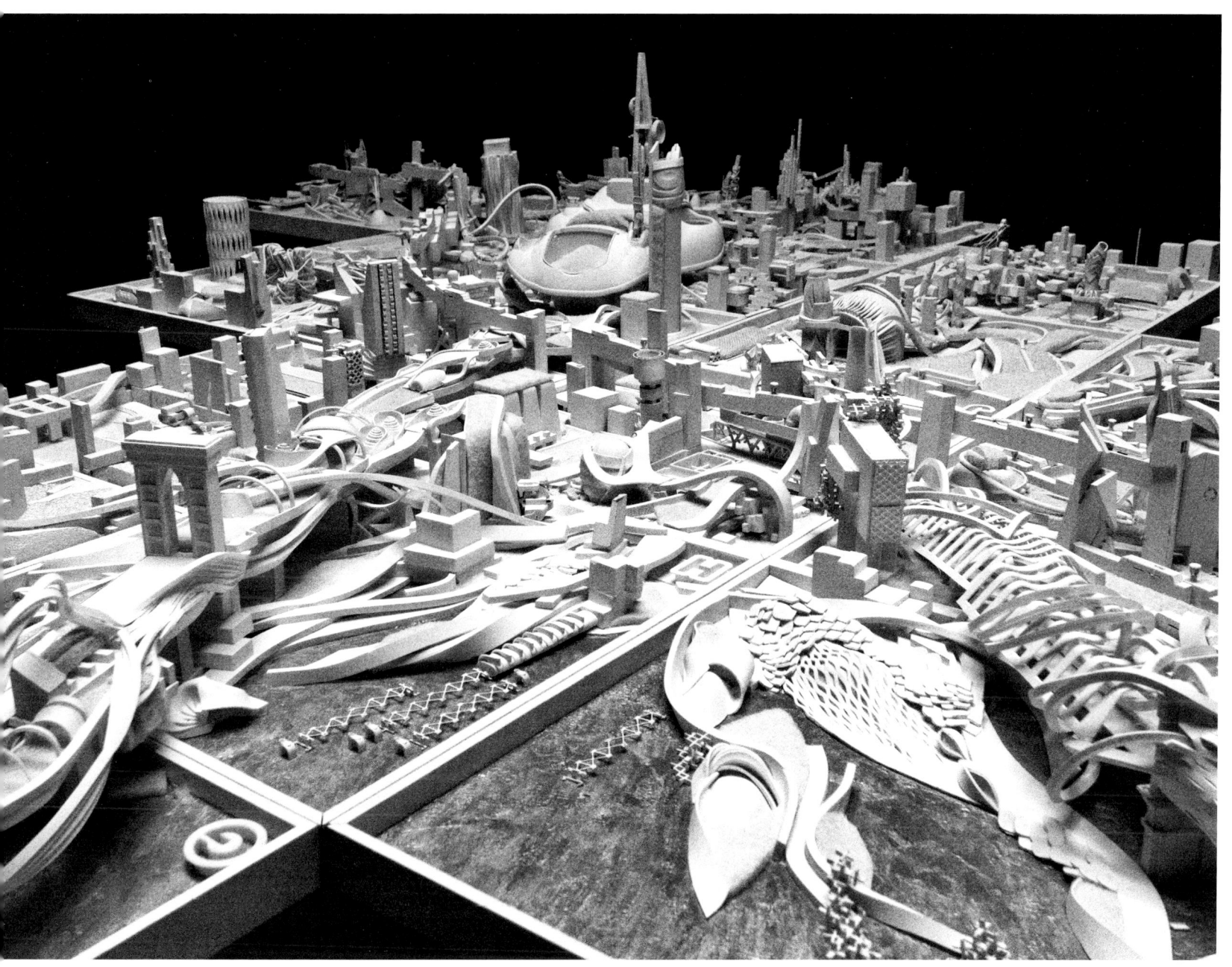

Project Title:
URBANEERING BROOKLYN 2110 CITY OF THE FUTURE

Architect:
Terreform ONE + Terrefuge (Mitchell Joachim, Maria Aiolova, Melanie Fessel, Dan O'Connor, Celina Yee, Alpna Gupta, Sishir Varghese, Aaron Lim, Greg Mulholland, Derek Ziemer, Thilani Rajarathna, John Nelson, Natalie DeLuca)

Envisioned Project Location:
Brooklyn, USA

Envisioned Completion Date:
2110

WHERE AND WHEN
This project *Urbaneering Brooklyn*'s primary assertion for Brooklyn a century from now is that all its necessities will be provided within its physical borders. An "intensified" version of Brooklyn has been designed, that supplies all vital needs for its population. In this version of the city, food, water, air, energy, waste, mobility, and shelter are radically restructured to support life in various forms.

BASIC CONDITIONS
Terreform ONE's strategy includes the replacement of dilapidated structures with vertical agriculture and housing merged with infrastructure. Former streets would become sinuous arteries of livable space embedded with renewable energy sources, soft cushion-based vehicles for mobility, and productive green-rooms. Their urban plan uses the former street grid as the foundation for new networks. By re-engineering obsolete streets, one is able to install radically robust and ecologically reactive pathways.

KEY PRINCIPLES
The operations the project proposes are not just about a comprehensive model of tomorrow's city, but also provides an initial platform for discourse. The future will necessitate innovative dwellings coupled with a massive cyclical resource network. The future will happen regardless; how it will function is dependent on our forward planning and preparation.

THE TRANSCENDENT CITY ECOTOPIA EMERGING

Project Title:
THE TRANSCENDENT CITY
ARCHITECT:
Richard Hardy
ENVISIONED PROJECT LOCATION:
The Biosphere
ENVISIONED COMPLETION DATE:
An alternative future

WHERE AND WHEN
The concept of a future sustainable city is developed for a society that is currently not responding effectively enough to the dangers of climatic and environmental change. Transcendence in this case refers to a point in time between our current Earth and the "ultimate" Earth, when artificial intelligence has reached, or surpassed, that of the human intelligence.

BASIC CONDITIONS
The *Transcendent City* explores the concept of a technological singularity, where humans may have evolved to transcend our carbon-based bodies, forming a hybrid system with the artificial machine, and in turn overcoming our biologically determined limitations. The project attempts to highlight the impact of information technology on society, the realization of the environmental crisis, and the worrying lack of effective action. It suggests the role of the city as a critical component in the development of a sustainable future and questions the relationship of humanity to nature that we have been taught to think of as separate. It attempts to suggest the conception of artificial intelligence as a necessity in humanity's future evolution and questions, therefore, whether we should embrace emerging technology in order to engage with the problems of sustainability and the city.

KEY PRINCIPLES
The *Transcendent City* is an autonomous, artificial machine that extends across the earth, adapting to the natural eco-systems it encounters, while deriving its energy from the renewable resources available at each particular site. The system's goal is to maintain homeostasis within itself—either a closed or open system's property, that regulates its internal environment and tends to maintain a stable, constant condition—whilst maintaining homeostasis within the greater system, known as *Gaia*. Its processes are engineered on the molecular scale by nano-technology, controlled by molecular computers that monitor and analyze the environment. To date, molecular engineered architecture remains a theoretical proposition, however recent research and advances in the field of nano-technology prove that its introduction is inevitable. Carbon nanotubes can be combined together to form an array of kinetic structures that also have the ability to function as circuits for computation, so the transfer of information and the city structures can be realized as fully synonymous. *Structure* and *circuit* are seamlessly merged together to form a hierarchy of mechanical components that, when combined together, form an "autopoietic" machine.

Project Title:
SOAK CITY
Architect:
Crab Studio
(Peter Cook, Gavin Robotham, Lorene Faure)
Envisioned Project Location:
East London, UK
Envisioned Completion Date:
The near Future

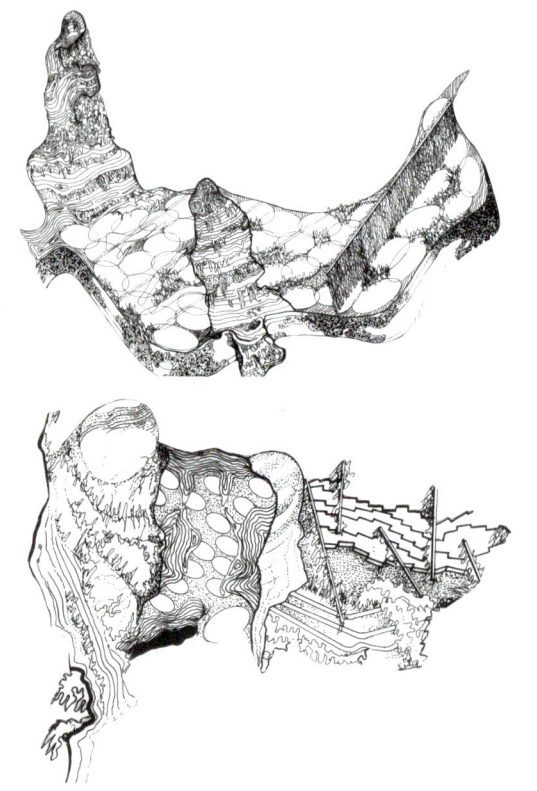

WHERE AND WHEN
Crab Studio's *Soak City* project envisions a future scenario for the city of London, in which the British capital is largely submerged under water as a result of global warming.

BASIC CONDITIONS
The project continues, and develops the investigations made by Peter Cook and Gavin Robotham at the Venice Biennale of 2004 when the architects devised a series of semi-planted structures for East London.

KEY PRINCIPLES
The context of a new infrastructure for *Soak City* relies, to begin with, on solid, high-density "blockhouses." The blockhouse development would be followed by a series of hybrid "stacks" that could contain various semi-vegetated typologies that deliberately cross-pollinate between the categories of apartment/workshop/refuge/clinic/studio/random-occupancy space, and could drift in and out of water and even drift on piles across boggy land. There would be the vague remnants of the present version of London and a stage-by-stage progression of the stacks and connecting bridges. The subsequent stage of the metamorphosis would occur as the Arctic ice-packs melt.

Đ. CHPT. III

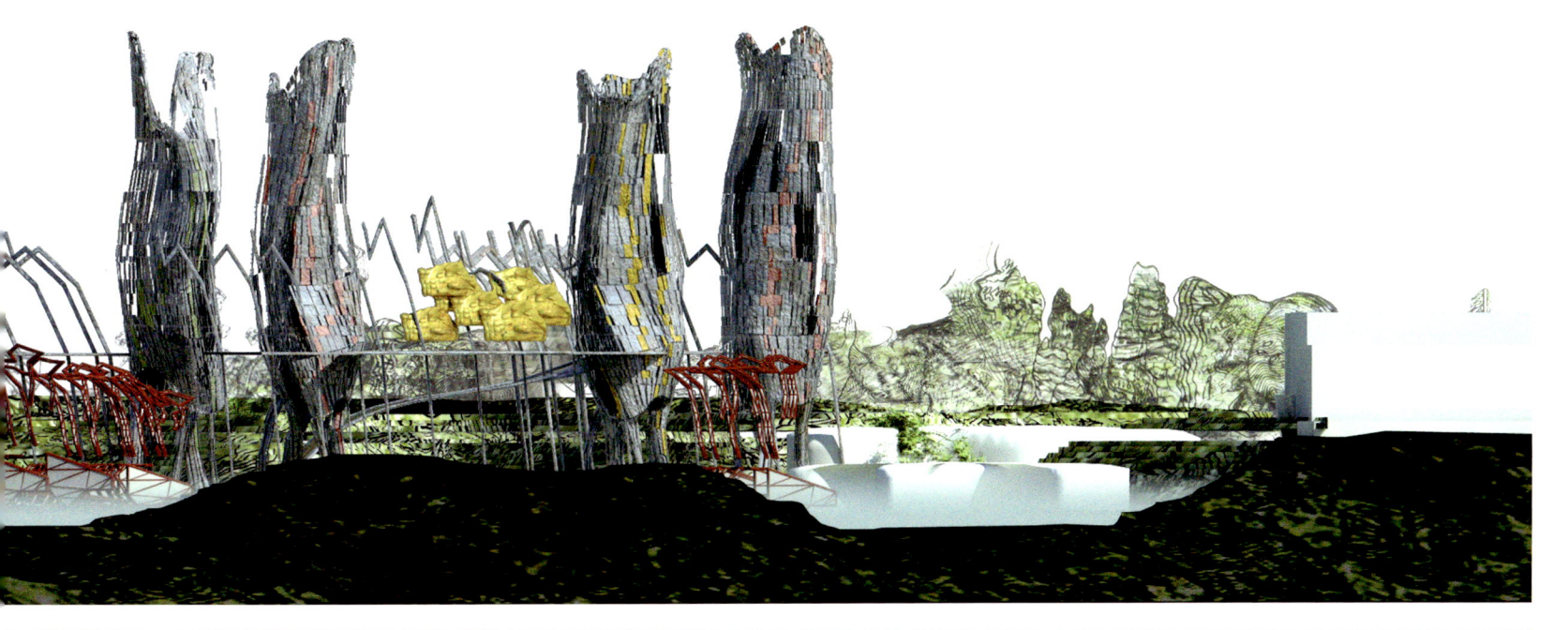

Project Title:
VEGETAL CITY

Architect:
Luc Schuiten

Envisioned Project Location:
Anywhere

Envisioned Completion Date:
An alternative future

D. CHPT. III
127

WHERE AND WHEN

The possible future worlds of visionary architect, Luc Schuiten, are committed to an ecological ideal that is concerned about both the future of the planet and about the living conditions of future humanity. Schuiten's thought process leads to the conception of new forms of architecture, based upon a poetic vision where built inventions and our relationship with nature play a dominant role.

BASIC CONDITIONS

Against the ominous backdrop of global climate change and the urgent call for the radical rethinking of our current consumerist mentality, Schuiten's *Vegetal Cities* demonstrate that the vision of a long lasting and bright future is possible for our planet through a new way of building based on a natural process called "archiborescence." A neologism based on the combination of the terms "architecture" and "arborescence" The latter describing a rooted tree in which all edges point away from the root. Schuiten considers our future lives as an attempt to reconcile and cooperate with nature, which will enable humanity to live in state of balanced harmony with our natural environment.

KEY PRINCIPLES

As part of Schuiten's creative journey in designing *Vegetal Cities*, he created diverse living scenarios, such as the *The Woven City,* in which all of the city's habitats are made with a kind of vegetative mesh produced by the root structure of a strangler fig tree. This fig tree may grow so large that high buildings can feasibly be built into it. Semi-transparent outer walls of the dwellings would be made from biotextiles, comparable to the silken thread material used for silkworms' cocoons or spiders' webs. These materials will also be able to capture solar power in order to supply the energy required for heating and electricity. People will move around within the city using suspended footbridges which will hang over the uncultivated plain below, thus allowing natural cycles to continue. In addition, *The City of the Waves* describes a city in continuous motion, which is constantly renewed through a slow progression around a lake where the migrations of its inhabitants follow the rhythm of the life of the city's main structure; the tree. The inhabited part of this urban forest would occupy almost a quarter of the circumference of the lake, with the remainder being made up of a forest, which will be mature enough for new dwellings to develop. The developing forest would extend over the bulk of the territory under the strict supervision of landscape-architects. The buildings the citizens will inhabit are designed like waves which face south towards a stretch of water at a lower level. These façades would act as large solar panels, the performance levels of which would be improved by the reflection of the sun's rays from the waters of the lake. Finally, *The Tree-House City* will be developed in a remodeled forest environment which will be adapted to the needs of a new way of life. The inhabitants will no longer be consumers of nature but operators of a new ecosystem, the management of which allows each of them to prosper and guarantees the long-term sustainability and development of the city. The external walls forming the façades of *The Tree-House City* will be made from a membrane made of translucent or transparent proteins, inspired by the chitin of dragonflies' wings. The floor slabs and the internal walls will be created using known techniques involving earth which will be stabilized using lime and will be reinforced by plant structures. These elements will constitute the thermal mass required for storing calories and redistributing heat. The building's natural ventilation is modeled on that of termite mounds. At night, the dwellings will be illuminated by bioluminescence, imitating the luminescence used by glow-worms at night or by certain types of deep sea fish.

Ð. CHPT. III

Project Title:
THE ECO-COMMUNE
Architect:
Richard Hardy
Envisioned Project Location:
London, UK
Envisioned Completion Date:
2080

enter the undergrowth to build a sustainable community for themselves within its midst. They reject the existing capitalist structures as shelter, and decide rather to dismantle and to reconfigure them to create a self-built commune. The abandoned buildings have become infiltrated by a variety of wildlife and plant-life. Species of vegetation have taken over entire tower blocks, loosening joints, and destabilizing supports, making the structures dangerously fragile, yet perfect for salvaging components. The community is a collection of like-minded individuals, who believe in the values of eco-communalism: an environmental philosophy based on the ideals of simple living, local economies, and self-sufficiency. Within their decentralized government there is a strong emphasis placed on agriculture, green economics and modern technology. The community is self-sufficient in the sense that it generates and recycles as much of its own energy as possible. Electricity is produced using sustainable methods including wind generators and salvaged photovoltaic panels, whilst potable water is extracted from the London Aquifer and recycled wherever possible.

KEY PRINCIPLES
Located on an open field where Leadenhall Tower once stood, the *Eco-Commune* comprises a central communal facility surrounded by a number of residential units and farmland. The commune grows organically in a series of defined phases, as the community desires greater capacity and function. This flexibility is facilitated by use of scaffolding as the buildings primary structure, which is then clad in a variety of pre-composed cladding systems that have been removed from the façades of the surrounding abandoned structures. The construction method is self-build and has a "bricolage" aesthetic. The *Eco-Commune* acts as a generator for further development and lures other like-minded scavengers. As time passes, the communes grow and a new "re-appropriated" skyline develops as more structures are dismantled as new communities develop.

WHERE AND WHEN
After the economic meltdown in 2008, the majority of the city's financial firms have become insolvent. The City of London in 2050 has become an abandoned ghost town, and nature has been left to repossess the iconic structures of its now redundant financial institutions.

BASIC CONDITIONS
Capitalism is waning and the British capital hangs in a state of imbalance. Attracted by the abundant materials and nature, a community of scavengers

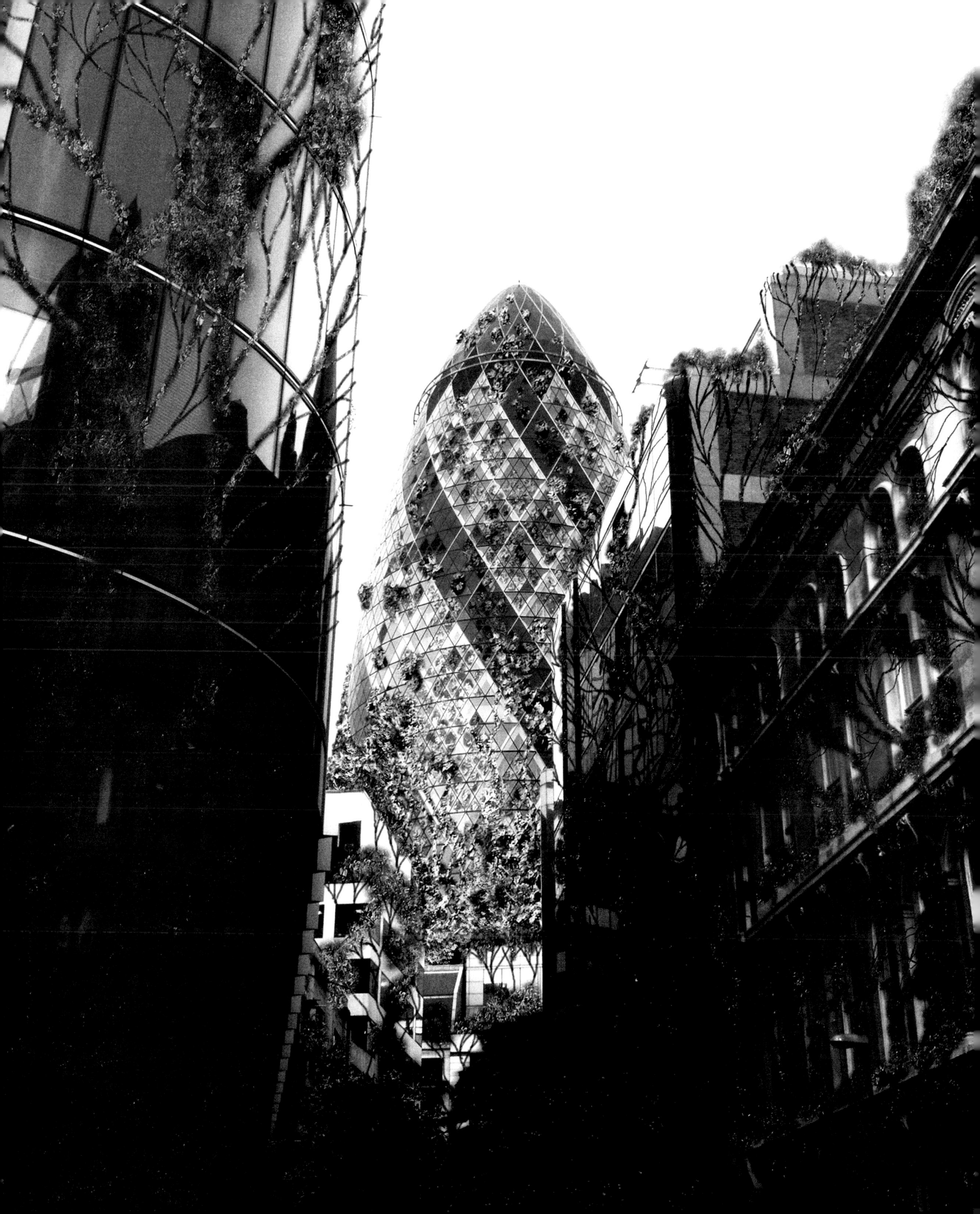

Project Title:
FOR ALL THE COWS

Architect:
CTRLZ Architectures (Francesco Cingolani, Massimo Lombardi)

Envisioned Project Location:
Dallas, USA

Envisioned Completion Date:
The near future

WHERE AND WHEN
Envisioned for Dallas, Texas this project, *For all the Cows,* by CTRLZ architectures, proposes the growth of a large interconnected social structure and a completely transparent model of energy and production above, dedicated solely to grazing fields for livestock as well as for cultivation.

BASIC CONDITIONS
The foundation of this project was the observation by the architect that concepts in architecture on sustainability and ecological growth are still used as tempting publicity spots to keep the present cut-throat capitalist system in place. Cingolani and Lombardi believe that architecture is, in fact, no longer about form and/or function, but rather that it is more about social connections and networking. The development of their network system, thereby shows that power resides in links and connections. As a result, architecture cannot solve the contemporary dilemma without creating relationships with people and the environments they occupy. The figure of the architect deals with the creation of spaces, society, energy, internet, and politics. CTRLZ aims to create more than merely a building, but a whole new model for society in which to live and work.

KEY PRINCIPLES
This project is about economic slow-down. It envisages the growth of interconnected social spaces and a transparent model of energy and production. Raised housing units would be "pixilated" in order to create a shared landscape that alternates private and public places; this would be the basis for the development of collaborative and social exchange. The ground level would remain free from any structures and would be allocated to the grazing of cattle and agricultural farms. From the base to the uppermost levels, the succession of functions related to one another would be (-1) commerce, (0) landscape and food cultivation, (2) housing, (3) public social places and finally, (4) energy collection on the top level. The project proposes a decentralized mode of living that would group production and consumption together. This arrangement would promote a transparent hyper-localized society, where the inhabitants could develop a consciousness about their energy footprint in terms of product waste and energy consumption.

Project Title:
CITY PIG
Architect:
The Why Factory
Envisioned Project Location:
The Hague, Netherlands
Envisioned Completion Date:
The near future

WHERE AND WHEN
This project by Winy Maas in collaboration with The Why Factory (TU Delft), focuses on urban pig farming in the town, Binckhorst, The Hague. The scheme was commissioned by Stroom Den Haag for their event: Foodprint Program, held in 2009–2010.

BASIC CONDITIONS
Pig farming used to be an integral part of urban life. Today, though, it has become an industry that is located outside of our cities, invisible, and unrecognized.

KEY PRINCIPLES:
City Pig explores the idea of bringing pig farming back into the city, and making it a visible and transparent part of our daily life. This might also be a solution to the ecological concerns about global food transport. The concept could also change the relationship we have with the food that we consume.

Project Title:
THE MOBILE MOUNTAIN CITY ZOO

Architect:
Tomorrow's Thoughts Today

Envisioned Project Location:
New York, USA

Envisioned Completion Date:
The near future

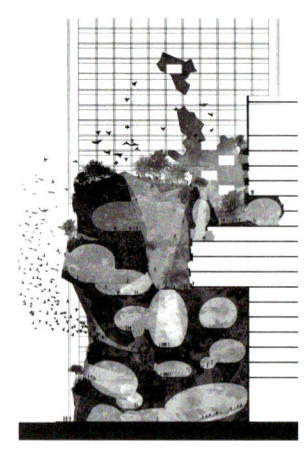

Infill section.

WHERE AND WHEN
This mobile urban zoo is envisioned for the city of New York, but could also be implemented in any other city around the globe.

BASIC CONDITIONS
Contemporary cities are no longer simply accidental homes for animals that have been displaced from their natural habitats. Cities can also be seen as hotbeds of evolutionary change, shaping the adaptations of their resident fauna, and providing an ideal stage where one might see animal behavior evolving at a pace rarely seen in the wild. As we begin to view our cities as worthwhile ecosystems, this project investigates the possibilities of a symbiotic relationship between two different systems of organization: technology and nature.

KEY PRINCIPLES
Resisting the *tabula rasa* conventions of current urban high-rise design, the project proposes a parasitic second skin to the existing city. Made from a mix of peat, moss and cement, the skin would be sprayed around the latent three-dimensional spaces of its host buildings and streets. Accumulating on existing service-cores, structural frames, and additional inflatable bladders, the infrastructure of the city would transform into a kind of artificial reef. The porous material would function as a water reservoir encouraging plant-life, and forming a new habitat for songbirds, bats, insects, as well as other small species. No longer would the natural world be something cordoned off in national parks and reserves. The inert and polluting city would become an agent in its own rebirth, where animals would be free to create their own habitats.

Project Title:
ZOO OF INFECTIOUS SPECIES
Architect:
David A. Garcia
Envisioned Completion Date:
2050

WHERE AND WHEN
The project, *Zoo of Infectious Species,* is proposed alongside the site of the first atomic bomb, Trinity, in the desert of New Mexico. The site sits next to a radioactive landscape, which is itself subject to another type of quarantine.

BASIC CONDITONS
Fear often transforms isolation into annihilation. However, dangerous or not, infectious species are part of the biological realm. Somewhere between Eden and a "garden of horrors," the visitor is allowed to enter only at their own risk, wearing a biohazard suit and following the most stringent bio-safety controls.

KEY PRINCIPLES
This zoo, built in an subterranean bunker made of concrete cylinders to secure containment, aims to concentrate the world's infectious species, while serving as an underground vault for virus and bacterial specimens. The landscape is hot and humid, filled with tropical forest flora, bathed in UV light while mechanically filtering exhaust air to the outside. In the interior, the deadliest of virus species, from ebola to malaria-carrying mosquitoes, are allowed to exist freely.

Project Title:
DOCHODO ZOOLOGICAL ISLAND

Architect:
JDS Architects

Envisioned Project Location:
Dochodo Island, South Korea

Envisioned Completion Date:
The near future

136   DOCHODO ZOOLOGICAL ISLAND   ECOTOPIA EMERGING

absence of urban development of the region. A pilot project has been developed to create a tourist region based solely on sustainable development, where nature and construction could function in equilibrium, feeding off one another. The resulting program brief is the establishment of a new zoo that would have the potential to strategically redefine an entire region. The natural island topography of peaks and valleys suggests the method for configuring the island's development. The low, flat plateau in the center of the island, which is currently covered with rice fields, would be the ideal location for the future zoo. The high mountain peaks are protected from development and are treated as nature preserves. The medium height terrain would be the site area available to build on. A datum height of 20 m has been selected, which defines a meandering contour-line across the entire island as the *locus* and boundary of the development. Everything above this 20 m mark would remain untouched and wild, whilst everything below could be transformed into a controlled nature reserve.

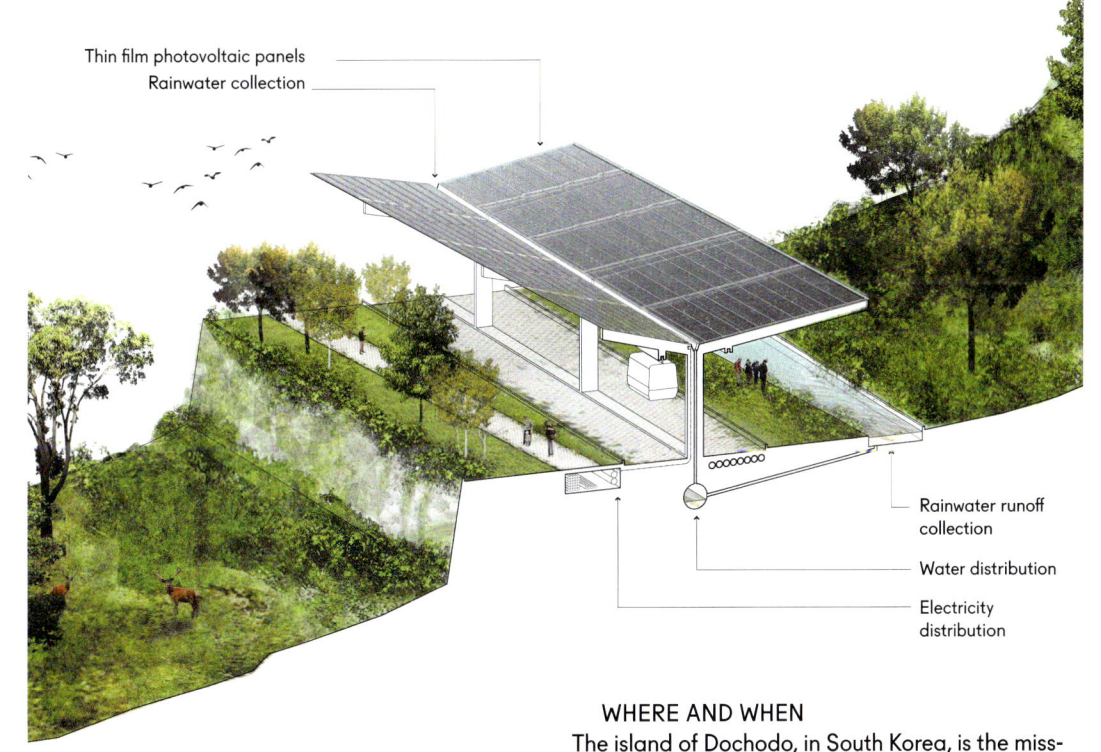

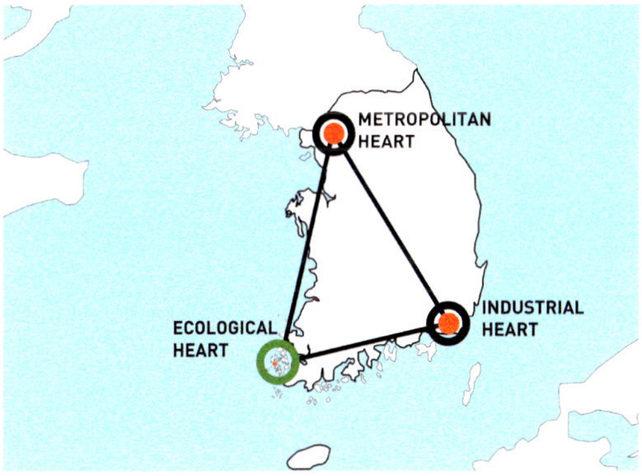

KEY PRINCIPLES

All infrastructure and program requirements (transportation, energy, water, waste treatment, and building systems) would be grouped within the development band, creating an "infrastructure green-belt." While the typical green-belt passively limits development, the infrastructure green-belt would actively enhance the surrounding ecology. Transplanted from the city to the countryside, the green-belt would act as sustainable infrastructure, and a machine to enhance the ecological health of the surrounding natural environment. Following a series of design principles, the island would only consume as much energy as it could produce. All energy will be gathered from renewable energy sources: solar, wind, wave, and bio-waste. Energy-generation will be embedded within the island development, reducing the loss of energy due to long-distance transmission. Rainwater would be collected and stored for use throughout the development. In the zoological sanctuaries and protected nature reserve areas, the characteristics of the natural pre-development hydrological system will be maintained as far as possible. The diverse functions on *Dochodo Zoological Island* would influence and become increasingly dependent on one another: architecture, infrastructure, and landscape would be integrated into a comprehensive ecology of exchange.

WHERE AND WHEN

The island of Dochodo, in South Korea, is the missing vertex of a triangle conscripted by the cities, Seoul and Bussan. Located on the southwest coast of Korea in the province of Mokpo, the most underdeveloped region of the country, Dochodo offers the potential to attract tourism from the surrounding Asian metropolises, especially from Shanghai.

BASIC CONDITIONS

Dochodo Zoological Island plays with the power of the void, and asks what can be done in an isolated place such as Dochodo Island with its lack of infrastructure, its low tourism levels, and its small population. It is precisely here where JDS architects envisage the island's potential for ecological growth in the

Project Title:
NATWALK 2.0
Architect:
Remote-controlled: Anton Markus Pasing
Envisioned Project Location:
New York, USA
Envisioned Completion Date:
An alternative future

WHERE AND WHEN
Envisioned for New York City, Natwalk 2.0 by Anton Markus Pasing, is a giant robotic machine that enriches the built environment with natural species. Natwalk 2.0 is the follow-up advancement of Pasing's Natwalk 1.0, which was designed 1993.

BASIC CONDITIONS
Against the backdrop of a general dissatisfaction with the slow pace of ecological change and the arrogance of the political powers-that-be, the basic concept of Natwalk 2.0 is based on the assumption that, as technologically highly developed products of our species, machines will be more able to understand the significance of an ecological renewal than we human beings. Moreover, they will act with an ethical and social conscience. The origin of the machines is purposely disregarded.

KEY PRINCIPLES
Based on the principles of peace, love, nature, and narration, the idea of the Natwalk 2.0 is—in contrast to conventional approaches to typical architectural concepts—described with a brief, romantic and naïve story, reminiscent of a fairy tale. This approach is taken in order to activate the readers' known patterns of experience and to provide room for their ideas to flourish between the architectural drawing and the romantic narration. On the one hand, Natwalk 2.0 reintroduces the recurrent idea of the layered city, and on the other hand it creates a paradox. Of all things, it is huge, (allegedly) soulless machines that will transport natural artifacts back into the city on their backs and in their bellies, in order to make a point, and to challenge, once more, the parameters of human action. The aspect of conquest paraphrases our deepest human methods.

Glass dome

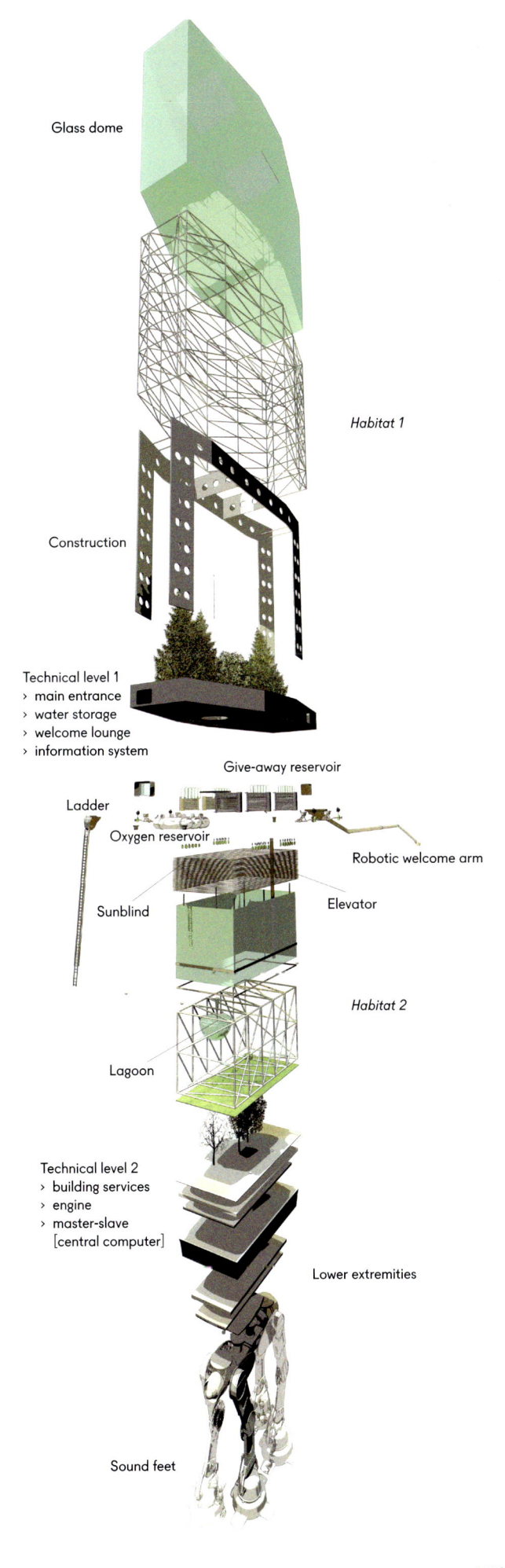

Habitat 1

Construction

Technical level 1
> main entrance
> water storage
> welcome lounge
> information system

Give-away reservoir

Ladder

Oxygen reservoir

Robotic welcome arm

Sunblind

Elevator

Habitat 2

Lagoon

Technical level 2
> building services
> engine
> master-slave
  [central computer]

Lower extremities

Sound feet

Project Title:
SPECIMENS OF UNNATURAL HISTORY: A NEAR FUTURE BESTIARY

Architect:
Tomorrow's Thoughts Today

Envisioned Project Location:
Anywhere

Envisioned Completion Date:
The near future

WHERE AND WHEN
This project, *Specimens of Unnatural History: A Near Future Bestiary,* projects itself out into the future population of an augmented wilderness of primeval specimens that breed and multiply, contaminating the landscapes of a time in the future.

BASIC CONDITIONS
Throughout history, humankind has invented monsters and myths as a way of coming to terms with phenomena we do not understand or cannot grasp. We have created fictional tales of the natural world whilst, at the same time, these tales we imagine chronicle the dreams and anxieties of everyday life. As the sun sets on our idealistic and preservationist views of the natural world, the slow burn of evolutionary change takes effect with its endless generations, duplicating and multiplying and gradually mutating until eventually variation comes to an end. As the designers stalk the savannas of the landscape of science fiction, robotics and neo-biological invention, they imagine encountering the novel reality of artificially engineered "monsters."

KEY PRINCIPLES
With these stuffed and mounted specimens from a new bestiary of unnatural history, Tomorrow's Thoughts Today sees a jump in the fossil record, an evolutionary leap, as the architectural interbreeding of biology and technology gives birth to a deviant nature. The result may be hopeful inventions, or unexpected off-shoots, wondrous possibilities, or dark, cautionary tales.

SPECIMENS OF UNNATURAL HISTORY   ECOTOPIA EMERGING

Project Title:
ACOUSTIC BOTANY
Architect:
David Benqué
Envisioned Project Location:
Worldwide
Envisioned Completion Date:
The near future

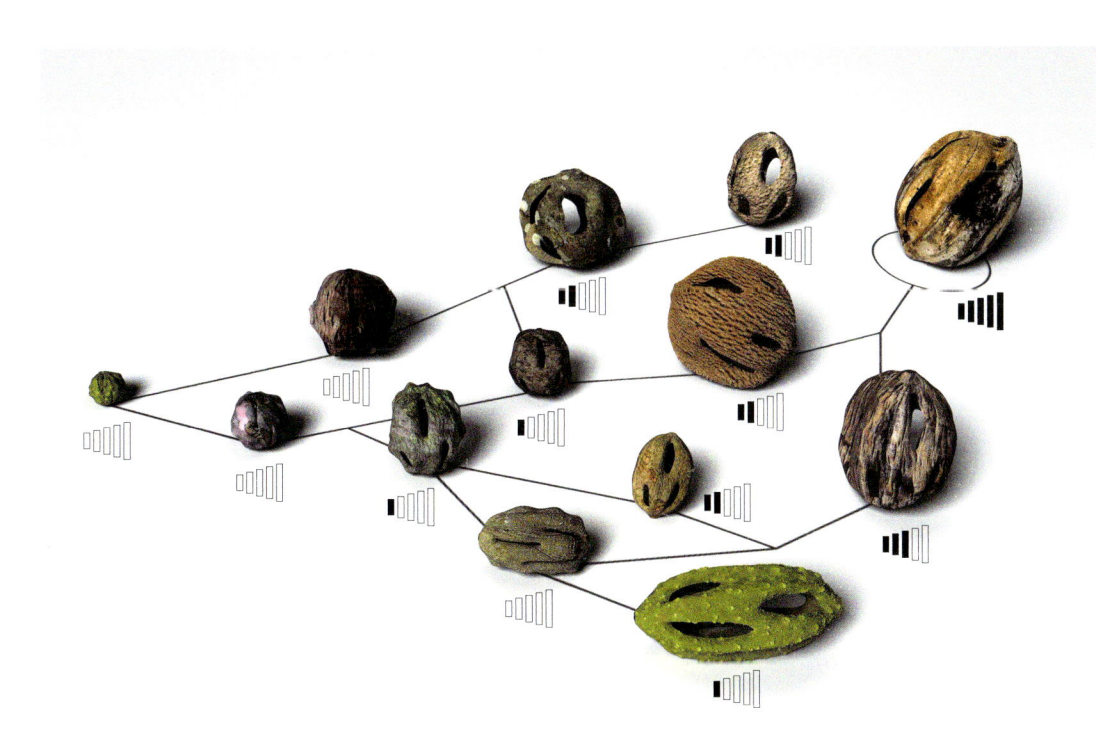

Lab Testing Rig: Factors like tension and temperature are modulated to fine tune the sound.

Desired traits such as volume, timbre and harmony are acquired through selective breeding techniques.

WHERE AND WHEN
This project envisions a genetically engineered sound garden.

BASIC CONDITIONS
The contentious debate about genetic engineering is currently focused on vital issues such as food, healthcare, and the environment. However, we have actually been shaping nature for thousands of years, not only to suit our needs, but also to suit our most irrational desires. Beautiful flowers, mind altering plants, and crabs that are shaped like human faces, all thrive on these desires, giving them a kind of evolutionary advantage.

KEY PRINCIPLES
Acoustic Botany proposes a future where genetic engineering and synthetic biology are used, not only to address vital issues like the environment, health, and our food supply, but also, where they are used to extend the age-old inclination of humans, to shape our environment to suit our aesthetic desires. Working specifically with the bioengineering of plants and using gardens, drug cultivation, and agricultural grafting as references, David Benqué imagines an acoustic garden created with science that will change its aural character throughout the seasons. By presenting a fantastical acoustic garden, a controlled ecosystem for entertainment purposes, the project explores our cultural and aesthetic relationship to nature, and questions its future in the age of synthetic biology.

HOME FURNITURE

PHILLIPS 66

35
69

ATM
CARWASH

Project Title:
AMESMM
Architect:
'AMID* architecture [cero9] (Cristina Díaz Moreno + Efrén García Grinda)
Envisioned Project Location:
Ames, USA
Envisioned Completion Date:
The near Future

WHERE AND WHEN
In the city of Ames, situated in the center of Iowa, a huge power station, set in the heart of the city, runs at full power. The project proposal, *AmesMM*, visually transforms the power station into a kind of landscape within the city: a living mountain.

BASIC CONDITIONS
Cristina Díaz Moreno and Efrén García Grinda's proposal, however, does not try and resort to a purely cosmetic, superficial treatment, to the influential power of images and the kitsch assembly of local materials. Their proposal responds by challenging established instruments and concepts of gardening, breeding of species, architecture, and the ecology of living. AMID* thus proposes a total covering of the structure with a blanket of roses, honeysuckle, and lights over the entire fragmented volumes of the power station. This new skin wraps around and adapts to the form at different heights, shrouding and unifying the façade elements with a unified silhouette and a single, common material. The covering reaches above the highest parts of the power station and transforms the building into a vertical garden with living and technological surfaces. The plant species chosen for the construction of this vegetative covering are a combination of rosebush creepers against a green and white background of honeysuckle. For this purpose the immense genetic material developed by the biologist, Griffith J. Buck, will be used. Buck managed to cultivate many species of roses, which he adapted to the harsh climate of Iowa. AMID* proposes to use gardeners' ancient techniques of genetic selection to create a modern, and novel image in the daunting presence of the power station.

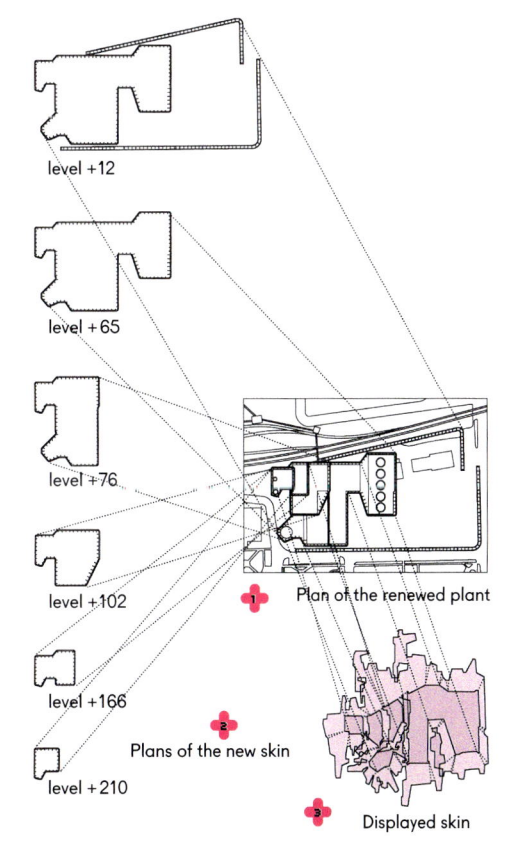

KEY PRINCIPLES
For the covering of the outer shell of the power plant, the architects propose to use the growth of the living matter as a foundation grid of recycled polypropylene pellets. Each grid has a structural box girder at its base containing the necessary subsoil to help the plants flourish, which is attached to the reinforced concrete walls of the power station. In order to facilitate pruning and maintenance by the gardeners, a perimeter pathway is cleared between the façade and the covering. The city Ames lies on the north-south migratory route on the North American continent. As in natural landscapes, the floral covering will attract various butterfly species. Simultaneously, the power station is converted into an open receptacle where a large variety of bird species will be able to nest, attracted by the water and the numerous swarms of insects hovering around the vertical garden. The power station will provide a wayside resting place for migrating birds and also an artificial alternative to the forests and wetlands that have been destroyed in this area in recent years. The combination of the existing power station and its new transformation produce an ecosystem that is subject to human interaction. Architecture and energy infrastructure converted into living systems using bio-engineering techniques to produce a "magic mountain"—a natural monument that is artificially generated.

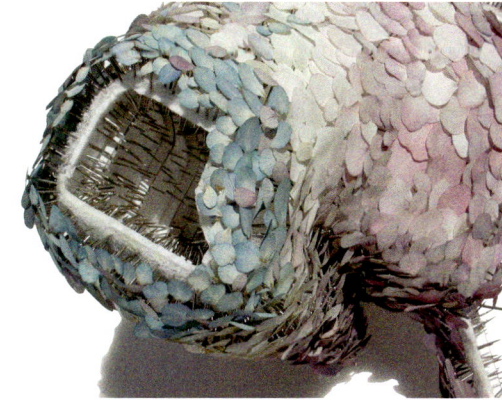

Project Title:
EVOLVING SKYSCRAPER
Architect:
Vahan Misakyan
Envisioned Project Location:
Yerevan, Armenia
Envisioned Completion Date:
In several decades time

WHERE AND WHEN
Evolving Skyscraper is envisioned to be realized in roughly seventy years from now, in the future Armenia, in the city of Yerevan. The immediate surrounding is the historic city, which will preserve only the best examples of architecture and demolish any buildings, which "pollute" the urbane environment: aesthetically or ecologically. The urban environment will be greener and be more in harmony with nature.

BASIC CONDITIONS
The *Evolving Skyscraper* is embedded within a greater future society, uniting humanity as well as preserving nature and cultural identity rather than ruining nature and suppressing, or ignoring, cultural ideology. Society of the future will hopefully have improved, especially with regard to the perception of beauty and ugliness; what is aesthetic and what is unaesthetic. The evolution of the aesthetic judgment of society is one of the key ameliorations that should become visible thanks to the improvement of the built environment.

KEY PRINCIPLES
The main concept of *Evolving Skyscraper* is architecture and aesthetics. The project consists of several parts: the "concept of skyscraper" as the central focus whilst the building complex, includes the Performing Arts Center with a new transportation hub as an additional part of the scheme. The *Evolving Skyscraper* consists of an assemblage of structural geodesics that form three piercing towers linked by habitable bridges above and below. Different programs, including offices, residences, and hotel would be located in each tower—the geodesics would change in scale and configuration depending on the program. The bridges would be used as commercial and recreational areas for the public. One of the main ideas of the proposal is to soften the transition between the vertical and the horizontal planes by creating surfaces that "peel off" from the ground and that could transform into habitable areas. A transportation hub for the city would emerge from one of these structures, while a secondary structure would serve as a bridge and a recreational park. Another key feature is the idea of the continuous growth of the skyscraper. Before reaching the visualized "final phase" of the construction there could be multiple prior stages, which could also be continued after the official construction phase is completed. The building is designed with the latest ecological technology. An "intelligent" membrane would control the amount of light incidence, through mechanical openings, and could also be used to reduce heat and provide natural ventilation. This membrane would also be equipped with rainwater collection systems, photovoltaic cells, and wind turbines.

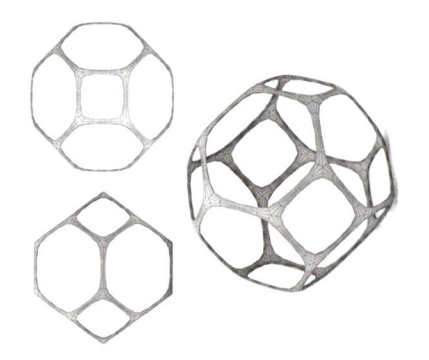

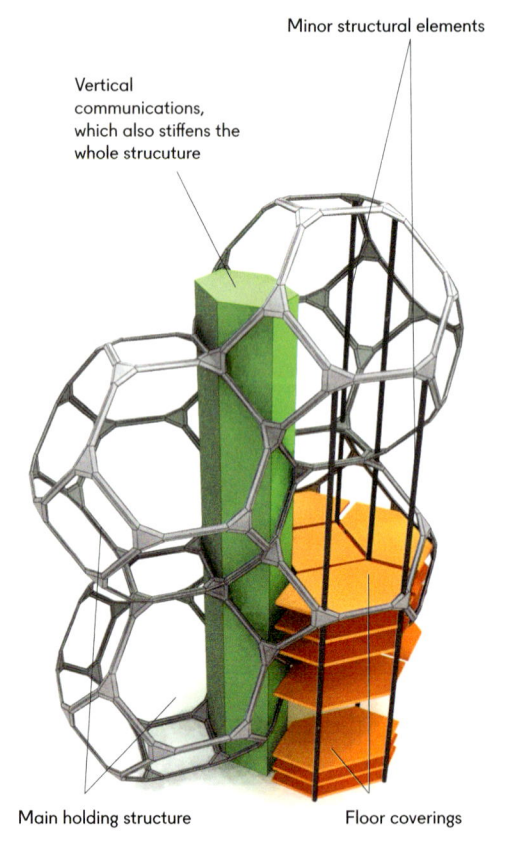

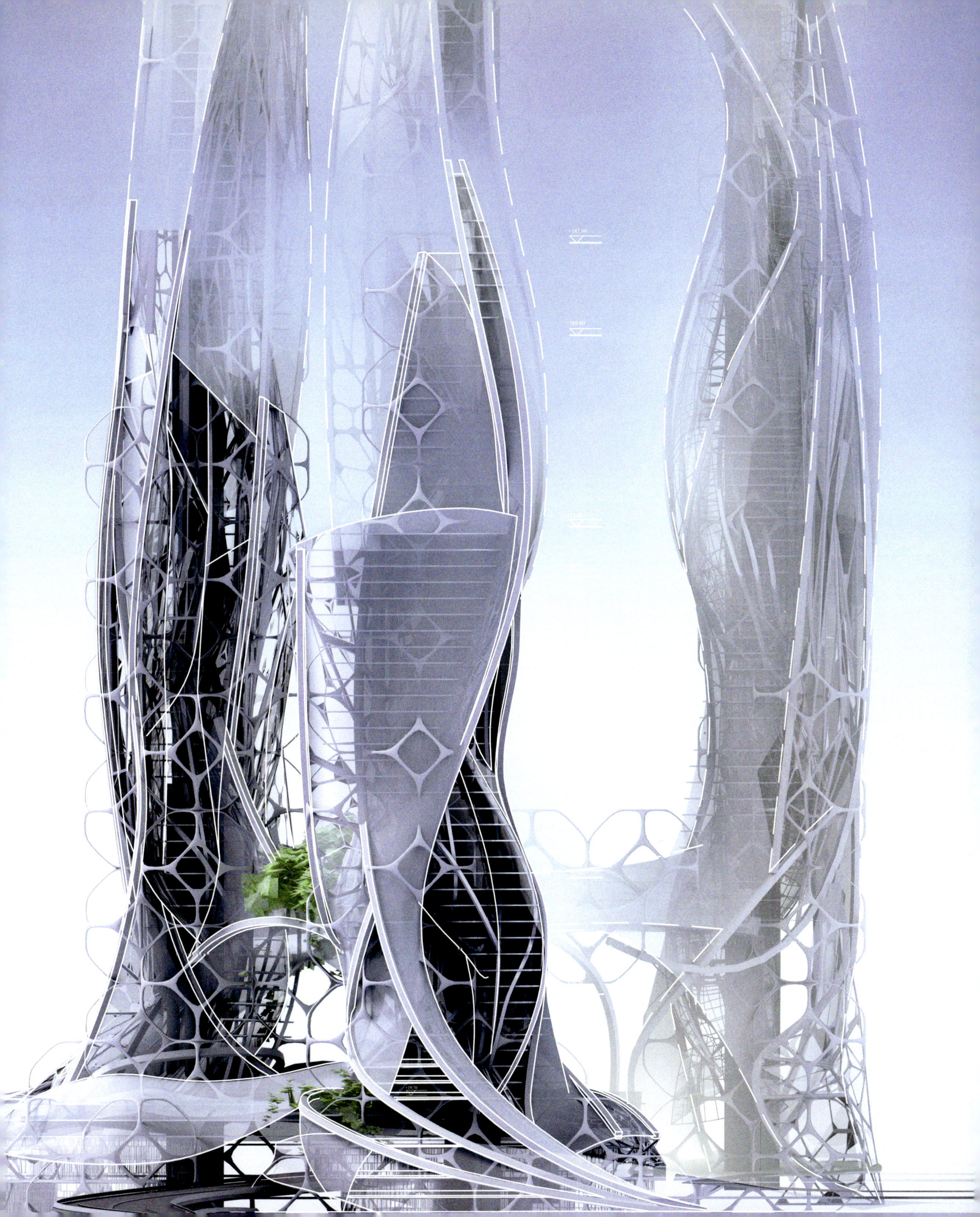

Project Title:
FRESHWATER FACTORY
Architect:
DCA/Design Crew for Architecture (Nicolas Chausson, Gaël Desveaux, Jiaoyang Huang)
Envisioned Project Location:
Almeria/Spain
Envisioned Completion Date:
The near future

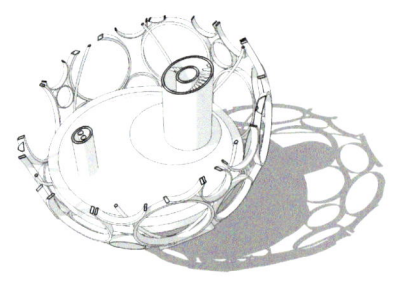

WHERE AND WHEN
Envisioned for Almeria in Spain, a province located in the south of Spain, along the Mediterranean coast, this project, *Freshwater Factory,* proposes a 280 m high and 12,000 m² tower designed to produce freshwater to irrigate the cultivated lands standing at its base. The region of Almeria is where most European fruits and vegetables are cultivated throughout the year—the sun shines here for as many as 250 days per year! Hundreds of greenhouses cover more than 90% of the region, spread over the landscape.

BASIC CONDITIONS
Although water is ubiquitous on earth, 97% is salted and 2% is solid, in the form of ice. In actual fact there is a mere 1% left of liquid fresh water—the UNO and the World Water Council estimate there might well be a water crisis by the year 2030, affecting half the worldwide population. Availability of fresh water will, doubtless, be a major issue in the twenty-first century. Indeed the production of liquid intake for a human being requires 3,000 liters of fresh water daily and the overall rate of fresh water use requires 64 billion m³ annually. Farming makes up for 70% of the worldwide fresh water consumption. Design Crew for Architecture's proposal is a completely new building: an innovative response to sustainable development and the upcoming challenges we are bound to face.

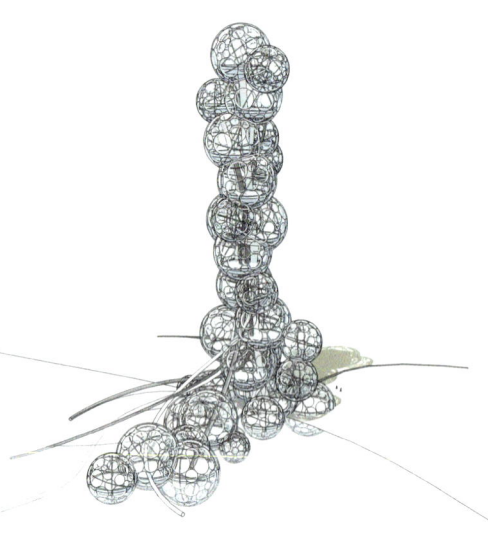

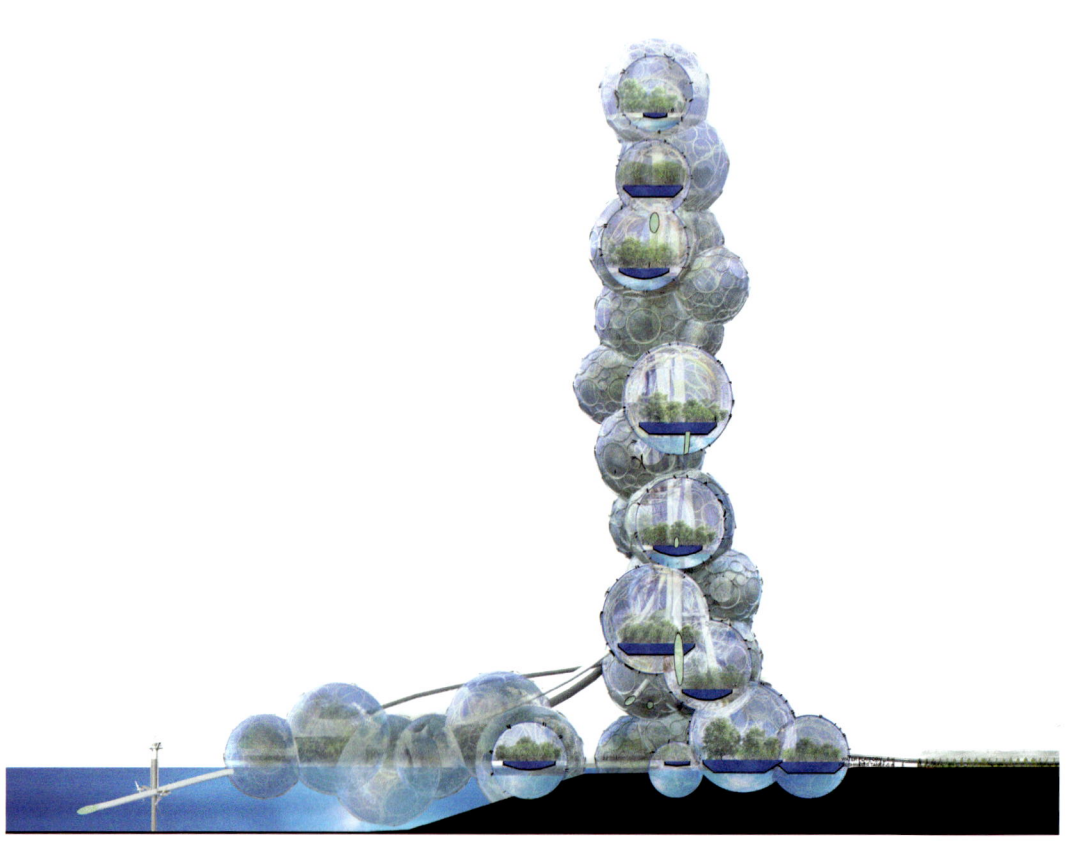

FRESHWATER FACTORY — ECOTOPIA EMERGING

KEY PRINCIPLES

Freshwater Factory proposes a novel solution for farming needs: this dome shelters a fresh water factory. A vertical tower would be made of several circular tanks filled with brackish water. These tanks would be held in spherical greenhouses. The brackish water would be brought up in the tower by tidal-powered pumps. The network of water pipes would be incorporated in the tower's main structure. The tanks would be planted with mangroves, which have the unique ability to flourish in brackish water and to "perspire" freshwater. This freshwater "perspiration" would evaporate in the greenhouse and condensate during the night into dew on the spherical polymer wall, to be collected in a fresh water tank. Thanks to the fact that the water is stored at altitude, the fresh water produced could be distributed over the fields by gravitational flow. The total surface of the tower would be one hectare—a single hectare of cultivated mangroves should be able to produce as much as 30,000 liters of fresh water per day. The design is the direct expression of the concept and has a realistic structural logic. The main structure of the tower would be constructed in concrete. It is conceived as a basic post-and-floor building principle. The levels would work as horizontal bracing in the structure as with many buildings. The posts would be larger than in common skyscrapers, as water pipes and circulation are integrated into them. The architectural expression of the proposed greenhouses is inspired by the geodesic domes Buckminster Fuller built in the late 1960s. The greenhouses would have a light, metallic structure that would be independent from the concrete structure of the tower. The primary structure would be made of large rings that would work interactively. The secondary structure would be made of smaller rings that would work in compression. The greenhouses, therefore, have an independent self-supporting structure.

Project Title:
400K PODS
Architect:
Federico Pedrini, Elia De Tomasi, Filippo Mazzaron, Alessandra Pepe, Silvia Sandor
Envisioned Project Location:
Barcelona, Spain
Envisioned Completion Date:
The near future

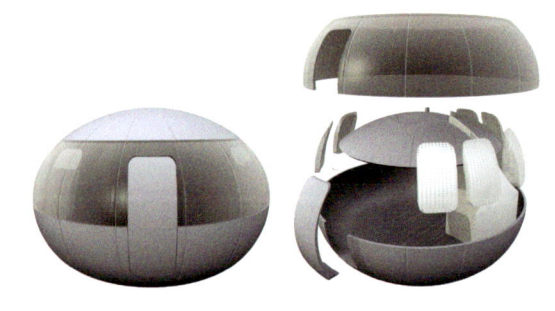

WHERE AND WHEN
This massive housing project, *400k Pods*, offers living and work space for 400,000 new inhabitants for the Spanish city of Barcelona.

BASIC CONDITIONS
The concept behind the project is to provide basic infrastructure, a "core" which will stand like a tree trunk in a forest providing vertical circulation and point access to the utilities grid. Each unit can be conceived as a fully independent sort of hanging villa, which can be easily assembled, produced, and mounted on demand, as well as provide privacy. The overall effect would be unusual and striking. Rather than forcing collective living, "collectiveness" would be created by the simple accumulation of the pods over time.

KEY PRINCIPLES
The hanging system for the "living-pods" is envisioned as a kind of a central trunk. The pods would be stacked on cantilevered beams, which would also serve as foot-bridges connecting the horizontal circulation to the vertical interior of the trunks. The tree could have various heights (40–60 m), each holding a proportional number of units, to create a forest-like effect. The cell would be constructed with a shell structure similar to the hull of a ship, with an optimal internal layout, similar to that of a caravan or a boat. Costs would be minimized thanks to the serialization of the production of the pods. Moreover, the proximity of the nearby railway could be used to reduce the transport costs of construction elements even further. The landscape created by the scheme would blend with the surrounding vegetation and maximize green areas for the inhabitants and for any passersby. The design would provide extensive views of nature from the apartments, and provide an optimal amount of shade, sun, and ventilation. Services and car-parks would be located underneath artificial mounds, thereby reducing excavation costs and clearances as a succession of open plazas connected to ground level. The pods would be hung between the "branches" of the buildings. The pods would receive light from above, as well as shade and coolness from the park below.

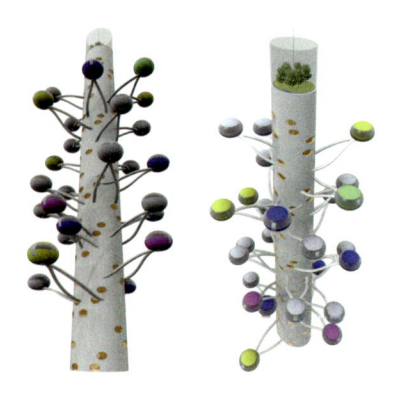

Project Title:
SEAWATER VERTICAL FARM
Architect:
studiomobile
(Antonio Girardi, Cristiana Favretto)
Envisioned Project Location:
Dubai, United Arab Emirates
Envisioned Completion Date:
2018

WHERE AND WHEN
SeaWater Vertical Farm is set in Dubai where lack of fresh water and lack of locally produced fruit and vegetables, the high soil quality, as well as traffic congestion, and the problem of transport, make the idea of using urban sites for intensive cultivation more realistic. The site for this project is located in Ud al Bayda, a desert area adjacent to Dubai, where the city council is planning to dig a new canal by 2015.

BASIC CONDITIONS
Several months ago at the Copenhagen Climate Conference, the IPCC (Intergovernmental Panel on Climate Change) disseminated statistics about greenhouse gas emissions and their relationship to agriculture. The globalized food system is responsible for between 30% and 40% of global greenhouse gas emissions; whereas land clearance and deforestation is responsible for 12% of emissions, and packing, refrigeration, and transportation is responsible for producing up to 18% of greenhouse emissions. An amazing fact is that agriculture produces only about 8% of global CO_2 emissions. It is environmentally strategic to cultivate food near to where it will be consumed: i.e. the cities. In addition, large desalination plants consume a great amount of energy: according to the UN Food and Agriculture Organization, a cubic meter of fresh water produced by the desalination technology, (called reverse osmosis), requires a liter of fuel. This means that desalination is responsible for the release of large amounts of CO_2 gas, which contribute to climate change. The *SeaWater Vertical Farm* uses seawater to cool and humidify greenhouses, and to convert sufficient humidity back into fresh water to irrigate crops. Converting seawater to fresh water in the right quantities, and in the right places, offers the potential to solve all the issues described above.

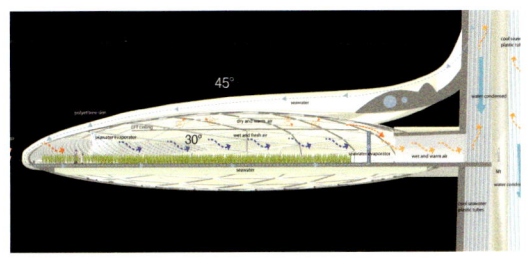

KEY PRINCIPLES
The *SeaWater Vertical Farm* uses traditional Arabic design strategies, which have arisen from the study of ancient building such as Iranian wind towers. The design provides for five cocoon-greenhouses fixed to five cantilevered branches that also transport and "nebulize" the seawater creating a humid and cool air flow, ideal for the growth of plant landscapes, like the environment of the equatorial forest. In these conditions crops require very little water as they are not stressed by excessive transpiration. As the air leaves the growth area it passes through the second evaporator which has seawater flowing over it. During this phase the humid air mixes with the warm, dry air of the ceiling inter-space. Thus, the air is made far warmer and more humid. No fans would be required: warm air is forced by the stack effect to flow upward through the central chimney. Here warm and humid air will condense when in contact with plastic tubes where cold seawater is pumped. Drops of fresh water will appear on the surface of the condensers ready to be recollected in a tank to hydrate the cocoon-greenhouses; the water can also be used for other purposes. In addition, the the growing process in the *SeaWater Vertical Farm* will use less than 90% water owing to the combination of "aeroponic" technology—the process of growing plants in an air or mistenvironment without the use of soil or an aggregate medium—and seawater desalinization processes. These processes are an effective, sustainable, and economic alternative to traditional desalinization plants, which are responsible for a significant amount of greenhouse gas emissions.

SEAWATER VERTICAL FARM ECOTOPIA EMERGING

Đ. CHPT. III

Project Title:
GALIJE
Architect:
MVRDV
Envisioned Project Location:
Galije, Montenegro
Envisioned Completion Date:
The near future

WHERE AND WHEN
On a piece of untouched, virgin coastline in Montenegro, barely a couple of kilometers from the monumental fishing village peninsula, Sveti Stefan, this project proposes a resort hotel that seems to be built into the undulating coastline.

BASIC CONDITIONS
Montenegro is a country which has a steadily growing tourist trade. This growth is thanks primarily, due to its rugged and unspoilt coastline. Some parts of the coastline have already been developed, but most of the coastline remains untouched. The client was determined to combine "exclusivity" with "sustainability" by embedding the project in its surrounding landscape. They were convinced that the attraction of the Montenegrin landscape would only be maintained by preserving its rugged beauty.

KEY PRINCIPLES
Creating an exclusive resort and constructing to a high standard was regarded as the best strategy to preserve the unique site. As a result, MVRDV designed the entire project as an offset to the terrain, and covered the landscape with a kind of "blanket" vegetative covering echoing the original landscape. Where a higher density was required the architects simply raised the "blanket" to create a hill. The iconic hotel is formed by cantilevering the "blanket" over the cliff to create an even more dramatic overhang. The flatter areas of the landscape would accommodate the villas, which would be arranged around private patios looking out at the ocean.

Project Title:
HUALIEN BEACH RESORT
Architect:
BIG/Bjarke Ingels Group
Envisioned Project Location:
Hualien, Taiwan
Envisioned Completion Date:
The near future

WHERE AND WHEN
The *Hualien Beach Resort* project is set within a former industrial and factory region which BIG proposes to convert into a luxury beach resort on the mountainous eastern coast of Taiwan.

BASIC CONDITIONS
The site has great potential with its spectacular views, thanks to its location on the coast, adjacent to the intersection of two river deltas. Taiwan's range of mountains can be seen to the west, the ocean to the east, and Hualien city to the north.

KEY PRINCIPLES
For the master-plan of the resort a language of green terraced landscapes was envisaged to create a kind of mountain terrain of commercial and residential units that would echo the mountains in the distance. The terraces would run east-west in order to frame the best views, while also creating an optimal shading system for Taiwan's hot and humid tropical climate. Low-angle, morning and evening glare from the sun would be blocked by the terraces, while favorable north-south light would be allowed into the units. Green roofs would further mitigate heat gain and, combined with the terracing, create a low-energy master-plan.

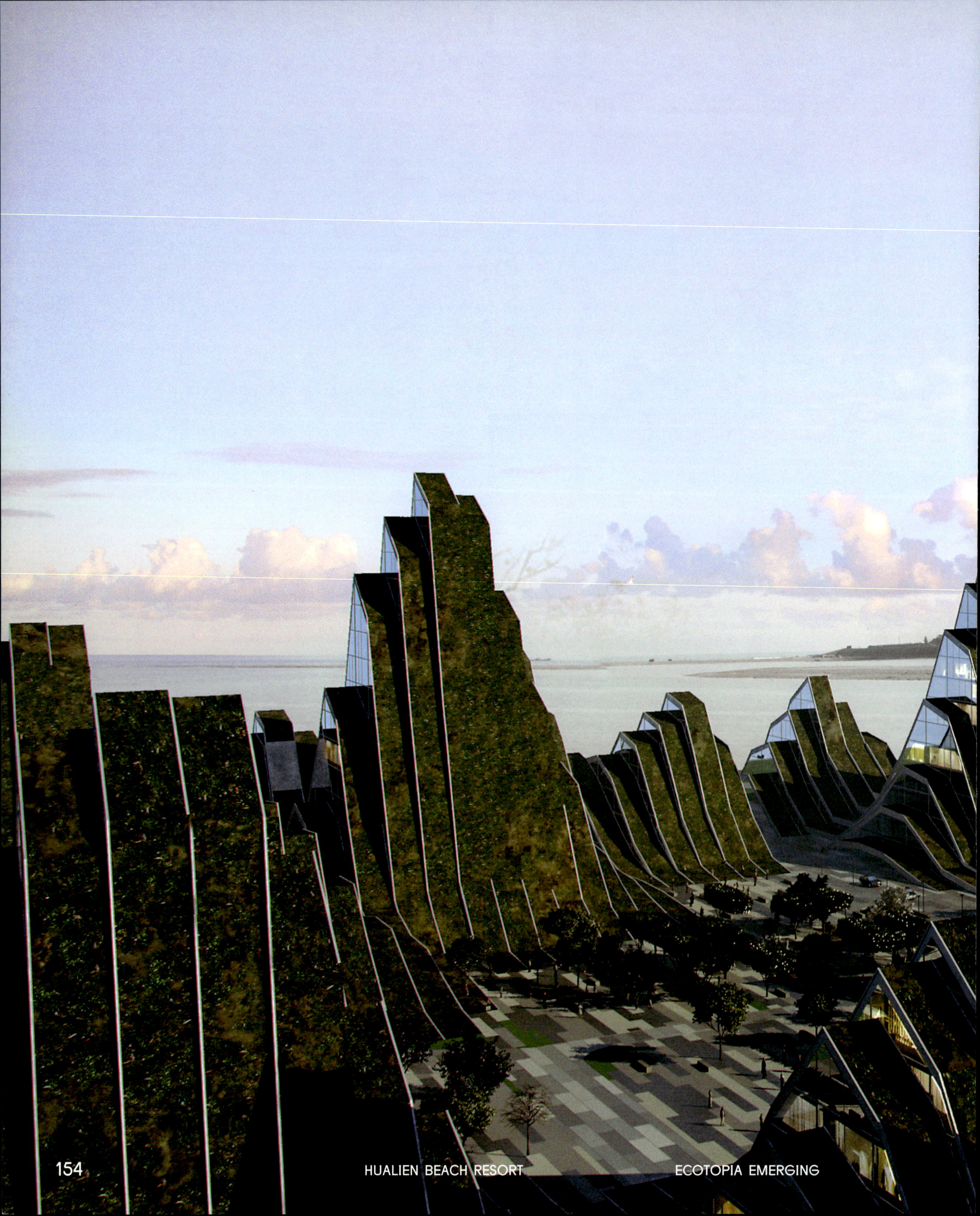

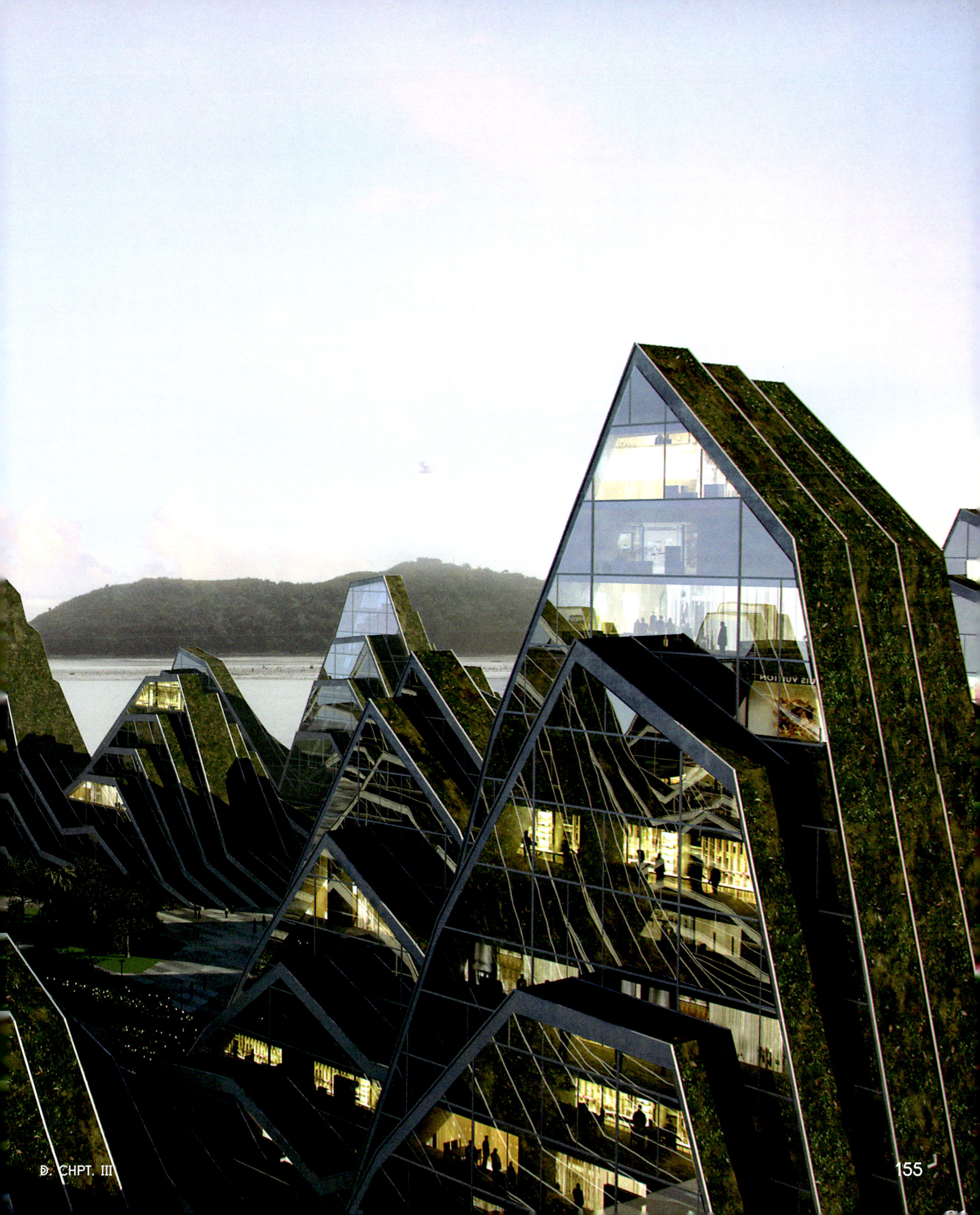

TECHNOLOGY MATTERS?

Reflecting upon the Impact of New Technology

In recent history media and technology have shaken the foundations of human culture and experience. Both offer compelling ways to explain cognitive and cultural changes, and present the enormous challenges our culture, our society, and our very conceptions of ourselves face. The projects shown here investigate new technologies suffused with utopian energy, and consider their significance in the way we might live and work in the future. Many of the architectural projects gathered in this chapter rely on technologies that do not yet exist, or spin-off technologies that derive from existing models or ideas. The multitude of concepts at the heart of these projects range from virtual engagements in cyberspace, all the way to new technological innovations that push the boundaries of human knowledge and experience. In the project, *New City*, Los-Angeles architect, Greg Lynn, envisions an architectural virtual world, which would respond to the emergence of social media through the design of a parallel virtual reality in which all of Earth's inhabitants reside in a single interconnected mega-city. Jürgen Mayer H.'s *A.WAY* project, predicts that urban spaces, buildings, people, and vehicles will all develop "clouds" of data and personalized information around them. He imagines that as citizens move around this digitally-augmented urban environment, their personal data and preferences would splash onto fields of information from the world around them, while cars would become tools for viewing and navigating this data. Rebuilding and expanding the contemporary city from decades of its own waste, Terreform 1's project, *Rapid Re(f)use*, on the other hand, involves specialized robots which would process garbage into usable building material, almost like three-dimensional printers spewing out recycled building material on a massive scale. Each one of these projects calls for the removal of frontiers between architecture and other disciplines, and desires an endless process of connectivity: an architecture that not only "thinks" in terms of buildings, but far beyond any conventional disciplinary boundaries.

"IT HAS BECOME APPALLINGLY OBVIOUS THAT OUR TECHNOLOGY HAS EXCEEDED OUR HUMANITY."

ALBERT EINSTEIN

164. *GEOtube* by Faulders Studio
166. *Dustyrelief/B_MU* by R&Sie(n)
168. *Rapid Re(f)use: Waste To Resource City 2120* by Terreform ONE & Terrefuge (Mitchell Joachim, Maria Aiolova, Melanie Fessel, Emily Johnson, Ian Slover, Philip Weller, Zachary Aders, Webb Allen, Niloufar Karimzadegan, Lauren Sarafan)
172. *Casa Pulpa* by Hodgetts + Fung Design and Architecture
173. *UL-9205* by Mas Yendo
174. *UL-9304* by Mas Yendo
175. *B1-9004 Hole in Water* by Mas Yendo
176. *The Big Mech & Co* by amid.cero9 (Cristina Díaz Moreno & Efrén García Grinda), with Colectivo Cuartoymitad
178. *Hypnosis Chamber* by R&Sie(n) with Benoit Durandin
181. *Water Flux* by R&Sie(n)
182. *Eco-Pod (Gen1)* by Hoeweler + Yoon Architecture and Squared Design Lab
186. *Coney Island* by Squint/Opera
189. *Fabulous Fabbers* by David Benqué
190. *A.WAY* by J. MAYER H. Architects
192. *New City* by Greg Lynn Form, Peter Frankfurt, Alex McDowell, and Imaginary Forces
194. *The Amber Clock from The 200 Year Continuum* by Christian Kerrigan
196. *The Industrialist Monks* by Dylan Cole

THEY PROMISED US JETPACKS!
Of Futures and Utopias

by MATTHIAS BÖTTGER and LUDWIG ENGEL
raumtaktik — office from a better future

raumtaktik — office from a better future pursue an investigation of space and spatial intervention. Raumtaktik's co-founder and architect, Matthias Böttger, and future researcher Ludwig Engel, focus on transformative processes in the urban context.

The future will arrive no matter what happens to us. Utopia, on the other hand, is a concept we have created in order to instigate innovation and change; to "make things happen." Within this logical twist, we will be able to find the inseparable connections and the profound differences between society's role in shaping our future and our utopia. The future will come regardless; it remains always ahead of us, no matter in which direction we are heading, no matter which path we choose to take. Utopia is always the mirage-like vision of what may be lying ahead at the end of one of these paths.

Considering this argument, it seems logical to refer to both terms—utopia and future—in plural only, because there is actually no singular future but rather many futures, there is not one single utopia, but rather myriads which can co-exist in many different future scenarios. Rather than forecasting futures by projecting linear developments of the past, it would be better to reflect upon our current understanding of global and societal dynamics, intellectually grasping the utopian aspects of what we would like our future selves to have attempted and to have achieved.

Our Phenomenal Civilization-Machine

In order to follow this approach, it is necessary for us to step back and take a look at the current state of our world and how it has arrived where it is today. For the better part of history, the Earth with all its resources has been available to only a small, fortunate fraction of its population and has adapted to their specific economic model. With the help of the planet's natural resources, the industrialized countries were able to establish a "phenomenal civilization-machine," as the social psychologist, Harald Welzer, coined it. A machine, run by fossil-fuels which provided incredible advances in science and technology, food and health systems, welfare society, security, and education. As the Athenian polis of ancient Greece, with all its intellectual and architectural magnificence, had heavily relied on slave labor, the economic model of "the global few" was based on the possibility of spatial externalization. Only the exterior was able to deliver the required resources for the "interior world of the capital," as the philosopher, Peter Sloterdijk, described this imbalance, in his account of the European script for globalization—the Eurocentric perception of what we regard as "world history."

The turning point came with globalization and its geographical inclusion of everyone and every place, through global capital and information streams. The globalized world no longer had an exterior to feed off, no exterior from which to draw the resources it required. Therefore, worldwide competition for natural resources and transport routes has grown into an open rivalry and, significantly, the exploitation of our planet has been relocated from *space* into *time*. Our ruthless depletion of the future planet will be the pitiful inheritance of future generations, making the future inhabitants of our planet the main victims of our obsession with development. We, who live now, will not suffer as much as those who will be left to pick up the pieces of our broken world. The present, in a way, consumes the future.

Ideal Islands in the Distance

When Sir Thomas More, Renaissance humanist, published his novel *De optimo rei publicae statu deque nova insula Utopia* in 1516, the consequences of globalization were a far-off reality; nevertheless, Sir Thomas was not content with the society of his time, either. Most often referred to by its abbreviated title, *Utopia*, his fictional work is believed to be the origin of the term, "utopia," widely used since then. Utopia consists of two sections in which More analyses the political system of his time. Through the eyes of the novel's protagonist, Raphael Hythlodeaus, More subsequently plots the ideal alternative society he envisions on the island he named *Utopia*. The story's clear fictional basis, combined with its eye witness, believable, first-person narrative, helped establish the literary genre of utopian fiction.

Though written in Latin, the name of the island where More placed his ideal society, was a play on the Greek word *topos* in combination with the prefix, deriving from *eu* or *ou*, both pronounced *u* in English. By playing with the prefixes—*eu* translates as *good* and *ou* as *non*—More lay down the foundation on which utopia would be defined from then on. It would always be a *good place* and a *non-place;* a place that was more than its author's reality, but a place that also did not either exist: a place the author desired but knew could never be.

More's choice for a Greek neologism is no coincidence. His attempt to criticize the social conditions of his time by making a "utopian" counter-proposal was closely related to Plato's dialogs *Timaios* and *Kritias*. In the Middle Ages, Plato's accounts of the ideal state, *Politeia*, and the island, *Atlantis*, had become legendary myths. More made use of the well known island-theme and linked it directly to his newly invented term *Utopia*. The far-flung, (almost) unreachable island, therefore, developed into an enduring metaphor for the pursuit of a certain kind of happiness—remotely located and beyond societies' norms.

Space and Time: Utopia and Uchronia

To begin with, the foundation of every kind of utopia had been regarded as the possibility of externalization in a geographical sense. As long as our world had not been discovered and mapped fully, there would always be the hope of a better life somewhere else, far from home. With the completion of "terrestrial globalization" as Peter Sloterdijk refers to the first circumnavigators and astrologists whose amazing discovery that the world is not flat, but indeed a sphere and therefore finite, meant that spatial externalization was no longer feasible. There was no place on Earth left unchartered, no untouched, virgin territory. With this realization, the idea of the existence of an ideal community on a far away island subsided.

According to the historian, Reinhart Koselleck, the year 1771 marked the first literary alliance of utopian fiction with the future. French writer, Louis-Sébastien Mercier, published his book *L'An 2440, Rêve s'il en fut Jamais*. Rather than fleeing to a distant place, the author remained physically in Paris, whilst mentally traveling forward in time. Mercier's visions had a profound impact on the confines of what utopia could be conceived as. Thereafter, the abstract future, became a "relief-space" which could endlessly be filled with the fantasies of authors, like the concept of time: indefinitely repeatable. This shift from utopia to *uchronia* (meaning *good time* and/or *non-time*) transformed the author of a future vision into the authentic producer of his own utopia. Since the future cannot be grasped, nor be proven, it became a genuine product of the author's imagination. As utopia no longer existed in a place that was reachable, it became connected to the circumstances of the present through time. Every *uchronia* had to assume chronological continuity. *Uchronia*, therefore, is not merely fictitious, but has to connect to the empirical present. In his novel, *L'An 2440*, Mercier did not simply imagine how he desired the future Paris to be and look like, rather he described precisely how Paris *will look like*, how it *will be* in the year 2440. Mercier presented his dreams for the future as fact.

Jetpacks! Again!

In a sense, *L'An 2440* set in motion something that Marxist philosopher, Ernst Bloch, observed almost two centuries later. While defending his concept of utopia in modern times against Theodor W. Adorno in their 1964 dispute, he stated that *utopia* had been passing into the realms of "science fiction." The genre of science fiction started to develop into our favorite form of reflection on society. Formal and fictitious constructions of the future in combination with utopian elements—such as desires, wishes, and hopes for a better world, as well as fear and apprehension towards non-utopian futures—science fiction became a poetic and an indirect form of social critique.

In order to fully gasp the connection of science fiction as an updated, revision of utopia, we shall turn once more to the past and to the role the *future* has played in it. *Future* returns throughout history as an idea-pool of reoccurring *topoi*, or often *outopoi*, disguised as replays of *eutopoi*. The future takes place as it becomes reality and immediately becomes the past. But some imagined *futures,* which do not occur, remain outside this change of time and linger in limbo around us as possible futures and desired utopias. So many fears and desires of people do not actually ever transpire. This undeniable fact leads us to the obvious insight that we cannot ever know what the future will hold. Nevertheless, this glaring fact has not hindered us from indulging in other, new future hopes and future fears, creating a graveyard of never-to-be-realized futures, tumbling through history. Consequently these ghosts of ideas cannot be destroyed but will return again and again as updated versions of themselves. In this way, everything that has ever been thought of can be reviewed for tomorrow's future. A good example of this recurrence is the *jetpack,* which has recurred in numerous guises: a science fiction novelty in the 1920s, a German wonder-weapon in WW2, a famous James Bond gadget, and even currently marketed by the *Jetpack International Corporation.* Almost a century later, the idea remains a contemporary visualization of future mobility—the *jetset, jetpacking* into the near future.

Utopian Windows of Opportunity at Present

As we have seen, in the course of the history of utopian thinking, the importance of *place* faded and was substituted by the notion of *time.* Utopia became the "universal remedy for the ever-concerned" (Georges Minois) who follow the imperative: "If the future does not exist, it shall be invented." Utopia appears as an absolute act of volition, not concerned with knowing what will happen, but reacting to various hypotheses. In this sense, *utopia* disregards transcendental and immanent principles, and creates visions of situations that have not yet happened but are nevertheless plausible. Historically—per definition—utopia remains worlds apart from our present, with a maximum amount of distance and the maximum amount of time between. This allows us to see utopias as simple visions, or as practical solutions, to immediate problems. The fascination with utopia lies in its innate ability to imagine the unthinkable: a society, a state, a communal environment of individuals that is organized utterly differently. Utopia as the *non-place* describes what we do not have, what we probably will never have, but can still imagine. The flaws of all utopias, we find in the creative gap that lies between the vision of the future, and the reality we live in. This gap can only be bridged by a miracle that, unfortunately, never occurs. Visions of the future, therefore, are inevitably utopian. They are shaped by our present circumstances, indicating the complexities of contemporary events, and illustrating the current state of our society. Each time another utopian ideal is ruined by the heavy burden of reality, the disappointment is great. Still, fears and hopes for the future continue to color utopian thinking, forming our approach to dealing with what has-not-yet-happened. This might be regarded as positive; after all, we only have to know that there is no use in following utopian concepts but that there are also great benefits in imagining utopian scenarios that will make the future open and shapeable—to stretch our minds. Only multiple, even opposing scenarios, can help us to imagine seemingly paradoxical futures.

News from Nowhere is Real News

Let us (re)turn now to the function of utopias: this subjective perspective on the world provides a means of escape to a place of hope, a purposefully vague ideal to counterbalance reality's hyper-complexity. Yet utopias are also created with the intention of changing contemporary patterns of these hyper-complex realities, to indulge in a process of "objectively" transforming current society from a subjective standpoint. Utopia functions as a form of escapism and a form of change. This may appear paradoxical to a single entity at first glance. However, for the historian, Lewis Mumford, for example, the compensatory and transformative functions of utopia are not paradoxical. The core function of utopia is social progress. Mumford quotes the French writer, Anatole France, to illustrate his point: "Without the Utopians of other times, men would still live in caves, miserable and naked. It was Utopians who traced the lines of the first city… Out of generous dreams come beneficial realities. Utopia is the principle of all progress, and the essay into a better future."

Utopia cannot be understood in the restrictive manner of one single solution for all problems, but rather functions as the constant production of utopia; as a key to the door of otherwise unthinkable futures. The mistake humankind has repeatedly made is taking a single utopian idea too literally; as a manual to follow in order to achieve a prospective better society. Rather than reflecting on different utopias and their purpose or on contemporary criticism, its author attempted to shed light upon utopias that have been misused, by claiming to know what this "better future" might be—that it is indeed better and not just another variation of the future. Ideological dictators of a specific utopia have been witnessed to follow their rigid line of "future history," a one-way street into the singularly "true" future. This has proven to be dangerous historically, mainly as it ignores reality. A vision of an alternative reality should never be misunderstood as reality itself. As we have seen, utopias can only work as a commentary on current issues and on contemporary hopes. Yet it lies in the nature of human beings to look endlessly for signs of what tomorrow might bring. Utopia offers the possibility to dream, to visualize, to narrate, to imagine the impossible, and can therefore develop the power, as a catalyst, to kick-start a process of change. We cannot start changing without the prospect of something in the future—either something we want to avoid or something we want to achieve—or even reflectively continuing on the path we have chosen. Consequently, we cannot know the future but we do shape it by our present actions. After the fall of the Berlin Wall in 1989, the decline of most socialist economies, and the domination of capitalism on a global level, utopian thinking was temporarily abandoned until it was revived again, thanks to the ecological and financial crises in the beginning of the third millennium. It seems now, imperative to open up this window of opportunity to envision alternative and hopeful futures. The shaping of the future by political decisions and individual initiatives cannot be left to projecting past, or less-than-ideal paths into the future, but to create alternatives, options, and futures to look forward to. It seems that in particularly dire situations, dreams and hopes are even more important. To consider the future means to come up with more utopias—again and again, never to give up. But, never forget… the path into the future is never a direct line!

GEOTUBE

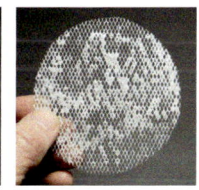

Deposits of primarily halite, gypsum, and aragonite form some of the major subsurface hydrocarbon reservoirs in the Middle East. Against this background, the vertical surfaces of the *GEOtube* tower, with an open structure and an exposed membrane skin, are continually condensed with salt water via an external vascular water system. The result is a continual uniform growth of salt-crystal deposits on the huge and highly visible surfaces of the tower.

KEY PRINCIPLES

GEOtube is a novel kind of tower, based on a pattern design for the structural system that is created by tracing the planar surface deformation generated by large wind tube openings. Sprayed with water from the Persion Gulf, its structural skin is entirely grown rather than constructed; the skin is continually formed rather than fully completed. The structure is also created locally rather than imported from afar. As the water evaporates and salt- mineral deposits aggregate over time, the tower's appearance transforms from a transparent veil to a glistening white vertical plane. Salt-crystals produce air saturated with healthy negative ions. The concentration of negative ions is naturally higher around waterfalls and by the ocean—when water droplets are dispersed, an electrical charge is created. Research has proven the therapeutic values of salt-caves and their positive influence in the treatment of respiratory diseases. Saline water will be supplied to *GEOtube* tower via a 4.62-kilometer-long, subterranean pipeline. The incoming salt water will be distilled on site to increase saline levels, and filtered prior to distribution onto the tower surfaces.

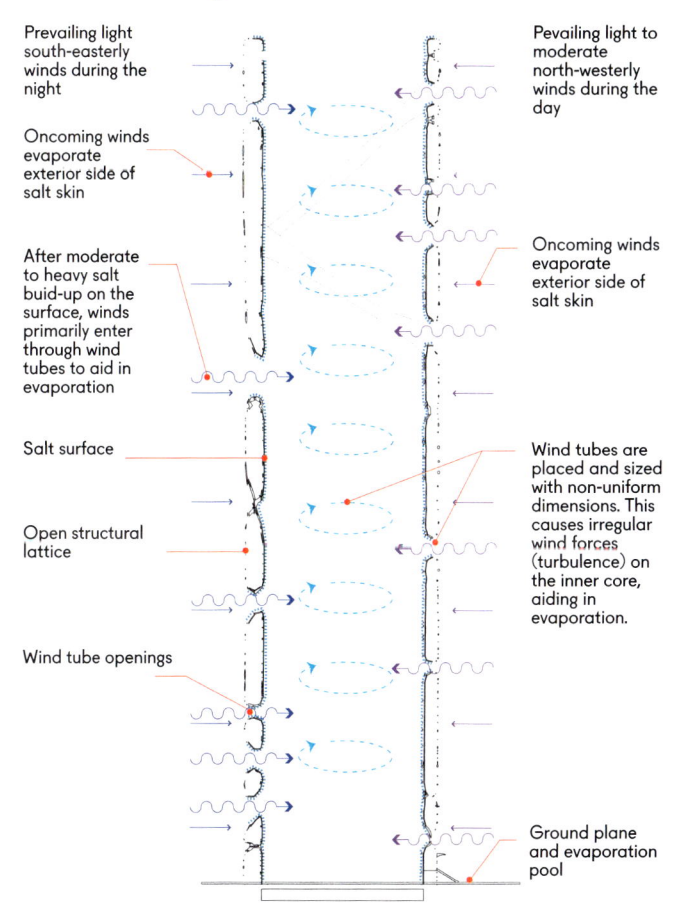

Project Title:
GEOTUBE
Architect:
Faulders Studio
Envisioned Project Location:
Dubai, United Arab Emirates
Envisioned Completion Date:
The near future

WHERE AND WHEN

GEOtube is a proposal for a new 170-meter-tall sculptural tower for the city of Dubai, which is situated in one of the most unique natural environments on Earth. The world's highest levels of salinity of seawaters are found in the Red Sea as well as the adjacent Persian Gulf. This is due to high evaporation rates in the region from high temperatures and low fresh water influx. *GEOtube* provides an identifiable architectural icon for the city, a specialized habitat for wildlife that thrives is this specialized environment, and an accessible skin for the harvesting of crystal salt.

BASIC CONDITIONS

Dubai's regional coastal plains, known locally as "sabkahs," are geological formations from salt flats created by extreme temperatures and humidity in combination with high water-salinity. The extreme climate variations experienced in the region, with thermal contraction at night and thermal expansion during the day, leads to polygonal surface-cracking.

Building section showing wind vectors

Project Title:
DUSTYRELIE*F*/B_MU

Architect:
R&Sie(n)

Envisioned Project Location:
Bangkok, Thailand

Envisioned Completion Date:
The near future

WHERE AND WHEN
Design proposal for a 5,000 m² contemporary art museum in Thailand's capital city, Bangkok.

BASIC CONDITIONS
The *Dustyrelief* project was developed on the basis that dust can be attracted to an electro statically-charged surface in order to obtain an imprint of the levels of contamination and dust that pollute the sky around Bangkok. This imprint would reveal the atmospheric context in which the project is set. In this type of mega-city the presence of the ghostly "breeding dust" is hardly unique; high levels of pollutants can also be found in many other cities where the contamination is over the healthy limits for the populace: for instance Mexico City, Manhattan, or Hong Kong.

KEY PRINCIPLES
R&Sie(n)'s proposal involves covering the building of the museum with an electro-magnetic skin to attract the dirt from the air. The pollution becomes a tangible layer that grows like fur on the exterior. A so called "random relief calculated by particles and *pixelization* of a grey ectoplasm under the grey, smoggy sky of Bangkok." As the building's aluminum envelope and electrostatic system collects the dust—particles of carbon monoxide—of the city, it intensifies the climate between the labyrinthine, white, cubic interior and the strange and provocative exterior.

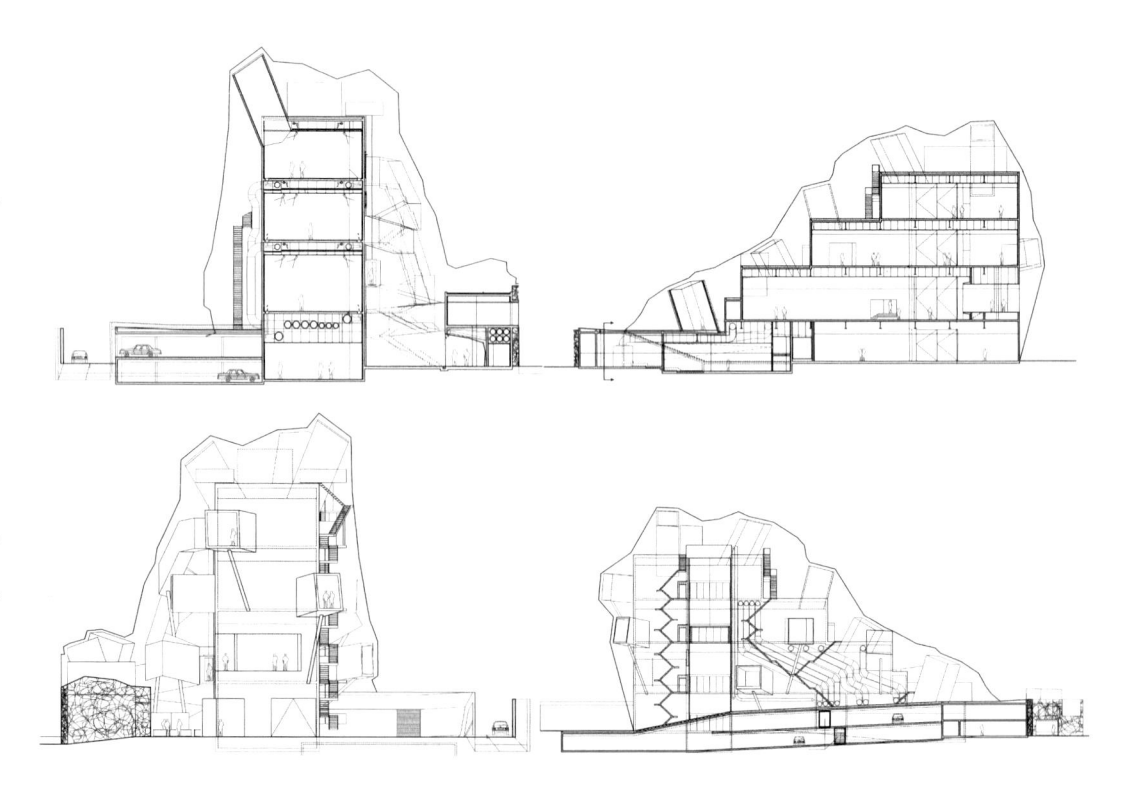

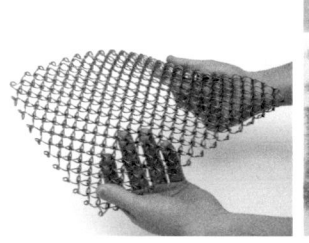

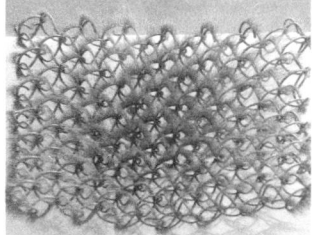

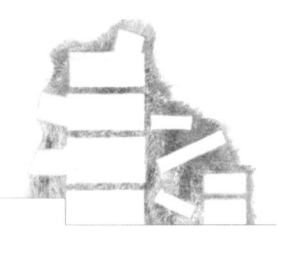

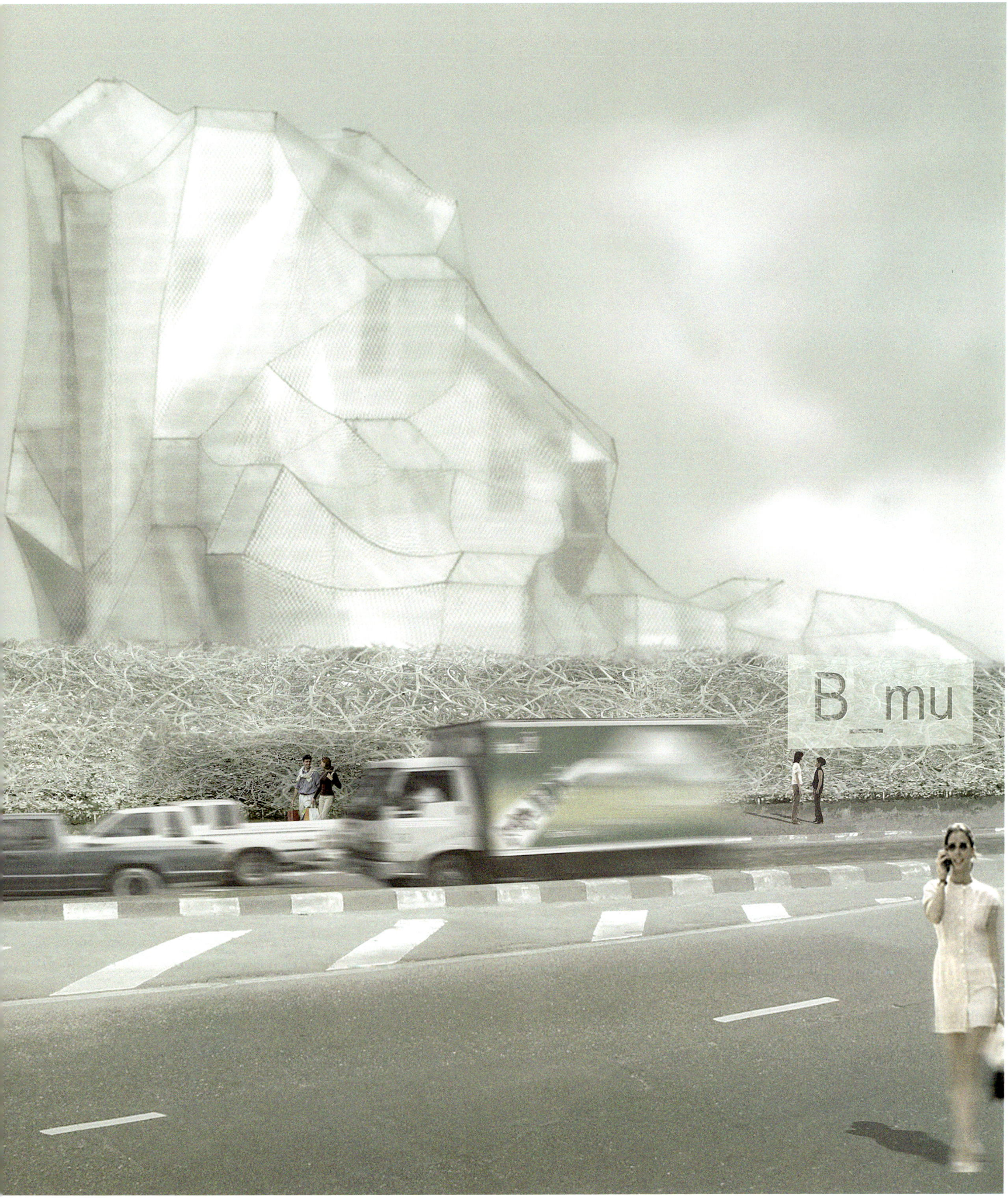
B_mu

166   RAPID RE(F)USE   TECHNOLOGY MATTERS

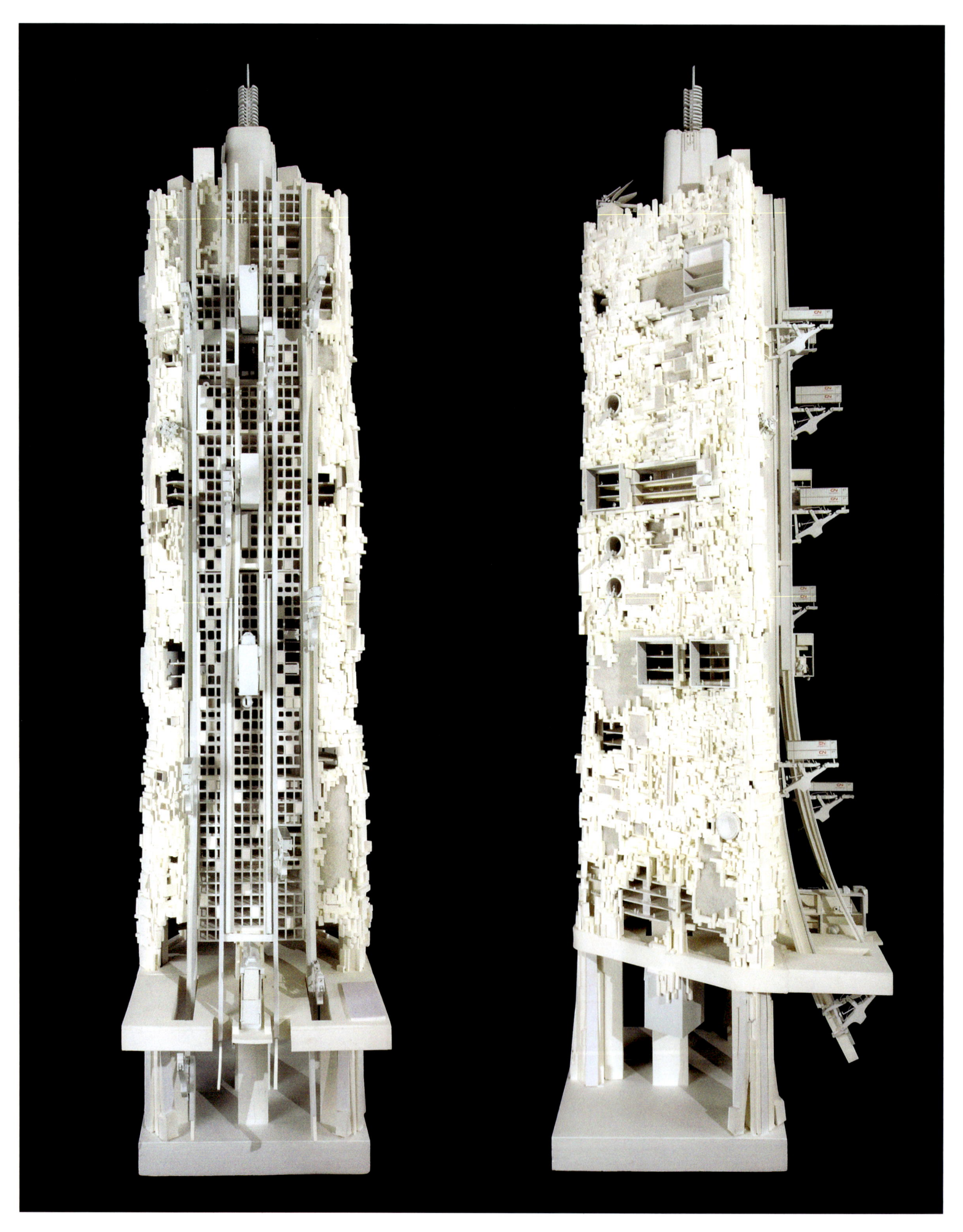

Project Title:
RAPID RE(F)USE: WASTE TO RESOURCE CITY 2120

Architect:
Terreform ONE + Terrefuge (Mitchell Joachim, Maria Aiolova, Melanie Fessel, Emily Johnson, Ian Slover, Philip Weller, Zachary Aders, Webb Allen, Niloufar Karimzadegan, Lauren Sarafan)

Envisioned Project Location:
New York, USA

Envisioned Completion Date:
2120

WHERE AND WHEN
New York City disposes 38,000 tons of waste per day. Most of this discarded waste material ends up in Fresh Kills Landfill before it closed. The *Rapid Re(f)use* project by Terreform ONE, proposes an extended New York reconstituted from its own landfill waste material. Their concept recreates the city by utilizing the waste at Fresh Kills Landfill.

BASIC CONDITIONS
With Terreform ONE's proposal, seven entirely new Manhattan islands could be recreated at full scale. Automated, robotic three-dimensional printers will be modified to process trash and complete the construction of the islands within decades. The design of the robots will be based on existing techniques commonly found in industrial waste compaction devices. Instead of machines that crush objects into cubes, these devices will have jaws that make simple shaped forms for assembly.

KEY PRINCIPLES
Different materials will serve specified purposes: plastic for fenestration, organic compounds for temporary scaffolds, metals for primary structures, etc. Eventually the future city will make no distinction between waste and material supply.

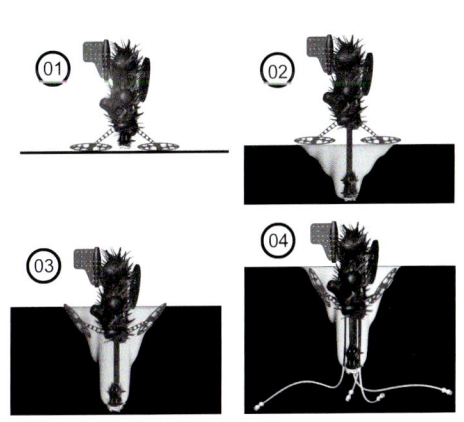

1: Scans surface, 2: Penetrates sub-layer, 3: Embeds in landfill, 4: Extends sensors, 5: Releases

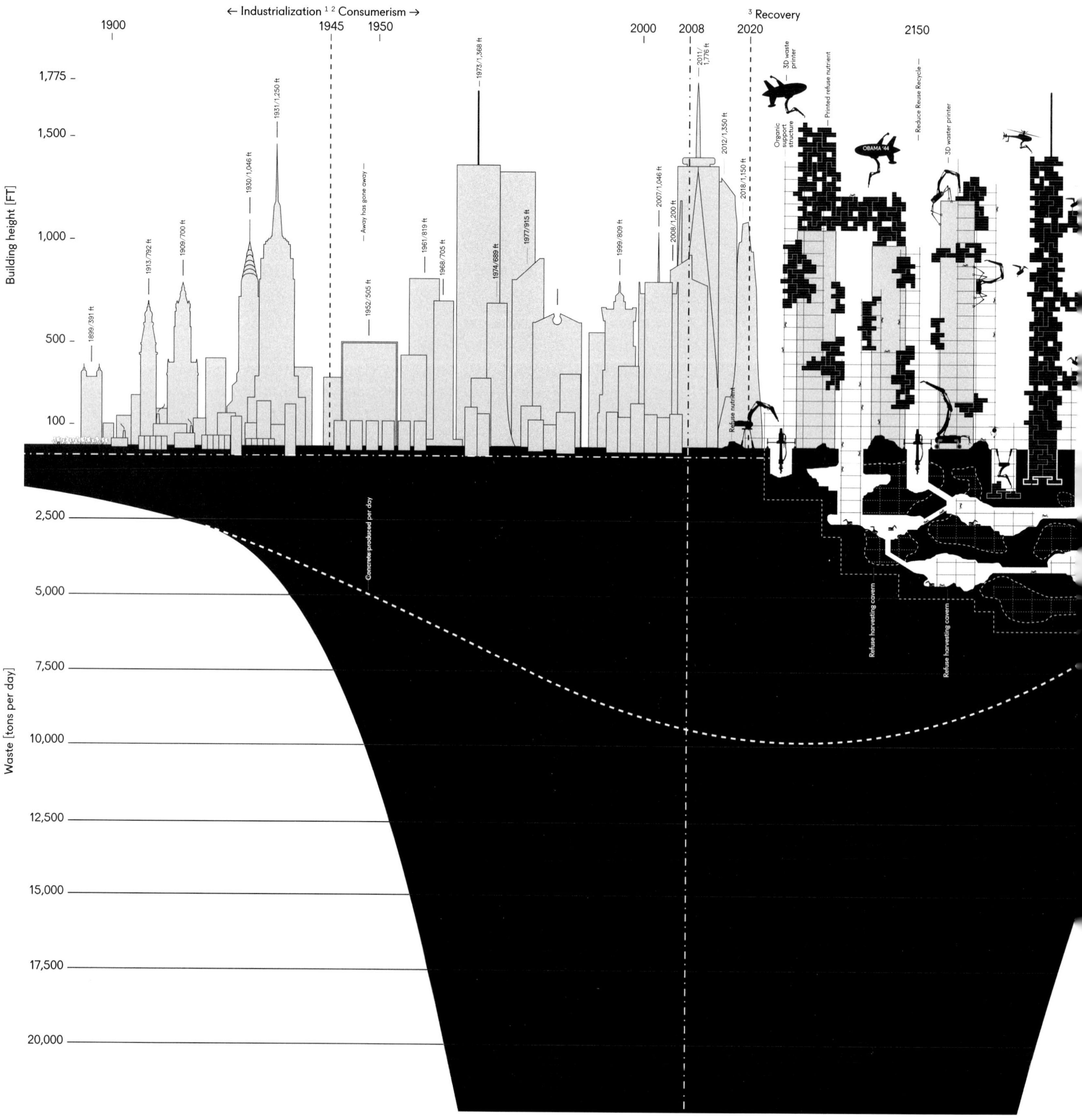

← Industrialization [1] [2] Consumerism →
[3] Recovery
1900
1945
1950
2000
2008
2020
2150
Building height [FT]
1,775
1,500
1,000
500
100
1899/391 ft
1913/792 ft
1909/700 ft
1930/1,046 ft
1931/1,250 ft
Away has gone away
1952/505 ft
1961/819 ft
1968/705 ft
1973/1,368 ft
1974/689 ft
1977/915 ft
1999/809 ft
2007/1,046 ft
2008/1,200 ft
2011/ 1,776 ft
2012/1,350 ft
2018/1,150 ft
Refuse nutrient
3D waste printer
Organic support structure
Printed refuse nutrient
OBAMA '44
Reduce Reuse Recycle
3D waster printer
Waste [tons per day]
2,500
5,000
7,500
10,000
12,500
15,000
17,500
20,000
Concrete produced per day
Refuse harvesting cavern
Refuse harvesting cavern

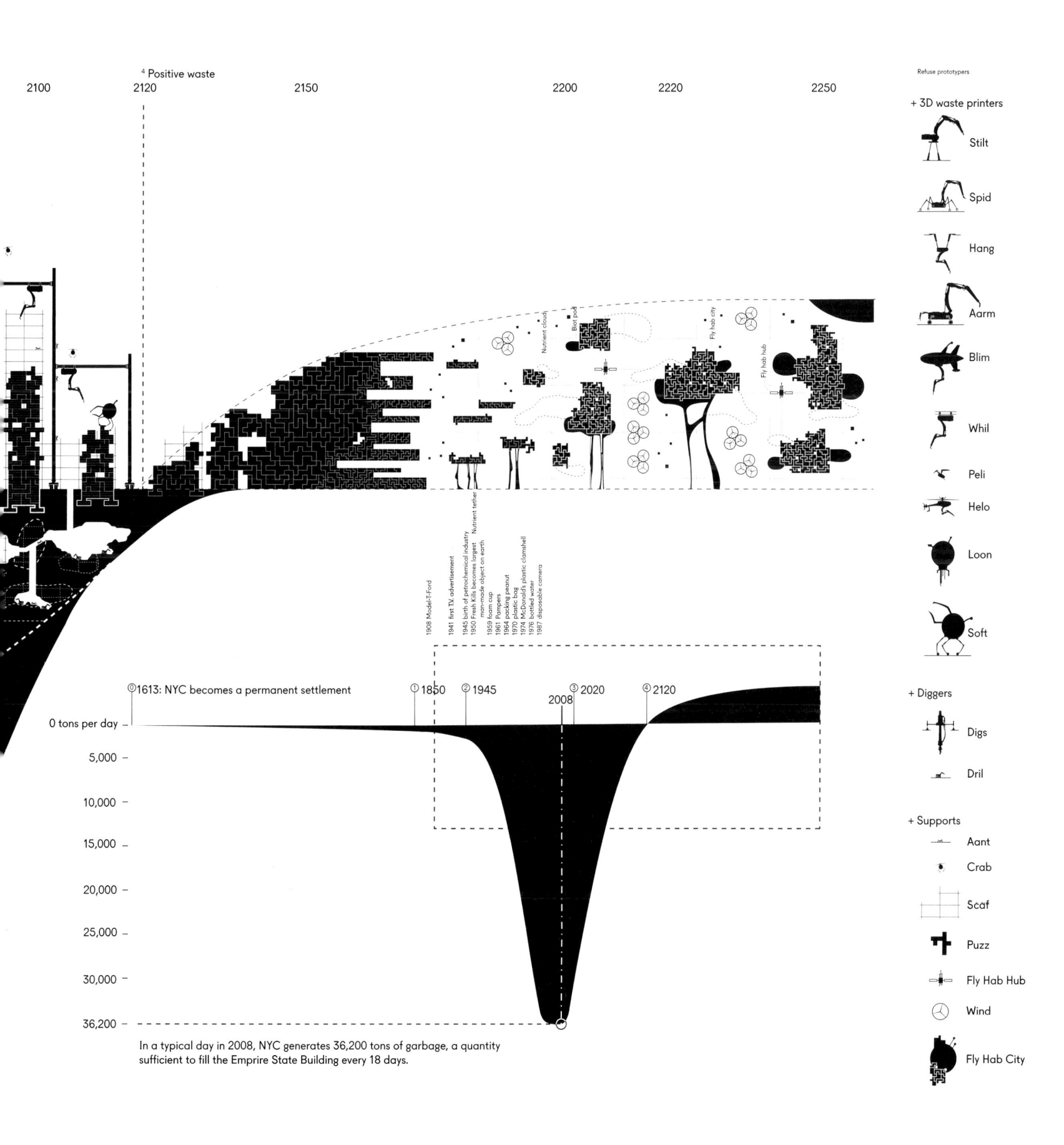

Refuse prototypers

+ 3D waste printers
- Stilt
- Spid
- Hang
- Aarm
- Blim
- Whil
- Peli
- Helo
- Loon
- Soft

+ Diggers
- Digs
- Dril

+ Supports
- Aant
- Crab
- Scaf
- Puzz
- Fly Hab Hub
- Wind
- Fly Hab City

2100 2120 2150 2200 2220 2250

4 Positive waste

Nutrient cloud
Biot pod
Fly hab city
Fly hab hub
Nutrient tether

1908 Model-T-Ford
1941 first TV advertisement
1945 birth of petrochemical industry
1950 Fresh Kills becomes largest man-made object on earth
1959 foam cup
1961 Pampers
1964 packing peanut
1970 plastic bag
1974 McDonald's plastic clamshell
1976 bottled water
1987 disposable camera

⓪ 1613: NYC becomes a permanent settlement   ① 1850   ② 1945   2008   ③ 2020   ④ 2120

0 tons per day
5,000
10,000
15,000
20,000
25,000
30,000
36,200

In a typical day in 2008, NYC generates 36,200 tons of garbage, a quantity sufficient to fill the Empire State Building every 18 days.

P. CHPT. IV

Project Title:
CASA PULPA
Architect:
Hodgetts + Fung Design and Architecture
Envisioned Project Location:
Applicable world-wide
Envisioned Completion Date:
The near Future

WHERE AND WHEN
Casa Pulpa was created in response to the global crisis in housing. The project has found a way to provide shelter to families in developing countries on a *where-needed, when-needed* basis. By utilizing the machinery to process waste and convert it into a form which could be molded to useful configurations, Hodgetts+Fung speculated that a "nomadic housing production factory" might literally go where ever needed, acting as a hybrid collection facility and production resource. The *Pulpa* would leave behind components which local labor could assemble.

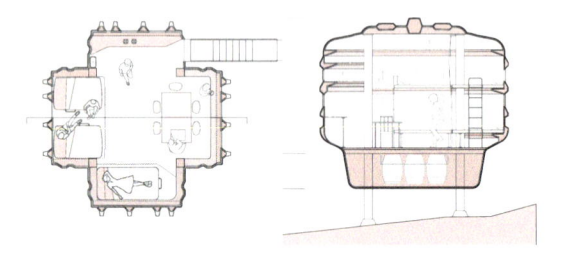

BASIC CONDITIONS
As has been well documented, there are vast areas in places such as Sierra Leone and Luanda, where waste has accumulated with little or no prospect for reclamation. The materials and design of *Casa Pulpa* were conceived to tap into this resource, while avoiding the additional costs of transport and processing normally associated with remediation and recycling. With the knowledge that there are hygienic concerns which obviously have to be addressed, the architects envision a "train" of vehicles operating in unison to sort, pulp, sanitize, enrich, apply, mold, dry, and assemble building panels. The panels themselves are conceived as incorporating simple interior amenities, such as ledges, shelves, and apertures which can be employed however the resident choose. Furthermore, panels are designed to be three-dimensional architectural elements which incorporate roofing, walls, and other features into a single, molded component.

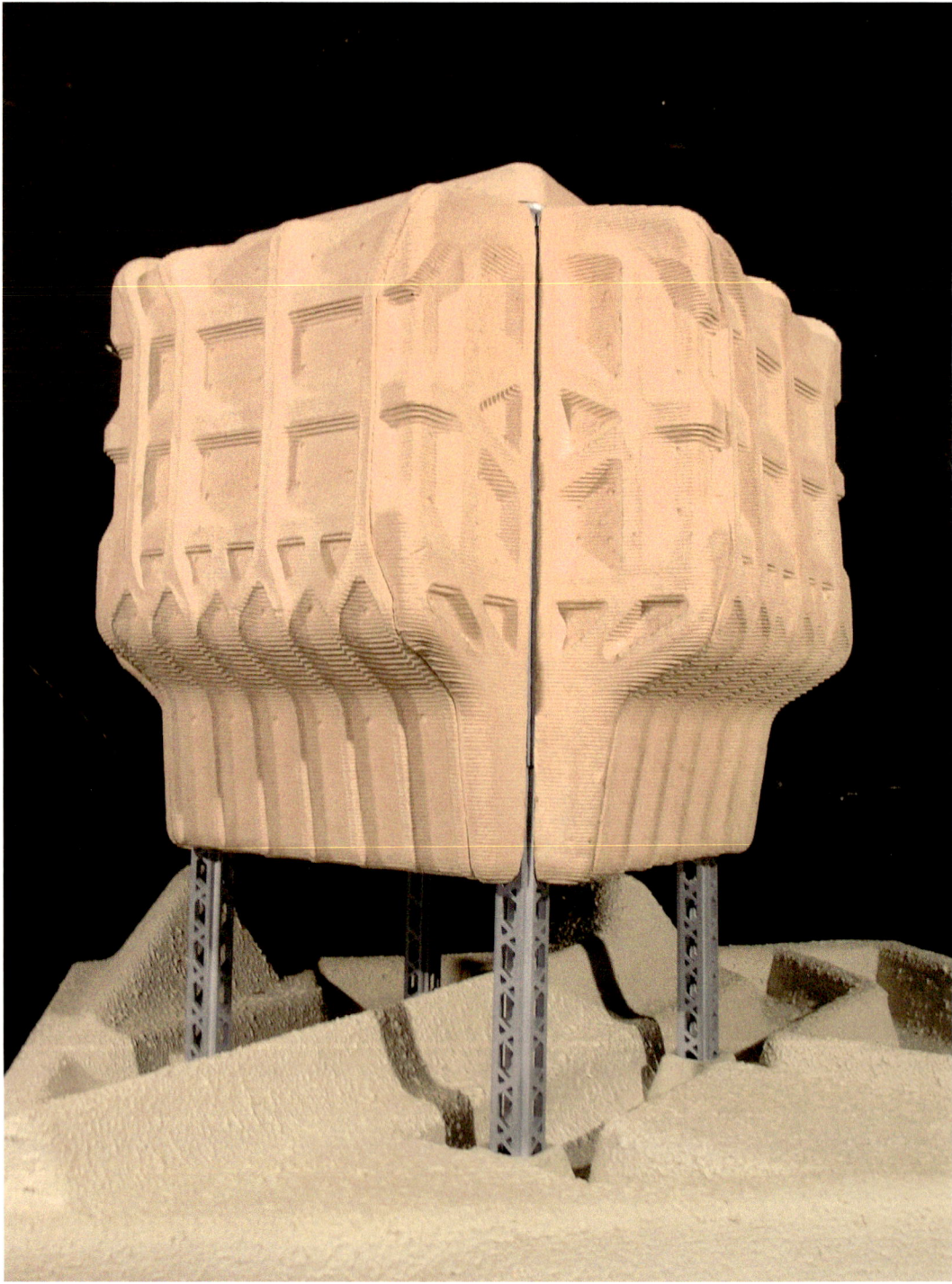

KEY PRINCIPLES
The configuration of the project reflects Hodgetts+Fung's research into the structural properties of pulp, which indicated a surface deformation which mirrors and defines anticipated stress patterns. Using these principles, it was possible to design the pulp shell with useful attributes, which also provides structural integrity. A lightweight steel sub-frame formed from 13 mm diameter steel rods, creates a network of attachment possibilities, which support the pulp moldings at strategic points. Thus, the aesthetic and structural objectives were not unlike those in comparable thin-skinned industrially-produced objects such as automobiles and aircrafts, which exploit the strength developed in monocoque structures to achieve both aims simultaneously.

Project Title:
UL-9205
Architect:
Mas Yendo
Envisioned Project Location:
Mobile
Envisioned Completion Date:
The near future

WHERE AND WHEN
UL-9205 is a compact and autonomous urban survival apparatus that shelters its occupants and provides them with a physical and a spiritual respite from the stressful modern world.

BASIC CONDITIONS
Modern science, politics, and economics have granted us an extraordinary capacity to abstract, understand and grasp the concrete realities of life. However, at the same time, this "abstraction" leaves us with a troubling sense of rootlessness and alienation. For those of us who live in dense, urban environments this anxiety is intensified even further by the alienating and cut-throat pressures of mass culture.

KEY PRINCIPLES
As a "zero anxiety" space, *UL-9205* creates atmospheres that are intended to restore the occupant's own sense of individuality and calm. *UL-9205* can be easily transported and installed. With a footprint of only 5,6 m² the pod would fit easily into tight spaces. Furthermore, no on-site assembly is required. To ensure the individual's privacy and autonomy, *UL-9205* would be clad with welded steel panels and designed to be as self sustaining as possible. The space would be soundproof—with absolutely no infiltration of noise from the outside world.

to incline up to 8%. An interchangeable, rotating footing-disk can be adjusted to individual needs, thereby completely eliminating the need for site preparation. The flatbed and the living space above it are connected with a 1,5 m ball-bearing platform that can rotate 360 degrees. The 37 m² of photovoltaic panels (PVP) would be able to adjust position in accordance with solar movements so that the panels would remain perpendicular to the sun's rays, and would produce enough electricity to power the unit. Water would be provided from condensation on the rear of the PVP. An organic-waste management system (OWMS) is able to decompose around 1,5 tons of human waste and other organic-waste material annually.

Project Title:
UL-9304

Architect:
Mas Yendo

Envisioned Project Location:
Globaly applicable

Envisioned Completion Date:
The near future

WHERE AND WHEN
UL-9304 is a mobile habitat and urban living-unit that could be situated anywhere in the world.

BASIC CONDITIONS
The bulk of Mas Yendo's work speculates on new technology and how it plays a central role in the way in which architects and planners embrace new ideas. The advancement and convergence of seemingly unrelated sciences, such as biochemical engineering, coupled with the growing consciousness of environmental issues, furthered by the development of computer aided design, served as an inspiration for Yendo's project.

KEY PRINCIPLES
UL-9304 boasts a living space of approximately 13 m² held on a flatbed chassis. Four hydraulically controlled footings at each corner allow the unit

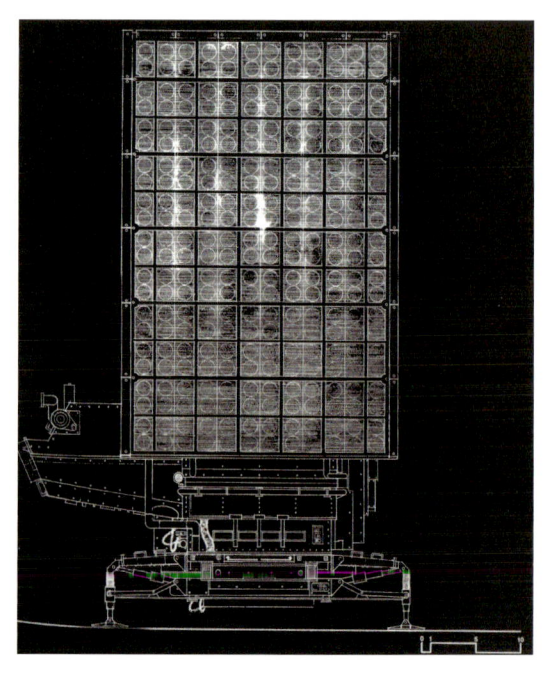

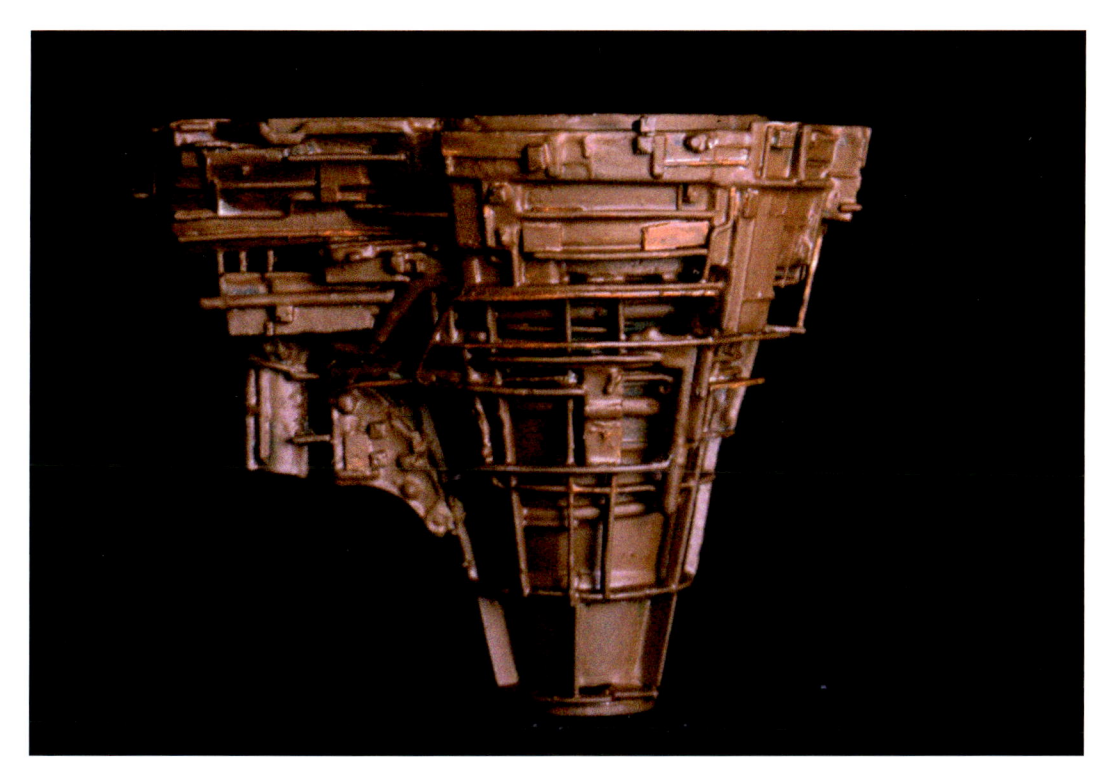

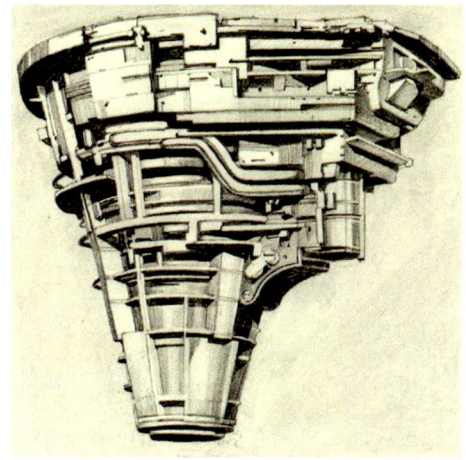

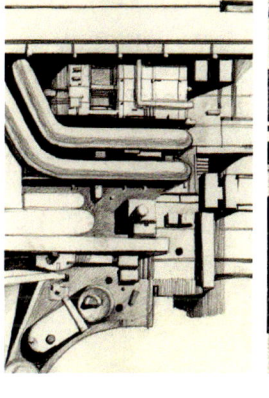

Project Title:
B1-9004 HOLE IN WATER

Architect:
Mas Yendo

Envisioned Project Location:
Sagami Bay, Japan

Envisioned Completion Date:
The near future

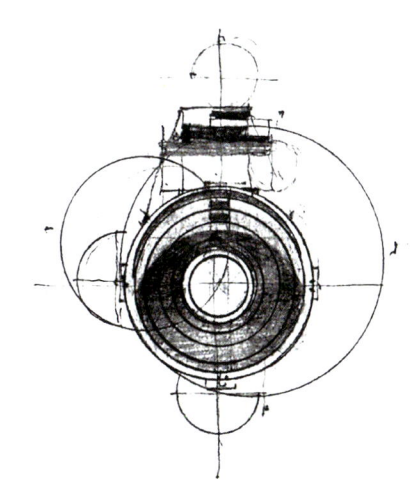

WHERE AND WHEN

Mas Yendo's *B1-9004* is an experimental prototype for the Sagami Bay ecosystem. This bay, which forms the lower portion of Tokyo Bay, stretches 113 km west of the Miura Peninsula to the town of Manazuru. The bay, which is dotted with sandy beaches and quiet fishing villages, is shaped like a bow, with the Sagami River flowing into its center. Beneath the sea, Jogashima, Kagemi, Enoshima, and Oiso Spurs spread like fingers to then drop abruptly, 1,500 m to the Sagami Trough Basin. 32 km south of the bay, the flow of the deep ocean current, known as Kuroshio, sweeps the Izu Peninsula and travels north. This particular current originates at the equator and brings along migrating fish and microscopic organisms with it. The combination of the extraordinary depth of the bay and the tropical ocean current fosters a diverse and highly concentrated ecological system.

BASIC CONDITIONS

Sagami Bay's proximity to Tokyo, coupled with a convenient mass-transit system that includes the world's fastest bullet-train, has resulted in the recent increase in population and land use. The environmental impact of this development on the bay area's ecosystem includes beach erosion, pesticide contamination, and sewage run-off. This has obviously had dangerous effects on the system's macrobiotic organisms, barnacles, plants, crustaceans, birds, mammals, and fish. Multiple artificial reef systems would be required to reverse this destructive trend. The project, *B1-9004*, is also a reaction to the usual methods of preserving and designating natural reserves. These methods (parks and reserves for example) may halt further development, but they are largely already overdeveloped. Furthermore, when one considers our advanced understanding of the complexity and interrelated structure of nature in its entirety, such bureaucratic efforts seem fragmented and ineffectual.

KEY PRINCIPLES

B1-9004 would have a radius of nearly 6 km, and self-gyrates 24 times per hour. A satellite positioning device (GPS) and three on-land markers that activate multiple jet-thrusters would keep *B1-9004* stable on all its axes. The project is a large artificial reef system that would maximize the ocean's capacity to renew itself and sustain life. It encourages macrobiotic activity by pumping air through nearly 145 km of pipes that wrap around its perimeter. This process would result in the growth of crustaceans and barnacles, which, in turn, would lead to habitation by larger organisms. Eventually *B1-9004* would be completely covered with living organisms to form a wonderfully complex eco-environment.

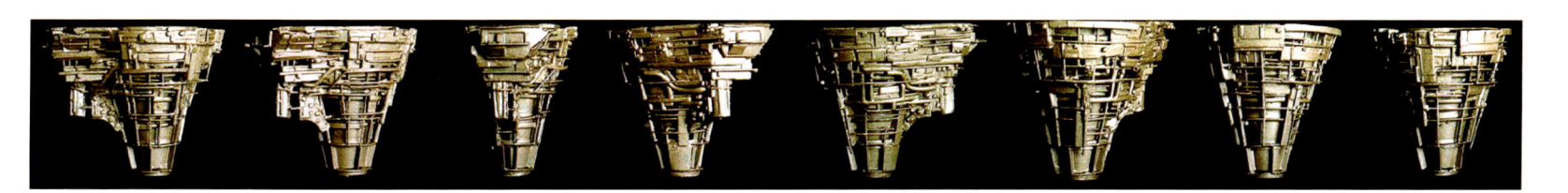

Project Title:
The Big Mech & Co

Architect:
amid.cero9 (Cristina Díaz Moreno & Efrén García Grinda), with Colectivo Cuartoymitad

Envisioned Project Location:
Madrid, Spain

Envisioned Completion Date:
2008–2026

P. CHPT. IV   175

Serie 01: Digital deconstruction platform

WHERE AND WHEN

The scene is set in the Gran Via in Madrid, where there will be cyclical periods of destruction conducted by the *Big Mech & Co.* machines. The premise of the intervention, by amid.cero09, is directly related to the most interesting and also the most disturbing images of Gran Vía, which depict the destruction of the Spanish city. The images illustrate a fascinating scenario of systematic demolition overlaid with the quotidian scenes of ordinary life in a typical European capital. Madrid's Gran Vía is not much more than one of the many small-scale replicas of the transformed center of Paris undertaken by Georges-Eugène Haussmann during the Second Empire. In a process of forced removals of the population, the working masses of Paris were displaced and banished to the periphery: an attempt also to control rioting and to facilitate the mobility of the repressive force. One of the most fascinating attempts at self-governance during European history, the *Paris Commune,* was crushed with astonishing ease, thanks in part to Haussmann's surgical engineering of urban space; his dissections and amputations. This clinical social engineering can be read as a brutal example of what the Austrian economist, J.A. Schumpeter, called the innovative process of destruction: "Capitalism is nothing more than a constant process of creative reorganization regulated by cyclical periods of destruction."

BASIC CONDITIONS:

By extrapolating the urban concepts of Haussmann in time; turning around and purging them of any clinical or repressive elements, the destruction of the Gran Via could become an incubator of "freedom-spaces," exhumed from their coffins and brought back to life with the communards. In the late nineteenth century, the city was widely regarded as sick, antisocial, dangerous and unsightly; a toxic and corrupt place that needed to be tamed, cured and beautified through purifying destruction. Cities can be regarded as nothing but a continuous process of construction and demolition that sees cultural, economic, and social opportunity of renewal in selective destruction. Amid.cero9 imagines the extension of the process of the Gran Vía today by converting it into a kind of anti-replica. It looks for opportunities in the destruction of the urban fabric and the treatment of its waste, in order to create a reverse process of urban transformation, which could utterly transform the city. One could "celebrate" the destructive process as inverted constructions and convert them into a standardized, creative, and inclusive process. One could then test the new concept of public space, merging it into an architecture, set in the cultural world of urban social groups and subcultures.

KEY PRINCIPLES

Four series of gigantic machines would consume buildings and spew out monuments and ecosystems. The first series would be digital "de-fabricating" machinery of buildings and infrastructure, while the second would chew buildings and would crush any materials. The *Landscape Plotters,* the third series would plant, irrigate, and compost a new landscape on the destructed landscapes. The final process would create topography from the destruction and fabricate *Instant Monuments.* A huge destruction mechanism, classification process, fermentation and plantation will transform the toxicity of the urban fabric in strips of ecosystems and *Instant Monuments*. In the void left from the destruction, local organic communities will erect buildings that will respond to emerging social groups and urban subcultures. Madrid will gradually be destroyed. Thereby, the architects question whether a review of the "Haussmann" treatment of Gran Vía II, and the conversion of its waste might become a viable alternative to the toxicity and the substandard quality of the 10,000,000 m² of housing built in Spain in the last decade?

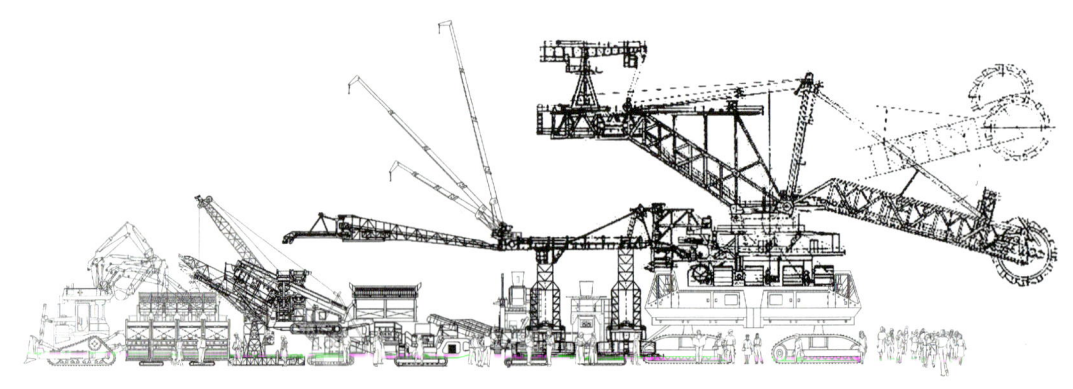

Alzado serie 02: Building chewer

THE BIG MECH & CO

TECHNOLOGY MATTERS

P. CHPT. IV

177

Project Title:
HYPNOSIS CHAMBER
Architect:
R&Sie(n) with Benoit Durandin
Envisioned Project Location:
Paris, France
Envisioned Completion Date:
2005

P. CHPT. IV

WHERE AND WHEN

R&Sie(n) together with the architect, Benoit Durandin, created the *Hypnosis Chamber* at the Modern Art Museum in Paris under the guidance of hypnosis specialist, Francois Roustang. The group set up a chamber where experimental hypnosis, individual sessions for the research, and an exhibition project entitled, *I've Heard About* took place.

BASIC CONDITIONS

R&Sie(n)'s investigative approach to architecture focuses on developing topographical experiments—cartographic distortions and territorial mutations—in order to explore the relationship between building, context, and humans. Each project is a process, a dynamic device which has the tenacity of a parasite that uses every means offered by its host, in this case architecture, to perform an ecologically useful function.

KEY PRINCIPLES

The *hypno-chamber* is produced as an indoor chamber, an immersion zone, where an hypnosis session has been registered that help citizens to escape from their alienated social condition. It has been created as an "hetero-topian" cognitive room, that allows the visitor dive into a "wake-up dream," filled by vocal information on a new kind of urbanism: artificial growth of extruded urban housing—both generative and robotic—where new cities are constructed using robotic processes by feeding and scavenging off the "carcasses" of the older, dying cities. Confronted with visions of urban-planning approaches, based on growth, and scripts, and algorithmic procedures, the visitor of the chamber, is supposed to feel like a nerve-ending inside the organic and self-determining, expanding structure. The immersive *Hypnosis Chamber* consist of video monitors, booking services, three-dimensional movies, and robotic drawings and plans that reveal the source-code of the generative program at the heart of R&Sie(n)'s work.

Project Title:
WATER FLUX
Architect:
R&Sie(n)
Envisioned Project Location:
Evolène, Switzerland
Envisioned Completion Date:
The near future

WHERE AND WHEN
For the *Maison des Alpes* and a public foundation, R&Sie(n) architecture studio proposed a project they called *Water Flux* as a design for an art museum and alpine ice-research station.

BASIC CONDITIONS
The organic, confronting architectural projects of the practice, R&Sie(n), are concerned with the relationship between building, context, and humans. The architect, François Roche, from the Paris-based firm, explains his concept of "spoiled climate," chameleon architecture, which links and morphs the human body to the body of architecture by creating a "re-scenario" of the rules of nature. The designers have used speculations and fictions in their design and thinking processes.

KEY PRINCIPLES
The *Water Flux* building is the result of a long process that moves from the initial digitization of the envelope of a traditional habitat, to carving out hollows within the volume as if it were an ice cavity, but in this instance in solid wood. As water and ice ebbs and flows according to the changing seasons, the building's ice façade freezes and melts and forms a pond in front of the building. The entire building is constructed by CNC machine-processing, five-axe drill in solid wood (2,000 trees, extracted over two years from forest upkeep) and reassembling the manufactured the 180 pieces on site. Furthermore, the project aims to re-activate the local economy in the region with 50% of the annual wood production of the region of Evolène village within two years.

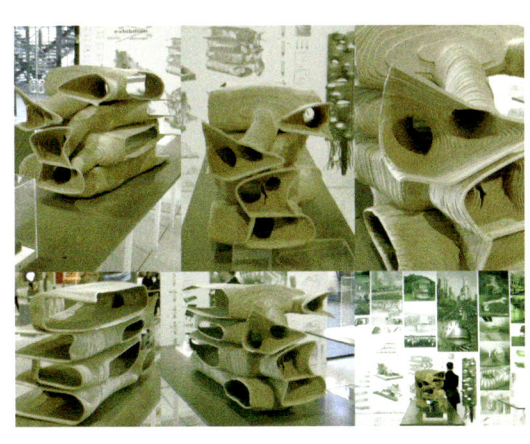

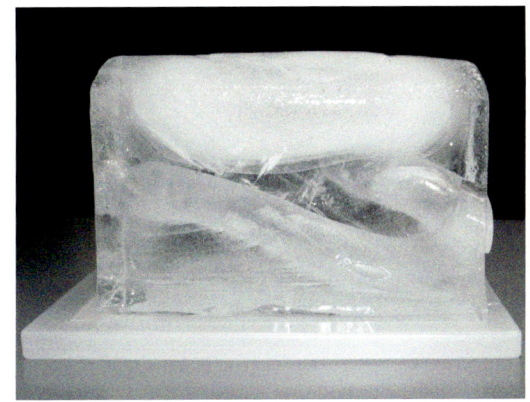

Project Title:
ECO-POD (GEN1)
Architect:
Höweler + Yoon Architecture and Squared Design Lab
Envisioned Project Location:
Boston, USA
Envisioned Completion Date:
The near future

WHERE AND WHEN
Taking advantage of the stalled construction site at Downtown Crossing in Boston, *Eco-Pod* is a proposal to stimulate the economy as well as to stimulate the ecology of downtown Boston.

BASIC CONDITIONS
Eco-Pod (Gen1) proposes a temporary algae bioreactor and new public venue built with custom-made prefabricated modules. The pods will serve as a source of bio-fuel, and as flexible micro-incubators for research and development programs. As an open structure which could reconfigure, the voids between the pods would form a network of vertical public parks and botanical gardens which would house unique plant species. Micro-algae is one of the most promising bio-fuel crops of today, yielding over 30 times more energy per acre than any other fuel crop. Unlike other crops, algae can even grow vertically and on non-arable land. The production of micro-algae might well be the only viable method by which we can produce enough fuel to replace the world's current fossil-fuel usage. Algae farming requires sugar and cellulose to create bio-fuels thereby simultaneously helping to reduce CO_2 emissions, since the algae replaces CO_2 with oxygen during photosynthesis. While bio-reactor processes currently remain in an experimental phase, recent advances in algae oil extraction and low-energy, high-efficiency LEDs, make the algae bio-reactor a promising prospect on the renewable energy horizon. In addition to being an active bio-reactor and a local source of renewable energy, the *Eco-Pod* would also be a research incubator in which scientists could test algae species and methods of fuel extraction, as well as new techniques of using low-energy LED lighting for regulating algae growth cycles. The central location of the *Eco-Pod*—the public and visible nature of the research—would allow the public to experience the growth of the algae and the energy production processes. As a productive botanical garden, it would

also function as a pilot-project, a public information center and a catalyst for ecological awareness.

KEY PRINCIPLES
An on-site robotic armature (powered by the algae bio-fuel) is designed to reconfigure the modules to maximize algae growth conditions and to accommodate evolving spatial and programmatic conditions in real-time. The flexible modular units would allow the structure to transform in order to meet changing programmatic and economic needs. The continuous construction on the site would transmit a subtle message of construction activity and economic recovery. *Eco-Pod* is an anticipatory architecture, capable of generating a new micro-urbanism that is local, agile, and carbon net-positive. This proposal envisions the immediate deployment of a "crane-ready" modular structure which could house experimental and research-based programs. Once funding has been found for the original architectural proposal, the modules can easily be disassembled and redistributed to other vacant sites, testing new proposals, and developing initiatives with other communities. Designed with flexibility and the ability to reconfigure the nodes, the modularity of the units anticipates future deployments elsewhere. An instant architecture, designed with an intention towards its afterlife, this is a "pre-cycled" architecture. In their ongoing, synergistic scenario, the growth of the algae propels, and is propelled by, technologically enabled developments that literally and metaphorically "grow the economy."

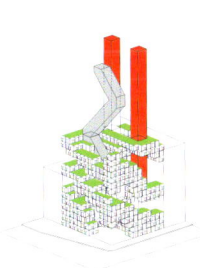

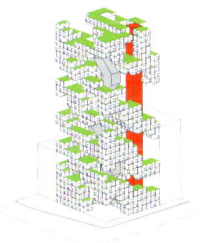

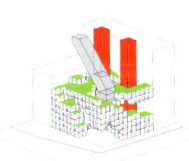

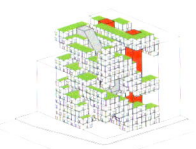

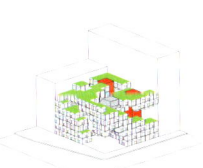

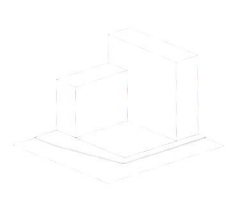

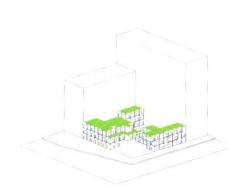

ECO-POD (GEN1)

P. CHPT. IV

Project Title:
CONEY ISLAND

Architect:
Squint/Opera

Envisioned Project Location:
New York, USA

Envisioned Completion Date:
The near future

186　　　CONEY ISLAND　　　TECHNOLOGY MATTERS

P. CHPT. IV
187

WHERE AND WHEN
Coney Island is a peninsula, in southernmost Brooklyn, New York City; it has a beach on the Atlantic Ocean. The area was previously a major resort and site of amusement parks that reached its peak of popularity in the early twentieth century.

BASIC CONDITIONS
Commissioned by The Municipal Arts Society in New York, these still images portray a fantastical projection of how Coney Island might appear in the future. Squint/Opera's creative impetus to create these images was to counter an existing proposal by a developer to turn the area into a condominium estate. Squint/Opera's desire for Coney Island to retain its former funfair/"pleasure-seekers" atmosphere that it is known for, as well as for a return to the levels of popularity it reached in its heyday a hundred years ago.

KEY PRINCIPLES
The concept calls for Coney Island to become the main stage for New York City, providing a platform for small and large performances and events in conjunction with its role as an amusement destination. The idea, which would include a variety of indoor and outdoor facilities, could be implemented immediately and would take advantage of the tracts of undeveloped land on Coney Island, a large portion of which is currently vacant or only operating as street-level parking. The concept also offers a thematic focus for the long-term redevelopment of Coney Island and creates a link to a point in the future when it could be implemented. By positioning Coney Island as a venue for small and large events all year-round, new visitors can be attracted, creating economic activity in the process. The concept, Coney Island, is intended to serve as a spring board to generate momentum for the district in the near future.

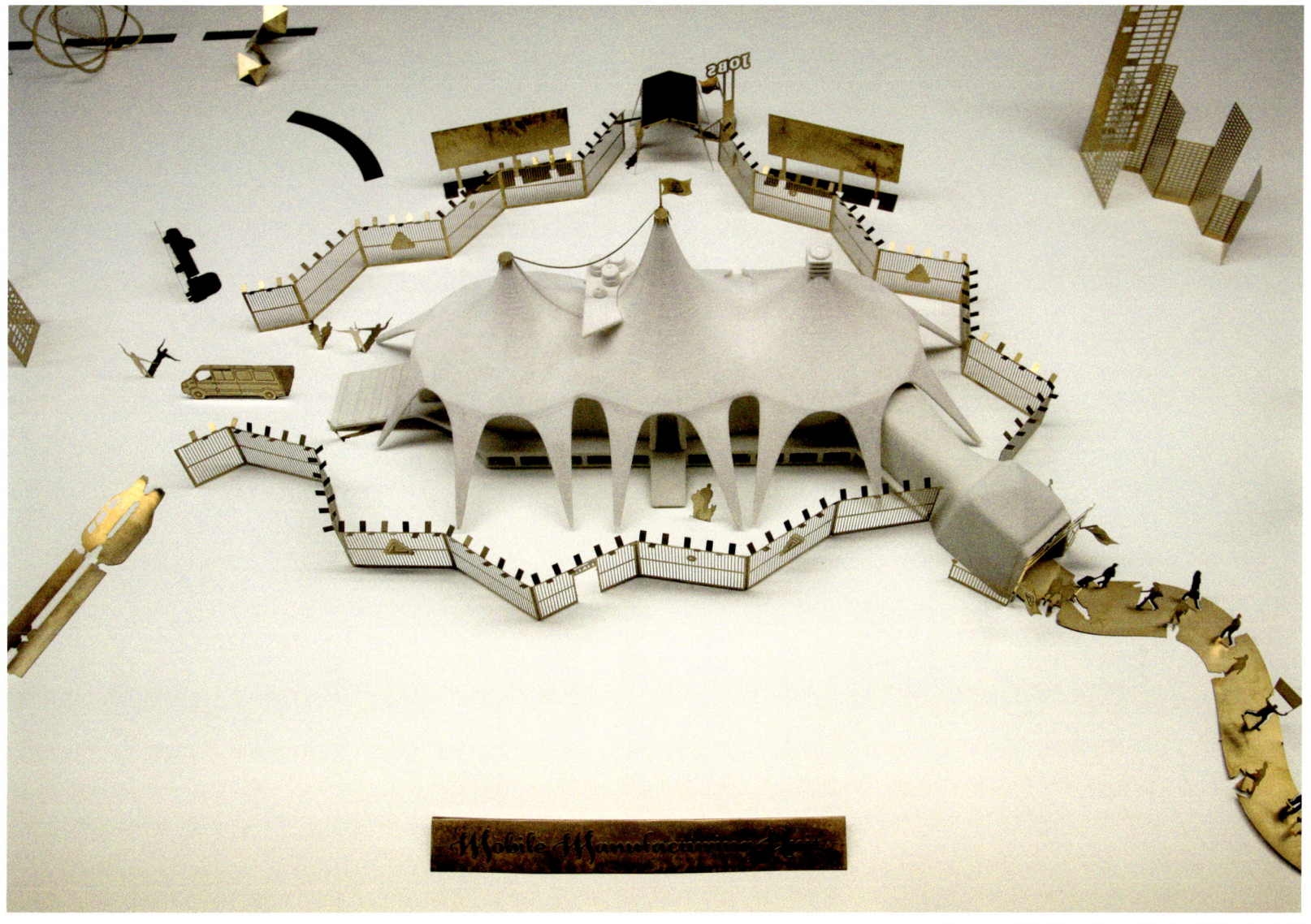

Project Title:
FABULOUS FABBERS

Architect:
David Benqué

Envisioned Project Location:
Anywhere

Envisioned Completion Date:
Anytime

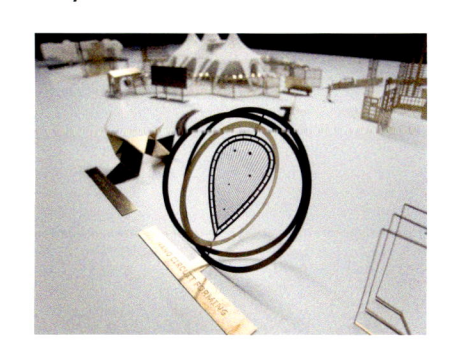

WHERE AND WHEN
This mobile manufacturing unit—commissioned by the Engineering and Physical Sciences Research Council as part of the *Impact!* exhibition at the Royal College of Art in London, in March 2010—will tour the country as a corporate factory, setting up in cities for a few months at a time. As the population welcomes a new source of goods, jobs, and manufacturing techniques, *Fabulous Fabbers* will be celebrated as an event.

BASIC CONDITIONS
Factories are coming into town! They are moving away from the unseen fringes, and into the heart of our cities. Advances in micro-scale engineering point to a global revolution where local, disposable factories will be able to produce hi-tech goods on our very doorstep.

KEY PRINCIPLES
Fabulous Fabbers wonders what shapes this new way of "making things" might take within our urban landscape. From garage-workshops to circus-like temporary structures, from street vendor stalls to vagabond encampments, this project explores factories of the future and envisions what our relationship to them might be in the future. It holds the exciting prospect of taking back ownership of the tools of our production.

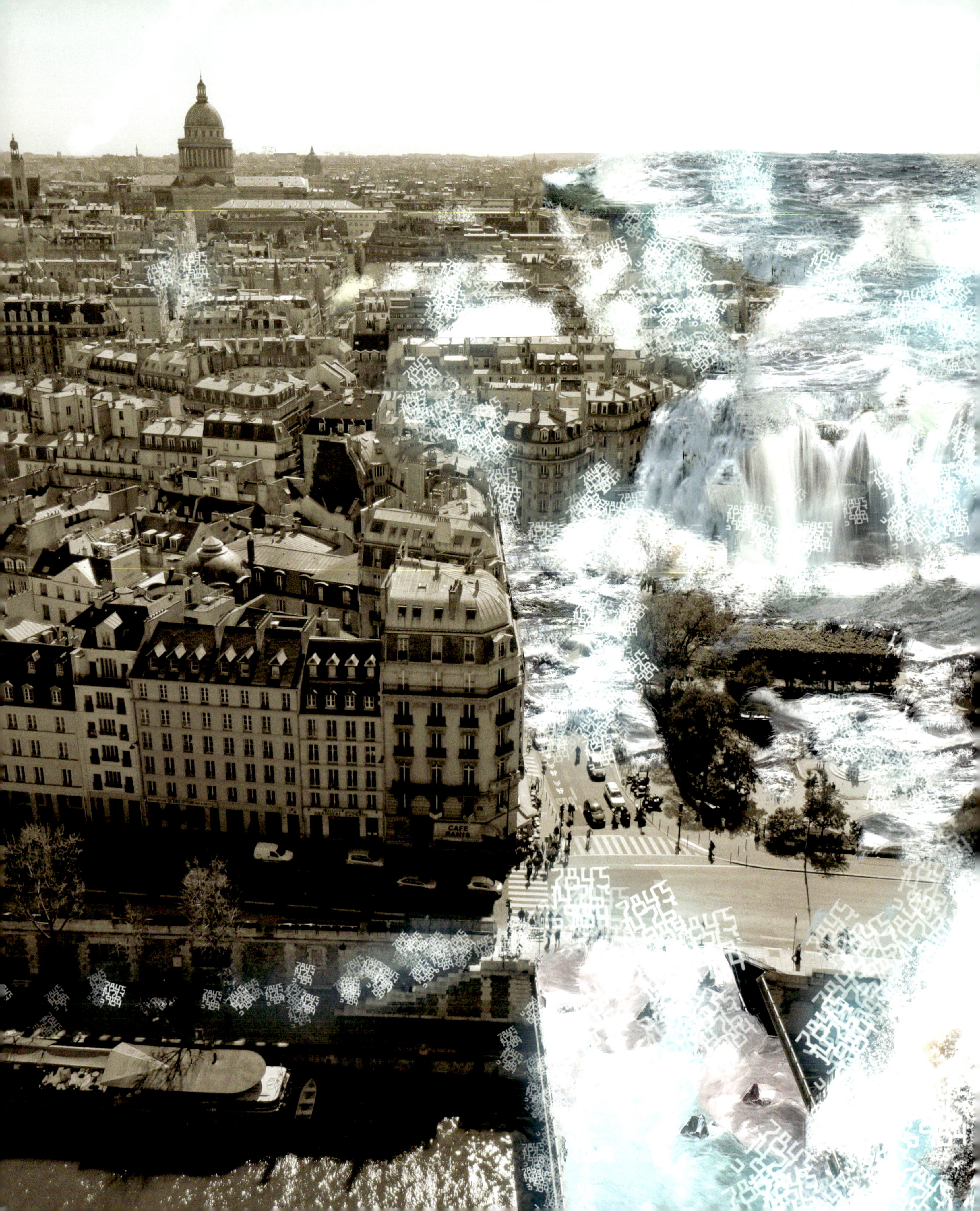

Project Title:
A.WAY
Architect:
J. MAYER H. Architects
Envisioned Project Location:
Across the globe
Envisioned Completion Date:
2030

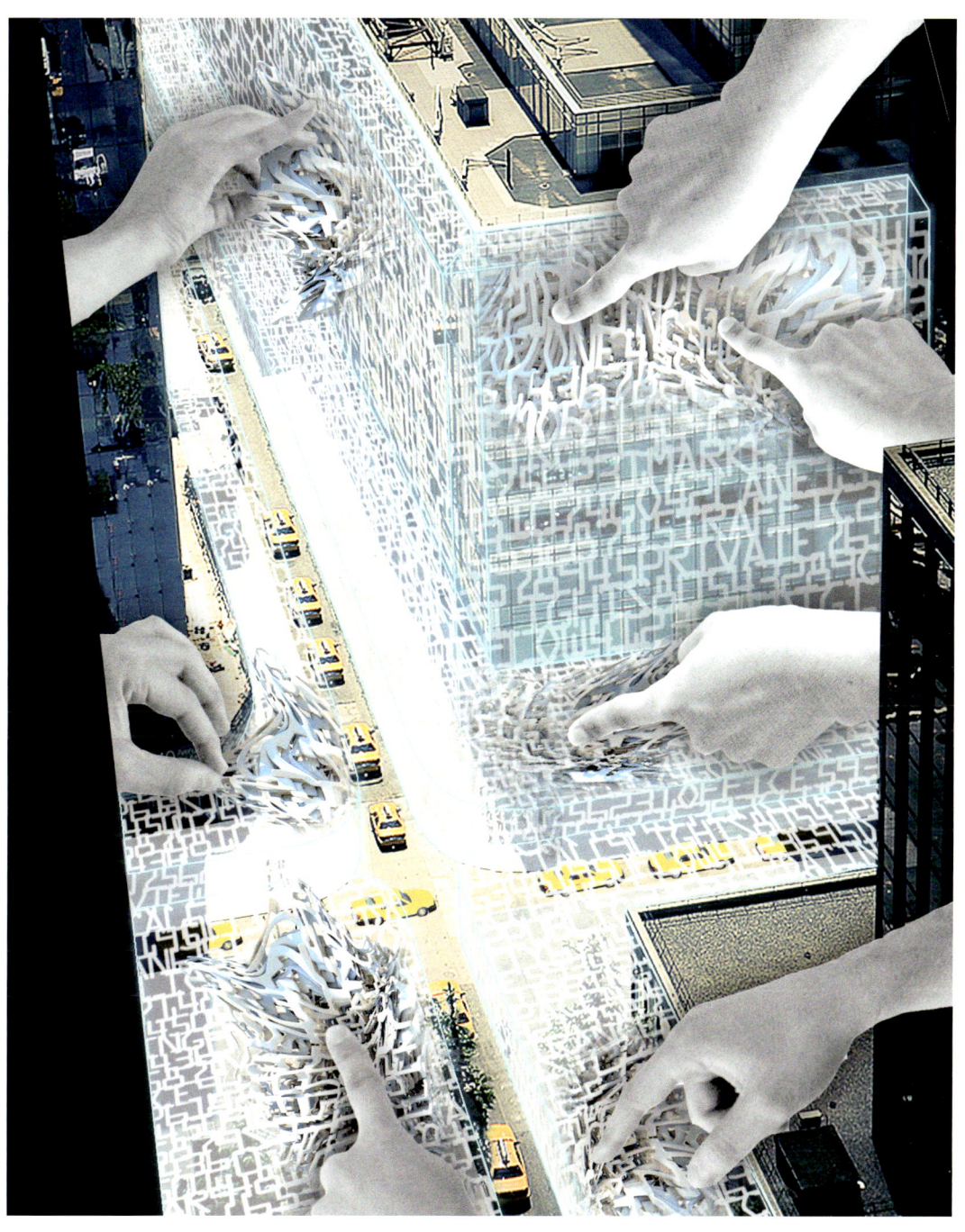

WHERE AND WHEN

The project, A.WAY, is a vision for mobility in cities in a couple of decades from now. The project was the winner of the *Audi Urban Future Award 2010—Building a Vision for 2030*. In the not-too-distant past, in the mid 1980s, scientists discovered a hole in the ozone layer, which forever altered the way in which we think about our environment and our future. From that time on, consumption, production, and mobility were regarded critically. With the proliferation of digital technologies in the early twenty-first century, and the fact that electricity is the main source of energy supply, means that our cities are free from heavy pollution and congestion; and have become more green, clean, quiet and efficient.

BASIC CONDITIONS

Visions of the future have always included speculation about mobility and transportation. Urban designs of the twentieth century proposed playful and sometimes even naïve visions of flying cars and underwater urban settings. Novel ways of zooming around galaxies, excursions to the center of the Earth, living in submarine worlds, time-traveling, beaming through different universes, tele-transporting, injecting and traveling through the blood-stream of a human body, populated our former visions of the future. Perhaps in the long-term, we might yet experience these fantastical modes of transportation. Individual mobility became strongly linked to developments of digitally augmented urban spaces, automated driving and personalized data-exchange between the human body and its environment. Traffic engineering since the twentieth century has been a constant flow of development. There was no longer any need for parked vehicles; pedestrian areas regained their place from cars. Repercussions were seen on a social, economic, as well as an ecological level. Surveillance and technology related to surveillance transformed the city and its inhabitants into a steady flow of data, blurring the boundaries between body, automobile, and architecture.

KEY PRINCIPLES

New forms of perception and performance have arisen from digital technology. Advanced technology has allowed each one of us to selectively accept, or reject, individual aspects of the city. The car has transformed from being a viewing machine for maneuvering in traffic, towards a sensory machine. Driving through the city today puts our senses and sensibilities into the foreground, and allows us to interact with the urban context in completely new ways. We interact, we move along temporary roads, we float through the city in automobiles which have been turned into a mode of social media. This instant personalization caters for anyone's interest. One is on the move, one is here and there. There remains the possibilty of a collapse of all systems that might come as a surprise, and that will keep us going, and force us to improvise, invent, and advance. If, at that point, cities prove once more to be flexible, adjustable, and able to transform and survive, then we will live "happily-ever-after" under a protective ozone layer again

Project Title:
NEW CITY

Architect:
Greg Lynn Form, Peter Frankfurt, Alex McDowell, and Imaginary Forces

Envisioned Project Location:
Online

Envisioned Completion Date:
Continuously updated

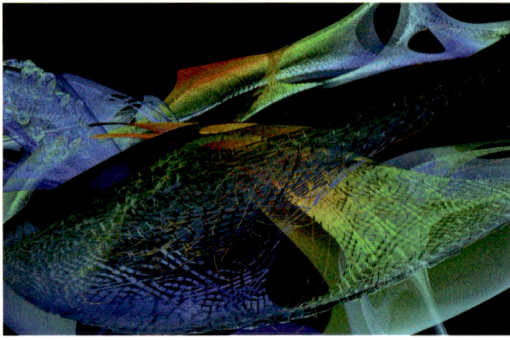

WHERE AND WHEN
New City regards the world as a city. Greg Lynn and his colleagues have mapped the topology of the earth onto a virtual, folded manifold. The architects have envisaged a denser, more connected, urban place of historical, geographical, architectural, economical, cultural, social, and intellectual intersections and interactions. Real-world data creates architecture in a constant, unpredictable, evolutionary manner. The team imagines a place that would dissolve the boundary between the real and the virtual. The *New City* would be experienced as all-encompassing but not fantastical. The project would change the world as we experience it currently. It would be a place of science fiction, a cinematic playground of discovery that would be virtually human, where untold stories would unfold to create dynamic new histories.

BASIC CONDITIONS
New City represents a place that would merge and erase borders. The movement and behavior of its inhabitants would reflect the dynamic motion in, around, and through the city. The unique social characteristics of the real world would be dynamically merged and mixed into new unpredictable syntheses. The scheme would provide a way to experience and populate a new architecture, which would be built to reflect the physical laws of a manifold city in motion. *New City* would be simultaneously diurnal and nocturnal. Absorbing data from real and imagined worlds, it would engage and extend our perception and experience via continuous conversations. Here, mutable laws of nature would divulge new stories. Condensed into virtual space, *New City* is tangible yet not tangible, visible yet invisible, physical yet ethereal, and yet, nevertheless, clearly present.

KEY PRINCIPLES
New City is a model for today; a place of perpetual transformation and self-generation, a new way to reflect on our Earth. It represents a new blueprint of urbanism that would engage contemporary communication, density, lifestyle, and globalization, structured in an ideal urban and architectural space.

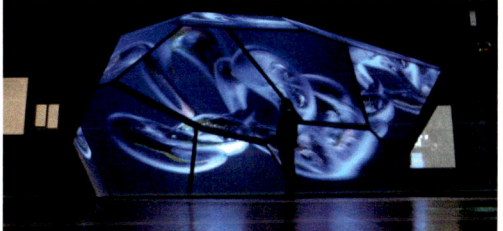

Gallery view of Greg Lynn's New City in Other Space Odysseys: Greg Lynn, Michael Maltzan, Alessandro Poli.

P. CHPT. IV 193

Project Title:
THE AMBER CLOCK FROM THE 200 YEAR CONTINUUM

Architect:
Christian Kerrigan

Envisioned Project Location:
West Sussex, U.K.

Envisioned Completion Date:
Sometime

WHERE AND WHEN
In Kerrigan's visual narrative, *The Amber Clock*, he constructs a fictional project of constructing a ship over two centuries on the site of Kingley Vale in West Sussex in one of the last remaining yew forests.

BASIC CONDITIONS
Defined as a symbiotic, fictive performance, the development of a ship over 200 years, the *Amber Clock*, displays the choreography between a natural system of growth and the artificial presence of human-made interventions.

KEY PRINCIPLES
Using three-dimensional drawing technology and historic references to the existing site, combined with professional "dendro-chronological" expertise, Kerrigan creates an integrated description of this mythology. The weave of the myth consists of the descriptive fictional-narrative written alongside drawings to contextualize the description by depicting typological characteristics for each stage of the mythology. As such, Kerrigan explores the possibilities of time in relationship to technology and the natural world. In his narrative, artificial and natural systems are choreographed. The natural production of resin is harvested from the yew trees as a novel way of measuring time.

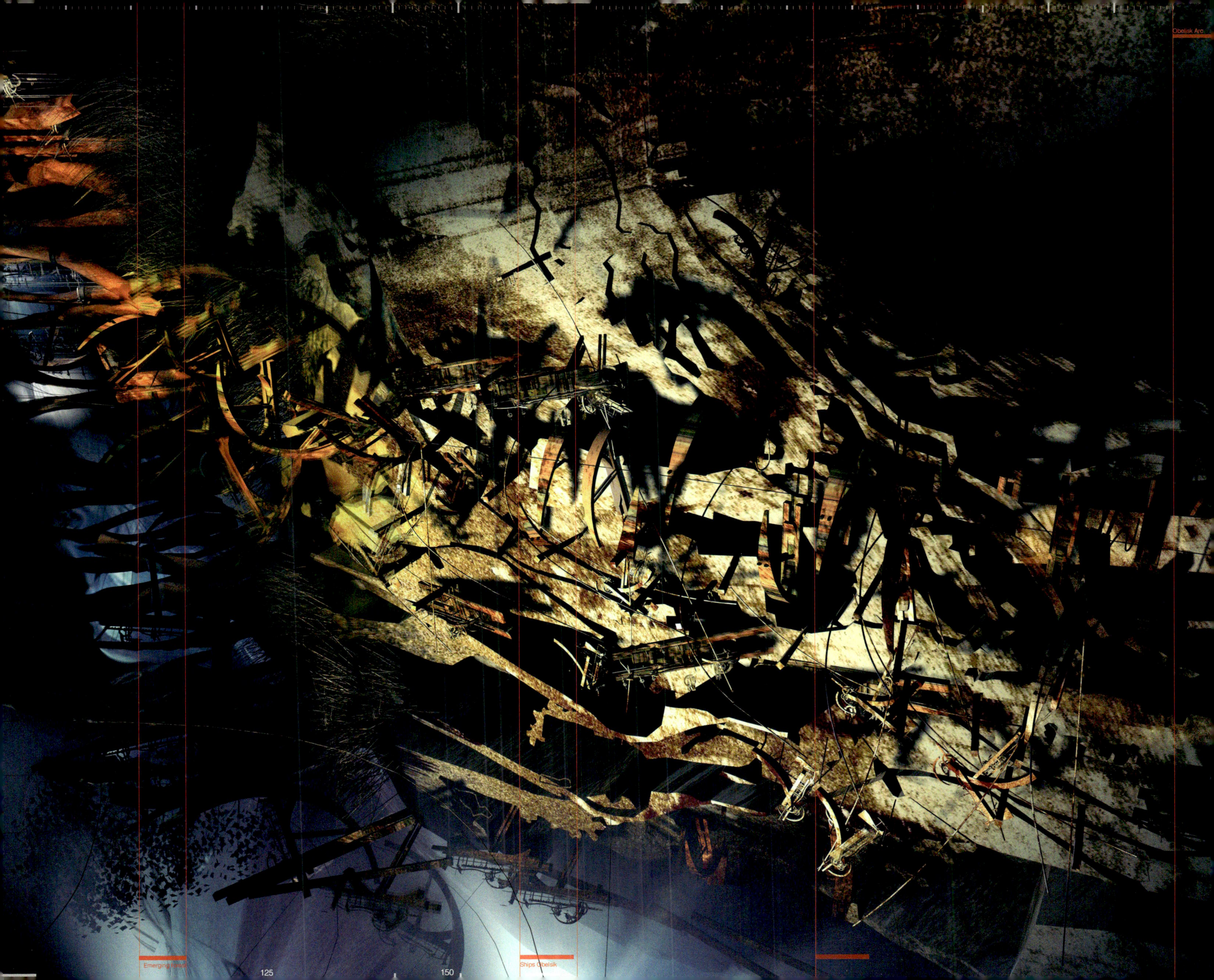

Obelisk Arc
Emerging forest
125
150
Ships Obelisk

Project Title:
THE INDUSTRIALIST MONKS
Architect:
Dylan Cole
Envisioned Project Location:
Sirius 8
Envisioned Completion Date:
2389

WHERE AND WHEN
After the success of the resort city on the planet, Sirus 7, many of the laborers might well grow disillusioned with the hedonistic lifestyle of the tourists and wealthy visitors. They might choose to found a reclusive colony on the colder neighboring planet, Sirius 8.

BASIC CONDITIONS
The workers will found a civilization based on personal denial and higher, spiritual pursuits. The colonists will embrace the challenge of a raw, newly discovered planet to satisfy their new ascetic principles. They will start by drilling into the planet to harness the heat and energy from the large pockets of volcanic gas. Upon continued subterranean exploration, the workers will discover valuable minerals and ores, which will be used in the construction of the resort city on Sirius 7. Realizing that they will need certain goods to sustain their colony, they will start trading with Sirus 7. The trade will grow and industry will grow. Huge refineries and structures to house the workers will need to be built. Any aesthetic principles for the design of the resort city will be rejected in favor of pure functionality.

KEY PRINCIPLES
Many of the structures will actually be giant engines operating massive drills and pumps. All the exposed beams, pipes, and mechanics will have a kind of beauty of their own. Not all the workers will remain true to their original ideals. As with any religion or civilization, corruption will rear its ugly head. An upper class will emerge on Sirius 8, with charismatic leaders exploiting the more gullible workers. The ruling class, who will live in penthouse apartments on top of their skyscraper engines of industry, will become wealthy by skimming off profits and exploiting the monk's labor.

SKY HIGH

Elevating the Possibilities of Vertical Habitation

Taking the utopian idea to new heights, the chapter entitled, *Sky High,* engages in the discussion of vertical architecture and the city, and proposes advanced aviation systems for the future. The chapter explores the possibilities and the implications of high-rise living in all its kaleidoscopic, creative facets, and looks at new kinds of spatial and functional relationships between tall, habitable buildings and the voids between them. By "reaching for the sky," the intellectual flights-of-fancy of the projects featured here, somehow continue the never-ending design of the Tower of Babel, one of our primordial metaphors of architecture and construction. For instance Daekwon Park's modular system and its symbiotic superstructure for sustainable skyscrapers, Nicolas Mouret's power-generating 380-meter-high mobile tower, *Phyte,* "dancing" with the winds, or MIT's *Senseable City Laboratory's* proposal for a light-weight, transparent tower, created with a cloud of inflatable, light-emitting spheres. *The Cloud* is depicted as a delicate, yet robust, filigree of hardy high-tech components, its materials familiar, whilst their composition radically new and innovative. Some of the projects attempt to conquer gravity through air travel towards the final frontiers of space—the ultimate projection of all that is new and unknown—some of the other projects featured here fly even higher still. For example Studio Lindfor's reflections on self-sufficient machine-like dwellings—the *Cloud Skippers*—that would drift and glide in the clouds, all the way, to Anton Markus Pasing's massive super-structures entitled, *Autonomous Objects,* which would float in zero-gravity, Christian Waldvogel's extreme-case, *Globus Cassus* project, that presents a conceptual transformation of Planet Earth into a far larger, hollow world with an ecosphere on its inner surface, or Alicia Framis' all-encompassing, multi-disciplinary cultural investigation of lunar space in her project, *MoonLife.* This to name but a few of the projects shown in this publication: utopian projects that re-think concepts of architecture, city, and mobility in novel and refreshing heights of thought and creativity.

"ONLY THE SKYSCRAPER OFFERS THE WIDE-OPEN SPACES OF A MAN-MADE WILD WEST, A FRONTIER IN THE SKY."

REM KOOLHAAS

204. *Urban Forest* by MAD Architects
208. *Habitat Solare* by R Architects LLP (Kenneth Loh and Michelle Lim)
210. *Tower of Droplets* by Crab
212. *Valdrade* by metamorphOse
214. *Plug Out* by WORKac
215. *Locavore Fantasia* by WORKac
216. *Biornis Aesthetope* by Ballistic Architecture Machine
217. *Symbiotic Interlock* by MTS (Meta-Territory_Studio)
218. *Engineered Biotopes* by Anthi Grapsa & Konstantinos Chalaris
220. *Phyte* by Nicolas Mouret
221. *Beautiful Minds* by MAD Architects
222. *Superstar: A Mobile Chinatown* by MAD Architects
224. *Hyrdogenase Algae Farm to Recycle CO_2 for Bio-Hydrogen Airship* by Vincent Callebaut Architecture
226. *Cloud Cities/Air-Port-City* by Tomas Saraceno
227. *The Cloud* by The Cloud Team
230. *Zeppelin's Swarm* by Hector Zamora
232. *Cloud City* by Studio Lindfors
233. *Cloud Skippers* by Studio Lindfors
236. *Migrating Floating Gardens—Airscape Architecture* by Rael San Fratello Architects
238. *ChicagoSkyScrapesback* by Mila Studio (Jakob Tigges)
239. *Autonomous Objects* by Remote-controlled
240. *Moon Life Project* by Alicia Framis
241. *The Barbarian Spaceport* by NaJa & deOstos
243. *Inflatable Ice* by R&Sie(n)
244. *Luna Ring* by Shimizu Corporation
245. *Lunar hotel* by Hans-Jurgen Rombaut | Lunar Architecture
246. *Globus Cassus* by Christian Waldvogel

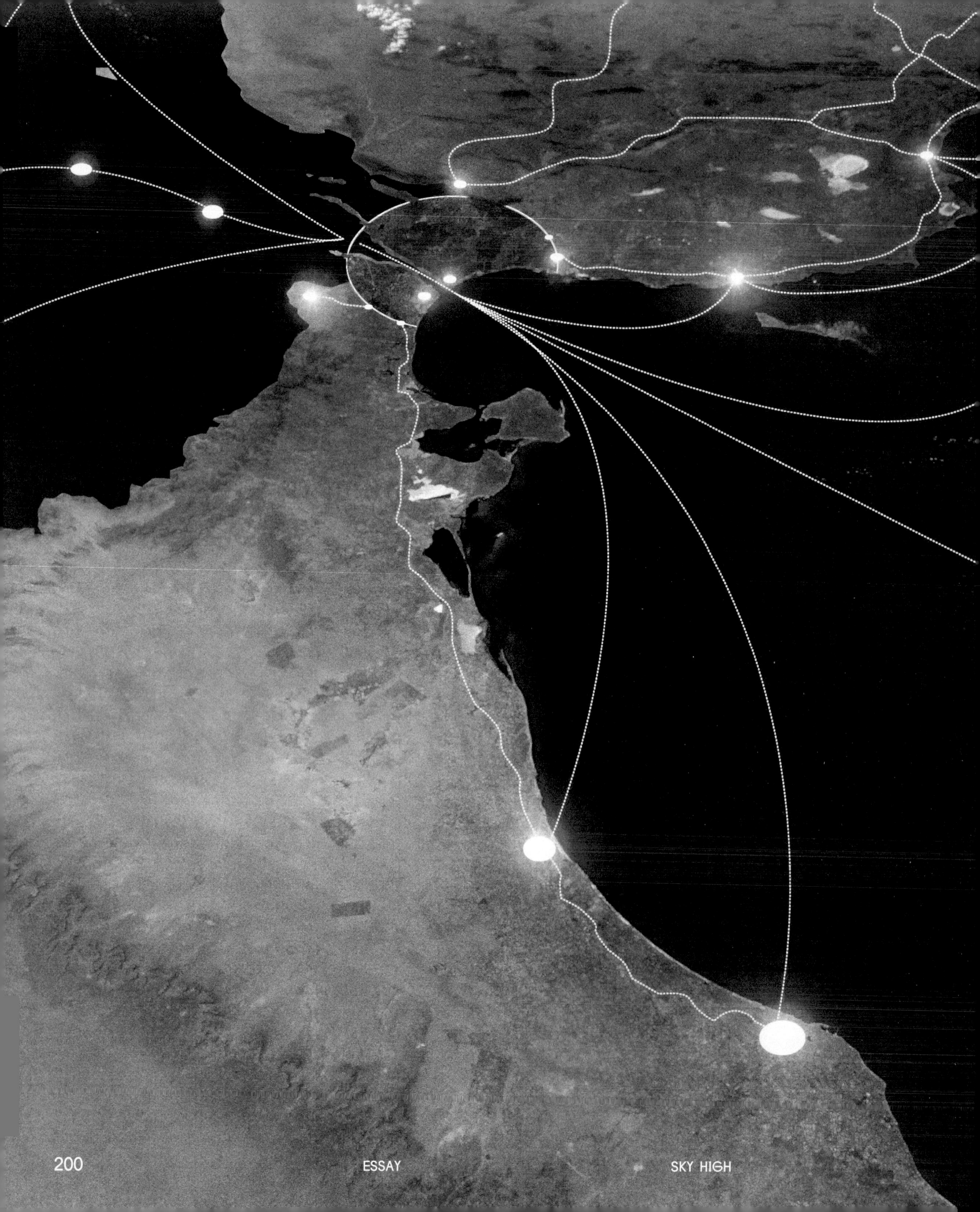

THE WHY FACTORY:
A Project on Visionary Cities

by ULF HACKAUF

Architect Ulf Hackauf focuses on the technical sociological aspects of innovation, resources, and planning processes. Since fall 2007, he has been teaching and researching at *The Why Factory (T?F)*, run by *MVRDV* together with Delft University of Technology.

Close your eyes and picture the city of the future. Do you see towering skyscrapers and flying cars? Or Robots? Advanced computers that can control the climate, the built environment, and human behavior? This is the standard mythology of the clinical, automated, technocratic, gadget-dominated future that has been conceived for us by science fiction novels, television shows, comic books, and Hollywood films. It is also the image of the future that has been seared into our popular consciousness. The far-reaching influence of these poignant images means that they go beyond merely depicting images of the future, and projects them further into the realm of actively determining the future of our cities. From Jules Verne's 1886 vision of man landing on the moon, to George Orwell's 1949 depiction of ubiquitous surveillance systems; what starts as a fantasy in the imagination of the creator, later becomes reality. Should architects and urban planners, not then be the creators of these fantasies and realities? The people who imagine how we will live in the future?

The Why Factory is a global think-tank and research institute, initiated and run by MVRDV in collaboration with Delft University of Technology and headed by professor Winy Maas. The focus of the Why Factory is the Future Cities Research Program, a series of models and visualizations for cities of the future. The Why Factory tries to reclaim the image of the future. It is a project; a campaign for visionary cities, and a studio for the production of research-based utopias.

A Larger Scale

Much of today's architectural discourse focuses on surprisingly small-scale projects. Previously the most successful project-architects were given the largest commissions, while smaller projects were given to architects, who worked on a smaller scale. Nowadays, it is no longer so. While Pritzker Prize-winning architects design vodka bottles and jewelry, unknown developer-architects design and build entire cities from scratch in the Middle East and China. Projects smaller than 1,500 m² dominate architectural magazines, whilst large projects of over 100,000 m² mostly remain in the shadows; out of the limelight. At a time of complex global challenges and paradigm shifts, the "small-scale" becomes a comfortable retreat. Architects and planners should, though return to the large-scale and address the challenges of big cities. There is a need for "utopia": for well thought out scenarios on a large scale rather than merely disconnected, small ideas.

The Lack of Vision

Visionaries have been working on utopian models of cities, countries or societies since Thomas Moore's 1516 novel, *Utopia* and Sir Francis Bacon's 1623 publication, *New Atlantis*. However, in the recent years, visions of utopias seem to have disappeared.

The search for future visions has all but been ceased in the current century. As quoted by American counter-culture writer Stewart Brand, best known as editor of the Whole Earth Catalog, in his publication *The Clock and the Library*, the computer scientist and co-chairman of the *Long Now Foundation*, Danny Hills observed in 1993:

> "When I was a child, people used to talk about what would happen by the year 2000. Now, thirty years later, they still talk about what will happen by the year 2000. The future has been shrinking by one year per year for my entire life. I think it is time for us to start a long-term project that gets people thinking past the mental barrier of an ever-shortening future."

For many years the enchanted, millennium year 2000 represented *The Future*. Once the year 2000 arrived, and after we had survived it, the will and motivation to speculate about the way we might want to live in the future receded.

Instead, images of the future became pessimistic. Overpopulation, climate catastrophes and finite resources shape the general somber image of the future. Images of what can go awry outnumber more optimistic visions of what is possible and what we might achieve. Today, *dystopia* seems, all too often, to win the upper hand over utopia.

The Power of Imagination

Utopias are not envisaged for entertainment, fortune-telling or a purely realistic prediction of the future. The power of utopia is to influence development and create future concepts. Once an idea is clearly described, it can become a goal to work towards. We have witnessed this in visionary literature, internet, space travel or endoscopic surgery, which were described by utopian writers like John Brunner, Jules Verne, and Isaac Asimov long before the technology was present to realize them. Visions are necessary to give technical and social development direction, and goals to work towards. Utopias have the power to become our future reality.

Model Cities

The Why Factory attempts to challenge this doom and gloom with the production of new utopian models of the future. Models that are more than "less," that go beyond negative restriction and dare to have a positive vision of the future once again. The architects do not ignore current global challenges. Today's problems and challenges have to be part of our future visions and are often catalysts for their solutions. But the visions should not merely illustrate the problem, they should also address how the problem might be dealt with in the future. At the core of the Why Factory's endeavors are *model cities*. Their *model cities* address global challenges and respond with complex images of future cities. Themes for model cities range from the *Sustainable City (Green Dream)* or the *City of Sufficiency (Austeria)* to urban visions on the future of the leisure society (*Death of Leisure City*) and speculations on the impact of technological innovation (*Robotic City*). A model city does not imply that the topic has to be approached solely on an urban-scale. Individual projects range from proposals for regional, urban networks, architectural interventions, to small, detailed designs. For each invention, the impact on the city is calculated and illustrated. The aim is to create a complete and complex image of the city of the future. The result is a project that is visual and illustrative on the small-scale, and that provokes discussion and debate on the large-scale.

Quantified visions

The Why Factory's *model cities* aim at creating visions, which are not merely for entertainment, but which have a relevant, meaningful impact in the public realm. Therefore, the cities need to have a scientific foundation. At the start of each *model city* project calculations are made and visual statistics are established. They illustrate the scale of the problems which the *model city* addresses. In the project *Foodprint Manhattan,* we calculated the total amount of food, which the city consumes daily and how much land is needed to produce this food. This initial step of visualization is already revealing and critically questions many small-scale urban farming projects, which may be effective in a social sense but do not provide a significant enough contribution to the total consumption of the city. The utopian designs that are generated use these calculations, which provide the *model cities* with scale and give them relevance.

A Factory for Utopia

The production of utopia requires rigorous, thorough work. Hence the name chosen: the *Why Factory*—a factory for future visions. Researchers and students work in collaboration on the recherche and design of these future visions. Technically, there is no pure course work which the students produce at the Why Factory; rather their studies form part of a larger framework. Being part of the utopian project gives the students' work a relevance to the wider world and more significance than a singular study can usually achieve. However, at the same time, it requires a collective effort and the ability to position their work in a larger framework. The research and design studios of the Why Factory, therefore tend to start with a collective exploration of a given topic. A lot of the work at the studio is done in smaller teams along with regular group discussions. This approach is often different from the previous experience of the students. It requires one to focus not only on one's own work, but also to see and to develop it in relation to the ideas and work of the rest of the group.

This collective approach also requires careful management and direction of the process. Common parameters have to be fixed, and it has to be agreed upon where the project will use real, current possibilities and where it will speculate on future developments. In the Why Factory's 2006 *Skycar City* project, the speculative assumption was that flying cars, as shown in utopian images since the beginning of the twentieth century, will be manufactured and widely available before the year 2030. This was the agreed assumption from which various studies developed: studies on the shape of the future flying vehicle, on the future of parking, the disappearance of streets and asphalt, and on the three dimensional complexity of the city accommodating five million people, which is based on flying cars. Besides the base component—the flying car—it was also necessary to agree on the setting of the urban vision: do people still travel to work or will they mainly work from home? Does the abstract city include production facilities, or is it a model of a service based economy? Factors which may be discussed in detail in other projects are fixed as a fundamental setting for the visionary project.

At some point, the utopian projects require collective editing. Whether the results are presented in a single event, an exhibition or in a publication, the utopian visions are shown as a kind of a narrative. The sub-studies require editing in order to find their position within the complete story. The visionary project can thus be comprehended by, and accessible to, a wider audience. Building the narrative and telling the story is integral to each studio. It allows for the utopian project to leave the realm of academia and engage the public in discussion, open a discourse, and paint a bigger picture that is worthwhile to work towards.

> *The Why Factory's Future Cities research programme explores possibilities for the development of our cities by focusing on the production of models and visualizations for cities of the future. The results of this research programme are being presented in a series of books—the Future Cities Series.*

Project Title:
URBAN *F*OREST
Architect:
MAD Architects
Envisioned Project Location:
Chongqing, China
Envisioned Completion Date:
The near future

scale urbanization on such a massive scale should ideally not only push economic growth and material prosperity, but also foster the evolution of the city's cultural essence. Chinese cities have gone through the process of starting from almost nothing, to high-speed development following contemporary Western urban patterns. Nowadays, the overall economic infrastructure has influenced the direction of future development towards inland China. MAD's project questions, how one might discuss the future of architecture in Chinese cities on the basis of an Eastern Naturalist perspective in the current context of China's unique economic, social, and global background. It asks how to give city dwellers the opportunity to experience nature despite the steady dwindling of its green zones in the face of the ever-growing concrete jungle.

KEY PRINCIPLES
Throughout the process of contemporary Western urbanization, skyscrapers were the symbol of technological competition, prime capital, and the formal "enslavement" of the powerful and the rich. Sustainable ecology became more of a demand for comfort; while the yearning for a return-to-nature was ignored. MAD's *Urban Forest* draws inspiration from the perspective of nature and human-made objects in Eastern Philosophy; it ties urban city life with natural outdoor experiences. The form of the architecture mimics a mountain, shifting in a dynamic, yet holistic rhythm, becoming a continuation of nature. Unlike its preceding counterparts, the *Urban Forest* no longer emphasizes the vertical force, it rather concentrates on the multi-dimensional relationships within complex anthropomorphic spaces: multilevel sky-gardens, floating terraces, and minimal, yet well-lit nesting areas. The architectural form dissolves into fluid spatial movements between air, wind, and light. In this environment, people would encounter nature bursting with unexpected surprises. The fusion between the spirit of Eastern humanism and urban public spaces pioneers the design of a sustainable multi-dimensional city. The *Urban Forest* will not merely be a piece of mediocre urban design, but rather an artificial organ that will live and breathe new life into the steel-and-concrete-filled city center.

WHERE AND WHEN
By the close of 2009, MAD had completed the concept design of a 385-meter-high metropolitan cultural complex in the city center of Chongqing: The *Urban Forest*. MAD proposed a new architectural concept for the course of Chinese urban development—to realize a sustainable multi-dimensional high-rise within China's newest municipality. The *Urban Forest* would allow nature to be incorporated into the high-density urban environment, to evoke a feeling for nature which was lost in the ancient oriental world and to bring it back to modern city dwellers.

BASIC CONDITIONS
To give one a clear indication of the incredible rate of economic growth in western China: the city area of Chongqing is more than twice the size of Beijing, Shanghai and Tianjin combined! Macro-

Open office plan

Duplex office plan

8 m structure line

6 m structure boundary

8 m structure line

Core

8 m   8 m

Structure strata

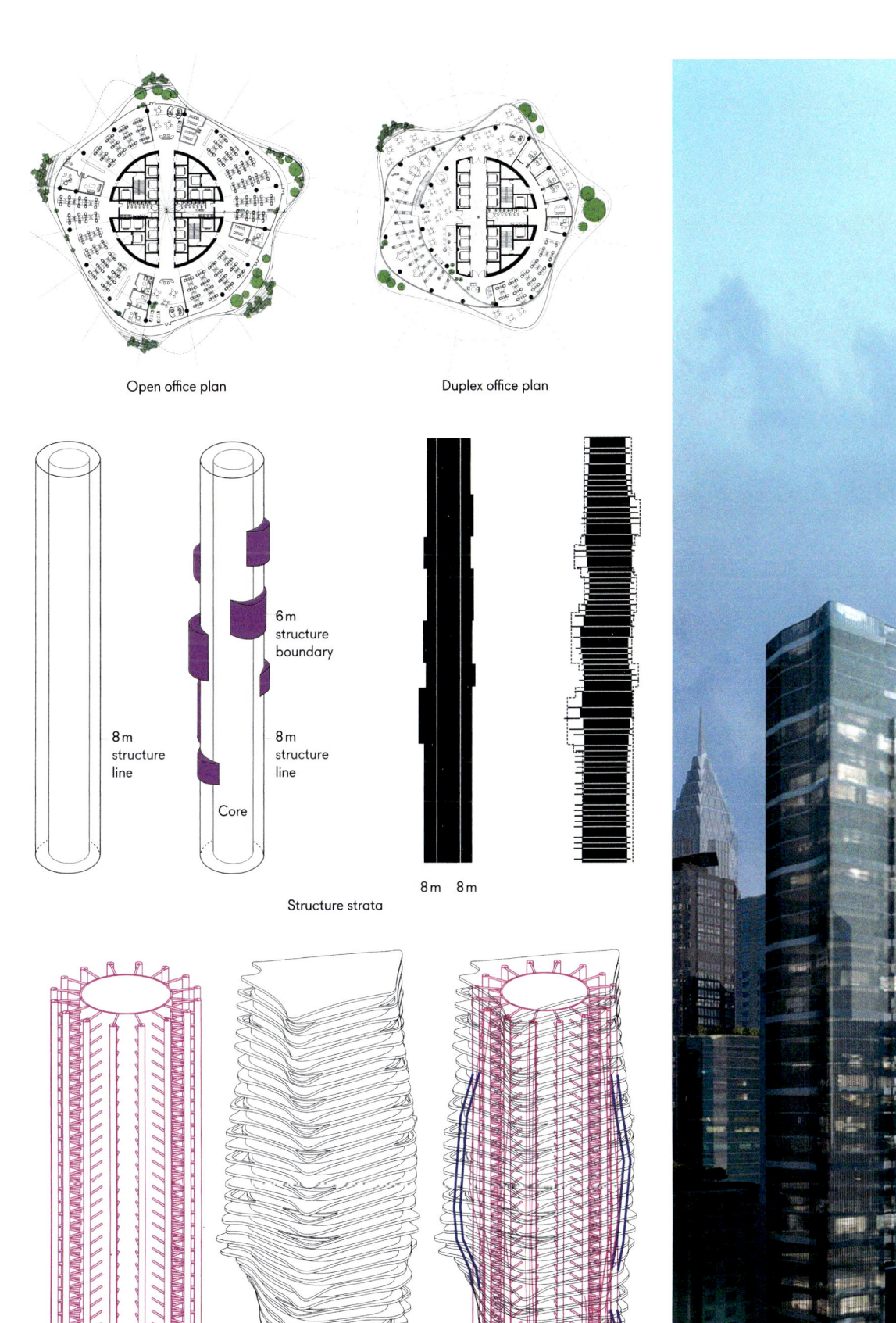

Conventional structure

Floorplates

Additional structure

CHPT. V

205

URBAN FOREST　　　SKY HIGH

CHPT. V

HABITAT SOLARE SKY HIGH

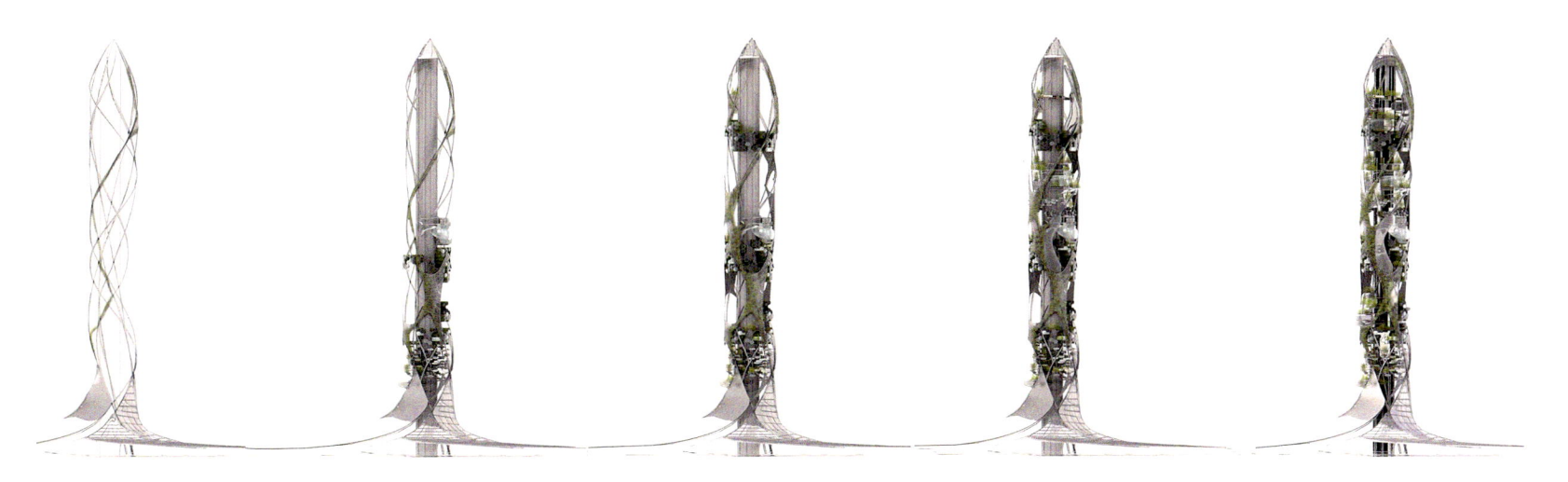

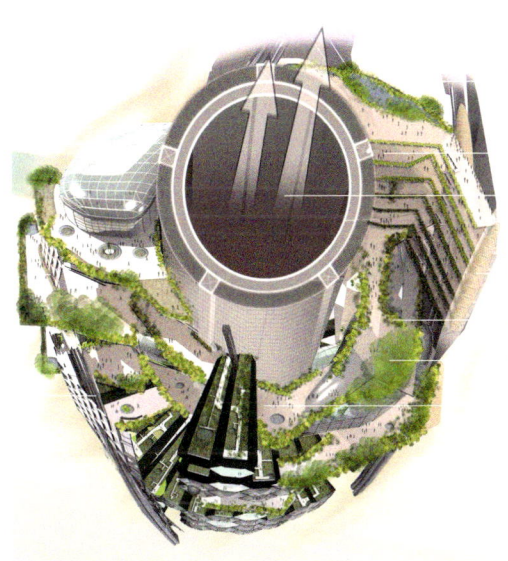

Structure labels: Dew/water harvester; Structural/splinal circulation paths; Service cores; Solar updraft core; Transport pods; Walk/ramp ways; Green buffer spaces.

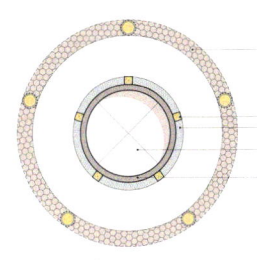

Structure callouts: Self-supporting fullerenes (secondary structural frame); Service lifts; Service core (utilities and support facilities); Thermal shaft; Solid hollow tube updraft tower (primary structural frame).

Structure

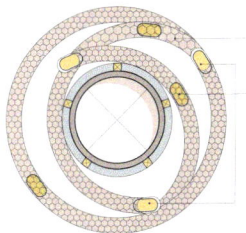

Transport System callouts: Self-supporting structural frame; Vertical splinal transport (transport capsules).

Transport System

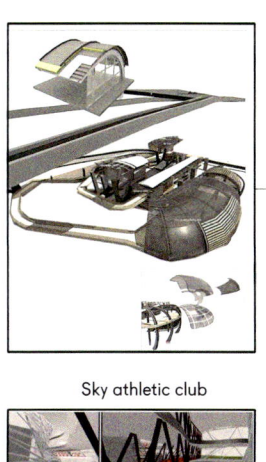

Sky athletic club

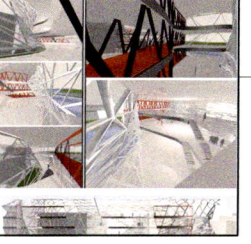

Exhibition center

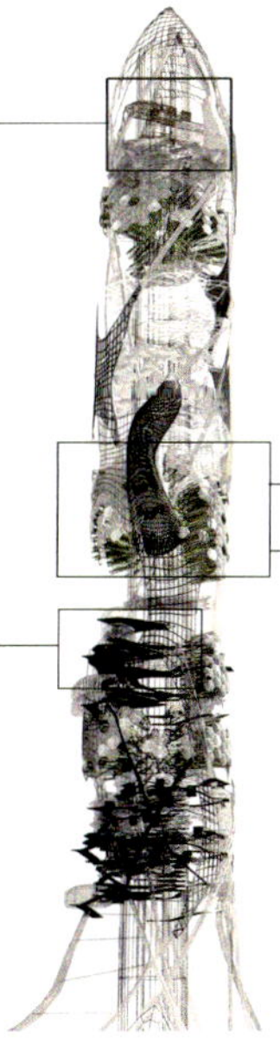

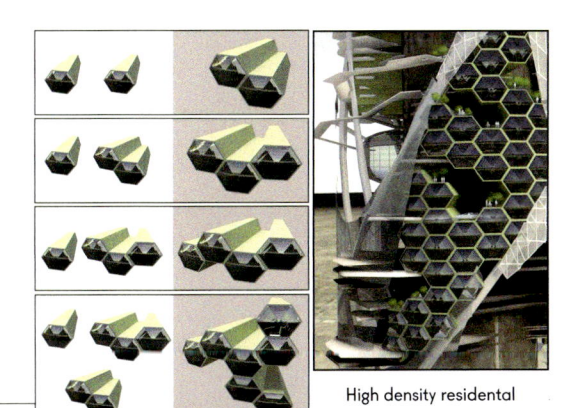

High density residental

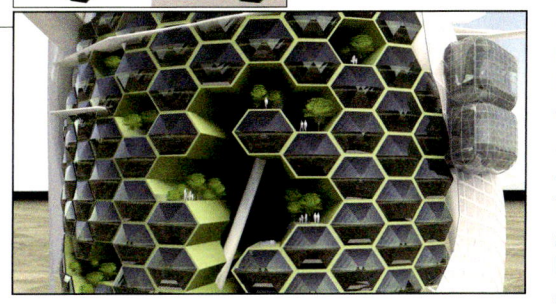

Project Title:
HABITAT SOLARE
Architect:
R Architects LLP
(Kenneth Loh and Michelle Lim)
Envisioned Project Location:
Globaly applicable
Envisioned Completion Date:
The near future

WHERE AND WHEN
Designed by Kenneth Loh and Michelle Lim, this project *Habitat Solare* is an investigation into a new prototype of solar-powered towers for urban settlements worldwide.

BASIC CONDITIONS
In striking imagery this project combines the ideas of a vertical garden with a mixed-use development plan. Ideally, the tower would grow and develop over years in an organic manner as the gardens and open space mature, leaving the exterior rather unstructured without any cohesive architectural presence. The designers' vision was that a series of these *Habitat Solare* towers could provide sustainable housing for urban environments, whilst also helping cool the environment.

KEY PRINCIPLES
The entire façade of the edifice would be covered with a thin membrane of solar cells as well as a water collector system. The main idea is to develop a green building with different types of functions. The building core would be a hollowed cylinder that would move hot air from the façade surface and create micro-climates for gardens, fields, and recreational areas. Residential units for low, medium, and high density would be attached to a continuous ramp or street. Along the entire structure there will be "pockets" of different sizes and materials for cultural and educational areas. The building would be connected to an underground cistern with a power plant. Rainwater would be collected, filtered, stored, and used to produce sufficient energy for the entire community.

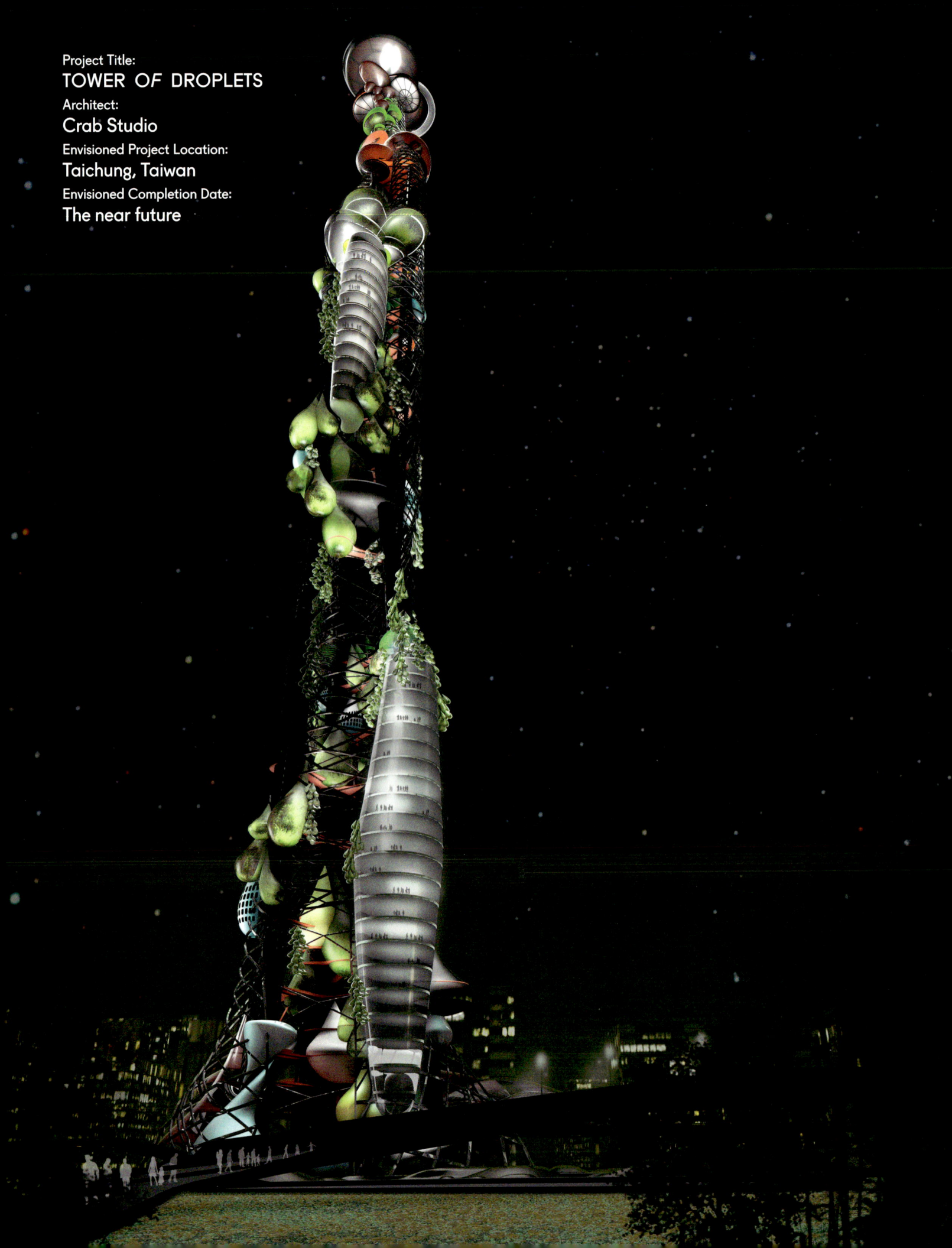

Project Title:
TOWER OF DROPLETS

Architect:
Crab Studio

Envisioned Project Location:
Taichung, Taiwan

Envisioned Completion Date:
The near future

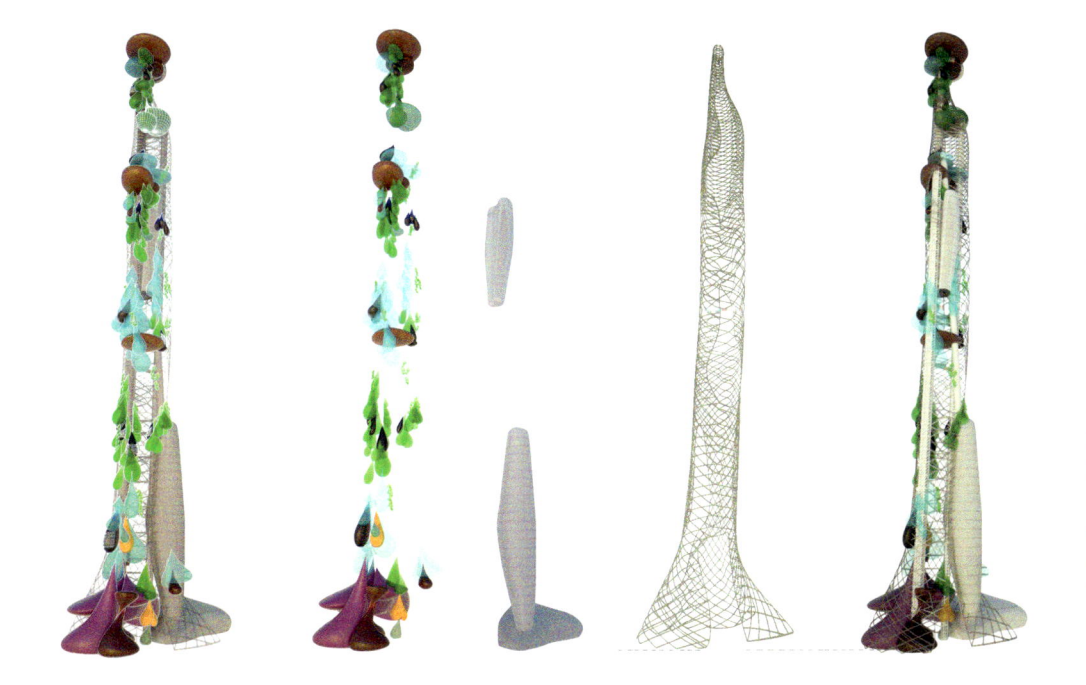

WHERE AND WHEN
Tower of Droplets is a prize-winning proposal for the Taiwan Tower international competition, chosen from a submission of 237 entries from 25 countries. The government of Taiwan envisions this tower to be a new landmark for the metropolis, where visitors will be treated to a panoramic view of the park, the city, and the natural surroundings beyond.

BASIC CONDITIONS
Based on a brief that focuses on sustainability, the Crab Studio proposal features a tower that conceives the growing of algae in layers of droplets, which will house a multi-functional space. The design of the entire tower is driven and inspired, on the one hand, by the creation of energy, or as the architects put it, "Living energy, which should be visible energy." On the other hand, the project focuses on the activity, presence, and formation of the droplets, thereby functioning as primary elements of the design process, as well as informing the overall scheme. A large proportion of the tower is open to the public so that they might view the process at close quarters. The daily state of vegetable husbandry will even be visible from the lifts. A variety of different combinations of plantation and localized environment will be distributed over its length.

KEY PRINCIPLES
The structure of the *Tower of Droplets* is comprised of a series of steel lattices that encircle the steel elevator cores, while the droplets form cages with membrane skinning. Divided into three observation levels: the upper level will overlook the mountain range, the mid-level will contain areas of hydroponic vegetation growth, which will enable public viewing of plants and processes, whilst the lower-level will house aviaries and aquaria. Furthermore, office and exhibition zones will enrich the functional diversity of the building. The algae grown on the tower—when watered and filtered—will provide biomass, creating food for fish, and nutrition for plants, as well as for making paper, and biofuel for powering engines. The tower would provide approximately 10,000 m² of algae, the tower would produce around 3,000,000 liters of oil and several thousand tons of biomass annually. The same structure could be further developed with accumulated income to a maximum of double the surface, thus creating up to 6,000,000 liters of oil per annum.

CHPT. V — TOWER OF DROPLETS

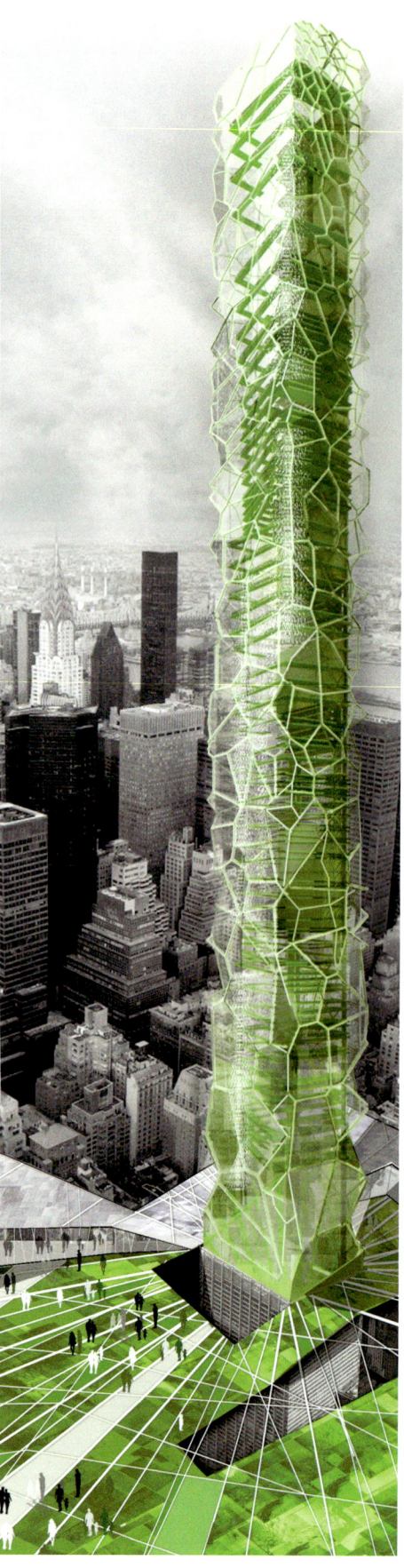

Project Title:
VALDRADE
Architect:
metamorphOse
Envisioned Project Location:
Manhattan, New York, USA
Envisioned Completion Date:
The near future

WHERE AND WHEN
The project, *Valdrade*, is located in the dense urban center of Manhattan in New York; the project aims to find answers to the problems related to the city density with innovative ways of thinking, using new technology, materials, and novel construction systems.

BASIC CONDITIONS
The proposal aims to underline a series of specific problematic issues related to the urban system of Manhattan's point; issues such as its mono-functionality, its high density, high energy consumption, high waste and pollution production. Although *Valdrade* has been conceived as a kind of utopia, its hypothesis is based on careful analysis in a concrete context, in order to find new urban strategies based on an innovative approach, which pushes the boundaries of our actual society and building technology even further. However, *Valdrade* is not defined as a project

that can only be conceived in a specific time-frame. The goal is broader and far more abstract: envisioning the future.

KEY PRINCIPLES

Valdrade creates a new definition of a high-density urban space, based on three inter-dependent factors: density, sustainability, and diversity. The concept expands as an "upper city" above the existing "lower city" with zero ground occupation. The purpose of *Valdrade* is the compensation of deficiencies of existing structures. The "upper city" would not only have the capacity to sustain itself, but would also serve as a plug-in generator that would "quench" the energy needs of the "lower city" creating an integrated network that would create the necessary balance in the urban life of Manhattan. Whilst this infrastructure is currently situated off-shore in suburban areas, forming part of the urban sprawl and energy expenditure, the proposed plug-in structures would create positive energy poles that would compensate the over-consumption of the existing building fabric. The infrastructure would also provide various ways of recycling, in order that the entire cycle could be reversed, so that one person's waste would become another person's raw material and energy source. In order to achieve such a complete and dynamic balance between the urban areas, self-sufficient generators would be combined with a variety of technology that would complement one another according to specific weather conditions. This infrastructure will include a photovoltaic membrane, wind turbines for the production of electricity, "lagooning" waste water purification, recycling areas for various types of waste, recycling, and production of recycled paper, compost and gas production by the use of methane. The lower city would act as a kind of parasite of the ecosystem, while the upper city would feed the lower city by drawing a green vegetative, permeable layer between the two cities. It would generate a new public space in the basements of the apartment towers and would re-establish a closer proximity to the level of the upper city, while it would also provide a buffer zone between the two cities. The layer would shelter and feed the local fauna by providing flora in abundance to fulfill the needs of the animals. At specific locations, the layer between the cities, would expand and would offer new infrastructure for the public that would create additional urban diversity. The infrastructure would act as new attraction nodes that would stimulate connections, exchanges, and synergy between the two cities.

The façades would be constructed with double-layer "smart" membranes that would be composed from facets that would react to their environment. Each facet would take its cue from a natural element which would function according to the uses and to the aims of the membrane.

Facet 01 is inspired from chloroplast cells that would purify the city's air, by using photo-catalytic smart materials, which would react to UV rays in order to absorb traffic pollution or break down CO_2 molecules.

Facet 02 would be composed of flakes which would react to humidity and would spread out from the façade plane, and collect rain water as a pinecone does.

Facet 03 would act as the stoma acts, which is found in the epidermis of plants and would be used for gas exchange. It would be a flexible airway, going through the membrane of the housing. Its ability to open and close would enable the inhabitants to ventilate their own spaces.

Facet 04 would be a double skin containing fog, which would change from opaque to transparent. On the outside membrane, it would enable the housing units to protect themselves from the sun at the same time as it would allow light to penetrate inside. On the patio membrane, the inhabitants would simultaneously manage to acquire the desirable degree of intimacy and privacy.

Facet 05 drew its inspiration from the finely veined structure of a butterfly's wings, and how they function. It would be composed of photovoltaic facets which would follow the trajectory of the sun.

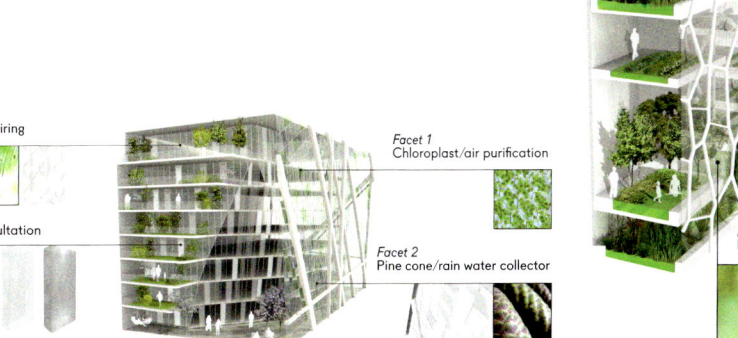

Facet 3 Stoma/airing
Facet 4 Fog/occultation
Facet 1 Chloroplast/air purification
Facet 2 Pine cone/rain water collector
Facet 5 Butterfly wing, solar energy

CHPT. V

Project Title:
PLUG OUT
Architect:
WORKac
Envisioned Project Location:
New York, USA
Envisioned Completion Date:
The near future

WHERE AND WHEN
This project, *Plug Out*, envisions a possible future of Manhattan's Greenwich South neighborhood.

BASIC CONDITIONS
WORKac were assigned a site whose access to sunlight was blocked by a large building immediately to the south of the site. WORKac noticed that the space above—an extremely wide ten-lane boulevard called West Street—was unutilized. Thus, the architects proposed a series of experimental, new housing typologies, stacked on top of one another in a 45-storey building, expressed as independent sections, which rotate around the building's central core and out over West Street.

KEY PRINCIPLES
This "Swiss Army Knife" design takes full advantage of sunlight and views, and allows the rooftops of each section to evolve into a different ecosystem, from urban farms, to campgrounds, to streams and rivers. The idea is that the building could also provide the necessary ecological infrastructure for Greenwich South neighborhood, allowing it to "plug out" from the city grid and perform a kind of "urban dialysis" filtering and cleaning water, and producing enough energy which could then be fed back into the surrounding district. The tower's core, would link the various sections with its structure and its vertical transportation. The core would also contain all the infrastructure, which would be divided into waste and water systems down one side, and heat-producing systems moving up the other side, crisscrossing at several points. On the water/waste side, rainwater would be harvested for toilets, irrigation, hydroponic farming, laundry, and fish farming. Grey-water would be purified in a grey-water wetland and recycled in toilets and irrigation. Black- water would be cleaned and recycled in a treatment facility and pumped back up the tower to be used for cooling the energy systems. Heat and energy could be created in several ways: via composting, a waste-to-power incinerator, geothermal heating, solar powered façades, wind-turbines, as well as a co-generation plant. Excess heat would be used to create public baths, a yoga center and heated earth for the urban campgrounds, allowing year-round use. At the top level of the building would be the Eco-Research School, called, *PS 2030* in honor of the mayor's *PlaNYC 2030*.

Project Title:
LOCAVORE FANTASIA
Architect:
WORKac
Envisioned Project Location:
New York, USA
Envisioned Completion Date:
An alternative future

WHERE AND WHEN
WORKac's version of vertical farming, *Locavore Fantasia*, is the result of an invitation by *New York* magazine to submit ideas for a vacant lot in lower Manhattan in New York City.

BASIC CONDITIONS
The apartment building, topped with a working farm, brings the farm back to the city by stretching it, concertina-like, vertically. The scheme concentrates on the notion of urban farming and attempts to make the contemporary city more sustainable by slashing the distances needed to transport produce to the store.

KEY PRINCIPLES
The project combines migrant farmers' housing in a series of stepped terraces with a farmers' market and public space situated below. The terraces allow the cultivation of different crops; fallow land would be used as greens for small golf courses, thereby doubling the surface of the site. Four large water tanks would collect rainwater for irrigation. The entire project would be supported, literally, by art with sculptures by Brancusi holding up the vertical farm.

Project Title:
BIORNIS AESTHETOPE
Architect:
Ballistic Architecture Machine (Martha Schwartz)
Envisioned Project Location:
Lower Manhattan, New York, USA
Envisioned Completion Date:
The near future

WHERE AND WHEN
The project, *Biornis Aesthetope*, was developed for the client, Goldman Sachs, as an urban landscape in the ultra-dense area of Lower Manhattan. The project was designed as an alternative to current green-roof technologies, which although "green," nevertheless do not support more than simple sedum plants. In *Biornis Aesthetope*, the architects at BAM envision the entire roof-scape of Manhattan as a potential landscape that would host a carefully chosen range of flora and fauna. The specific design parameters of the project balance a matrix of structural, economic, and aesthetic considerations with the aim of supporting an avian ecosystem for the Atlantic Coast flyway. People who occupy the surrounding towers will be able to observe the *Biornis Aesthetope* as it transforms through the seasonal and migratory cycles. Furthermore, monitors installed in the feeding and nesting areas, along with data of species migration, will be linked to the adjacent sky-lobby.

BASIC CONDITIONS
The technology of *Biornis Aesthetope*, and its applicability to existing structures, is already mature and ready for application. Political hurdles, including airspace rights in dense urban zones, still remain. It is also rather rare to find clients such as Goldman Sachs, who have both the means and the generosity to build a landscape within the city that is not accessible to humans.

KEY PRINCIPLES
Biornis Aesthetope will attach to the roof of an existing 12-storey mixed-use building, utilizing existing column points to create a fully-spanning roof structure. Structural latticework sculpted as a "meadow and tree" transforms a 21,000 m² rooftop covered with vents and ductwork into a park landscape accessible only to birds and insects. The *Meadow*, an undulating surface of structural mesh, is filled with a matrix of material "plugs" including 85% and 15% organic soil mixes, water pools, gravel, perforated metal, and glass. Infill materials are positioned according to structural loading conditions and the need to create a "refueling station" attractive to birds. The migrating birds would be attracted to land on the roof after perceiving adequate landing space (green) and water (reflective, blue). The *Tree*, a tetrahedron structure, creates ideal resting conditions for 12 species including diurnal raptors, songbirds, and owls. Ornithologists at Harvard and Cornell universities selected the target species based on their cohabitation potential and popularity within the species that travel the Atlantic Coast flyway. With bird-houses built and located according to the specific "tastes" of each bird species within the *Tree*, the birds can rest and scan the *Meadow* for berries, insects, and other prey.

Project Title:
SYMBIOTIC INTERLOCK
Architect:
Meta-Territory_Studio (Daekwon Park)
Envisioned Project Location:
Chicago, USA
Envisioned Completion Date:
The near future

WHERE AND WHEN
Skyscrapers started to be built in cities like Chicago and New York towards the end of nineteenth century. Over a century has passed since then, and in the meantime skyscrapers have become ubiquitous in city centers worldwide. Although skyscrapers are truly an achievement of modern technology and vision, the urban spaces that are created by them seem to be fragmented, limited and insensitive to the natural environment. The project, *Symbiotic Interlock,* is envisaged in this urban context; it investigates a possible way to unite the isolated city blocks by inserting a multi-layered network of public space, green-space, and nodes for the city.

BASIC CONDITIONS
The fundamental approach for this project is to create an *evolution,* rather than a *revolution.* The key concept to this approach is not to create new structures by replacing existing buildings, but rather to respect the context by inserting a secondary layer of architecture/infrastructure which would be overlaid onto the existing structures of any dense urban fabric. The proposed architectural system aims to contribute towards creating self-sustainable cities, particularly the central city core. Along with many aspects, creating more public space and green space (parks and urban farms) in this dense environment was both important as well as challenging for the team. The strategy that the team has taken in this project was to expand vertically, by utilizing existing skyscrapers and the voids between them.

KEY PRINCIPLES
The key principle of this project is to create an architectural system/infrastructure that would create a symbiotic relationship with the existing fabric of the city. The existing skyscrapers would become the primary structure for the system to be attached to; the scheme would provide a network of connections, public spaces, and green-spaces between the high-rise buildings. Energy would also be exchanged in a symbiotic way by wind-turbines, which would generate electricity in order to be self-sustainable. Any excess energy could be sent to other buildings or to the city grid. The components of the proposed project would be modularized for mass production; each module and component would be compact enough to be prefabricated in a factory, to be easily assembled on-site.

Project Title:
ENGINEERED BIOTOPES

Architect:
Anthi Grapsa & Konstantinos Chalaris

Envisioned Project Location:
Pireaus, Greece

Envisioned Completion Date:
2010

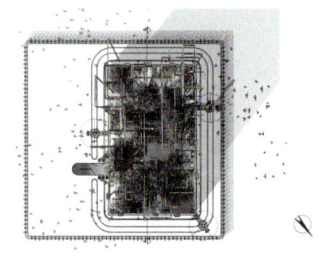

WHERE AND WHEN
Engineered Biotopes is the design proposal for the *Piraeus Tower 2010—Changing the Face/Façades Reformation* Competition by London-based architects, Anthi Grapsa and Konstantinos Chalaris.

BASIC CONDITIONS
The Greek city of Piraeus has a very low proportion of open green spaces to the number of its inhabitants compared to European standards. The architects' proposal, *Engineered Biotopes*, for the façade conversion of Piraeus Tower, intends to take advantage of technology to optimize the adaption of nature on the building surface. Using modern agricultural techniques in the construction of the building, the proposal allows nature to flourish with the help of plants and birds that already exist around the city.

KEY PRINCIPLES
The expression of the façade varies through its vertical ascent. On the exterior of the first two levels, a plant nursery consists of a matrix of glass tubes which would be used to nurture seedlings. From a distance these would appear as a shimmering texture, reflecting light onto the street and catching the attention of passersby. Levels 3-22 would consist of small biotopes that would produce low-level vegetation for the workers and visitors of the building. This system would consist of a robotic crane and bespoke designed modules where plants could be grown. The crane would be connected to a computer, which would re-position the modules depending on the weather conditions, sunlight, and water consumption. If a crop were to receive too much sunlight, the module would be transported to the shade, either horizontally or vertically, until it found the optimal position. The close proximity of the modules to the inhabitants of the building challenges the conventional distancing of humans from nature within cities, and poses the question: "Can humankind compromise and forego some of his/her personal space for the sake of nature?" The movement of these modules creates a kind of urban choreography, a microcosm of the dynamic movements of Piraeus Port, where containers and ships are constantly reconfigured. The formation of the proposed façade projects the horizontal city grid of the surrounding area onto the vertical expression of the building, linking the structure to its context, and creating a form familiar to the inhabitants of the region. At the summit, the roof structure facilitates the colonization of the building by nature, allowing the growth of plants, while also attracting insects and birds.

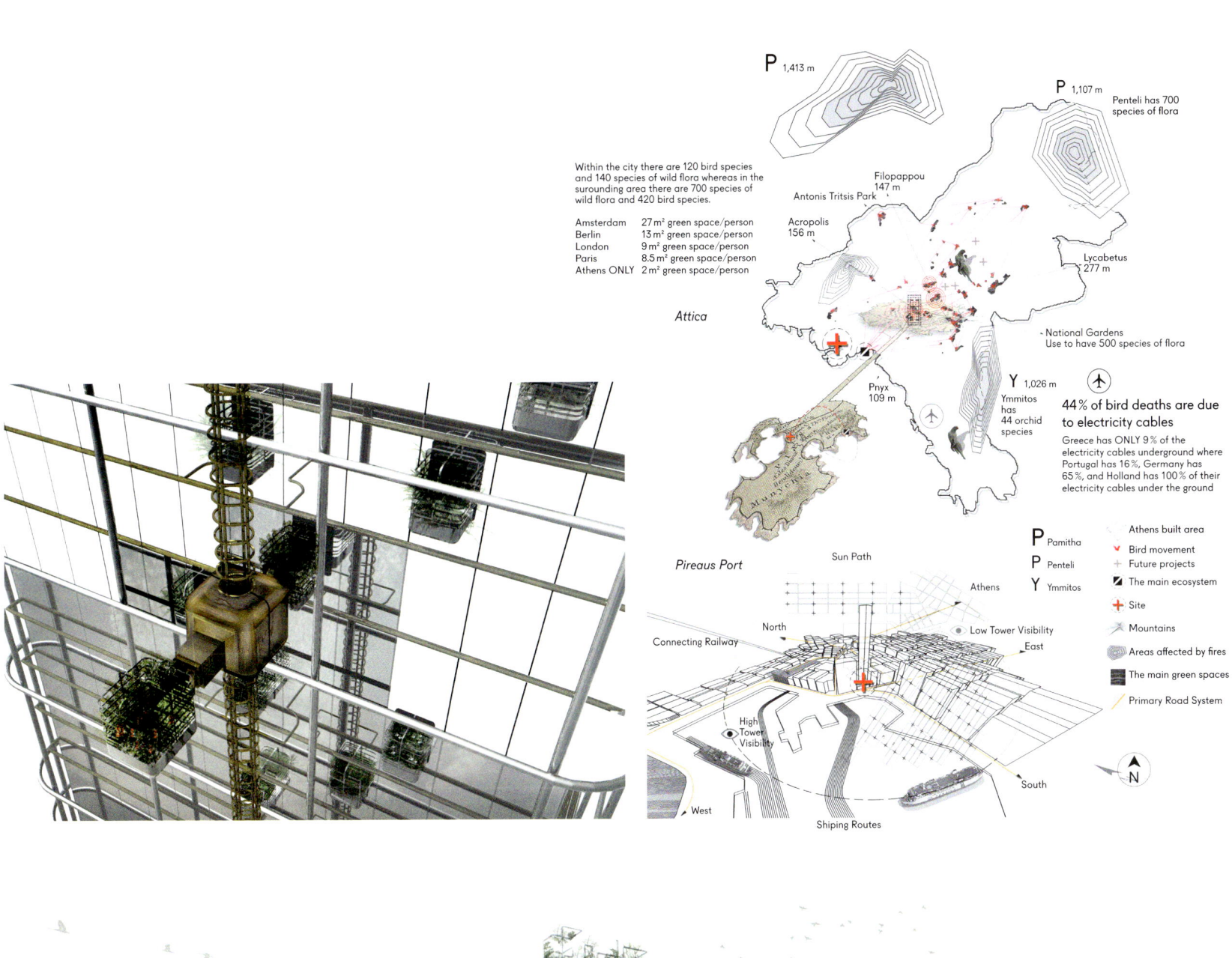

Within the city there are 120 bird species and 140 species of wild flora whereas in the surounding area there are 700 species of wild flora and 420 bird species.

Amsterdam	27 m² green space/person
Berlin	13 m² green space/person
London	9 m² green space/person
Paris	8.5 m² green space/person
Athens ONLY	2 m² green space/person

P 1,413 m
P 1,107 m
Penteli has 700 species of flora

Filopappou 147 m
Antonis Tritsis Park
Acropolis 156 m
Lycabetus 277 m

Attica

- National Gardens
Use to have 500 species of flora

Pnyx 109 m
Y 1,026 m
Ymmitos has 44 orchid species

44% of bird deaths are due to electricity cables

Greece has ONLY 9% of the electricity cables underground where Portugal has 16%, Germany has 65%, and Holland has 100% of their electricity cables under the ground

Pireaus Port

Sun Path
Athens
North
Connecting Railway
Low Tower Visibility
East
High Tower Visibility
West
South
Shiping Routes

P Pamitha
P Penteli
Y Ymmitos

- Athens built area
- Bird movement
- Future projects
- The main ecosystem
- Site
- Mountains
- Areas affected by fires
- The main green spaces
- Primary Road System

CHPT. V

219

Project Title:
PHYTE
Architect:
Nicolas Mouret
Envisioned Project Location:
Paris, France
Envisioned Completion Date:
The near future

WHERE AND WHEN
Nicolas Mouret's project, *Phyte*, was announced the winner of a competition held by the Foundation Société Tour Eiffel. *Phyte* proposes a 380-meter-high mobile tower at the culmination of Paris' Champs de Mars. Unfortunately, shortly after the announcement, Mouret was disqualified due his lack of formal architecture qualifications.

BASIC CONDITIONS
Phyte is the result of Mouret's reflections on the lack of natural environments in Paris. The designer searched for a way to balance and remedy this lack without the use of organic matter. Mouret's conclusion is that the city could be a huge expanse of static buildings, where the only movements would be the streams of traffic circulating through the city. He proposes nature as a synonym for perpetual motion. Mouret's tower, which would be made from ultra strong fiber-crete, would create movement in a seemingly frozen city. Another aspect for the designer was to take a stand, in the way that Gustave Eiffel's works did, and build with resources that Eiffel would not have had at his disposal in his lifetime. It seemed almost impossible for Mouret to be able to conceive of a building 380 m high that could function with only a single foundation. Mouret conveys this by stating: "The stance of this moving tower would give life to Paris, reminding us of natural movements like the dance of the grass, the flow of the waves, or clouds of sand in the desert."

KEY PRINCIPLES
According to Mouret, the project is entirely feasible: the construction would consist of eight monobloc structural members 50 m high, which would be articulated by *gimbals* and *guys* that would ensure stability while still tolerating rotating movement. The members would be made from fiber-concrete tubes filled with ultra strong fiber-crete and would support spoke-like beams with triangulation, stiffened and tied by tension cables. The mechanical energy of the rocking tower would generate sufficient electricity to supply the building's lighting. Thus *Phyte* becomes epiphytic, lighting up to the rhythm of its movements and creating a spectacle similar to that observed in certain planktons, glow-worms or fish.

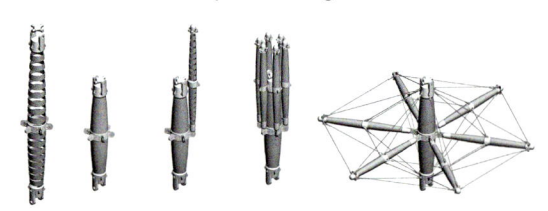

WHERE AND WHEN
Inspired by the picturesque natural landscape of Ansan, the project *Beautiful Minds* seeks to create something artificial and intelligent in response to it. On a programmatic level, this project proposes a cultural center for Ansan.

BASIC CONDITIONS
Beautiful Minds represents the brain-center and the imagination of the city; a place where one can celebrate and develop ideas across every intellectual discipline, from religious, to artistic, and scientific thought.

KEY PRINCIPLES
The building is organized as a loosely shaped pyramid. Larger facilities, such as lecture halls, churches and galleries, occupy the base of the building, grouped in a configuration that mirrors the patterns of the human brain: rational, mathematical facilities are located on one side of the structure, while more intuitive, imaginative disciplines, occupy the other. Intimate learning environments are scattered above and between them, creating opportunities for unexpected encounters and environments to foster the synthesis of new ideas across intellectual boundaries. At the very top of the tentacles are *Inspiration Pods*. Suspended high above the noise, pollution, and commercialism of the city, these represent the "mind" of the building. Offering a clear, aerial view of the city and its activities below, the pods will provide the perfect environment for students and visitors to contemplate.

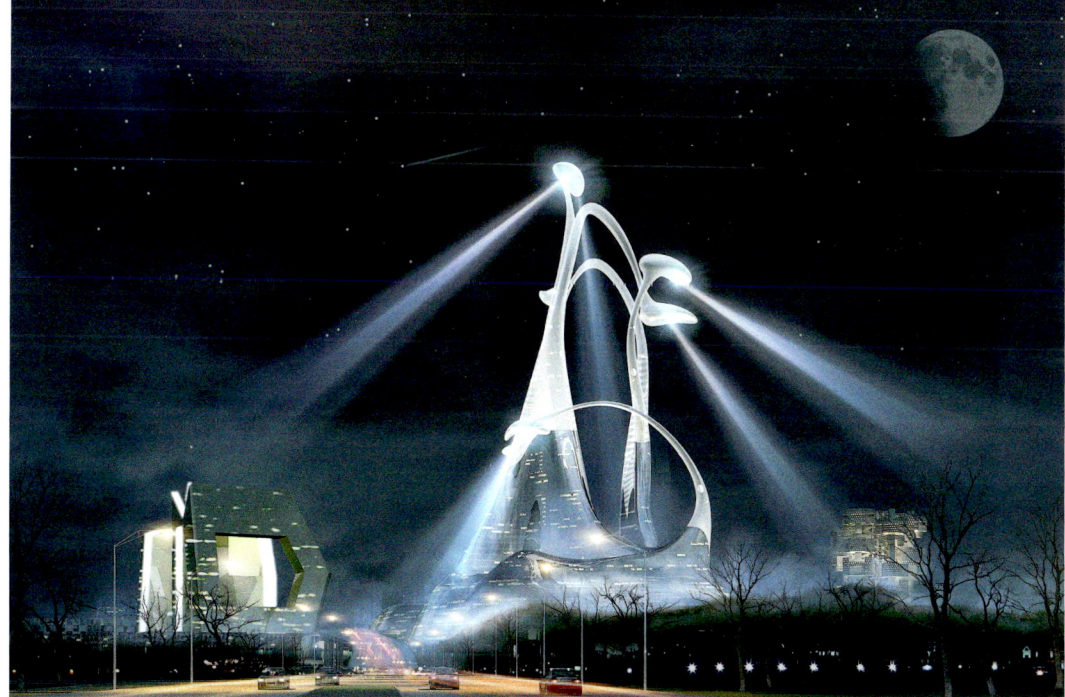

Project Title:
BEAUTIFUL MINDS
Architect:
MAD Architects
Envisioned Project Location:
Ansan, Korea
Envisioned Completion Date:
The near future

Project Title:
SUPERSTAR: A MOBILE CHINATOWN

Architect:
MAD Architects

Envisioned Project Location:
Chinatowns worldwide

Envisioned Completion Date:
The near future

WHERE AND WHEN
As a mobile Chinatown, the *Superstar* is envisioned to land in any Chinatowns in cities around the world. The *Superstar*'s first destination will be the periphery of Rome. The *Superstar* will provide an unexpected, ever-changing future embedded in the eternal past.

BASIC CONDITIONS
Along with shopping malls, petrol stations and fast-food restaurants, the old Chinatown renders all cities similarly boring and uninteresting. There is nothing more than streets flanked by a multitude of restaurants and pseudo traditional buildings, representing a kitsch representation of contemporary China with no real life within it. It is a kind of an historical theme park that poisons the urban space. There has to be a kind of shock therapy to remedy this situation. *Superstar: A Mobile Chinatown* is MAD's response to the redundant and increasingly out-dated Chinatowns that are found in so many western cities. As opposed to the rather higgledy-piggledy patchwork of poor construction, the *Superstar* is a fully integrated, coherent, and above all, modern upgrade of the twentieth century model of Chinatown. MAD's Chinatown will be a place where one can enjoy Chinese food, quality goods, and cultural events; a place to create and produce, where people can use workshops to study, design, and realize their ideas.

KEY PRINCIPLES
Superstar: A Mobile Chinatown is like a benevolent virus that would release new energy between unprincipled changes and principled steadiness. *Superstar* could land on any corner of the world, exchanging new "Chinese" energy with the environment where it has landed. *Superstar* would be self-sustaining; it could grow its own food, would not require any resources from the host city, and would recycle all of its waste. It would be a living place, with an authentic Chinese atmosphere, which would also accommodate health resorts, sports facilities, reservoirs filled with drinkable water, and even a digital cemetery in memory of the deceased. *Superstar* would be a traveling party on a mega-scale that could journey to the host city every four years. *Superstar* is a kind of dream that could house up to 15,000 people: there would be no hierarchy, no ruling class, but rather only a fusion of technology and nature, future and humanity.

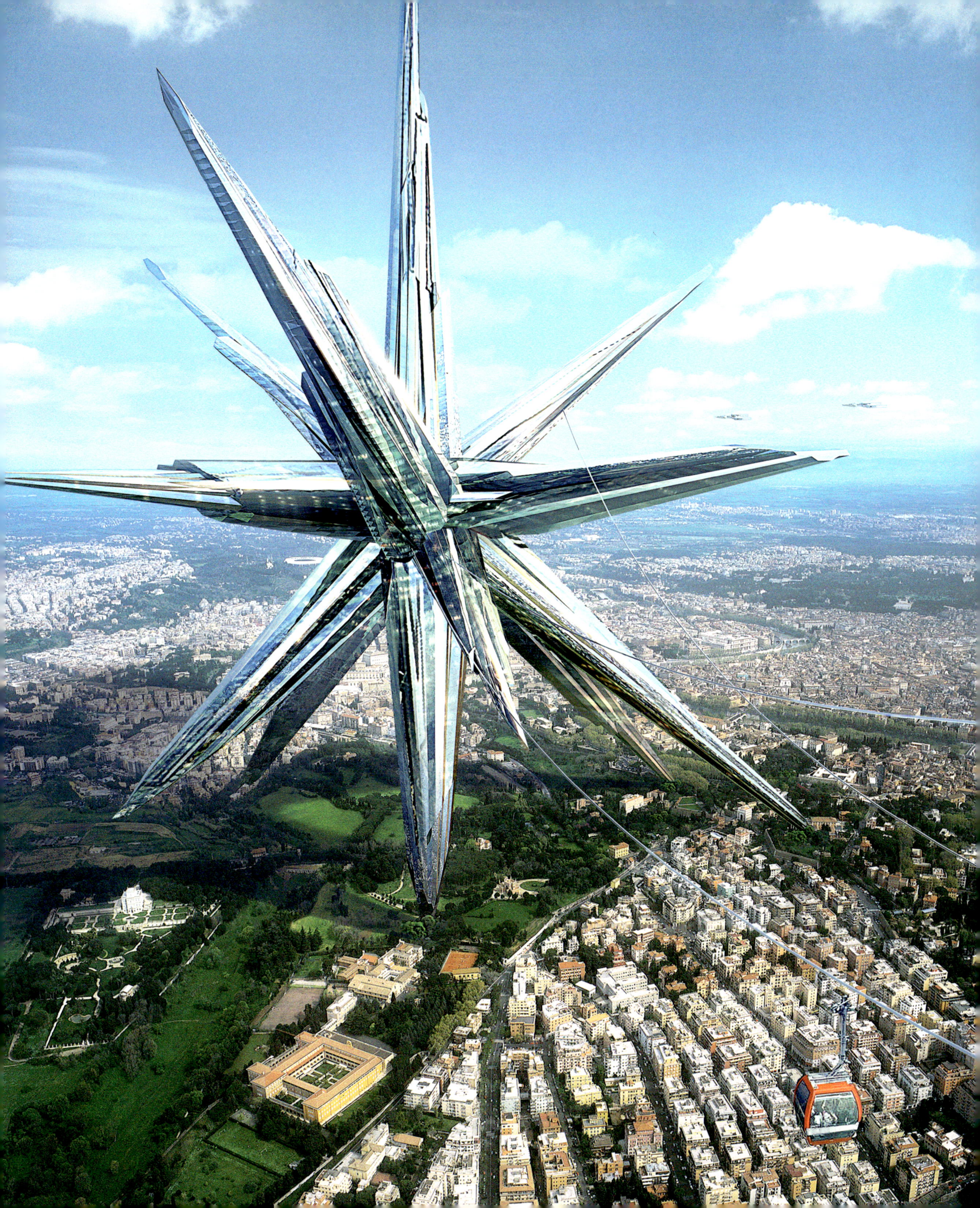

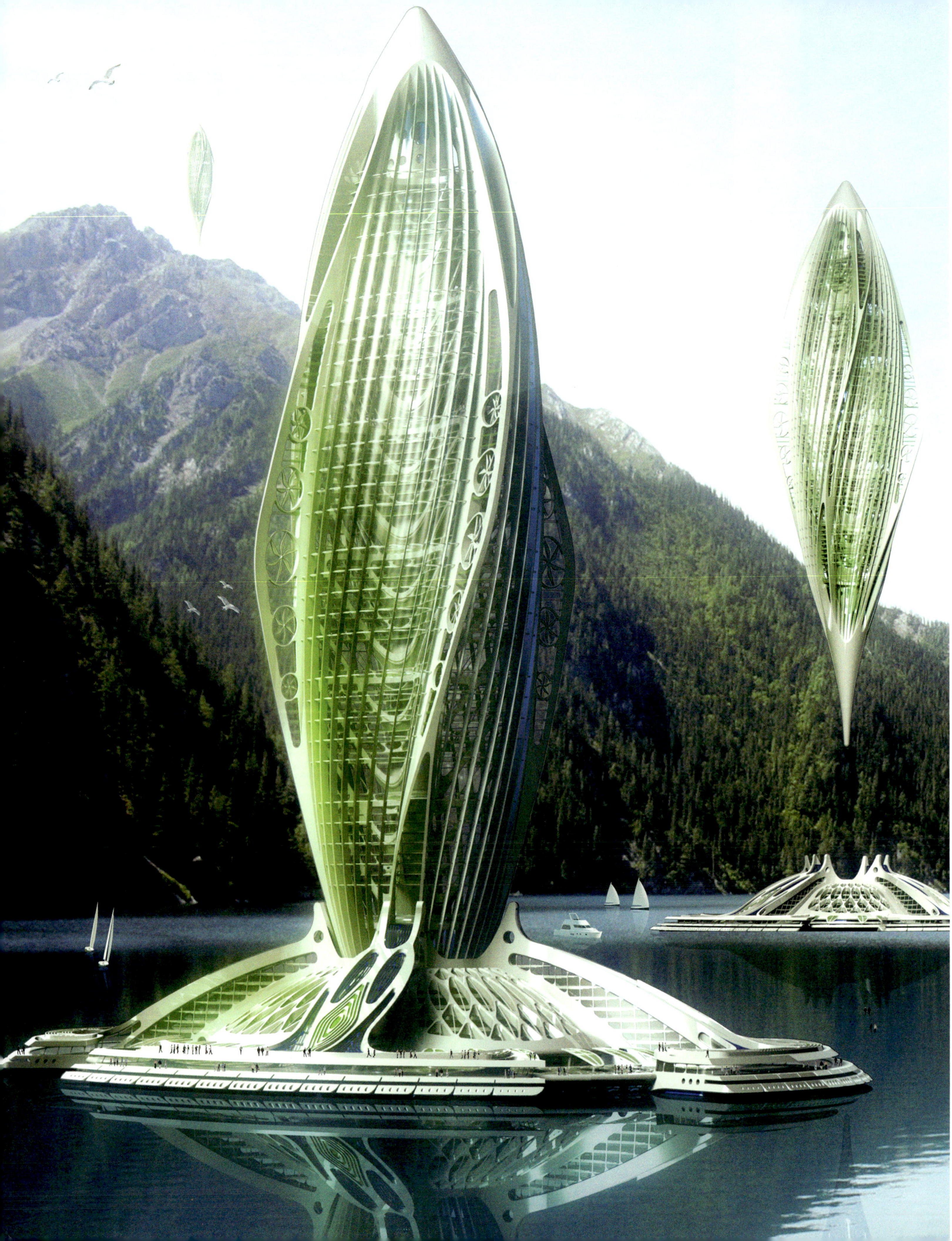

Project Title:
HYRDOGENASE ALGAE FARM TO RECYCLE CO_2 FOR BIO-HYDROGEN AIRSHIP

Architect:
Vincent Callebaut Architecture

Envisioned Project Location:
Worldwide

Envisioned Completion Date:
2015 – 2030

WHERE AND WHEN
The *Hyrdogenase* is an algae farm, which can recycle CO_2 for a bio-hydrogen airship. The project is set in the near future against the backdrop of a decrease of worldwide fuel production due to fossil fuel shortages, which will result in new forms of bio-fuels revolutionizing future sustainable land and air resources.

BASIC CONDITIONS
Positioned somewhere between engineering and biology, *Hydrogenase* is one of the first pioneering bio-mimicry projects which draws its inspiration from the beauty and the shapes of nature, whilst also drawing from the qualities of nature's raw materials and nature's ability to self-process and reproduce. The fact that hydrogen is able to produce electricity and bio-fuels without emitting CO_2 or other polluting substances, makes it a very promising source of clean energy. Already at the end of the twentieth century scientists discovered that sulphur micro-seaweed transform from the production of oxygen (classical photosynthesis) to the production of hydrogen. In the same way in which a growing tree uses solar radiance to manufacture organic material, the architects at Vincent Callebaut aim to produce dihydrogen (i.e. gaseous hydrogen) by photosynthesis from living micro-organisms as seaweed does from the *Chlamydomonas reinhardtii* family, that possesses enzymes of the type hydrogenase. This process could produce an estimated at 1,000 liters of hydrogen per 330 grams of chlorophyll per day, whereas for example, colza produces only about 1,000 liters of oil per hectare. According to industrial statistics, a hectare of seaweed could produce 120 times more bio-fuel than a hectare of colza, soya or sunflower.

Moreover, a farm cultivating seaweed is a miniature biochemical power station which would be able to absorb CO_2 as a primary nutrient by photosynthesis accelerated by producing hydrogen in vitro or in bioreactors. This natural process, nourished by our waste, would be able, therefore, to recycle up to 80 % of carbon gas and NOx (nitrogen oxides also impact heavily on the greenhouse effect) under the sun's radiation, in seaweed or seawater pools.

KEY PRINCIPLES
Hydrogenase marks a new generation of state-of-the-art hybrid airships. The airborne ships will be dedicated to humanitarian missions, rescue operations, installation of platforms for scientific studies, and of course, to the transport of air freight. Complementary activities would also be available: entertainment, eco-tourism, hotel, human transport, air media coverage, as well as territorial water-surveillance. *Hydrogenase* is a jumbo-jet vessel that will fly at an average height of 2,000 m. The airship would measure close to 400 m high and have a volume of 250,000 m³. It would be able to carry up to 200 tons of freight at a speed of 175 km/h. The semi-rigid non-pressurized airship will stretch vertically around a tree-like spine that aerodynamically twists to its widest 180 m diameter dimension. Forming a kind of flower-bud ready to open, the spaces divide diagonally beneath the shape of "petals" that embrace the main zones of activities: housing, offices, scientific laboratories, and entertainment. The stem around one of these functional "petals" would structure itself to accommodate the vertical circulation, the technical services, and the warehouses for the freight. These four habitable spaces will be enclosed between four great bubbles which will be inflated with bio-hydrogen, a renewable energy. These bubbles will be made with a rigid hull in a light alloy, shaped with twisted longitudinal beams, linked together by large rings. Each apex would end in a cone; the bottom end, the most sharpened, would have stabilizers and rudders incorporated to navigate depth and direction. This framework would be covered by a double layer of waterproof, fireproof, glazed canvas which will reduce air resistance. The voids between will be divided into "slices" where small helium-filled balloons will be situated. This helium "mattress" on the periphery will protect the balloons from bio-hydrogen and helium. As a docking station serves a floating farm, here will be an organic, purifying station composed of four carbon wells, in which the seaweed will recycle our carbonated waste. The purifying station will be dedicated to "feed" the airship organically with biohydrogen. The airship accommodates as much beneath the surface as on top of the sea surface. Echoing the quartet of wings on the pneumatic tower, four great arches will structure this circular platform and vertically distribute all the levels of the central ring. At the surface, these arches will be covered by thermal and photovoltaic solar shields, whilst beneath the water surface, they will be provided with 32 hydro-turbines which will be able to transform tidal energy of the ocean currents into electrical energy.

Project Title:
CLOUD CITIES/ AIR-PORT-CITY

Architect/Artist:
Tomas Saraceno

Envisioned Project Location:
Planet earth

Envisioned Completion Date:
Unknown; imaginary

WHERE AND WHEN
Cloud Cities/Air-Port-City is a project which explores the possibility of creating future cities by forming habitable cells on platforms that float in the air, morphing, and absorbing themselves together like clouds.

BASIC CONDITIONS
The cloud of platforms would move through the atmosphere, propelled by the wind, equalizing temperature and negotiating differences in pressure. The migration would be constant and sustainable. Lack of restrictions to movement between cloud cities would make travel anywhere possible. *Cloud Cities/Air-Port-City* seeks to challenge our current political, social, cultural, and military restrictions in an attempt to establish new concepts of co-operation and synergy.

KEY PRINCIPLES
Flying gardens within the city will transform as the city move. The geographic range of most plant and animal species is limited by climatic factors; any shift will have an impact on the organisms living there. The climactic conditions will change faster than the plants will be able to disperse to new, more suitable areas. A flying garden will generate different forms; the interior of the spheres will enclose enough air to lift the city off the ground; its ability to fly will depend on solar energy. The gardens will be populated with "airplants" (genus Tillandsia), indigenous to South America and Africa, which will derive their nutrition from the air, imbibing rain, dew, and whichever nutrients the air carries, through their leaf tissues. There is no root system for water and nutrient absorption so the plants are entirely air-sufficient. Like continental drift, the new cities will search for their positions in the air, allowing for more flexible and more dynamic border regulations (political, geographical, etc.) for a new space/cyberspace. These settlements will create new possibilities for communication, will save energy, and will allow people incredible mobility, thus permitting a constant redefining of boundaries, and of national, cultural, and racial identities from cloud computing to Cloud Cities/Air-Port-City.

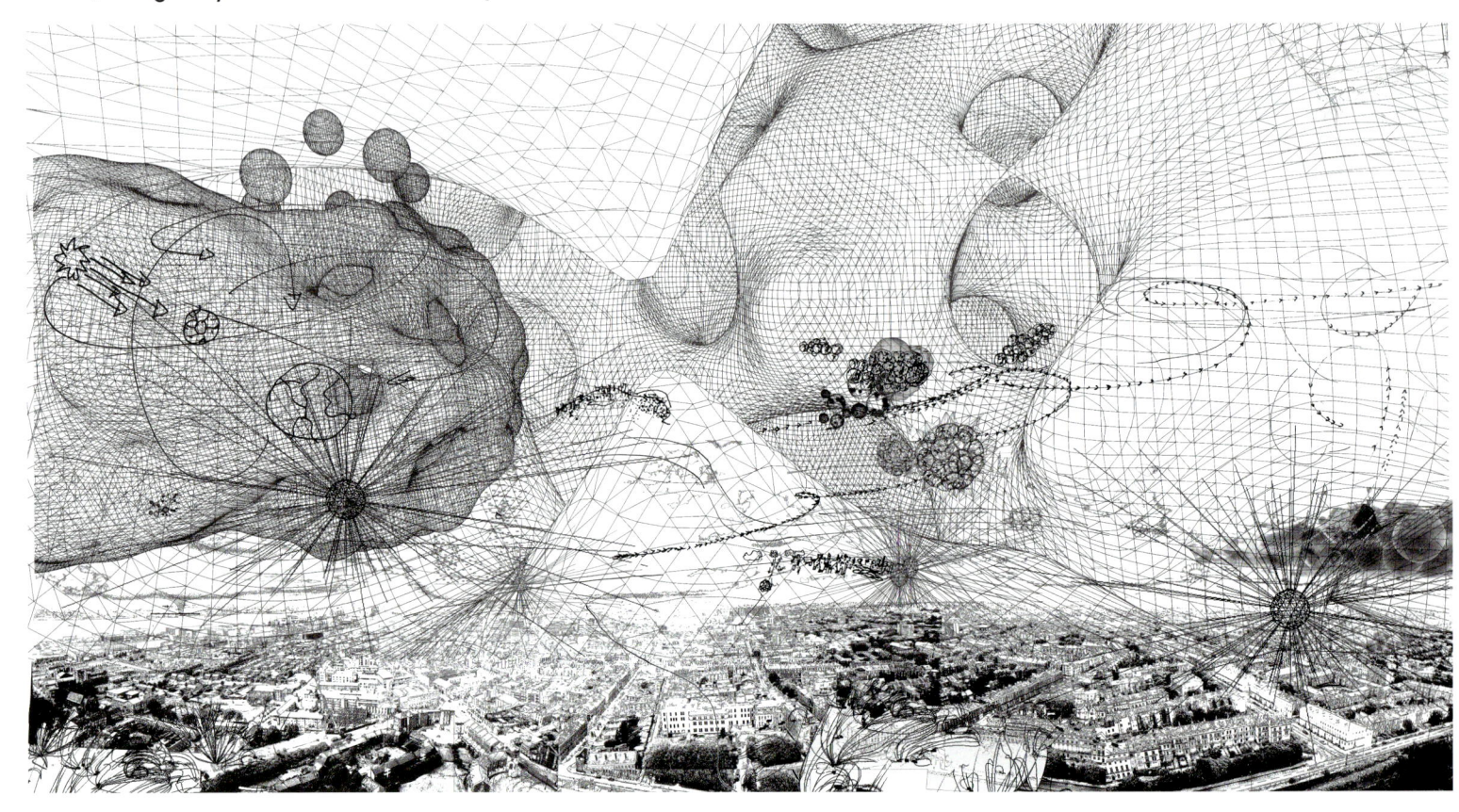

Project Title:
THE CLOUD
Architect:
The Cloud Team
(Multi-disciplinary team of architects, engineers and designers)
Envisioned Project Location:
London, UK
Envisioned Completion Date:
2012

WHERE AND WHEN
A team of leading architects and engineers has proposed the designs for *The Cloud*—a landmark structure to commemorate London's role as host of the 2012 Olympics. *The Cloud* was initially designed for the 2012 Olympic Park, although other sites in London are also currently being explored.

BASIC CONDITIONS
The lightweight, transparent tower, composed of a cloud of inflatable, light-emitting spheres, creates a spatial, three-dimensional display in the skies of London, which is fed by real-time information from all over the world. The structure is, as one of the project leaders, Carlo Ratti, head of the MIT Senseable Cities Laboratory, says: "A new form of collective expression and experience, and an updated symbol of our dawning age: code rather than carbon." Other members of the design team include: artist, Tomas Saraceno, digital designer, Alex Haw, lightweight-structures expert, Joerg Schleich, engineering group, Ove Arup, landscape architects, Agence Ter as well as the internet company, Google. Those advising the team include writer, Umberto Eco and MIT professor and artist, Antoni Muntadas.

KEY PRINCIPLES
Professor Joerg Schleich commented on the team's concept: "*The Cloud* is a delicate, yet robust filigree of reliable high-tech components, its ingredients familiar; their composition radically new." The LEDs in *The Cloud*, will be fed by real-time information, and will be able to be viewed from all over London—an aspect which was of particular interest to Google. "When Carlo Ratti approached our founder, Larry Page, we chose to collaborate because of his bold and visionary concept, and because the project tied in with Google's mission of organizing the world's information and making it universally accessible and useful," explained Matt Brittin, Managing Director of Google UK: "We particularly like the idea of *The Cloud* in the sky above London displaying information to the city and beyond—a powerful symbol for the openness and diversity of London, befitting the first truly digital Olympic Games." Moving inside *The Cloud* will be like floating inside a three-dimensional display, animated by information-feeds that could include energy use, spectator numbers, decibel levels, award updates, transport patterns, mobile phone activity, internet traffic, and much else more. "*The Cloud* develops our ongoing interest in the idea of the *civic-scale smart meter*, acting as a real-time feedback loop on collective urban activity," Dan Hill from Ove Arup explained.

228 THE CLOUD SKY HIGH

♣. CHPT. V

230 ZEPPELIN'S SWARM SKY HIGH

Project Title:
ZEPPELIN'S SWARM
Architect:
Héctor Zamora
Envisioned Project Location:
Venice, Italy
Envisioned Completion Date:
2009

WHERE AND WHEN
Mexican artist, Héctor Zamora's contribution to the Venice Art Biennial in 2009 was to create a life-sized zeppelin caught adrift between the two walls that form the Arsenale corridor. He also created a fictitious festival of airships above the city.

BASIC CONDITIONS
The installation, entitled *Zeppelin's Swarm,* also included a massive campaign to publicize a zeppelin fair that never took place. Zamora's project investigated the ways in which history is constructed in the public imagination via the use of this public space. From the participation of Venetian street artists to the contamination by viruses of internet media, Zamora managed to ensure that the imaginary zeppelin fair, as well as the real-life zeppelin, will occupy a place in the history of Venice.

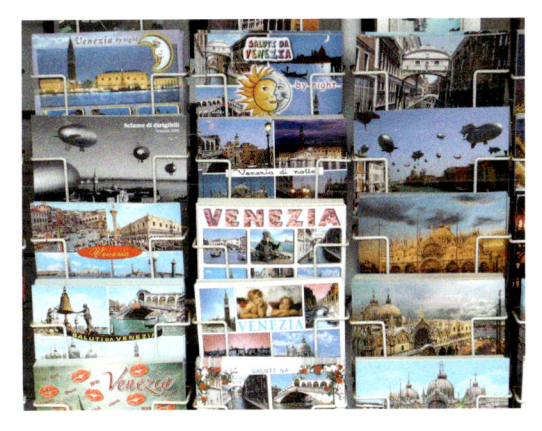

KEY PRINCIPLES
Due to the extreme site-specific nature of the installation, a strong connection was forged between history and place. This connection had a political aspect. Creating a falsified history is generally driven by a political desire to structure the past and influence political beliefs. Even when this need is absent, the interpretation of history inevitably retains political connotations. Therefore, even in the absence of any overtly political claim, the structure of Zamora's piece forces one to consider it as a political action. Nevertheless, *Zeppelin's Swarm* remains an experiment in the ability of the imagination to fly.

Project Title:
CLOUD CITY

Architect:
Studio Lindfors
(Ostap Rudakevych)

Envisioned Project Location:
New York

Envisioned Completion Date:
The near future

WHERE AND WHEN
Cloud City is a design proposal for *Post-Disaster Provisional Housing* for temporary housing solutions in the event of New York City being struck by a catastrophic coastal storm. It would house residents in a series of pre-fabricated, helium-filled balloons that would float temporarily above the flood-stricken city.

BASIC CONDITIONS
Though a somewhat unusual proposal, *Cloud City* is literally an uplifting experience that will allow communities to remain intact as they pull themselves out of the water. *Cloud City* is a continuation of the dream captured in the built form of the Empire State Building, the spire of which was constructed as a landing platform for dirigibles. The dream of floating amongst the clouds above, embodies a magical and ever-changing cityscape. The concept for *Cloud City* is based on the desire to allow people to remain in their community as close to their homes as possible, despite their dire circumstances. This would allow residents to remain an active part in the rebuilding of their community, while it would also foster a sense of security. The way to achieve this would be to literally float a layer of provisional housing over the damaged or destroyed portions of the city. Once airborne, the floating homes would allow construction crews below to work unimpeded, speeding up the recovery effort. This, in turn, would reduce cost overruns and unnecessary delays.

KEY PRINCIPLES
Inflatable homes would be pre-fabricated and would be stored in warehouses for deployment as required. Each home would consist of three basic components: a rigid core, an inflatable "bladder," and a timber platform. The inflated "bladder" would consist of two compartments, filled with pressurized helium (which is non-combustible). The pressurized gas would give shape to the tailored and stitched fabric shell, creating an open living space within. Made from recycled polyester fabric, the balloon would have a large surface area suitable for mounting flexible solar panels in order to generate electricity. Within this living space would be a rigid core, which would contain a space-efficient kitchenette and bathroom, along with plumbing and electrical services. The 28 m² living space would be open, and could be configured in many ways, with up to three bedrooms suitable for a family of four. The homes could be rapidly deployed with minimal site preparation. They are intended to "plug in" to existing utility services, and can be deployed by a team of four workers within roughly an hour. Once in place, access to the floating home is gained by lowering the entire home to the anchorage point (either a rooftop, or a temporary boardwalk). A hand-crank winch would guide the home down, to allow for the mobility impaired to gain easy access via a gangplank. The homes are minimally designed, in an effort to reduce overall fabrication costs. They are also fully reusable, and can be deflated and stored indefinitely.

Project Title:
CLOUD SKIPPERS
Architect:
Studio Lindfors (Ostap Rudakevych)
Envisioned Project Location:
Clouds (the Atmosphere)
Envisioned Completion Date:
The near future

WHERE AND WHEN
Over time a need is developed to harvest the Earth's resources more effectively. While some researchers might look to the ground for solutions, others might look up, finding enormous possibility in the Earth's atmosphere. By harnessing the tremendous energy of the jet-stream, they envision a new, improved way of living. Thus, the birth of *Cloud Skippers* began—a high-flying, free-roaming community of future nomads in the sky.

BASIC CONDITIONS
Imagine a community of adventurous pioneers who leave the Earth's surface to drift and glide amongst the clouds in machine-like dwellings; self-sufficient and free from the toils and trappings of everyday life as we know it. Such a community exists in the whimsical world of the *Cloud Skippers*.

KEY PRINCIPLES
By employing large wing structures and exceptionally long cables, *Cloud Skippers* hitch to the constant winds (100+ km/h) of the jet-stream, lifting entire communities up into the clouds. Fully-equipped *Cloud Skippers* glean the bounties of the Earth's atmosphere, both through electricity-generating wind-turbines, solar panels, and large funnels for rainwater collection. To sustain dwellers and livestock alike, residents plant and tend gardens enriched with organic composted waste. To stay afloat requires work. A delicate equilibrium must be maintained to remain anchored in the air. Abrupt shifts in weight can dislodge a *Cloud Skipper* from the jet-stream—low levels of rainwater storage or sloppy waste management, excessive hoarding or rapid shifts in population—any dramatic change may result in a loss of altitude, or worse, a precipitous fall to Earth. The unique emphasis on weight shapes a new economy with its own values and currency. Gravity banks deal in kilos of crops, or gallons of water, in lieu of more traditional monetary loans. As material over-consumption may have catastrophic consequences, money, as we currently know it, is redefined. *Cloud Skippers* must also take into account the constant shifting of the jet-stream's course. With no solid connection to the ground below, the idea of community is re-imagined. Assuming a nomadic nature, *Cloud Skippers* fly whichever way the winds buffet them. Through such trials and demands, a strong, fluid bond develops among the skippers in their efforts to survive in such a precarious environment. Balance is emphasized, manifested in a collective responsibility of the entire community and reinforced by personal discipline, as well as respect for the limits of one's environment, and the needs of one's neighbors.

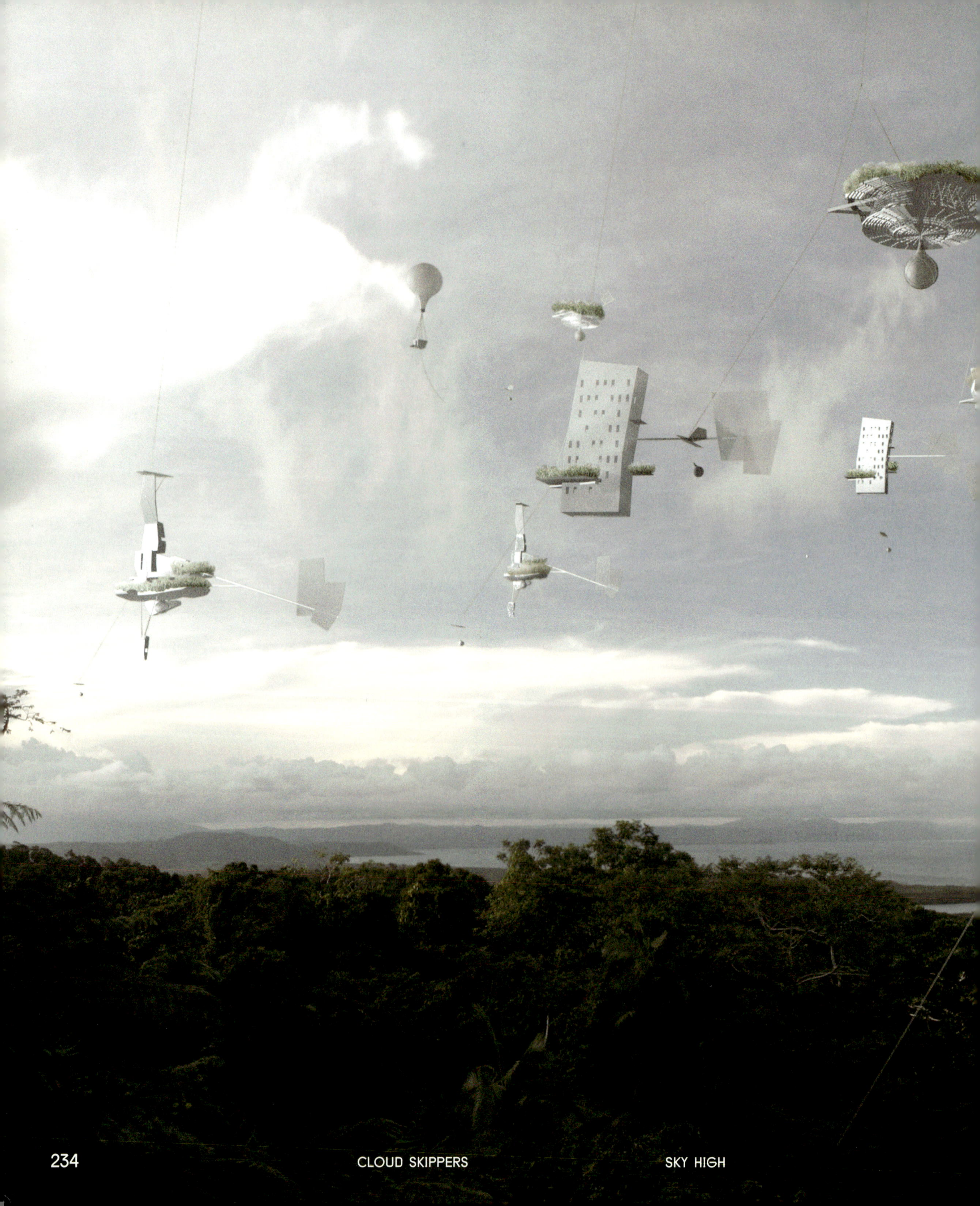

△. CHPT. V

MIGRATING FLOATING GARDENS
SKY HIGH

Project Title:
MIGRATING *FLOATING* GARDENS: AIRSCAPE ARCHITECTURE

Architect:
Rael San Fratello Architects

Envisioned Project Location:
Global urban areas

Envisioned Completion Date:
The near future

WHERE AND WHEN
Migrating Floating Gardens are a free-floating biomass infrastructure for the city of tomorrow. Today's demand for more ecologically responsible cities has provoked architects to seek new sites and new ways in which landscape can intervene in the urban fabric. *Migrating Floating Gardens* postulates the sky as being the next frontier for implementing green space in the contemporary metropolis.

BASIC CONDITIONS
Our relationship to the natural world in recent years has demanded an ever-expanding vision for the creation of green space in our urban areas. Given that we face a dearth of urban sites available for green space, might the next logical location for urban park landscapes lie in suspending them in the air? Might this *Airscape* posit a new territory for the aspiration for greener cities? Will theories of *Airscape Urbanism*, like *Landscape Urbanism*—which postulated that landscape is potentially superior to architecture in organizing complex systems in cities—supplant landscape as we know it? *Migrating Floating Gardens* is the next logical step in a history of urban landscapes that challenge our relationship to nature and the space in which this relationship takes place. The potential of these new landscape elements lies in their freedom from the constraints of, and the highly specific responsiveness to, diverse urban conditions. Through the introduction of air-born natural environments, an entirely new dimension of inhabitation would be made possible. The feasibility of the project lies within a trans-disciplinary collaboration involving robotic engineers, horticulturists, airspace activists, airship manufacturers, swarm-intelligence theorists, meteorologists, and perhaps, even architects and landscape designers. *Migrating Floating Gardens* are not only mobile gardens of biodiversity, but data-gardens, that collapse the distinction between the man-made and the natural, while both navigating and organizing the city as a biological and technological ecology.

KEY PRINCIPLES
These aerial gardens will be suspended from large, remotely controlled dirigibles or airships. A photovoltaic skin will power a host of sensors and receptors that will detect, record, and monitor relevant data, such as weather conditions, traffic patterns, pollution and noise levels, as well as other urban information. This energy-absorbing skin will also power a system of propulsion devices that will allow the floating garden to migrate physically, based on the conditions provided by the accumulated data. A pod of dirigibles would migrate within a city, moving towards areas where the heat island effect is the highest, they would also migrate seasonally, traveling to southern cities during winter months and northern cities during summer months to seek the most appropriate environments for sustaining life. In the evening, pods will return to a base within the city where they can refuel, rehydrate and process the data acquired in order to formulate future aerial agricultural plantations. Each inflatable craft will house thousands of smaller shallow water epiphytic plants attached to long tendrils including air plants and vines. Each individual plant attached to the long tendrils will have a host of sensors embedded in it that will be able to detect and chart velocity, wind, light, air quality, humidity and temperature. In addition, each plant is fitted with an individually propelled device that will allow it to detach and to act independently from its base. Controlled by GPS and GIS data and organized in flocking patterns, individual plants will be able to move through the city in swarms—a "smart mob" of collective intelligence—hydrating, providing shade, and bringing oxygen to spaces devoid of green in the city. The seething gardens will assume formations that provide shade and form new urban environments.

Project Title:
CHICAGOSKYSCRAPESBACK
Architects:
Mila Studio (Jakob Tigges)
Envisioned Project Location:
Chicago, USA
Envisioned Completion Date:
The near future

WHERE AND WHEN
The project which the *ChicagoSkyScrapesback* proposed is a patch of inclement weather as a new icon for the city that first invented the skyscraper 125 years ago. Instead of hovering at the summit of the skyscrapers, the sensual cloud suspends just above the ground. While a skyscraper tower is inevitably a demonstration of power through its sheer size, the patch of bad weather is a shared experience—you can choose to experience it or you can try and avoid it. You might decide to succumb to it, while most others might seek shelter inside—but everyone who remains outdoors gets wet in the rain.

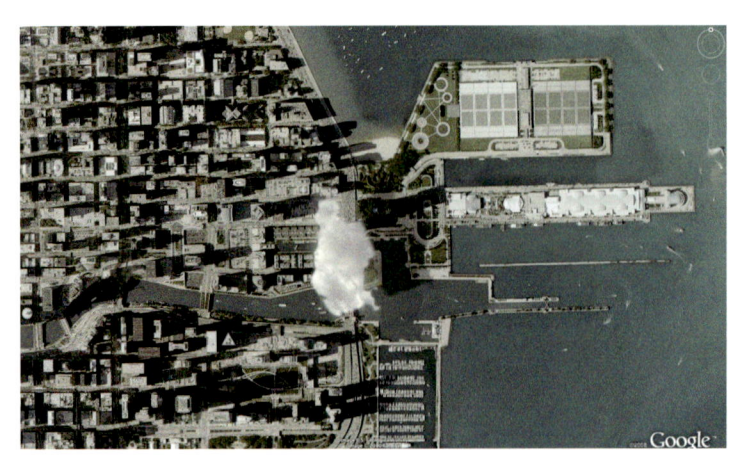

BASIC CONDITIONS
World-wide competition of major cities, the emergence of Asian cities linked to rapid economic expansion of the Far East, concurrently America's relative downturn, and—at present—the world financial crisis that has hit the United States harder than competing emerging economies, form the cultural background of this project. It is a response to the need for American cities to find new ways to deal with what seems to be a crisis; a crisis which might prove to be more permanent than the term suggests.

KEY PRINCIPLES
The permanent patch of inclement weather forms a quirky icon for a mighty but unpretentious city. It leaves the skyscrapers behind and moves from the construction of visual monuments to the creation of shared experiences as a new and more modest way of forming a common expression. The title hints at socio-cultural development and the current debate on sustainability. It partly refers, also, to the mythical power of nature.

Project Title:
AUTONOMOUS OBJECTS

Architect:
Remote-controlled (Anton Markus Pasing)

Envisioned Project Location:
Nowhere & everywhere

Envisioned Completion Date:
Sometime

WHERE AND WHEN
As a giant elevated mega-structure, *Autonomous Objects* is free from any intentional designation or destination.

BASIC CONDITIONS
Pasing's project explores the limits of architectural longevity and questions expectations and perceptions of architecture *per se*. It asks at what point space is no longer perceived as architecture, and in turn, what it requires to define architecture as architecture. As a result of this debate, Pasing created an animation that allows the observer to decide exactly what he/she is looking at: architectural space, random space, or free space?

KEY PRINCIPLES
Autonomous Objects are devoid of scale and context. No window openings, no dimensions, and no architectural details but only sound, light, and shape as a vision of what lies behind our endless search for home and shelter.

Project Title:
MOON LIFE PROJECT

Artist:
Alicia Framis

Envisioned Project Location:
Moon

Envisioned Completion Date:
The near future

WHERE AND WHEN
Moon Life Project, by Alicia Framis in collaboration with many others, proposes, four decades after the first human being set foot on the moon, that it is time for a more democratic, peaceful, artistic, and cultural investigation of outer space.

BASIC CONDITIONS
Moon Life focuses on the impact this might have on our daily lives; it examines the potentialities and the challenges of life on the moon, not only in the fields of architecture and design, but also for social, political, and public life. Prototypes and products developed by architects, designers, fashion designers, and musicians will be presented in the Moon Life Concept Store. In addition to this traveling "pop-up" shop with its ideas about daily life on the Moon, a catalogue with background and sales information could be published.

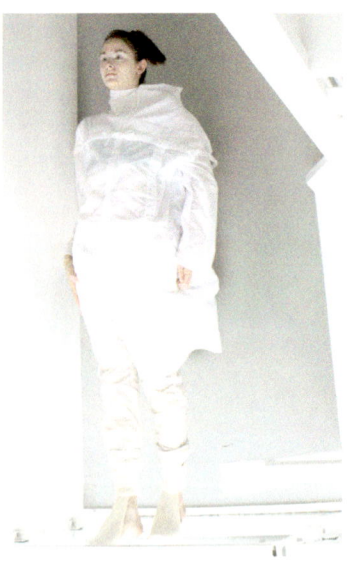

Paula Ampero and Maria Serret, *Moon Compass*

Marina Toeters, *Human & Child*

KEY PRINCIPLES
At the heart of this project lies the creative speculation on the possibility that humans might well be able to live in outer space in the future. Thereby, Framis' project acts as a stimulus for creativity from all disciplines, to envisage and design radical, but at the same time human concepts, for living in the extreme lunar environment.

Paula Ampero and Maria Serret, *Moon iGlove*

Atelier van Lieshout, *Moon Suit*

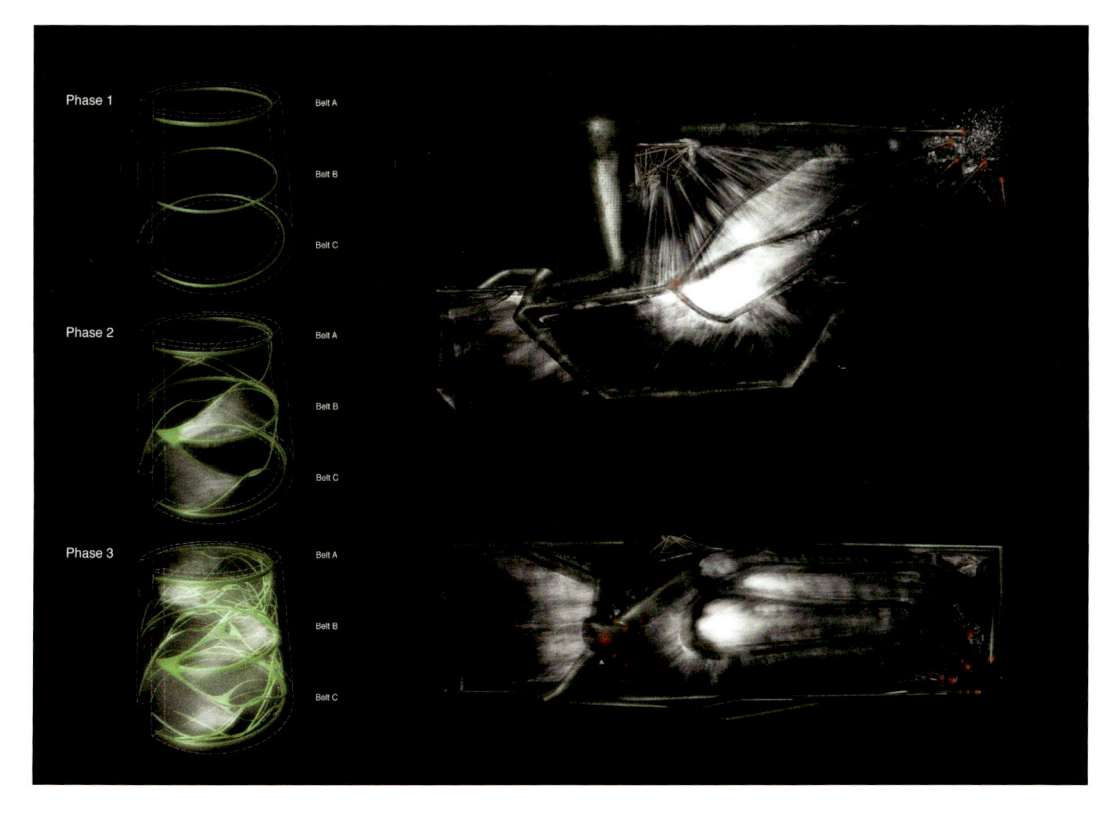

Project Title:
THE BARBARIAN SPACEPORT
Architect:
NaJa & deOstos
Envisioned Project Location:
Outer space
Envisioned Completion Date:
The near future

THE BARBARIAN SPACEPORT

WHERE AND WHEN

Over the past 15 years Asia has received both criticism and admiration for its enormous infrastructure projects, like, for instance the *Three Gorges Dam* on the Yangtze River in China. Developing nations like China strive for cosmopolitan and industrialized development, while trying to avoid breaking international treaties regarding human rights. During this period the world has watched not only the *internationalization* but also the *homogenization* of this society's cultural values and social patterns.

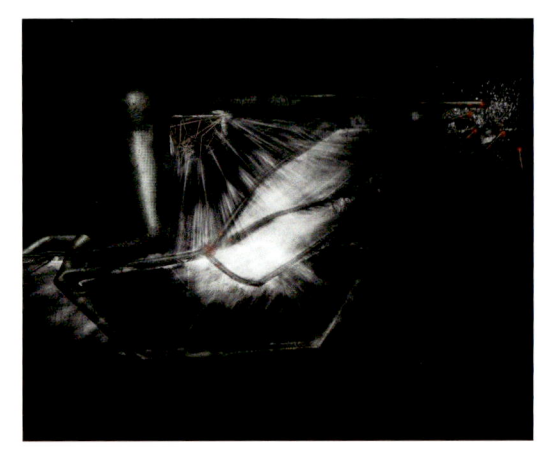

BASIC CONDITIONS

The Barbarian Spaceport is a contemporary reinterpretation of the Great Wall of China, which was started in the fifth century to separate the Chinese Empire from Barbarian invasions, a controversial military enterprise for security. *The Barbarian Spaceport* deals with the conditions of outer space where architecture is introverted, designed to enclose and protect the interior from its context rather than to connect to it. Being in constant production mode and under permanent construction, the spaceport gradually grows, but instead of expanding horizontally like the Great Wall, it rather develops spirally, sealing and always re-defining the perimeter of the port. The spaceport expands via the *Isothermal Dendritic Growth Experiment* (IDGE), a delicate experiment which expands under controlled gravity conditions. The spaceport houses an artificial environment where its inhabitants, displaced by the flooding of the Three Gorges, colonize the new structure which encircles it. In this hermetically sealed scenario, the space-borne industry is the infrastructure of survival.

KEY PRINCIPLES

The current design proposal utilizes the myth of "keeping up development" and its social impact to tackle the taboo of having *no national identity*. The concept of non-national borders and a cosmopolitan "axis-society" manifests itself in the architectural project by the structure and program involved in the design, and its response to an "outer" space.

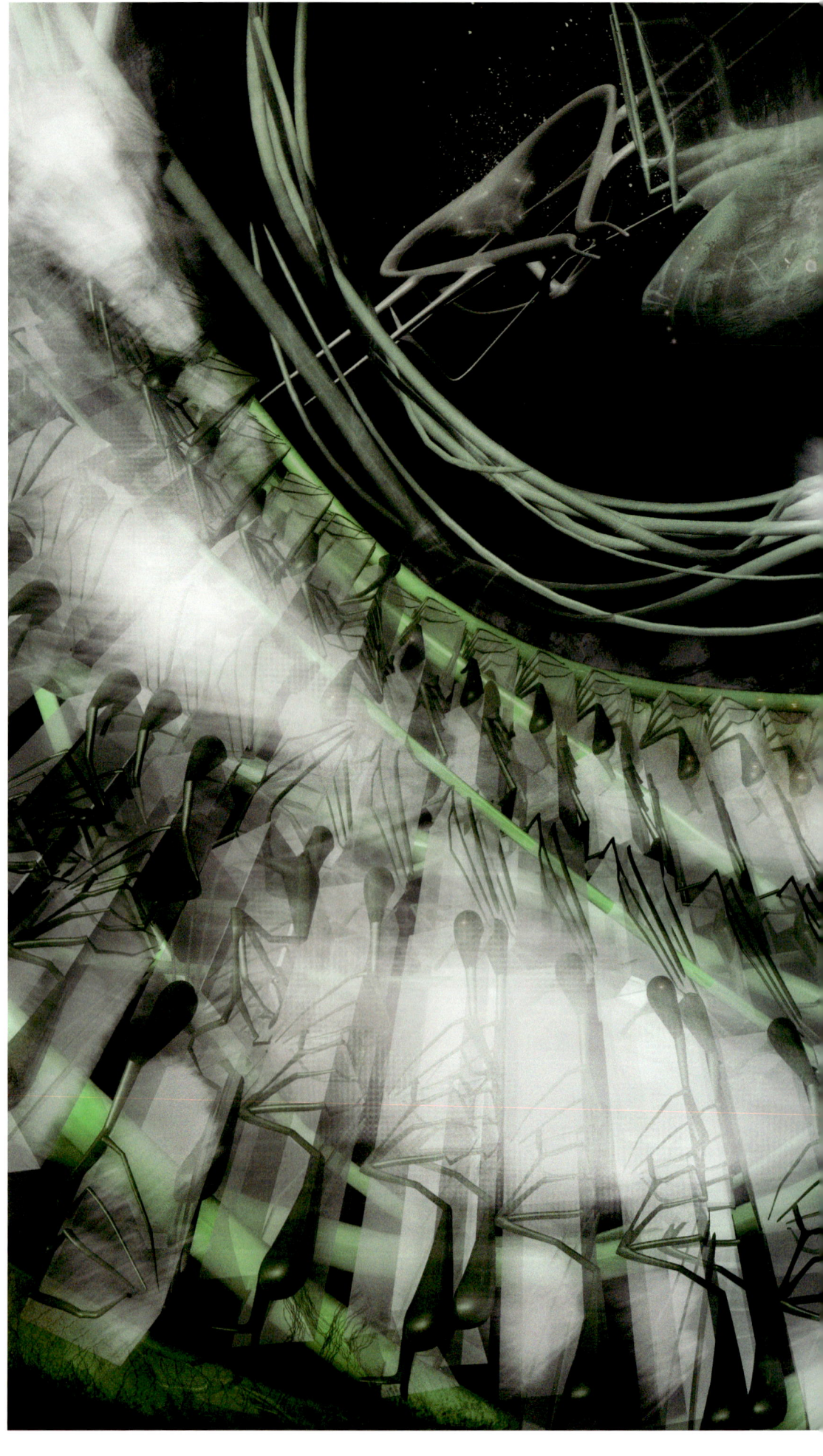

Project Title:
INFLATABLE ICE
Architect:
R&Sie(n)
Envisioned Project Location:
Planet Mars
Envisioned Completion Date:
The near future

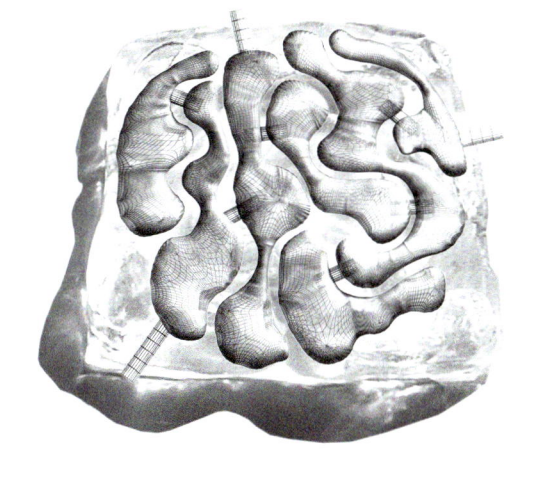

WHERE AND WHEN
The *Inflatable Ice* project, by R&Sie(n) in collaboration with NASA's Earth-Bioplex Unit in Houston, USA, and the Future Home Exhibition in Malmö, Sweden, has been developed as a design of a structure, which might colonize Mars.

BASIC CONDITIONS
Mars is the fourth planet from the Sun in the Solar System. It is often described as the "Red Planet," as the iron-oxide prevalent on its surface gives it a reddish appearance. Only recently, NASA's Mars Global Surveyor spacecraft has found evidence of water seeping to the surface of the planet. This significant discovery fuels hope for microbial life on the Red Planet. It might also make a human mission to Mars more conceivable.

KEY PRINCIPLES
For the design of structures on Mars, R&Sie(n)'s *Inflatable Ice* proposes the use of light inflatable environments using a high-tech, transparent skin to protect against cosmic radiations. After the transport of the deflated structures to Mars and their inflation on site, water from the soil would be extracted and dispersed on their exteriors. The frosted water on the skins of the inflated structures would then serves as both solar and wind protection.

CHPT. V · INFLATABLE ICE

Project Title:
LUNA RING

Architect:
Shimizu Corporation

Envisioned Project Location:
Moon

Envisioned Completion Date:
2035

WHERE AND WHEN
Luna Ring proposes lunar solar-power generation via an 11,000 km-long and—eventually—400-kilometer-wide belt of solar cells around the lunar equator. The generated electric power will be transmitted to the Earth from the side of the Moon that faces the Earth.

BASIC CONDITIONS
Shimizu's proposal is regarded as a major paradigm shift in energy consumption that would open the door to a sustainable society and aim at the indefinite coexistence of humankind and Earth. A shift from the economic use of limited resources to the unlimited use of clean energy is (or, at least, should be) the ultimate dream of every informed person. The *Lunar Ring*, Shimizu's lunar solar-power generation concept, translates this idealistic dream into reality through ingenious ideas and advanced space technology. The project proposes to utilize the inexhaustible, nonpolluting solar energy—the ultimate source of green energy—that would allow nature as well as humankind to prosper alongside one another indefinitely.

KEY PRINCIPLES
Based on mega-scale solar-power generation on the lunar surface, *Luna Ring* would transmit energy from the Moon to the Earth. The lunar equator is exposed to a consistent amount of energy from the Sun. Sunlight would be converted into electricity using solar cells from the electrical-power generation facilities located on the lunar equator. The electric power would be transmitted via cables to the near side of the Moon where it would be converted into microwave power and laser power in order to transmit energy to the Earth. At ground level, energy conversion facilities consisting of large-scale arrays of antennas—so called microwave power receiving antennas—and laser power receiving facilities would convert the transmitted solar energy into electric power. This electric power could then be supplied to the grid. Alternatively, energy could be converted into hydrogen to be used as fuel, or else stored; thereby creating a world where all human beings use energy at an equal rate. With the Sun revitalizing the Earth via the Moon, the *Luna Ring* promises a future in which a shift from fossil fuels to clean energy has been achieved, and unlimited clean energy can be used in vast quantities everywhere in the world. Furthermore, lunar resources will be used to the utmost extent possible in constructing the *Solar Belt*. Lunar soil can, for example, be used to make ceramics, glass, oxygen, concrete, and solar cells. Water could even be produced by reducing lunar soil with hydrogen that could be imported from the Earth. Cementing material could also be extracted from lunar mineral resources. These materials could be mixed with lunar soil and gravel to produce concrete. Bricks, glass-fiber, and other structural materials could also be produced via solar-heat treatments. In constructing the belt on the lunar surface tele-operated robots would play a vital role. These robots would perform various tasks, including surface leveling and excavation of solid strata. Machines and equipment from Earth would be assembled in space and would dock on the lunar surface for installation. A team of astronauts would support robotic excavation on site.

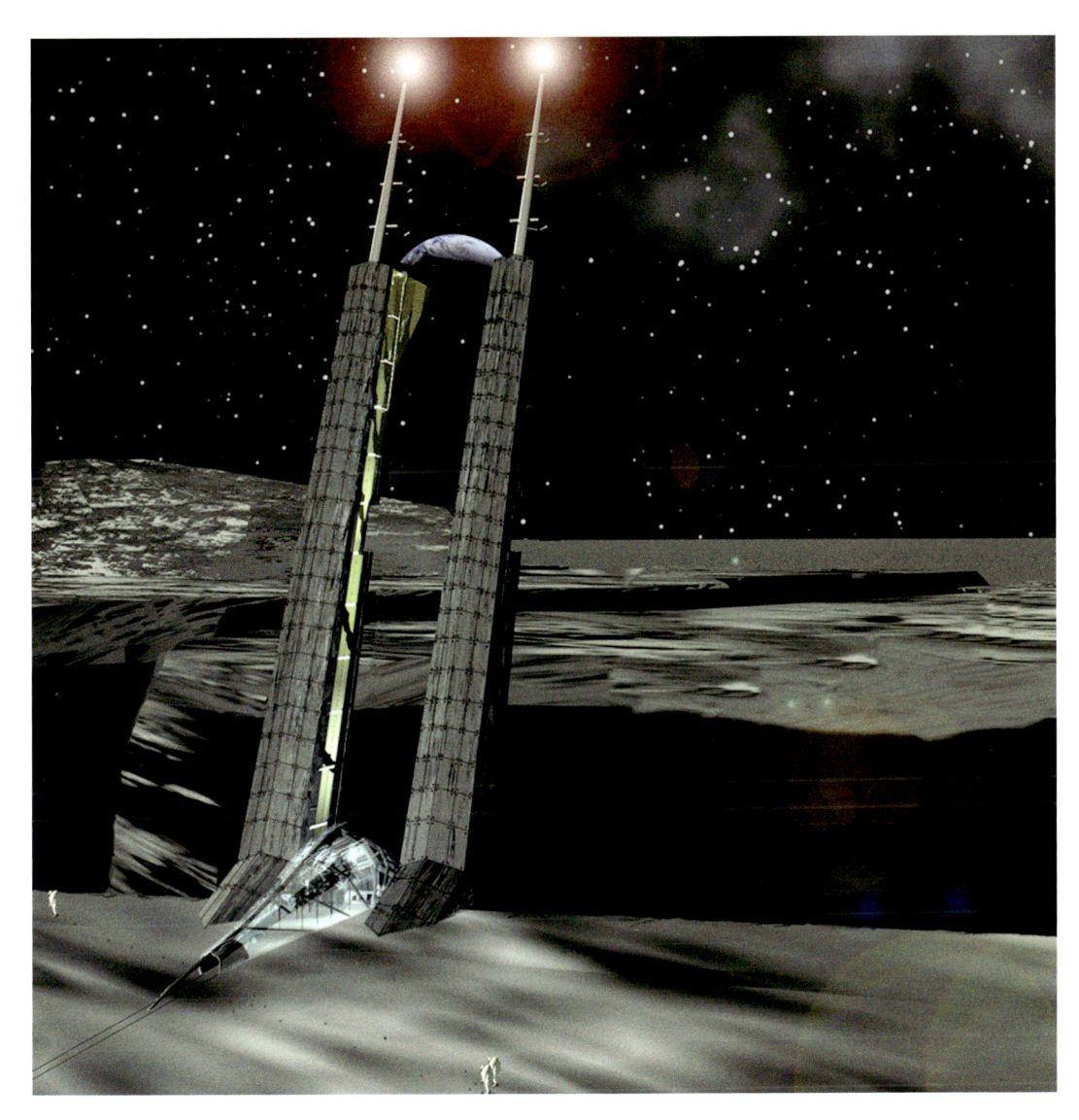

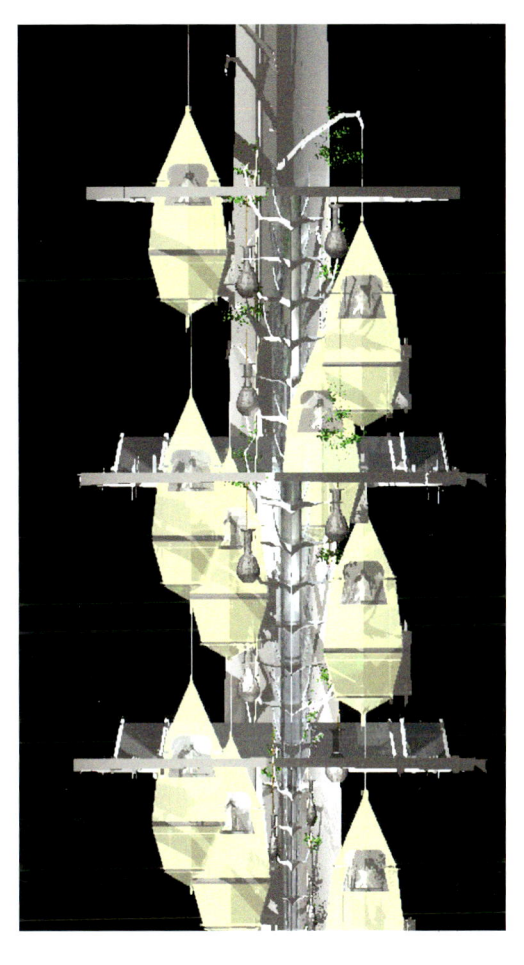

Project Title:
LUNAR HOTEL
Architect:
Hans-Jurgen Rombaut | Lunar Architecture
Envisioned Project Location:
Moon
Envisioned Completion Date:
The near future

WHERE AND WHEN
As the title suggests, the project, *Lunar Hotel*, proposes the construction of a 160-meter-high hotel on the surface of the Moon for approximately 200 guests and as many staff. Located in one of the numerous Moon canyons, the hotel would take full advantage of the depth of the canyon site.

BASIC CONDITIONS
The *Lunar Hotel* is no ordinary hotel where bedrooms branch of corridors. The views from the hotel would be, as one would expect, extraordinary. Every single moment the hotel guest will spend in the hotel will be extraordinary. The hotel will offer living-booths with optimal views across the surrounding extra-terrestrial, vast and dramatic lunar landscape, as well as of the Earth in the inky, black sky. However, the lack of atmosphere, deadly radiation, and extreme temperatures would pose a serious threat to humans in this harsh environment. The landmark structure counterbalances the harsh, inhospitable conditions. As a lighthouse demarcates safe passage in stormy seas, the high-rise structures would offer a focus point and a haven in outer space. In addition, compartmentalizing would be vital to assure the safety of visitors and staff. For that reason, part of the structure is situated beneath the Moon's surface. The staff would be accommodated in the subterranean section, where exposure to radiation is virtually zero. In case of an emergency in one of the towers, people could be evacuated to the adjacent tower which would have sufficient facilities to function autonomously.

KEY PRINCIPLES
Gravity on the moon is 1/6 of the gravity on Earth. Consequently a person who weighs 80 kilograms on Earth will weigh a mere 13,33 kilograms on the Moon. Lower gravity pull and the absence of wind pressure would also allow the design of an alien building. The dimensions of the building as a whole, as well as its structural elements (beams, columns, and staircases) could not be achieved on Earth. Moreover, the lack of cross-bracing structures would cause the building to collapse in similar circumstances on Earth. Although the two towers would appear to be similar from the exterior, they would differ significantly internally, as one tower would have a *physically*, and the other a *spiritually* orientated program. The dual tower would also fulfill safety concerns: if something went awry one could transport the visitors to the neighboring tower. Lacking the protection of a lunar atmosphere the building would be protected with an outer shell of a double layer of moon rock, 18 cm thick, and an inner shell, which would consist of a double layer filled with 35 cm deep water. The main protection required would be against radiation. The second protection required would be against the abrupt diurnal temperature swings (night time -140°C, day time approx. +160°C).

Project Title:
GLOBUS CASSUS
Architect:
Christian Waldvogel
Envisioned Project Location:
The entire Earth
Envisioned Completion Date:
Never

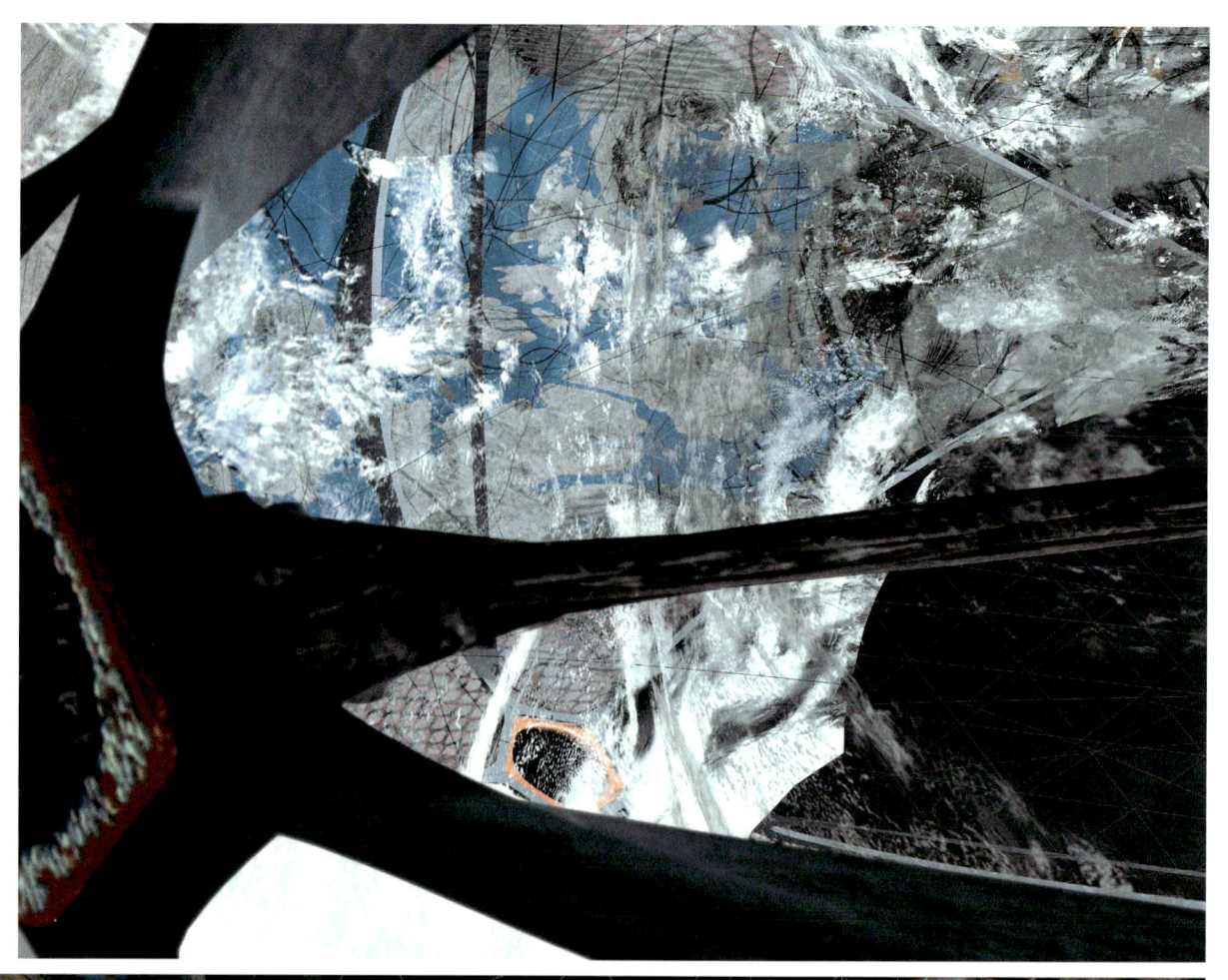

246   GLOBUS CASSUS   SKY HIGH

WHERE AND WHEN

Globus Cassus is a thought experiment: Earth's antipode, built using the entire Earth as a resource. Humans would live on the inside of this gigantic structure, *Globus Cassus,* which would be much larger than the Earth itself.

BASIC CONDITIONS

Calculations have proven that a hollow sphere with 45 times the surface area of planet Earth, and a shell membrane 150 km thick could feasibly be constructed from material available on Earth. The radius of this hollow sphere would be 42,378 km, and its structure would be that of a spherical, geodesic icosahedron. As there is no gravity inside a hollow mass, people on the inside would only experience centrifugal force, which works rather like gravity. However, as this only functions in equatorial regions, the sphere would be compressed to half its height and life would be restricted to the equatorial regions alone. Sunlight would penetrate through the diagonally configured, concave windows. In this way every point on the inhabited zones would enjoy approximately eight hours of direct sunlight every day. Habitable lakes of air would form around the equator. The new world would still be infinite, but in the form of a twisted, closed band. Land run around the world, rather than oceans. Humankind would have as much as nine times more living space than on Earth. Raw materials would be evenly distributed, with additional stocks available at the airless poles. Egalitarianism would permeate the world as an underlying principle and regulatory form of governance for societies. It would also define the social behavior of urban populations, creative principles in art, economic systems, and the way in which people and animals will live alongside one another. Justice, equality, tolerance and sensitivity will form the cornerstones of this world model.

KEY PRINCIPLES

Four satellites would be positioned in orbit and would be precisely orientated above the new planet. These satellites, also known as cable nodes, would be made from mono-molecular silicon. They would grow towards and away from the planet as slender, fixed cables by means of a crystal-synthesis process. Pits would be dug on the Earth to the quarry areas. Here material from the Earth's crust would be mined and taken up to the cable nodes in the lifts within the towers. Robotic construction machines would first build the horizontal equator support into the geostationary orbit. These supports, built in high-tensile silicon foam, would each connect to towers anchored to the Earth, thus forming the first rigid section of the load-bearing system that would span the Earth. The skeleton framework would be assembled with strict symmetry and balance. Transfer hoses would lead outwards from the drill holes, through them tempered magma would be pumped to the skeleton. There it would be expanded to form the 150 km thick vacuum-porous shell. The window domes would then be fitted. Extracting building material would reduce the Earth's mass and thus also its gravitational pull. Water and air would be hurled outwards and caught there; an ecosphere would form on *Globus Cassus.* People and animals would move to the new world in the towers and lifts. Earth would be completely mined to complete the construction of the poles. The inner structure of the shells would consist of a bracing structure, and an amorphous secondary structure that would support the expanded magma. Morphological landscape forms would be applied to the interior of the completed equator structure. Once water arrives, the surface would be articulated with a network of gullies, hollows, and basins to form a system of rivers, lakes, and seas. The quartz glass for the window domes would be made from Earth's mantle silicates, using solar energy. The domes would be held in tension according to the qualities of the glass. This would reduce the size of the interior space, and would concentrate the two atmospheric oceans at the equator.

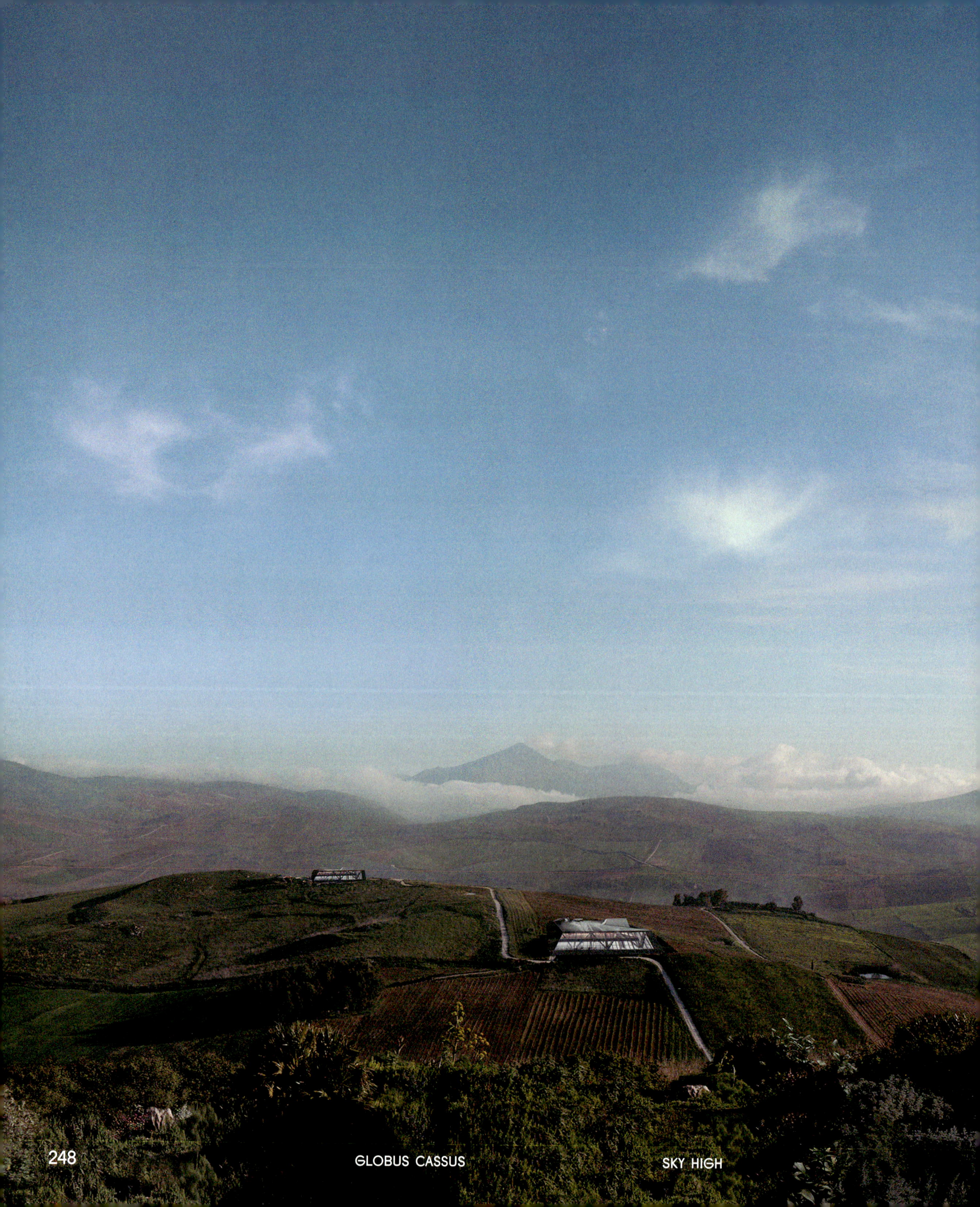

♣. CHPT. V   249

A

ALICIA FRAMIS
Spain, www.aliciaframis.com

Project Title:
Moon Life Project

Photo/Image and additional credits:
© VG Bild-Kunst, Bonn 2010

Page:
240

AMID.CERO9
Cristina Díaz Moreno,
Efrén García Grinda
Spain, www.cero9.com/amidmagazine

Project Title:
I *AmesMM*
II *The Big Mech & Co*

Photo/Image and additional credits:
AMID.cero9 + Colectivo Cuarto y Mitad + © Fundación Telefónica. Exposición Laboratorio Gran Vía

Pages:
142 – 143, 174 – 177

ANNE HOLTROP
Netherlands, www.anneholtrop.nl

Project Title:
Floating Gardens (spa)

Photo/Image and additional credits:
Courtesy of the artist

Pages:
68 – 69

ANTHI GRAPSA
Anthi Grapsa &
Konstantinos Chalaris
UK, www.arch-memories.co.uk / www.chalaris.co.uk

Project Title:
Engineered Biotopes

Pages:
218 – 219

ANTHONY LAU
UK, www.cyclehoop.com / www.tonylaudesign.com

Project Title:
Flooded London

Photo/Image and additional credits:
Masters project at the Bartlett School of Architecture, University College London

Pages:
76 – 79

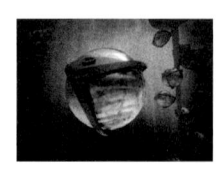

ARUP
Alanna Howe,
Alexander Hespe
United Kingdom, www.arup.com

Project Title:
Syph. The Oceanic City

Photo/Image and additional credits:
FloodSlicer

Pages:
82 – 83

ATELIER VAN LIESHOUT
Netherlands, www.ateliervanlieshout.com

Project Title:
Slave City

Photo/Image and additional credits:
Atelier Van Lieshout

Pages:
54 – 55

B

BALLISTIC ARCHITECTURE MACHINE
China, www.bam-usa.com

Project Title:
Biornis Aesthetope

Photo/Image and additional credits:
Ballistic Architecture Machine

Page:
216

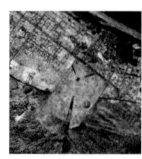

BEHRANG BEHIN
USA, bbehin22@yahoo.com

Project Title:
Stack City

Photo/Image and additional credits:
Landscape consultant for urban-scale model: Theodore Hoerr

Pages:
46 – 49

**BIG/
BJARKE INGELS GROUP**
Denmark, www.big.dk

Project Title:
Hualien Beach Resort

Photo/Image and additional credits:
BIG

Pages:
153 – 155

C

CDMB ARCHITECTS | Christophe DM BARLIEB
Germany, www.barlieb.com

Project Title:
Green Desert Mine

Photo/Image and additional credits:
Christophe DM BARLIEB

Project Title:
Vardø Arks

Photo/Image and additional credits:
C. Barlieb, M. Seitz, C. Lara

Pages:
50, 70 – 71

CHRISTIAN KERRIGAN
Ireland, www.christiankerrigan.com

Project Title:
The Amber Clock from The 200 Year Continuum

Photo/Image and additional credits:
Christian Kerrigan

Pages:
194 – 195

CHRISTIAN WALDVOGEL
Switzerland, www.waldvogel.com

Project Title:
Globus Cassus

Photo/Image and additional credits:
Christian Waldvogel/Pro Litteris, © VG Bild-Kunst, Bonn 2010

Pages:
246 – 249

CRAB STUDIO
Peter Cook &
Gavin Robotham
United Kingdom, www.crabstudio.co.uk

Project Title:
I *Soak City*

Photo/Image and additional credits:
Design Team: Peter Cook, Gavin Robotham, Lorene Faure

Project Title:
II *Tower of Droplets*

Photo/Image and additional credits:
Design Team: Peter Cook, Gavin Robotham, Jenna Al-Ali, Nuria Blanco, Lorene Faure, Selma Johannson, Michael Kaverne of Buro Happold

Pages:
124 – 125, 210 – 211

CTRLZ ARCHITECTURES
Francesco Cingolani, Massimo Lombard
France, www.ctrlzarchitectures.com

Project Title:
FOR ALL THE COWS

Page:
132

D

DANIEL DOCIU
USA, www.tinfoilgames.com

Project Title:
Gandara/Guild Wars Nightfall

Pages:
98–99

DAVID A. GARCIA
Denmark, www.davidgarciastudio.com

Project Title:
I *Urban Sky Link*
II *Dead Websites Archive*
III *Quarantined Library*
IV *Sustainable Iceberg Living Station*
V *Zoo of Infectious Species*

Photo/Image and additional credits:
Architect David A. Garcia

Pages:
28–29, 56, 75, 104–105, 135

DAVID BENQUÉ
UK, www.davidbenque.com

Project Title:
I *Acoustic Botany*
II *Fabulous Fabbers*

Pages:
141, 189

DCA/ DESIGN CREW FOR ARCHITECTURE
Nicolas Chausson, Gaël Desveaux, Jiaoyang Huang
France, www.d-c-a.eu

Project Title:
Freshwater Factory

Photo/Image and additional credits:
DCA

Pages:
146–147

DYLAN COLE
USA, www.dylancolestudio.com

Project Title:
The Industrialist Monks

Pages:
196–197

F

FAULDERS STUDIO
Thom Faulders
USA, www.faulders-studio.com

Project Title:
GEOtube

Photo/Image and additional credits:
<u>Images</u>: Faulders Studio. <u>Design team</u>: Thom Faulders, Jason Chang, Charles Lee, Devin Rutz, Scott Blew

Pages:
162–163

FEDERICO PEDRINI
Federico Pedrini, Elia De Tomasi, Filippo Mazzaron, Alessandra Pepe, Silvia Sandor
Belgium, www.fedepedrini.info

Project Title:
400k Pods

Photo/Image and additional credits:
nonms

Page:
148

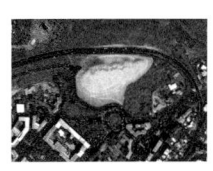

FORREST FULTON ARCHITECTURE
USA, www. forrestfulton.com

Project Title:
Lace Hill over Yerevan

Photo/Image and additional credits:
<u>Project team</u>: Jared Fulton, Andrew C. Bryant, Derrick Owens

Pages:
36–39

G

GIACOMO COSTA
Italy, www.giacomocosta.com

Project Title:
Consistenze & Persistenze

Pages:
26–27

GREG LYNN FORM
Greg Lynn Form, Imaginary Forces, Alex McDowell
USA, www.glform.com

Project Title:
New City

Photo/Image and additional credits:
Courtesy of Greg Lynn Form and Imaginary Forces, Richard Perry, and New York Times, Ari Marcopoulos. Gallery view of Greg Lynn's New City in Other Space Odysseys: Greg Lynn, Michael Maltzan, Alessandro Poli (2010). © Centre Canadien d'Architecture, Montréal

Pages:
192–193

H

HANS-JURGEN ROMBAUT | LUNAR ARCHITECTURE
Netherlands, www.lunararchitecture.com

Project Title:
Lunar Hotel

Photo/Image and additional credits:
H-J Rombaut- Lunar architecture

Page:
245

HÉCTOR ZAMORA
Brazil, www.lsd.com.mx

Project Title:
Zeppelin's Swarm

Photo/Image and additional credits:
<u>Photography</u>: Hector Zamora.
<u>Posters</u>: Campo, Photomontages.
<u>Image</u>: Antonio Zanon. <u>Edition</u>: Renato Ferro Diego Girondi

Pages:
230–231

HODGETTS + FUNG DESIGN AND ARCHITECTURE
USA, www.hplusf.com

Project Title:
Casa Pulpa

Photo/Image and additional credits:
Craig Hodgetts

Pages:
170

HOLLWICH KUSHNER LLC (HWKN)
Matthias Hollwich, Marc Kushner
USA, www.hwkn.com

Project Title:
I *Skygrove*
II *MEtreePOLIS*

Pages:
91, 120

HÖWELER+YOON ARCHITECTURE
USA, www.hyarchitecture.com

Project Title:
Eco-Pod (Gen1)

Photo/Image and additional credits:
Design: Höweler+Yoon Architecture/Squared Design Lab. Image credit: Höweler + Yoon Architecture/Squared Design Lab

Pages:
182–185

I

IAN+ WITH MARCO GALOFARO
Italy, www.ianplus.it

Project Title:
Micro-utopie

Photo/Image and additional credits:
Project for the Biennale Valencia 2004. Propriety of Frac Centre Orleans, Carmelo Baglivo-Luca Galofaro with Marco Galofaro

Page:
74

IWAMOTOSCOTT ARCHITECTURE
USA, www.iwamotoscott.com

Project Title:
City of the Future: Hydro-Net SF2108

Photo/Image and additional credits:
IwamotoScott Architecture

Pages:
92–93

J

JDS ARCHITECTS
Denmark, www.jdsa.eu

Project Title:
Dochodo Zoological Island

Pages:
136–137

JOHN WARDLE ARCHITECTS
Australia, www.johnwardle.com

Project Title:
Multiplicity

Photo/Image and additional credits:
Design Team: John Wardle Architects and Stefano Boscutti. Image credit: FloodSlicer

Pages:
22–24

JÜRGEN MAYER H. ARCHITECTS
Germany, www.jmayerh.de

Project Title:
A.WAY

Pages:
190–191

K

KOBAS LAKSA
Poland, www.kbx.pl

Project Title:
Roller Coaster Warsaw

Page:
53

L

LUC SCHUITEN
Belgium, vegetalcity.net

Project Title:
Vegetal City

Pages:
126–129

M

MAD ARCHITECTS
China, www.i-mad.com

Project Title:
I *Urban Forest*

Photo/Image and additional credits:
MAD Architects. Project Manager: Ma Yansong, Dang Qun. Design Team: Yu Kui, Diego Perez, Zhao Wei, Chie Fuyuki, Fu Changrui, Jtravis B Russett, Dai Pu, Irmgard Reiter, Rasmus Palmqvist, Qin Lichao, Xie Xinyu

Project Title:
II *Beautiful Minds*

Photo/Image and additional credits:
Project Manager: Ma Yansong
Design team: Jtravis Bennett Russett

Project Title:
III *Superstar: A Mobile Chinatown*

Photo/Image and additional credits:
Project Manager: Ma Yansong, Dang Qun, Yosuke Hayano.
Design team: Chen Shuyu, Fu Changrui, Zheng Tao, Fernie Lai, David William Nightingale, Matthias Werner Helmreich, Bryan Alan Oknyansky, Zach Hines, Tom James

Pages:
204–207, 221, 222–223

MAGNUS LARSSON
UK/Sweden, www.magnuslarsson.com

Project Title:
Dune—Arenaceous Anti-Desertification Architecture

Photo/Image and additional credits:
Magnus Larsson with Alex Kaiser, Fredrik Nordbeck

Pages:
44–45

MAS YENDO
Japan, www.masyendo.org

Project Title:
I *UL-9205*
II *UL-9304*
III *B1-9004 Hole in Water*

Photo/Image and additional credits:
Mas Yendo

Pages:
171, 172, 173

MATSYS
USA, www.matsysdesign.com

Project Title:
Sietch Nevada

Photo/Image and additional credits:
Design: Andrew Kudless. Visualization: Nenad Katic, Tan Nguyen, Pia-Jacqlyn Malinis, Jafe Meltesen-Lee. Model: Benjamin Barragan

Pages:
42–43

METAMORPHOSE
Belgium, www.metamorphose-architecture.weebly.com

Project Title:
Valdrade

Photo/Image and additional credits:
metamorphOse

Pages:
212–213

MCGAURAN GIANNINI SOON (MGS) WITH BILD ARCHITECTURE, DYSKORS, AND MATERIAL THINKING
Australia, www.mgsarchitects.com.au

Project Title:
Saturation City

Photo/Image and additional credits:
Team: McGauran Giannini Soon (MGS), Bild + Dyskors, Material Thinking. Design Team: MGS – Eli Giannini, Jocelyn Chiew, Catherine Ranger; Bild—Ben Milbourne; Dyskors—Edmund Carter; Material Thinking—Paul Carter. Image credit: McGauran Giannini Soon (MGS), Bild + Dyskors, Material Thinking, FloodSlicer

Pages:
94–95

MILA STUDIO
Jakob Tigges
Germany, www.mila-berlin.com

Project Title:
I *The Berg*

Photo/Image and additional credits:
Image Credit: Jakob Tigges

Project Title:
II *ChicagoSkyScrapesBack*

Photo/Image and additional credits:
Design Team: Sean Pepe, Nino Tugushi, Jakob Tigges. Image Credit: Jakob Tigges

Pages:
34–35, 238

META-TERRITORY_ STUDIO
Daekwon Park
USA, www.daekwonpark.com

Project Title:
Symbiotic Interlock

Photo/Image and additional credits:
Daekwon Park

Page:
217

MVRDV
Netherlands, www.mvrdv.nl

Project Title:
Galije

Photo/Image and additional credits:
MVRDV, © VG Bild-Kunst, Bonn 2010

Page:
152

N

NAJA & DEOSTOS
UK, www.naja-deostos.com

Project Title:
I *The Hanging Cemetery of Baghdad*
II *The Barbarian Spaceport*

Photo/Image and additional credits:
NaJa & deOstos

Page:
25, 241–242

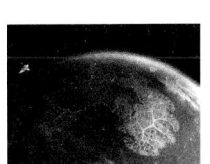

NH ARCHITECTURE
Australia, www.nharchitecture.net

Project Title:
Aquatown

Photo/Image and additional credits:
Design Team: NH Architecture & Andrew Mackenzie. Image credits: FloodSlicer

Page:
96

NICOLAS MOURET
France, www.nicolasmouret.com

Project Title:
Phyte

Page:
220

NL ARCHITECTS
Netherlands, www.nlarchitects.nl

Project Title:
Cruise City, City Cruise

Pages:
72–73

O

OFF ARCHITECTURE
France, www.offarchitecture.com

Project Title:
Rethinking the Bering Strait

Pages:
106–109

OFL ARCHITECURE
Italy, www.francescolipari.it

Project Title:
Silk Road Map Evolution

Pages:
30–33

ONOFFICE
Portugal, www.onoffice.no

Project Title:
Turbine City

Photo/Image and additional credits:
onoffice

Page:
89

P

PROTOCOL ARCHITECTURE
USA, www.protocolarchitecture.wordpress.com

Project Title:
Recovering Berlin

Photo/Image and additional credits:
Protocol Architecture. Under the guidance of professor Ed Keller (Columbia GSAPP)

Pages:
40 – 41

R

R ARCHITECTS LLP
Kenneth Loh, Michelle Lim
Singapore, www.rarchitects.net

Project Title:
Habitat Solare

Pages:
208 – 209

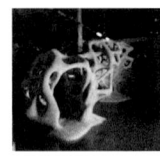

R&SIE(N)
An architecture «des Humeurs»
François Roche, Stéphanie Lavaux, Kiuchi Toshikatsu, associated to Stephan Henrich, François Jouve
France, www.new-territories.com

Project Title:
I *Dustyrelief*
II *Hypnosis Chamber*
III *Water Flux*
IV *Inflatable Ice*

Photo/Image and additional credits:
R&Sie(n) / Le Laboratoire / 2010. Scenario, design, production: R&Sie(n). Process and Robotic Design: Stephan Henrich. Mathematical Process: François Jouve. Computations: Winston Hampel, Natanael Elfassy, some help from Marc Fornes Design & Process of physiological collect: Gaëtan Robillard, Frédéric Mauclere, Jonathan Derrough. Nano-récepteurs scénario: Berdaguer et Péjus. Microneedles: Mark Kendall "The Lift": Delphine Chevrot, Takako Sato. Physiological Interview: Candice Poitrey. Text Natural Machine: Chris Younes. Architect: Jiang Bin, Laura Bellamy, Rosalie Laurin. Photography: Matthieu Kavyrchine

Pages:
164 – 165, 178 – 180, 181, 243

RAEL SAN FRATELLO ARCHITECTS
Ronald Rael, Virginia San Fratello
USA, www.rael-sanfratello.com

Project Title:
Migrating Floating Gardens – Airscape Architecture

Photo/Image and additional credits:
Rael San Fratello Architects

Pages:
236 – 237

REMOTE-CONTROLLED: Anton Markus Pasing
Germany, www.remote-controlled.de

Project Title:
I *Natwalk 2.0*
II *Autonomous Objects*

Photo/Image and additional credits:
Vladislav Delay

Pages:
138 – 139, 239

RICHARD HARDY
United Kingdom, www.rhardy.co.uk / www.weareom.com

Project Title:
I *The Transcendent City*
II *The Eco-Commune*

Pages:
122 – 123, 130 – 131

ROOM11/Scott Lloyd, Aaron Roberts, Katrina Stoll
UK, www.room11.com

Project Title:
iP2100 (Island proposition 2100)

Photo/Image and additional credits:
Design Team: Scott Lloyd, Aaron Roberts (room 11) and Katrina Stoll
Image credits: Scott Lloyd, Aaron Roberts (room 11) and Katrina Stoll

Page:
51

S

SENSEABLE CITY LABORATORY
MIT Senseable City Lab
USA, www.senseable.mit.edu

Project Title:
The Cloud

Pages:
227 – 229

SHIMIZU CORPORATION
Japan, www.shimz.co.jp

Project Title:
I *Green Float*

Photo/Image and additional credits:
Green Float Team of Shimizu;
Project Manager: Mr. Masaki Takeuchi

Project Title:
II *Luna Ring*

Photo/Image and additional credits:
Luna Ring Team of Shimizu;
Project manager: Mr. Tetsuji Yoshida

Pages:
88, 244

SILU YANG
xxxx, yangsilu520@googlemail.com

Project Title:
The Religious City

Pages:
100 – 101

SPEEDISM
Belgium/Germany, www.speedism.net

Project Title:
I *Happy Consensus Land*
II *Doomdough*

Photo/Image and additional credits:
© Speedism (Julian Friedauer + Pieterjan Ginckels)

Pages:
57, 58 – 59

SQUINT/OPERA
UK, www.squintopera.com

Project Title:
Coney Island

Photo/Image and additional credits:
Squint/Opera

Pages:
186 – 188

STÉPHANE MALKA ARCHITECTURE
France, www.stephanemalka.com

Project Title:
Self Defense

Page:
52

STRAWN.SIERRALTA
USA, www.strawnsierralta.com

Project Title:
Lake Effect – Chicago 2106

Photo/Image and additional credits:
Strawn.Sierralta Team: <u>Project Managers:</u> Karla Sierralta and Brian Strawn. <u>Team:</u> Prince Ambooken, Tiffany Daniels, Iker Gil, Jo Hormuth, Julie Michiels, Annie Mohaupt, Siamak Mostoufi, Diego Sierralta, Daniel Vasini. <u>Engineering:</u> IBC Engineering Services

Page:
90

STUDIO LINDFORS
USA, www.studiolindfors.com

Project Title:
I *Aqualta*
II *Cloud City*
III *Cloud Skippers*

Photo/Image and additional credits:
Studio Lindfors

Pages:
66 – 67, 232, 233 – 235

STUDIOMOBILE | FAVRETTO + GIRARDI ARCHITETTI
Antonio Girardi, Cristiana Favretto
Ital, www.studiomobile.org

Project Title:
SeaWater Vertical Farm

Photo/Image and additional credits:
Courtesy Favretto+Girard

Pages:
149 – 151

T

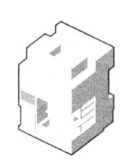

TAYLOR MEDLIN
USA, www.tgmedlin.com

Project Title:
Towards a New Antarchitecture

Photo/Image and additional credits:
Taylor Medlin

Pages:
102 – 103

TERREFORM ONE
USA, www.terreform.org

Project Title:
I *Future North: Ecotariums in the North Pole*
II *Urbaneering Brooklyn 2110 City of the Future*
III *Rapid Re(f)use: Waste To Resource City 2120*

Photo/Image and additional credits:
Mitchell Joachim, Jane Marsching, Makoto Okazaki, Maria Aiolova, Melanie Fessel, Dan O'Connor

Pages:
97, 121, 166 – 169

THE WHY FACTORY (T?F)
Winy Maas, Ulf Hackauf, Pirjo Haikola, Bas Kalmeyer, Tihamer Salij
Netherlands, www.thewhyfactory.com

Project Title:
I *Giant Water Lilies*
II *City Pig*

Photo/Image and additional credits:
Copyright by The Why Factory, visualisation by Wieland & Grouwens, Rotterdam

Pages:
84, 133

TOMAS SARACENO
Germany, www.t-saraceno.org

Project Title:
Cloud Cities/Air-Port-City

Photo/Image and additional credits:
Courtesy of the artist and Andersen's Contemporary, Tanya Bonakdar Gallery and pinksummer contemporary art

Page:
226

TOMORROW'S THOUGHTS TODAY
USA, www.terreform.org

Project Title:
I   *Where The Grass Is Greener*
II *The Mobile Mountain City Zoo*
III *Specimens of Unnatural History: A Near Future Bestiary*

Pages:
116 – 119, 134, 140

V

VAHAN MISAKYAN
Armenia, www.vahan-architecture.com

Project Title:
Evolving Skyscraper

Photo/Image and additional credits:
Vahan Misakyan

Pages:
144 – 145

VINCENT CALLEBAUT ARCHITECT
France, www.vincent.callebaut.org

Project Title:
I   *Physalia: A Positive Amphibious Energy Garden to Clean European Waterways*
II *Lilypad: A Floating Ecopolis for Climate Refugees*
III *Hyrdogenase Algae Farm to Recycle CO_2 for Bio-Hydrogen Airship*

Pages:
80 – 81, 85 – 87, 224 – 225

W

WORKAC
USA, www.work.ac

Project Title:
I *Plug Out*
II *Locavore Fantasia*

Pages:
214, 215

UTOPIA *FOREVER*

Visions of Architecture and Urbanism

Edited by ROBERT KLANTEN, LUKAS FEIREISS
Text and Introduction by LUKAS FEIREISS
Essays by MATTHIAS BÖTTGER, LUDWIG ENGEL, DARRYL CHEN, ULF HACKAUF, GEOFF MANAUGH, DAN WOOD, and AMALE ANDRAOS

Cover by FLOYD SCHULZE for Gestalten
Cover photography by BIG/BJARKE INGELS GROUP
Layout by FLOYD SCHULZE for Gestalten
Assistance by MATTHIAS HÜBNER for Gestalten
Typeface: Fugue by RADIM PEŠKO

Project management by JULIAN SORGE for Gestalten
Production management by NATALIE REED and JANINE MILSTREY for Gestalten
Copy-editing and proofreading by ANNA ROOS
Printed by SING CHEONG PRINTING LTD, Hong Kong
Made in Asia

Published by Gestalten, Berlin 2011
ISBN 978-3-89955-335-2

© Die Gestalten Verlag GmbH & Co. KG, Berlin 2011
All rights reserved. No part of this publication may be reproduced or transmitted in any form or by any means, electronic or mechanical, including photocopy or any storage and retrieval system, without permission in writing from the publisher.

Respect copyrights, encourage creativity!

For more information, please visit www.gestalten.com

Bibliographic information published by the Deutsche Nationalbibliothek.
The Deutsche Nationalbibliothek lists this publication in the Deutsche Nationalbibliografie; detailed bibliographic data is available online at http://dnb.d-nb.de.

None of the content in this book was published in exchange for payment by commercial parties or designers; Gestalten selected all included work based solely on its artistic merit.

Gestalten is a climate-neutral company and so are our products. We collaborate with the non-profit carbon offset provider myclimate (www.myclimate.org) to neutralize the company's carbon footprint produced through our worldwide business activities by investing in projects that reduce CO_2 emissions (www.gestalten.com/myclimate).

myclimate
Protect our planet